ART, ARTISTS, AND ART EDUCATION

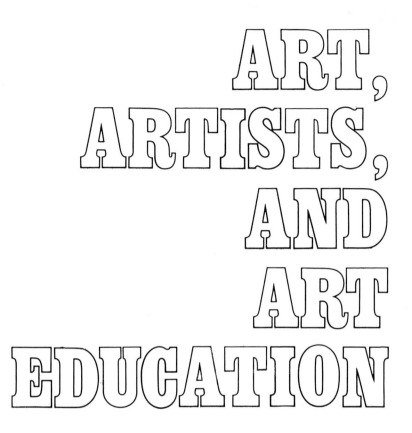

ART, ARTISTS, AND ART EDUCATION

Kenneth M. Lansing
University of Illinois

McGraw-Hill Book Company

New York, St. Louis, San Francisco, London, Sydney,
Toronto, Mexico, Panama

ART, ARTISTS, AND ART EDUCATION

Dedicated to the memory of Viktor Lowenfeld

PREFACE

This book is dedicated to the memory of a great teacher. To those who studied under him, Viktor Lowenfeld was an inspiration. Through his lectures, his writings, and his personal conversations he offered a wealth of provocative, enlightening, and practical information. But more important by far is the fact that he gave his students a sense of the mystery and excitement that can be found in art education. To be inspired in such a way is to possess one of the prime requirements for teaching and learning.

Therefore, my purpose in writing this book is to help classroom teachers and art teachers to find in art education some of the same mystery and excitement that have meant so much to me. In addition, I should like to assist those same teachers in the development and application of a reasonable philosophy of art education. As I make this attempt, however, I do not expect the reader to accept my philosophy completely or without question. But I do hope that he will use his mind as well as his heart as he accepts or rejects the ideas that are presented.

The book is different from other textbooks in art education because it has a philosophical foundation as well as a practical orientation. It also covers such uncommon topics as the nature of the artist, evaluation, the supervision of art in the public schools, and research. Furthermore, it is the only textbook in art education to present behavioristic objectives for the preprimary, primary, intermediate, and junior high levels of the elementary and secondary schools.

Although the book is written for both classroom teachers and art teachers, certain chapters are more appropriate for one than for the other. Chapters 4, 6, 11, and 12, for example, are not essential for the classroom teacher, whereas the art teacher should find all the chapters helpful and important. Some of the material in the book will be difficult for both the classroom instructor and the art teacher because it is commonly neglected in courses on art education. But the writer has found that teachers in training enjoy and prefer thought-provoking textbooks as well as stimulating discussions. Consequently, difficult topics or controversial issues have not been avoided.

Finally, the author believes that students as well as teachers are entitled to know the reasoning that underlies the organization of a textbook or a course. It helps them to understand why certain topics are discussed, and it helps them to see where they are going. For that reason a more detailed account of the purpose of each chapter is presented at the end of Chapter 1. VII

Acknowledgments

All writers are influenced in some way by other persons, and this writer is no exception. He is deeply grateful to Professor Kenneth Beittel of Pennsylvania State University for reading the entire manuscript and for making valuable suggestions. Special thanks also go to Professors M. Slade Kendrick of Cornell University and Harold Schultz of the University of Illinois for reading portions of the manuscript and for offering helpful comments on the writing and the illustrations. Professor Harry Breen and George Hardiman of the University of Illinois and Professor Laura Chapman of Ohio State University were helpful in responding to certain ideas and to problems that the author encountered along the way. Any weaknesses that remain in either the content or writing of the book, however, are solely the responsibility of the author.

Professor Barry Moore of Illinois State University at Normal was of assistance in furnishing the nine illustrations credited to him; Muriel Christison and Deborah Jones of the Krannert Art Museum at the University of Illinois were helpful in obtaining photographs of works in the permanent collection; and Mrs. Betty Gunsalus was highly efficient in typing the manuscript.

Finally, the author is grateful to Alice, Jennifer, and Laura Lansing for their patience and understanding during the years it took to write the book.

TABLE OF CONTENTS

X

Key to drawings of the human figure appearing opposite the preface and on chapter openings

Preface: Jennifer Lansing's first drawing resembling the human figure, produced at the age of two years and ten months.

ART, ARTISTS, AND CONNOISSEURS

Part I

Chapter 1
INTRODUCTION

Teaching is an old and honorable profession. Like medicine, religion, and law, it tends to attract intelligent and idealistic young men and women who wish to make a significant contribution to the improvement of society. Many of them choose to offer their services as educators in the elementary and secondary schools, and in that group are thousands of art instructors and classroom teachers who are involved in one way or another with art education.

Teaching art to young people is one of the most rewarding experiences that an educator is privileged to enjoy. Like the teaching of any other subject, it helps a person to retain a youthful spirit with all its joys, sorrows, laughter, and tears. It does so, in part, because it permits the teacher to share in the excitement of Johnny's first bicycle, Mary's new dress, Bryan's black eye, and Janet's first date. It also requires a person to give aid and comfort to those who suffer from skinned knees, bumped heads, and broken hearts. In other words, it keeps the teacher close to the daily problems of childhood and adolescence, and as he attends *3* to such matters, he often discovers that his own problems disappear or seem less important. The total effect of teaching, therefore, is to keep the instructor young in spirit.

Furthermore, it is possible for a teacher to develop a whole new perspective on life just by sharing day-to-day experiences with boys and girls. He may discover, for example, that many youngsters would rather be in school with him than in any other place; or he may find that he has unintentionally done something to hurt the feelings of another person. Incidents of that kind frequently cause a teacher to realize that a great opportunity and responsibility rests in his hands. It is an opportunity to direct the immense energy of youth toward a good and significant life. And the exciting part of it is that the youngsters in our classrooms have the potential to raise our society far above its previous heights. What is the nature of that potential?

Among other things, young people are sensitive to dimensions of life that many adults have forgotten or have taken for granted. They hear and appreciate the whistle of a faraway train; they feel and enjoy the wind in their hair; and they study with great attentiveness the shapes of clouds, insects, and plants. In other words, young people pay attention to their environment and to the way it looks, feels, and sounds. They see the happiness and sadness in daily events and, without much difficulty, are moved to laugh or to cry. Obviously, they are sensitive to life; it impresses them, and they care about it. The extent of their observation and the depth of their concern is freely revealed in their conversations, their songs, and their visual symbols. Their expression is not only frank and intense, but the high quality of its content is an excellent sign that the potential for a good and significant life is present.

By helping youngsters to shape their expressive symbols more artistically, and by helping them to judge such symbols with taste, the art teacher increases their chances for self-fulfillment and ultimately contributes to the improvement of society. Seeing the evidence of that achievement is definitely the teacher's greatest reward. He sees it in the intensified beauty and expressive power of drawings and paintings; he hears it in the reasoned judgment of an aesthetic experience; and he feels it in the growing excitement of creative activity. In the long run, the teacher also receives satisfaction from demonstrations of good taste by the mature men and women who were once his students. Their accomplishments as artists, critics, and aesthetically sensitive citizens are indeed more gratifying than money and other materialistic rewards.

In addition to the satisfaction that comes from the growth and development of his pupils, the art teacher receives the benefit of pleasant professional relationships. He is privileged to work with colleagues who are unusually idealistic, intelligent, and conscientious. Most of them are so thoroughly dedicated to the betterment of society through education that they are almost indifferent to their own personal welfare. Consequently, teaching in the public school is relatively free from the competitive scheming and the tactics for self-promotion that are found elsewhere. The atmosphere is one of dedication to the common task of education, and a spirit of cooperation prevails. In such an atmosphere, a person develops lasting friendships that are highly valued.

Another good thing about teaching is that it is one of the few occupations in which a person can enjoy a high degree of independence. After all, the instructions that a teacher receives and the restrictions that are placed upon him are not large in number. Naturally, he must be on time for classes and meetings; he must adjust himself to the demands of the curriculum; he must assume his fair share of extracurricular duties; and he must create a personal image that is uplifting to those who meet him. But they are not difficult or unreasonable restrictions; they are the things that make a meaningful education possible and effective, while allowing the instructor complete freedom in the classroom. Rarely does a colleague tell anyone how to teach or how hard to work. Even the teacher's immediate superior, the principal, is usually more of a helpful assistant than a master or a disciplinarian. Consequently, the teaching profession generates feelings of personal significance, of equality, and of partnership among colleagues that are rarely found in other occupations. In short, the working conditions are good and satisfying.

Through the close association with young people and with fellow teachers, a person is encouraged to read extensively, to engage in interesting conversation, and to participate in cultural activities of all kinds. The encouragement is there because young people and teachers create an exciting atmosphere that is filled with curiosity and a desire for intellectual adventure. Teaching is therefore a stimulating profession that helps a person to lead a full life by keeping him mentally alert and up-to-date on the happenings of the day.

Finally, the teaching of art is probably more exciting today than at any time in its history. The Federal and state governments, as well as private foundations, are providing funds for the improvement of education in the arts. Some of the money will aid the development of art centers, professional publications, and experimental programs. Other funds will support a wide variety of research projects in museums, universities, and public schools. The funds will be made available to any teacher who can develop an acceptable proposal. Hundreds of projects are already under way and more are being planned. If they are successful, the possibilities are excellent for a dramatic improvement in art education.

The quality of professional meetings and professional journals has already improved. Thoughtful and inspirational speakers are becoming the rule rather than the exception, and writers of articles speak from their heads as well as their hearts. The effect is to stimulate thinking and to generate activity. In the colleges, for example, students are forming professional organizations that play a useful role in the education of teachers. They conduct orientation programs for new students, organize exhibitions, plan trips to professional conferences, and do many other worthwhile things. In the public schools, teachers are starting humanities programs, giving more depth to their courses, and making greater use of audio-visual aids and other teaching materials. Thus it is no exaggeration to say that the teaching of art is more exciting, more challenging, and more attractive than it has ever been before; it is a fine profession.

THE PROBLEMS IN TEACHING ART

Although the teaching of art is basically satisfying, it would be highly improper to give the impression that it is completely free from problems and frustrations. It has its share of obstacles, just as any profession does, and it is not wise to ignore their existence. In fact, it is much better for the future teacher to learn of these difficulties immediately, so that he can prepare himself to meet and overcome them. If he is able to do so, he certainly will help to raise the quality of education in America. For that reason, it seems appropriate to examine the problems of art education as they now exist. As we do so, however, it may seem that the disadvantages of teaching outweigh the advantages. If it appears that way, it is probably because of the author's special effort to make a complete *summary* of the difficulties encountered by hundreds of colleagues in art education. But the summary is *not* meant to indicate that each art teacher faces the full range of problems, and it is *not* intended to demonstrate that the problems outweigh the rewards. After all, the writer of this textbook would not have devoted nearly half of his life to the teaching of art if he did not believe that the work was worthwhile and thoroughly satisfying. Furthermore, he would not have written this book if he had not been excited about teaching and convinced of the great opportunities in store for those who enter the profession. With that thought in mind, let us now turn to the problems of art education.

Opposition

We like to say that art is already an important part of education in American public schools. Unfortunately, it would be more accurate to say that art instruction survives and that it sometimes enjoys a favorable place in the school curriculum. Artless or nearly artless schools continue to flourish even in the richest and most progressive states. Some of them are found, suprisingly enough, in college communities where strong cultural commitments might be expected to create a demand for art. And if youngsters are actually permitted to work with art materials, they often must do so without the guidance of a professional art teacher.

The fact that art is offered in some places and not in others, and the fact that artist-teachers are often not employed as instructors, indicates that there are differences of opinion regarding the importance of art as a part of general education. This, of course, is nothing new. The history of aesthetic education in America shows that the place of art in the educational structure has always been questioned. It was introduced to the public schools during the latter half of the nineteenth century, and since that time there have been endless numbers of educational watchdogs who have objected to what they call "paint, paste, and putter." They also have opposed the presence of "mud pies in our schools." It is clear from such statements that aesthetic education has achieved, in the minds of many people, the status of "glorified busywork," a status that is not likely to improve overnight. It is no doubt the result of a misunderstanding about the nature of art and its value to society. No individual or group can be blamed for that misunderstanding, for it is probably an outcome of our historical and consuming interest in economic, political, and technological achievement. But, whatever the cause, the average American is not familiar with the fine arts and is often suspicious of them. A condition of that kind constitutes an obstacle to art education in the schools.

As if that were not enough, the teaching of art also is opposed by a few educators and artists. This opposition is serious because it comes from the persons most capable of affecting the cultural values of the general population. Surely art will not be taught, or if it is, it will not be effective, if educators and artists are against it. Their opposition can take two forms. It can be active, open, and highly verbal, or it can be quiet and passive. The former, although troublesome, can be defeated with reason, sincerity, and hard work. But passive resistance to art is hard to overcome because the opposition does not care enough about aesthetic education to give it serious thought. The average educator usually offers that type of resistance. Like most laymen, he is probably the victim of a passive cultural attitude about art that has developed through the years, and he tends to perpetuate that attitude through the curricula of the colleges and the public schools. He helps to fashion a program of education in which the average student receives little or no instruction in the arts from junior high school through his senior year in college. This trend is continued by graduate programs in education that produce our principals, our superintendents of schools, our curriculum coordinators, and our professors. When these persons become public school and college administrators, the effect continues to be one of opposition to art because the thought of it seldom enters their minds. If it does, they tend to assign it a place in the curriculum that is equivalent to the place that it has had in their lives and the lives of people they know. Thus, through no fault of their own, the value of art is likely to elude them and ultimately escape our children. Since these children will be the educators of tomorrow, the cycle of passiveness will continue unless contemporary school administrators can be persuaded to introduce art instruction in all public schools. To persuade them, the future art educator must be able to show clearly and forcefully that art does indeed have a significant value for the individual and for society.

The artist's opposition to art instruction in the public school is more difficult to understand, but a partial explanation may be that most artists work at their profession because they feel compelled to, not because they feel that it has any special value for society. Some of them may view the art process as being personally worthwhile, but they are apt to overlook the value that it could have for others. In fact, they usually think of the art experience in the public school as a kind of training for future professionals, and they have a hard time thinking of it as a form of general education. If they do consider the value of art for society, they usually think of the finished product and the worthwhile effects that it might have. From that viewpoint the work of children becomes practically worthless to them because they feel that it is not profound, that it lacks skillfulness, or that it has some other deficiency. In other words, artists have a hard time thinking about the value of the art process and have difficulty finding anything that is worthwhile in nonprofessional art or child art. Perhaps the trouble is that they simply have not given much thought to the subject of education through art.

Other artists explain that art abilities are inherent and cannot be taught. But that does not seem to make sense, because most artists spend their lives as art instructors in colleges and universities. Faced with that contradiction, they often explain that things of consequence cannot be taught to children because youngsters simply have not lived long enough to understand or appreciate them. On the other hand, these same artists frequently complain that many adults have lived too long to learn or that their attitudes have already been developed. Other remarks reveal a similar confusion of views, but all of them give the impression that some artists oppose art education in the public schools because they feel that it is a hopeless cause. Such an attitude is, however, more apt to have developed as a result of their own ineffectiveness as teachers.

Most artists probably favor a good program of art education in public schools, and if they cry out against a program, they may be objecting to the content and method of instruction and not to the presence of art in the school curriculum. Opposition of this kind is more clearly understood, because art instruction, like anything else, is not always good. But dissatisfaction with content and method should move the artist to offer constructive assistance instead of mere criticism, which is easily interpreted by the layman as firm opposition. And if the layman and the educator think that the artist is clearly opposed to art education, they will feel that they are justified in their own opposition. Such a notion is definitely not a boon to the artist. After all, a good art program in the public school could be of great service to the artist because it is potentially more influential than any educational program in art at the adult level. It has superior potential because almost all the children in America go to public schools, whereas few of them reach the colleges and professional art academies. If the aesthetic taste of those youngsters can be raised, the taste of society will improve, and such improvements are clearly beneficial to the artist. The future art teacher in the public school must be able to convince the critical artist of such things if there is ever to be any hope of gaining his support. And he must also be able to show the unsympathetic artist that art is really valuable for society and that it is possible to teach it to children with significant results.

Distracting pressures

Any teacher will testify to the fact that the normal experience of teaching places a pressure upon the instructor. He has to struggle with the problems of what to teach, when to teach, and how to teach. He has to figure out how to operate efficiently within the organizational structure of a particular school or school system, and he has to cope with the problem of discipline. But the pressure of solving such problems is a pressure that every teacher expects to face, and it is generally viewed as a welcome challenge. There are other influences, however, that run counter to good art teaching. One example is the urging of parents to do things that are cute, pretty, useful, or *clearly* educational. Demands of this kind are usually based upon a misunderstanding about the nature of art. Surely, art is not cute, and in most instances it is neither pretty nor useful in the way that parents expect it to be. Nor is its educational effect always crystal clear, especially to the uninformed observer. The teacher may know that, but if he is sensitive and subjected to enough pressure, he may give in, no matter how unrealistic it is. The result is that education through art is replaced by education through something else, such as the potting of plants in eggshells. Education of this kind is more detrimental than beneficial. At least the potting of plants in eggshells has nothing to do with art, and by doing it under the name of art, children develop a concept of the subject that is completely erroneous. Thus the pressure that comes from parents is frequently a force that makes it hard for the teacher to teach art. It is distracting and keeps him from attaining the goals of art education.

Secondly, good art teachers are faced with pressure from uninformed administrators to do things that are quiet, clean, impressive, and correct. These are not unreasonable demands as they stand, but the trouble is that they usually mean absolute quiet, antiseptic cleanliness, showy products, and highly photographic pictures. Art can not be produced under conditions of absolute quiet, because moving around, hammering, sawing, and other soundproducing activities are often a part of the process. The uninhibited use of paint, paste, clay, plaster, sand, and similar materials also prevents antiseptic cleanliness. Furthermore, the work of children is not always big and impressive, nor is it highly photographic by nature. Most of it is likely to be quite ordinary or very much like the work produced by children for hundreds of years. But the administrator often likes a showy and photographic product because of its usefulness as publicity. Thus his requests are really demands for qualities that are foreign to the child and irrelevant to art and education. The reason behind this, once again, is an erroneous idea about the nature of art and the place that it should have in the lives of children.

Another pressure that the good teacher faces comes from the children themselves. They see things being done in other classrooms that have become a kind of tradition, and they also want to do them. Holiday projects and gifts for parents are good examples. But the number of such activities that are artistic and educationally worthwhile is very small. Furthermore, special days and holidays are so numerous that the teacher can easily center all his art instruction around them, giving the student no opportunity to experience the value of art in a broader context.

Finally, and extremely important, is the pressure on the teacher, from many sources, to produce as a professional artist, the idea being that an individual can hardly teach others to create artistically if he is not experiencing that form of creation himself. This is so apparent to most art educators that the idea is not seriously questioned. The problem arises over the degree of creative productivity that it is reasonable to expect. It is practically impossible, for example, to do a good job of teaching in the public school and produce art in competition with professional artists at the same time. This is the same as saying that a good science teacher can not make frontier discoveries in science and that a good English teacher can not write novels. They can not do those things because good teaching in the public school is a full-time job requiring all the energy an individual can muster. If the teacher does produce art on a professional level, his students, his colleagues, or his family will suffer. After all, there are only twenty-four hours in a day, and a person who is primarily interested in his own creative work will probably ignore the needs of his pupils or shirk the duties that he sould be sharing with his colleagues simply because a professional artist is devoted to art, not to education. Such a person will make valuable contributions to society through his work, but contributions to aesthetic education will be made by people who are primarily committed to education through art, that is, by dedicated art educators. Consequently, the teacher who is pressured to produce art on a professional level is being diverted from his primary task; he is being asked to do things that are not in the best interests of education.

Probably there are other pressures that act upon the art teacher and cause him to fail an as art educator, but the most distracting pressures are the ones that have been mentioned. To resist them or to eliminate them, we need self-confident teachers who are dedicated to education, knowledgeable in their subject, efficient at their job, and clear about their goals.

Traditional problems

As has already been said, teaching is one of the best of professions. Few jobs are more satisfying or more important. Yet, in all professions, there are troubles that have been around for a long time. Most of the ones associated with teaching are well known and need not be discussed extensively here. Low salaries, low social and academic status in a few communities, and the problem of maintaining privacy are commonly mentioned difficulties. The teacher is subjected to considerable criticism, to heavy teaching loads, and to growing class sizes. He is often required to keep attendance records, supervise lunch rooms, chaperone dances, sponsor clubs, and manage homerooms. In addition, he must keep up with his field of specialization through expensive work on advanced degrees or through independent study. Some educators avoid mentioning these problems to prospective teachers; others minimize the problems or say that these difficulties must be accepted as part of the job. Obviously, nothing of this sort is recommended here. Instead, the actual facts of life in teaching are presented, so that the prospective teacher will know what is ahead of him and what he must do to meet the challenge. If we shield him from the truth or minimize the problems that he will face, we do him a grave injustice; and if we tell him that he must accept the difficulties as inherent in the job, we tend to preserve an unsatisfactory state of affairs. Perhaps this is one of the troubles with education. Perhaps we have convinced future teachers that they must accept conditions as they are. If so, we have created a tragic situation, because the profession is in need of improvements that can be brought about only by persons who are not content with the status quo. We need individuals who will not only object to weaknesses and see them as problems capable of solution, but will also do something about solving them. We need teachers with vision, spirit, and courage.

QUALIFICATIONS FOR THE JOB

Obviously, the teacher who represents the visual arts in the public schools is faced with a tremendous job. He must teach art to children in such a way that all its benefits are received, and he must convince the opposition that art has value for the individual and that it should play a significant role in education. He must be able to explain as well as demonstrate. This takes an extremely capable person, but the schools can settle for nothing less. After all, the teacher is probably the only artist or artistically informed person that most children and their parents will ever meet. Thus the impression that the teacher makes can profoundly influence the future of art education in public schools and the future of art as a part of the American way of life. If the teacher is that important, what kind of a person do we need for the job?

The teaching of art to children is largely in the hands of classroom teachers and art teachers. In general, they both need the same qualifications, except that the art instructor should have more technical skill and a much more profound understanding of art and aesthetics. He will be expected to teach children, to guide the art program meaningfully, and to assist the classroom teacher who must concern himself with more than one subject. To do his job effectively, the art teacher must be skilled in at least one productive aspect of art such as drawing, painting, or sculpture. This is a very important requirement because it is unlikely that anyone will teach persuasively without the sureness and conviction that come from personal accomplishment. Skill of that kind does not grow out of a superficial exposure to many media, but it comes from hard work and prolonged association with a few. Having acquired skill in at least one medium, the teacher will find it helpful to have a working knowledge of several others. This is because of the need to offer a variety of media to children between kindergarten and high school. The exposure to several materials helps the children to learn more about common materials, tools, and procedures, and it helps to make art an interesting and exciting activity.

The art teacher should know something about children, about child art, and about the people with whom he works. The fact that an individual considers himself to be an artist does not automatically make him a gift to education. He must work with children who have different interests, understandings, and capabilities. Some of them will have personality problems, physical defects, and family problems, and few of those difficulties can be overcome by the instructor's artistic talent alone. Success with such children requires that the teacher be sensitive to them and to their needs. He must know enough about the characteristics of child art to recognize when growth is the result of physical and mental maturation and when it is the result of his teaching. He also must realize that administrators and fellow teachers will have special strengths and weaknesses and that their knowledge of art is not apt to be one of their strongest points. By the same token, the art teacher is not likely to be an authority in math, science, or the social studies. This means, in short, that all teachers must be willing to accept each other for their special strengths and to help each other with their weaknesses. Doing so requires tact, patience, and understanding; and these same characteristics are needed to work satisfactorily with mothers and fathers. Some parents, of course, will treat the art teacher as if he were a king; others will act toward him as an equal; and some will behave as if he were a servant. But much of his treatment from teachers and parents will depend upon his ability to get along with people who do not understand art. If he cannot get along with those who are unfamiliar with the subject, it is quite clear that he cannot teach art.

It is apparent that tact and good judgment are necessary requirements in teaching, but it is especially helpful if they are supplemented by a knowledge of the social, historical, and philosophical foundations upon which American education is based. This knowledge is helpful because the art instructor will be working in an educational system that has grown, changed, and developed over many years. Its present configuration is the result of social and historical events, philosophical ideas, and experimental trial and error. In other words, the educational system in America is basically not a haphazard construction; it has reasons for existing in its present state. If the new teacher is familiar with those reasons, he is not so apt to fight the system or to ignore it. This is not to say that the way of education should not be changed, but it means that change should be given considerable thought. If it is not, the effectiveness that has been achieved with the present system will deteriorate and chaos will replace it.

Finally, the art teacher must be familiar with the history of art; he must have a background in aesthetics; and he must be verbal. A knowledge of art history and aesthetics helps one to make judgments about quality in art; it provides a basis for discussing the significance of art in human history; and it helps one to develop a philosophy of art or a point of view. There is probably nothing more important or more fundamental for the art educator than a point of view about the nature of his subject. Without a philosophical orientation of some kind, the teacher has no basis for organizing an art program; he has no logical way of deciding what to teach or how to teach; and he has no reasonable way of evaluating student growth. In fact, he has no grounds for arguing that art should be taught at all. But it is an unfortunate fact that artists are often critical of anyone who develops an articulate point of view about art. The prospective art teacher should know what the objections are.

The first is that art is too personal and too elusive to submit to definition. But if art is so subjective, so mysterious, and so intangible that it can not be defined in some way, then it can not be taught. In fact, it would not be possible to create an environment in which it could grow by itself if a person did not know what he was trying to grow. A teacher would even be unable to decide what to say to his students because he would not know what to talk about. Consequently, the first objection seems weak.

The second objection to having a point of view about the nature of art is that it might result in a formula for the production or teaching of art. Such a formula or design might be harmful, and, without a doubt, the possibility of developing such a formula exists. But this possibility exists whether we thoughtfully work out a philosophy of art or whether we do not. We develop formulas, systems, or patterns for working and teaching because they enable us to do things efficiently and responsibly. The alternative to systematic behavior is chance behavior, and it is doubtful that anyone would advocate teaching on the basis of chance. Consequently, we must recognize the necessity for systematic teaching behavior, but we must guard against the development of a formula that leads to the production of something other than art. The point is that we are less likely to create a teaching pattern that leads in the wrong direction if we develop a reasoned point of view about the nature of art.

The teacher with a philosophy of art in mind is a person with great potential in education. But if he is unable to put his ideas and feelings into clear and coherent verbal statements, he is likely to fail as a teacher. After all, teaching is largely a verbal activity, and an instructor must be able to speak clearly, correctly, and authoritatively about art if he is to convince people that it has any value and that it has a place in the education of children. Without that ability to make sense with words, the teacher will be unable to justify his methods of teaching or his evaluative techniques, because he will not be able to relate them meaningfully to the nature of art. Developing a facility with words is therefore a goal that future teachers should try to achieve, although it may not be easy. Part of the difficulty is that some art instructors in the universities are highly inarticulate and seem to value that condition. Consequently, they give our future teachers the impression that students are taught simply by bringing them into the aura of the artist. Perhaps teaching does occur in that way from time to time, but it is a highly inefficient method. In fact, it often takes as long as four years for a student to *feel* the meaning that a professor intends when he makes such comments as "it does not work," "it is uninteresting," "it needs to be more organic," "the design is weak," or "the work is not sufficiently plastic." The public schools can not afford the inefficiency of such vagueness. Thus the future teacher must do all he can to obtain clarification from his instructors, and he must work diligently to became more articulate himself.

THE PURPOSE OF THIS BOOK

The primary purpose of this book is to help the teacher of art acquire a portion of the knowledge that is needed for success in art education. The first requirement is to develop a point of view about the nature of art, the value of art, and the nature of the artist. Chapters 2, 3, and 4 are therefore devoted to those topics. The subjects are very complex, and it is quite possible that the reader will disagree with the views expressed. But the purpose of the material is not to present the last word in aesthetics; the purpose, rather, is to demonstrate how a philosophy of art might begin to take form. If the reader recognizes weaknesses in the reasoning, he should try to repair them and create a better philosophy for himself. This will require critical study, classroom discussion, and additional reading in aesthetics, but it is the kind of work that is interesting and exciting to undertake.

After a point of view about art and artists has been considered, it seems appropriate to study the symbolic development of children and the various explanations for it. This will give the teacher an indication of what he can expect from children, and it will offer him the kind of information that he can pass on to parents. Such material often convinces parents and administrators that their criticisms of child art are completely out of place. Hence an attempt has been made to give the necessary information about symbolic development in Chapters 5 and 6.

A teacher may be able to speak convincingly about the subjects that we have just mentioned, but getting art instruction established more firmly in the public schools will require that he explain the need to *teach* art and the need to do so in the public schools. Then it will be necessary for him to show that art will contribute to the aims of education. Chapter 7 offers help in that direction.

But the aims of education are usually stated in broad, general terms that are not especially helpful to teachers, who need to have a reasonable list of goals stated in terms of behavior. In other words, they need to know how youngsters act when goals have been achieved, and they must also know how the goals of the sixth-grade teacher differ from those of the first-grade teacher. This information is provided in Chapter 7; it is based on the nature of art, the nature of the artist, and the developmental characteristics of symbolization. Along with it there is some information that should be helpful in developing an art curriculum in the elementary and secondary schools.

Chapter 8 covers the methodology of teaching art. It suggests ways of developing the necessary knowledge, attitudes, and skills in children. It is recommended that the future teacher study that chapter carefully to see how the recommended methods are related to the philosophy of art presented in Chapter 2. A person should be able to show how methods would change if a different philosophy of art were employed.

It is one thing to know *how* to teach, and it is another thing to know *what* is appropriate for teaching in the various grades. Consequently, Chapter 9 is devoted to suitable procedures, materials, classroom arrangements, and motivational topics. Then, in Chapter 10, we make an effort to help the teacher with the problems of evaluation and reporting to parents. Both of these problems are almost certain to puzzle a person, especially in the subject of art, but the conditions in education seem to demand a careful and conscientious evaluation and reporting system; that is the reason for offering help on the subject in this textbook.

Because the teacher of art is often given supervisory duties, it seems important to give him some aid in understanding the supervisor's job. Consequently, Chapter 11 is devoted to curriculum development, personnel relationships, in-service education, public relations, managing equipment and supplies, and professional obligations. The future teacher should not avoid this chapter, because it contains information that he is not apt to get elsewhere and presents several ideas that a good teacher should think about for quite a while.

Finally, the last chapter calls attention to the strengths and weaknesses of research in art education. It urges the teacher to be *interested* and *critical*, and it suggests things that he can do to get more for his money from those who report research.

From these comments, the reader can see that the text is fairly comprehensive in its coverage. The comprehensiveness is intentional because the author believes that art educators must get an allover impression of the things that a good teacher must consider and a notion of the things that he must do. Naturally, the book does not say everything that might be said about art education, but if it shows how a reasonable approach to the subject can be made, it has served its purpose.

QUESTIONS FOR DISCUSSION

1. College teachers of art compete freely with other professional artists. Why is it easier for them to do so than it is for the teacher of art in the public schools?

2. Some persons like teaching because of the security that it provides. In what way does it offer security?

3. Teaching positions in art can vary from one community to another. What are the names given to the various positions, and how do they differ?

4. What is tenure? What are the arguments for and against tenure?

5. What are the various professional organizations in art education? What is their function?

6. What are the names of the professional publications in art education? What is the nature of the content of each publication?

7. If college art students are not told about the problems of teaching art, they will not learn about those problems until they graduate and begin teaching. Why is that a bad practice?

8. What is the history of art education in America? Why is it important to know about the history of art education?

9. Make a list of ten recent textbooks that deal with teaching art to children. What are the basic differences among those textbooks?

10. What is your state doing to improve the quality of art education?

11. Ask for an interview with one or two of your local school administrators. What are the qualifications they look for in an art teacher? Do they believe in the importance of art in the school curriculum? Does the art program in that system reflect the administrators attitude toward art?

12. How many employment opportunities are available to college graduates in painting, sculpture, art history, industrial design, advertising design, crafts, and art education? What are the opportunities for each of the sexes? What are the beginning salaries? What are the average salaries likely to be after sixteen years? Is there any variety in the work? Are the working conditions pleasant? Would you be making any significant contribution to the improvement of our society if you accepted a position in any artistic profession?

13. How do state certification requirements affect the education of art teachers? How do college and university requirements affect the education of art teachers?

14. Work with children of all ages if you get a chance. Do you like the children? Would you enjoy spending eight hours a day with them? Five days a week?

15. In your opinion, could you more easily see the effect of your teaching in the elementary school or the secondary school? Why?

16. Why do you want to be a teacher? Be honest with yourself. Are your reasons really good ones? Will you be a credit to the profession?

SUGGESTIONS FOR FURTHER READING

Barzun, Jacques: *Teacher in America*, Little, Brown and Company, Boston, 1946.
One of the great books on teaching.

Cole, Natalie Robinson: *The Arts in the Classroom*, John Day Co., Inc., New York, 1940.
An old but famous text on art education written by an intuitive classroom teacher. It is inspirational in nature.

Conant, Howard, and Arne Randall: *Art in Education*, Charles A. Bennett Co., Inc., Peoria, Illinois, 1959.
This book presents a lot of practical information for the future teacher that is not available in other textbooks. It covers placement agencies, professional organizations, interviews, application procedures, classroom planning, art materials, and other important items.

Conant, James B.: *The American High School Today*, McGraw-Hill Book Company, New York, 1959.
A well-known book by one of America's great educators. It examines the weaknesses of our secondary schools, and makes recommendations for improvement. The place that Conant gives to art education in the secondary school is not a prominent one.

Hubbard, Guy: *Art in the High School,* Wadsworth Publishing Company, Inc., Belmont, California, 1967.
An excellent book on art in the secondary school.

La Mancuso, Katherine: *Source Book for Art Teachers*, International Textbook Company, Scranton, Pennsylvania, 1965.
This little book offers a wealth of practical information that should be helpful to the beginning teacher.

Lanier, Vincent: *Teaching Secondary Art*, International Textbook Company, Scranton, Pennsylvania, 1964.
This is one of the few books available on the teaching of art in the secondary schools.

Lindstrom, Miriam: *Children's Art*, University of California Press, Berkeley, 1957.
A short paperback book that provides a fine, inspirational introduction to the teaching of art.

Logan, Frederick M.: *Growth of Art in American Schools*, Harper and Brothers, New York, 1955.
The only book of its kind that is available. It covers the history of art education in

America, but it includes education in the colleges and museums as well as education in the public schools. Each art teacher should have a copy in his library.

Mathias, Margaret: *The Beginnings of Art in the Public School*, Charles Scribner's Sons, New York, 1924.
Prospective teachers should have an acquaintance with art education of the past. This fine little book shows what the leaders in art education were thinking in the 1920s.

Merritt, Helen: *Guiding Free Expression in Children's Art*, Holt, Rinehart and Winston, Inc., New York, 1964.
A short paperback book that provides a good introduction to art education.

Viola, Wilhelm: *Child Art*, Charles A. Bennett Co., Inc., Peoria, Illinois, 1944.
All teachers of art should be familiar with this old classic. It mentions the methods of teaching used by the father of child art, Franz Cizek.

Wachowiak, Frank, and Theodore Ramsay: *Emphasis: Art*, International Textbook Company, Scranton, Pennsylvania, 1965.
For a glimpse at contemporary art education in the elementary school, we recommend this text because it is a recent one. A very practical book.

Chapter 2
THE NATURE OF ART

Before teaching art to children it is necessary to develop a reasonable point of view about the nature of art. Unless it is explained or defined in some way, the teacher has no logical basis for deciding what he should do with his students, no way of knowing whether they have been successful in judging or producing art, and no meaningful standard for the evaluation of his own teaching.

As he develops an explanation of art, the teacher will discover that many other persons have struggled with the same task. And if he examines their work, he will find that their definitions of art are not the same. They are different, at least in part, because the things we call art have changed considerably through the years, or, to put it another way, the definitions vary because the concept of art is open and subject to change. In fact, the continued expansion of the concept to include new and different referents or art forms has led not only to new and different definitions, but has caused certain philosophers to conclude that a perfect or real and true definition of art is a logical impossibility. It is   *25* impossible because a real and true definition of the term must specify the properties that are necessary and sufficient to identify and include all art and separate it from all nonart, and this can not be done when the concept to be defined is open to change.[1]

Although a real and true definition of art may be impossible, it still is absolutely essential for the teacher to develop an explanation of some kind if he is to operate efficiently and avoid the production of nonart in his classroom. Probably the best that he can do is to create an *honorific* definition, one that treats the concept of art as if it were closed. In other words, he may have to develop an explanation that restricts the notion of art to certain honored or preferred forms despite the fact that experts may refer to other things as art in the course of everyday experience. Accepting such a task as necessary and reasonable, we shall proceed with the development of an honorific definition, and we shall begin by assuming that most scholars would agree that art is creative. But what does it mean to be creative? What is creation? What is creativity?

WHAT IS CREATIVITY?

Sir Herbert Read, one of the most outstanding contemporary writers on art, says that creation "should imply the calling into existence of what previously had no form or feature."[2] This means that creation should involve the making of something out of nothing or the production of form out of formlessness. In that sense, the word is frequently applied to the act of divine power which brought this world into existence out of nothing. But the possibility of a similar achievement by human beings is difficult to accept because a state of nothingness or formlessness is unknown to modern man. As far as we know, new form develops only through the rearrangement of things that already exist.

[1] The impossibility of a real and true definition of art is explained by Morris Weitz in "The Role of Theory in Aesthetics," *Journal of Aesthetics and Art Criticism*, vol. 15, no. 1, pp. 27–35, September, 1956.
[2] Herbert Read, *Education through Art*, Pantheon Books, Inc., New York, 1958, p. 113.

Pl. 1
John Marin, *From the Bridge,
New York City*. Wadsworth Atheneum,
Hartford, Conn. Several color
illustrations appear in Chapters 1
through 4. Which of the depicted
objects are works of art, and which
are art objects of the highest quality?
Why? Chapters 2 and 3 should help
answer those questions.

Therefore, the words "creation" and "creativity," when applied to the formative activity of man, do not imply the making of something from nothing, but they mean essentially the same thing as invention. According to Read, invention implies "previously existing objects or facts, with the mind as merely an agent that arranges or combines them in a new order."[3]

So far, form has been mentioned without being defined. *Form is the shape that something takes.* The producer of that shape or form is a creator, and the act of producing the form is referred to as creation. The word creation also may be used to designate the final product, the new form. Creativity, like creation, is a noun that refers to the act of bringing new form into existence, but it is not used to designate the final product. In another sense, however, it is employed in referring to the ability to act creatively. Thus we say that we develop creativity when we develop the ability to act creatively, and a person who acts creatively is said to be creative. The word creative is therefore an adjective that is used to describe the process, the product, and the individual who produces new form.

It may be interesting to say that creativity, as a process, is the rearranging of forms that already exist in a new configuration. But a more useful definition of the process would specify the forms that are rearranged during the creative act. To think of those elements as existing outside the human organism is to forget the function of the human mind. Without the mind, few elements are likely to be rearranged except by accident or by evolution. Thus the initial organization of new form occurs in the mind, while the existence of combined elements in a new form outside the human organism merely indicates that creativity has taken place. If, however, the initial organization of existing elements does occur in the mind, what are the dimensions of mind that can be combined? The position taken in this text is that the basic elements or dimensions of mind are concepts and emotions. Hence *creativity is the process of rearranging concepts and emotions in a new form, and it is also the ability or the disposition to do*

[3] *Ibid.*

so. The evidence that such an act has occurred and that someone possesses the ability to engage in it is simply the materialization of a new form.

WHAT IS ART?

Men, by custom, have referred to certain man-made creations as works of art. This indicates that they think of the art product as being sufficiently different from other new forms to deserve a special name. How does it differ?

First, *the art product is unlike other created objects because it is primarily for aesthetic experience.* According to Gotshalk, aesthetic experience is "simply intrinsic perception, or attention to an object or field preeminently for the apprehension of the full intrinsic perceptual being and value of the object or field."[4] In other words, an aesthetic experience is the experience a person has if he pays attention to something for the purpose of grasping the meanings or values that reside in its visual appearance, its sound, its tactile quality, its taste, or in all its sensuous dimensions. If this is so, anything can be experienced aesthetically. We can focus our attention on the sensuous aspects of a thumbtack, a tree, an automobile, a girl, or a work of art for the purpose of apprehending whatever values reside there. But a work of art is the only created product that is intended to serve primarily as the focus of aesthetic experience. Thus we may conclude that a microscope is not a work of art even though it can be experienced aesthetically. It is not an art object simply because it is not intended to serve first and foremost as a subject for perceptual concentration and appreciation. Its major function is to magnify things.

Second, *the art object is different from other created forms because it has a structural organization or design that is pleasing, whereas the nonart object may or may not have a pleasing structure.*

[4] Denman W. Gotshalk, *Art and the Social Order*, Dover Publications, Inc., New York, 1962, p. 3.

To have that pleasurable quality, a man-made form must be organized in such a way that most of the persons who perceive it are attracted to it and have no desire to change it; or to put it another way, the organization must be such that changes other than very minor ones would reduce the attraction of the object or make it irritating and unpleasant to perceive.

It is important, however, to emphasize that the pleasurable quality of which we speak is a quality that resides in the compositional structure of a work of art, but not necessarily in the content or the concepts and emotions that are presented. This means that the nature of content or the nature of what is being communicated should not influence decisions about whether a particular form is a work of art. After all, the concepts and emotions presented by Brueghel's *Wedding Dance* (Figure 2.1) are pleasant, and the content of Picasso's *Guernica* (Figure 2.2) is not; yet, both are considered works of art. In each of these instances it is the pleasurable nature of the composition or the way in which the object is put together that causes it to be called a work of art.

Although most artists and critics probably would not argue strenuously about the notion that art is primarily for aesthetic experience, they might disagree more vigorously about the idea that the structure of art must be pleasing to the senses. The author of this textbook, however, contends that pleasurable structure is an identifying feature in art because he believes that art as a term is commonly used to designate examples of elaborate or refined expression as opposed to ordinary presentations of concept and emotion. And if there were no difference between the compositional or syntactical structure of art and that of nonart, it would be extremely difficult, if not impossible, to separate the refinements of expression from expression itself.

Assuming, therefore, that art products are different from other products in the two ways that have been mentioned, it follows that the process of making them is also different from other instances of creativity. At least the process of art must have a different intent behind it, and that intent is to make structurally pleasing forms that are primarily for aesthetic experience. Furthermore, the process must involve attentiveness to the

Fig. 2.1
Pieter Brueghel the Elder,
The Wedding Dance. 1566.
Tempera on panel, 47 × 62 in.
Detroit Institute of Arts.

aesthetic dimension of the emerging form. This means that the creator must pay attention to the concepts and emotions that he intends to present and to the organization or composition of the presentation. In other words, he must attend to the values or qualities that reside in the appearance of the new form.

From the foregoing comments, we may say that *art is the rearranging of concepts and emotions in a new form that is structurally pleasing and primarily for aesthetic experience.* A new public form that possesses those characteristics is called a work of art, and it proves that creativity of the artistic type has occurred.

QUALITY IN ART

To discuss the matter of quality in art, it seems helpful to return to our original definition of creativity. On the basis of that definition, we may say that creativity occurs in all areas of human activity and that all humans are creative. The proof for such an assertion is that all persons either talk, dance, write, cipher, sing, gesture, paint, build, or act in some other way to produce new form in the routine of daily existence. But this does not mean that all form-giving acts, all form-giving persons, and all man-made forms are equally significant. Writing a book is considered to be more creative than arbitrary hole digging; the inventor of a new vaccine is said to possess more creative ability than a person who produces new forms on a punch press; and an original painting is more highly regarded than a copy. In other words, the references we make to creativity imply that some instances of it are more significant than others and that it is on a value continuum. The problem is how to distinguish the more valuable from the less valuable examples of creativity. Solving this is an important problem because the betterment of the individual and his society depends upon the development and the use of the most valuable creative processes, abilities, and products.

Offhand one might think that creativity could be judged by the number of products produced, but the trouble with that notion is that all people produce large quantities of form in the course of ordinary, everyday experience. And if we say that a person is highly creative, we do not mean that he talks a lot or draws a lot. We mean that his acts, abilities, and products are achievements within a given domain of formative behavior that lead more significantly toward the goals of that domain than other instances of creativity. Consequently, we must determine the goals of artistic creativity if we are to judge the quality of formative behavior in art and the quality of the art product.

It is common to hear people speak of the language of art.[5] When they do, they usually mean either or both of the following: (1) that art is expression that *conveys* concepts and emotions; or (2) that art is expression that *symbolizes* concepts and emotions. The first meaning indicates that art acts as a kind of communication, and the second suggests that it serves simply as a presentation of concept and emotion without any desire for communi-

[5] For an interesting discussion of art as a form of discourse, see Charles W. Morris, "Science, Art, and Technology," *The Kenyon Review*, vol. 1, no. 4, pp. 409–423, 1939.

cation. To say that art acts as communication is to imply that its goal is to satisfy the needs of the artist *publicly* by developing in the observer an understanding of the concepts and emotions that are embodied in the art product.[6] But to say that art serves to present meaning without any intent to communicate is to suggest that its aim is to satisfy the needs of the artist in a more *private* manner. The needs that are apt to be satisfied in such a private way are numerous and vary from one person to another. An artist might use his art in a secluded way to think more clearly or to gain a better understanding of himself and the world around him; or he might use it entirely as a source of pleasure or as therapy.

Assuming that the aim of artistic creativity is either the satisfaction of needs through communication or through a more private presentation, it may therefore be concluded that artistic quality is determined by the degree to which the intended goal is achieved. And if the aim is some kind of private satisfaction for the artist, then the best judge of artistic quality would probably be the artist himself. Other persons can and do judge quality in art of that kind, but they are apt to have two problems. First, they are likely to have difficulty finding out what specific kind of satisfaction such art was supposed to have given its creator. Second, they are likely to have trouble detecting changes in behavior or increases in the satisfaction of personal needs. Judging quality in private art is therefore more appropriately the province of professionals in psychology or psychiatry who are trained to make such decisions.

The art that is much more familiar and more suitable for judgment by the general populace is the kind that is offered to the public for purposes of satisfying certain needs through communication. If it were not meant to communicate or to convey concepts and emotions, there would be no reason for displaying it in public. Consequently, the quality of such art may be ascertained by estimating the degree to which the communicative

[6] For a more complete explanation of the nature of the observer's understanding, see R. G. Collingwood, *The Principles of Art*, The Clarendon Press, Oxford, 1938, pp. 109–111.

Pl. 2
A poster design entitled
"Pretzel." (Photo courtesy
Anheuser-Busch, Inc.) Is this object
a work of art? If so, is it a work of
high quality? Why?

Pl. 3
Robert Indiana, *Louisiana*. 1966.
Oil on canvas, 70 × 60 in.
Collection, Krannert Art Museum,
University of Illinois, Champaign.
Is this object a work of art?
If so, is it a work of high
quality? Why?

Fig. 2.3
Morris Graves, *Guardian.*
1952. Oil on canvas, 48 ¼ × 32 in.
Collection, Krannert Art Museum,
University of Illinois, Champaign.

ART, ARTISTS,
AND CONNOISSEURS

content is understood by the observer. Making such a judgment, however, is full of problems which will be discussed below. But, first, what are some of the qualities in a work of art that are likely to affect the observer's understanding of its content?

To begin, a full understanding or appreciation of even the most elementary concepts and emotions is largely dependent upon the structural organization of the presentation. If the composition is unusually pleasurable to perceive, the observer may give the work whatever degree of careful attention is required to conceive its meaning. But if the arrangement offers no more than minimum pleasure, the observer is apt to pass it by or study it superficially, which keeps him from grasping its full significance. Thus any estimate of quality in art must be based in part upon the degree of pleasure to be obtained from structural arrangement. If we use that notion in appraising Morris Graves' *Guardian* (Figure 2.3), we find the painting to be of high quality because the

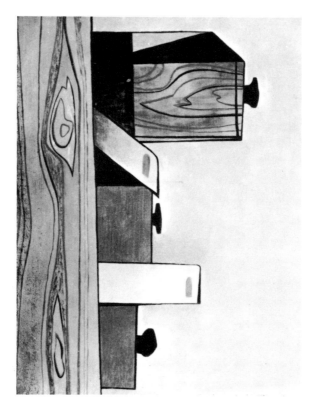

Fig. 2.4
Chest of Drawers.
This painting by the author has a disturbing composition. It does not balance, and most observers have the desire to turn the painting so that the left side is at the bottom.

organization of the work is very appealing. The painting by the author in Figure 2.4, however, is not of such high quality because there is in the painting a noticeable degree of imbalance that is irritating. In fact, it is so disturbing to a few observers that they have taken the painting off the exhibition wall and placed it in a different position on the floor.

Another factor that is likely to affect the observer's understanding of content in art is the complexity of that content. If it is relatively simple, it will be easier to understand than concepts and emotions that are more complex. But this does not mean that simple content is an indication of high quality in art. Most of us would attach the label of high quality to art that has succeeded in making us understand profound, elaborate, or complex concepts and emotions; we would do so because it is generally agreed that communicating profound information is more difficult than conveying simple information. Furthermore, *the ability to conceptualize complex material is the primary trait that separates human beings from the lower animals.*[7] Therefore it seems reasonable to expect evidence of that trait to appear in anything we call superior human achievement. If we accept this view, we may conclude that quality in human art increases as the content of the work increases and becomes more profound or complex. And if the content of a given art object remains extremely simple, there is no good reason for valuing that work more highly than the product of a lower animal.

A third factor that affects the observer's understanding of

---

[7] The only animal other than man that is capable of making drawings and paintings is the chimpanzee or ape. During the last fifty years, experiments have shown that chimpanzees or apes can make drawings and paintings that are similar in content and organization to the scribbles of children and to the work of certain adult abstract expressionists. The similarities are so great, in fact, that chimpanzees and children have won prizes in adult exhibitions. In those instances, however, the content of the adult art was very elementary, and as a result the work was low in quality. Ordinarily human art is superior and should be superior to chimpanzee art because chimpanzees are able to present no more than the most elementary concepts of color and mass while human beings are able to produce configurations that reveal intricate notions of color, shape, texture, space, and volume. Unlike chimpanzees, human beings are also able to create forms that present concepts of terror, sadness, tree, man, banana, and other moods, events, or objects.

For a more thorough account of the picture-making behavior of apes and its relationship to human art, see Desmond Morris, *The Biology of Art*, Alfred A. Knopf, Inc., New York, 1962.

Fig. 2.5
David Aronson,
Joseph and the Ishmaelites. 1954.
Encaustic on canvas, mounted
on panel, 38¼ × 48⅜ in. Collection,
Krannert Art Museum,
University of Illinois, Champaign.
The content of this work
is highly complex.

Fig. 2.6
George Mathieu,
A la Mémoire de Mathieu
de Vendôme, Régent de France.
1952. Oil on canvas, 38 × 76¾ in.
Collection, Krannert Art Museum,
University of Illinois, Champaign.
Compared to the content of the
painting in Fig. 2.5, the content
of this work is very simple.

content in art is the novelty of that content. If the communicative material in the art object is entirely new to the observer, he will have difficulty understanding it; if it is familiar, he will grasp it much more easily (Figures 2.7, 2.8). Contemporary art, for example, is often hard to understand because it frequently presents new information, while art of the past is less difficult to appreciate because its content has become familiar through long exposure, study, and discussion. Thus it is important, in estimating artistic quality, to reserve judgment on a work of art if the content of that work is new and difficult to grasp. Perhaps longer and more careful study will produce an appreciation of concepts and emotions that were previously unknown. If that happens, we may conclude that the quality of the art is unusually high. A judgment that the work is low in quality would be justified, however, if the content of the work could not be understood by expert observers even after careful and prolonged study.

A fourth element that affects the observer's understanding

Fig. 2.7
Sir Jacob Epstein,
Head of Wynne Godley. Bronze;
ht., 19 in. Collection, Krannert Art
Museum, University of Illinois,
Champaign. The content of this
work is familiar to most observers.
Consequently, they can understand it.

Fig. 2.8
Julius Schmidt. Untitled.
1960. Bronze, 14½ × 28 in.
Collection, Krannert Art Museum,
University of Illinois, Champaign.
The content of this work is novel
and relatively difficult for most
persons to understand.

of content in art is the *relationship* of the compositional structure to what appears to be the *intended* content of the work. If one element does not seem to be compatible with the other, the total effect of the work is unpleasant and confusing. As an example, imagine a figurative painting that, on the whole, looks soft, gentle, feminine, and warm; then imagine one or two portions of the painting as being harsh, hard, sharp, and cold. Imagine, also, that the latter qualities do not seem to be in keeping with the figure that they describe or with the other figures. The form and the *intended* content of the painting therefore seem inconsistent, contradictory, and disturbing. And the chances are that most observers will find the total configuration confusing and unpleasant. In such cases, the work may not be art at all, or if it is, it is low in quality.

Having discussed the factors in the art object that are likely to affect understanding or successful communication, we shall turn our attention to the problems that beset the observer in identifying art and estimating its quality.

THE PROBLEMS OF RECOGNIZING AND EVALUATING ART

Although a definition of art and a scheme for judging its quality have been offered, it is clear that identifying art and estimating its significance will not be easy. One of the problems that may arise in identifying works of art is how to determine if an unfamiliar object is intended primarily for aesthetic experience. Fortunately, the problem is not especially hard to solve because it is perfectly reasonable to assume that an object is primarily for aesthetic experience if it is placed on display without appearing to serve any function other than to be perceived and understood.

A second problem that will arise for the observer is how to decide if the goal of art in a given instance is communication. The problem is an important one because the average observer lacks the qualifications for judging art that is not intended for communication. But, once again, the problem is relatively easy

Pl. 4
Finger painting by the
chimpanzee Betsy. (Courtesy
Baltimore Zoo.) Is this
object a work of art?
If so, is it a work of
high quality? Why?

to solve because it is logical to assume that a work of art is meant to communicate through aesthetic experience if it is placed on *public* display. If it was not intended for communication there would be no reason for displaying it in public.

Another difficulty in identifying and evaluating art is apt to develop when the observer attempts to judge the pleasurableness of composition. At that time he may discover that a structural arrangement that pleases one individual may not please another to the same degree. And if that happens, how can he decide if an object is a work of art or art of high quality?

Obviously, an acceptable judgment of composition must be based upon a standard of organization that most persons would find pleasing, and Herbert Read has wisely suggested that the structure of nature comes closer to meeting that requirement than anything else.[8] In other words, a dispute over the pleasurable quality of composition might be solved by comparing the forms and relationships in the questionable object with the elemental forms and relationships found in nature. If there is a similarity, we may predict that the structural arrangement of the object will be pleasing to the majority of persons who view it, and in that case we may also conclude that the object possesses one of the two characteristics that identify art as art.

When we say that the most pleasing composition is the one that comes closest to the natural structural order of nature, we do *not* mean that the most appealing product is destined to be a naturalistic imitation of nature or a photographic reproduction of the changing surface qualities in nature. We *do* mean, however, that the most attractive composition is likely to be the one that contains proportions (such as those in the human skeleton), shapes (such as the teardrop, the crystal, the seed), and spatial relationships (such as bean to pod) that are similar to the proportions, shapes, and relationships found again and again in the structure of natural things.[9] Living with these natural forms as we do every day means that we feel "right" and comfortable

---

[8] Read, *op. cit.*, p. 16.
[9] For a wonderful account of the elemental forms in nature, see D'Arcy Thompson, *On Growth and Form* (John Tyler Bonner, ed.), Cambridge University Press, Cambridge, 1961.

in their presence. We have *learned* to like them. Thus it seems appropriate that their structural organization should serve as a standard in judging the composition of man-made form.[10]

Still other standards that might be employed in solving disputes over composition are the principles of perceptual organization. We know, for example, that certain configurations are difficult to perceive with clarity, and we know that other arrangements create tensions that can be very disturbing if they are not counteracted. Imbalance, for example, is irritating, and so is confusion between figure and ground. More will be said about such matters in Chapter 4, but the point is that certain principles of perceptual organization exist. If principles that lead to a kind of comfortable but dynamic equilibrium have been used, the composition of a new form should be pleasing to a wide assortment of people.

Most persons, of course, are perfectly capable of deciding if an object is intended for aesthetic experience, and they should be able to determine if an object's compositional structure is fundamentally pleasurable to perception. But they frequently have trouble judging composition simply because they habitually allow the pleasing or displeasing nature of the content to influence their decisions. If they could ignore the content, they could judge the basic structural organization adequately and *identify* art with relative ease.

A much more difficult task for the average observer, however, is the judging of *quality* in art. To estimate quality adequately, the observer must be sensitive to *nuances* of compositional structure and must have a broad background of experience with art and with life. Without those qualifications he is likely to be incapable of understanding new or unusual content or complex

---

[10] When we say that natural forms are pleasing to the senses, we refer to the more common forms that have not suffered from accident, genetic breakdown, or some other atypical occurrence. Thus we refer to the proportions, shapes, and relationships found in a normal, healthy tree and not to the configuration of a tree that has been distorted by fire, lightning, or genetic malfunctioning.

Forms that result from accident or from other atypical natural causes are likely to be displeasing in structure simply because they are so uncommon that we have not been able to get accustomed to them. We have not learned to like them.

concepts and will probably fail to recognize the presence or absence of compatibility between form and content. And if the observer is incapable of doing such things, he is not qualified to judge the degree to which the artist has been successful in communicating concepts and emotions.

In short, the understanding that art evokes is as dependent upon the observer as it is the artist. Also, the qualifications for judging art vary from one observer to another. Consequently, some persons will grasp the content of a particular work of art and others will not, which will lead to a dispute about the quality of the work. When this occurs, the observer obviously faces a difficult problem in making a judgment. How can he estimate quality when such differences of opinion exist? Probably the best that he can do is to turn the problem over to experts, connoisseurs, or arbiters of taste. Such persons are sensitive and learned observers who have devoted their lives to the study of art and to aesthetic perception, and they also possess a wide background of experience in the stream of life. If they can not adjudicate matters of identification and quality, we may conclude that a reasonable estimate can not be made.

THE APPLICATION OF THIS PHILOSOPHY TO ART INSTRUCTION

Now that a philosophy of art has been presented, it is appropriate to ask how it applies to the teaching of art in the elementary and junior high schools. That question can be answered briefly and in general terms at this point, but it will be answered in far greater detail in the second half of the book. By offering a short response here, however, we intend to show that a philosophy of art is highly *practical* and that it has *important implications* for art education. If we can do that, the reader should not be tempted to disregard the theoretical foundation of art as irrelevant or as a waste of time. Hence we shall begin by showing how our definition of art applies to the teaching of art.

We have said that art is the rearranging of concepts and emotions in a new form that is structurally pleasing and primarily for aesthetic experience. If we accept that view, it is clear that the potential artist must have concepts and emotions to rearrange, and they must be important enough so that he will want to rearrange them and clear enough so that he will be able to rearrange them in a new form. Therefore the art teacher's job is to help his students develop and clarify their concepts; it is also his job to make the concepts so interesting and exciting that his students will want to give them a visual form.

If the new form is to be structurally pleasing, then the second thing that the teacher must do is to help the student learn what it takes to make a pleasurable visual composition. The teacher might use nature, the principles of perceptual organization, and compatibility between form and content as standards for his own judgment of structural arrangement.

The third fundamental task for the teacher is to make sure that his students make their new forms primarily for aesthetic experience; but that is not a difficult job. It simply means that students must be required to make forms that act merely as the focuses of attentive perception and serve no purpose other than communication. In other words, the teacher must have his pupils make forms that are primarily for perception and not for something else.

Naturally the teacher also wants to help his students create art forms of the highest quality that they are capable of producing. To do so, he must help them to increase the pleasurable effect of structural organization by getting them to create greater nuances of formal arrangement within their compositions. He must get them to present concepts that are as complex and profound as youngsters of their age are able to produce, and he must do what he can to get them to present novel or at least original concepts. He also must help his students to see and become sensitive to instances of incompatibility between form and content. If they can not see such discordant elements, they obviously cannot correct them.

In conclusion, it is important to point out that the definition of art offered in this chapter can be of further practical value to the teacher, especially when he wishes to decide if a proposed project is truly an art project. If it is an art activity, it should permit the student to give visible form to his own concepts and emotions. Coloring dittoed drawings, for example, and following step-by-step systems for making an Easter bunny do *not* allow the student to give form to his own ideas and feelings. Consequently, they are not art projects and should not be used as such in the elementary and secondary schools.

SUMMARY

In this chapter, creativity is described as common form-making behavior, not as a special or unique activity practiced by rare individuals. Art is recognized as one kind of creative behavior, and the quality of that behavior is measured by the degree to which it succeeds in reaching its goal. The aim or goal of publicly displayed art is said to be the observer's understanding of the concepts and emotions that are presented in the art object.

Having offered such a point of view about the nature of art, it is important to show that art is valuable to the individual and to society. Consequently, we shall turn our attention to such matters in the chapter that follows.

QUESTIONS FOR DISCUSSION

1. Must art communicate? What do we mean by communication? What is necessary for communication? If a form communicates nothing, how can we be sure it exists?
2. If people seem to disagree about the nature of art, does that mean that it can not be adequately defined? What is an adequate definition?
3. If art is so personal that it can not be defined, how can we teach it?

4. Find three or four definitions of art. What are the strengths and weaknesses of these definitions?

5. Using the scheme for judging artistic quality that is presented in this chapter, compare the work of Rubens with the work of Franz Kline. Compare the work of Toulouse-Lautrec with the work of Pieter Brueghel. What are the results? In which instance is it more difficult to determine the better work? Why?

6. According to our definition, an automobile tire is not a work of art. If an artist mounts it on a pedestal and puts it in a museum, does his action make it a work of art? Why?

7. If art is created primarily for aesthetic experience, is it correct to speak of the designed cereal box as a work of art? Why? Is this a difficult question? Why?

8. If visual presentations of concept and emotion are on a quality continuum from nonart to bad art to fine art, where would you place children's drawings on that continuum? Why? Would you have to know anything about the capabilities of children or about their drawings to make the foregoing judgment fair and accurate? Why?

9. If a person happens to grow up in an ugly man-made environment, would that affect his standards for judging art? Why?

10. Teachers often have children make impressions of their hands in plaster for them to bring home for Christmas or Mother's Day. Is that an art project? Why?

11. It seems reasonable to say that high-quality human art is more humanistic than ape art. If you believe this to be so, in what way is it more humanistic?

12. Some people believe that philosophers are the only persons who are qualified to talk about the nature of art. If this is so, what are the implications of that position for the teaching of art?

13. If difficulties are encountered in making judgments about art, who should be consulted? Who are the experts in art?

SUGGESTIONS FOR FURTHER READING

Bell, Clive: *Art*, Chatto & Windus, Ltd., London, 1927.
Chapter I is a milestone in the history of art criticism. Very readable.

Gombrich, E. H.: *Art and Illusion*, Pantheon Books, Inc., New York, 1960.
A famous art historian offers a different and stimulating point of view about art.

Gotshalk, D. W.: *Art and the Social Order*, Dover Publications, Inc., New York, 1962.
This book offers a good account of the nature of aesthetic experience and covers other relevant topics with equal skill. Very readable.

Morris, Charles W.: "Science, Art, and Technology", *The Kenyon Review*, vol. 1, no. 4, pp. 409–423, 1939.
This essay deals with art as a unique form of language. A bit difficult for the beginner.

Rader, Melvin: *A Modern Book of Aesthetics*, 3d ed., Holt, Rinehart and Winston, Inc., New York, 1960.
A popular anthology that will introduce the beginner to the study of aesthetics.

Read, Herbert: *Education through Art*, Pantheon Books, Inc., New York, 1958.
Chapter 2 provides a natural follow-up to the book by Clive Bell.

Shahn, Ben: *The Shape of Content*, Harvard University Press, Cambridge, Massachusetts, 1957.
Chapter 3 is relevant to the material covered in this chapter. An excellent starting place for those who have no background in art. Written by one of America's best-known artists.

Vivas, E., and M. Krieger (eds.): *The Problems of Aesthetics*, Holt, Rinehart and Winston, Inc., New York, 1953.
This anthology presents many essays that are suitable for the student who is unfamiliar with aesthetics.

Weitz, Morris: "The Role of Theory in Aesthetics," *The Journal of Aesthetics and Art Criticism*, vol. 25, no. 1, pp. 27–35, September, 1956.
This essay explains why real and true definitions of art are impossible.

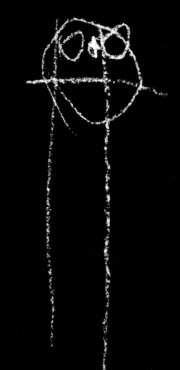

Chapter 3
THE VALUE OF ART

There is no point in discussing the nature of art for purposes of determining its place in the school curriculum unless it has value for the individual and for society. Since the time of Plato, scholars have attempted to explain its merit in philosophical terms, but their explanations have been difficult for most persons outside philosophy to understand. As a result, many persons do not accept art as an important element in their lives or in the general education of their children. If they permit it to be taught in the public schools, they allow it to play no more than a minor and relatively unimportant educational role.

The significance of the foregoing situation for art educators is that we must increase our effort to explain the values of art to the general population if we hope to retain and expand art instruction in the public schools. As we do so, we must offer our explanation in terms that most people will comprehend. In this textbook the first step in that direction is to suggest a standard that nearly everyone will accept as a reasonable measure for judging the worthiness of things.

In the last analysis, the value we assign to things depends upon the position we take regarding the ultimate goal of life. For most of us, *the primary purpose in living is the attainment of the good life*. According to Harry Broudy, a prominent educational philosopher, the "good life" is a state of existence characterized by physical well being, emotional security, excitement, and self-realization (or a sense of worth and achievement).[1] We accept that description, and as a result we assume that anything contributing to the attainment of such a life is valuable to the individual. Does the art process or product make that contribution?

THE VALUE OF THE ART PRODUCT

A work of art is valuable as an aid in the attainment of the good life *primarily* because it increases the opportunity for self-determination and stimulates self-realization. It does so simply because it is a model of the human condition, a model of concept and emotion that can be inspected and meaningfully interpreted by an observer. As a vehicle of communication, the art product permits the observer to perceive and to understand new possibilities for thinking, feeling, and imagining. Thus it increases his opportunities for self-determination and self-realization merely because it provides him with more information about life.

The pleasing or beautiful structural properties of a work of art tend to make the object especially effective as a source of information simply because beauty is alluring and persuasive. It not only attracts the observer to the content that exists metaphorically in the art product, but it causes him to be attentive and to accept the values that are presented. If a beautiful organizational structure were not present in the creations of Beethoven and Michelangelo, for example, it is almost certain that their work would not communicate so powerfully to so many people.

In its most highly creative form, the work of art is especially

[1] Harry S. Broudy, *Building a Philosophy of Education*, Prentice-Hall, Inc., New York, 1954, pp. 29–54.

Pl. 5
Hans Hofmann, *Apparition*. 1947.
Oil on reinforced panel, 48 × 57⅞ in.
Collection, Krannert Art Museum,
University of Illinois, Champaign.
Is this object a work of art?
If so, is it a work of
high quality? Why?

valuable because it is thoroughly humanistic. It is intricate in composition, complex in content, and novel in its presentation of concept and emotion. Hence the art object of high quality leads the observer away from an animalistic style of self-realization and directs him toward the fulfillment of his more human potentialities.

Considering the great effectiveness of art products in presenting or communicating the values of life, it is important that works of art be available to everyone and that they be of the highest possible quality. Any decline in the number of available art products would tend to reduce our freedom by decreasing our sources of information; and any deterioration in quality would not only limit our freedom but also lower the level of the culture by reducing the complexity of the humanistic concepts that people develop. It would reduce those concepts to a more elemental or animalistic plane.

The value of the art object in self-determination has been recognized for centuries by *small* groups of people, especially by heads of state. Hitler, for example, was well aware of the fact that a person can control large numbers of people if he can control the arts. By manipulating the various modes of expression, Hitler restricted the concepts that were made available to the people. With limited or selected information they were unable to develop themselves to a point where they could become a threat to the government.

In one respect, many of the culturally disadvantaged children all over the world are like the great mass of the people in Hitler's Germany. They lack a knowledge of the ideas and emotions that exist in the minds of men, and this, in turn, reduces their potential as human beings. That is why it is so important for culturally disadvantaged youngsters to be exposed to many works of art. After all, the artist is a manufacturer of possibility who puts the dimensions of mind into their most desirable public form so that they can be shared with others. Because we are able to learn from his communicative art product, and because the artist has controlled our learning to a certain extent through the organization of aesthetic elements, we may speak of the product as being educational. It is largely on the basis of this educational quality that art appreciation or the study of art objects is justified in the public school.

Unfortunately, education through the art product may not make a significant contribution to the good life if the content of the work is restrictive or commonplace. In a totalitarian society, for example, the artist is controlled. Consequently, his product presents the nature of things from the point of view of the state, and the possibilities for thinking, feeling, and imagining are curtailed. This means that the observer's opportunities for self-fulfillment are seriously limited, and he is not apt to become the man he could be.

In a free society, however, the art product does not necessarily provide the views of the state, nor does it simply mirror or reflect society. It presents the nature of things from the artist's personal and sensitive point of view. The artist is completely free to make use of his unusual sensitivity, which helps him to detect possibilities for being that are overlooked by the average man. It is important to point out, however, that such freedom also permits a person to create models that seem detrimental to the achievement of our goals. It allows him to make images of immorality and injustice, among other things; and if such models are accepted and imitated, the individual may not achieve the self-realization, the physical well being, and the emotional security that are characteristic of the good life. Nevertheless, most members of a free society would rather take that risk than submit to control of the arts or to censorship.[2] After all, the control of expression can easily lead to the subjugation of the individual even if he is educated. The undesirable aspects of *free* expression, on the other hand, are not so dangerous, especially if the individual is well schooled. They are less dangerous because education in a free society is itself uncensored and more capable of developing persons who can make wise judgments about the things they see and hear. Consequently, the members of a free society

[2] For a good account of the problem of censorship, see "Censorship—by Whom?" in Henry Ehlers and Gordon C. Lee (eds.), *Crucial Issues in Education*, Henry Holt and Company, Inc., New York, 1959, pp. 13–55.

are more apt to obtain the highly desirable values in art if they give their children a superior general schooling that includes aesthetic education among the fundamental subjects of instruction.

What has been said so far about the value of the art object could have been said about the products of all the arts. But what of visual art in particular? Does it make any contribution to the attainment of the good life that is not made by other works of art? If so, what does it do that is different?

Obviously, visual art offers the kind of information that can be embodied in visual images. This means that it provides at least two kinds of knowledge. First, it communicates the ordinary *discursive* type of information that is normally and more effectively transmitted by means of the spoken or written word; it says house, tree, sun, sky, red, blue, happy, and other things of a similar nature. If that were all it could do, however, visual art would have no more than a limited value. Hence it is the ability to offer the second, *nondiscursive* kind of knowledge that makes art so unique as a form of communication. Virtually all its nondiscursive content is *particular* in nature. By this we mean that visual art presents more than a general notion of treeness or blueness. It presents a particular kind of treeness and a particular hue, value, and intensity of blue. It also offers specific shapes, textures, and volumes. These are distinctive qualities that cannot be put into words, music, or gestures. They can be communicated only through visual images.

Furthermore, visual images are *presentational*,[3] which means that all the conceptual and emotional content that the artist wishes to convey is offered simultaneously, so that all the inner relationships are immediately available to the spectator. It shows him the relative positions of things and the precise qualitative relationship among colors, shapes, lines, and textures. Consequently, visual art not only gives the observer the particular qualities of individual formal elements, but it presents those qualities, all at once, in a specific contextual relationship. The

[3] For a more complete discussion of visual art as a nondiscursive and presentational form of symbolism, see Susanne K. Langer, *Philosophy in a New Key*, New American Library, Inc., New York, 1948, pp. 63–83.

exact meaning that results from the total context is another kind of information that cannot be offered through other expressive media. The arts of speaking and writing, for example, necessitate the stretching of content into sentences, paragraphs, and chapters. Words and sentences not only lack the peculiar meaningful quality of visual form, but occur in a context that must be perceived over a length of time. The same is true of the elements of music, drama, and the dance, where the final understanding of the whole is dependent upon the observer's memory of the parts as they occur

Fig. 3.1
Charles Burchfield,
The Four Seasons. 1949–60.
Watercolor on paper, 55⅞ × 47⅞ in.
Collection, Krannert Art Museum,
University of Illinois, Champaign.
Everything Burchfield wishes to say
about the four seasons is presented
simultaneously in this painting.

57
THE VALUE
OF ART

sequentially in time. Thus visual art provides the individual with certain meaningful particularities of experience that cannot be offered by the other arts.

Persons closely associated with visual art have always contended that they receive value from an aesthetic experience with the product. They have expressed the belief that such an experience is relevant to human life, but they have had great difficulty in convincing others. They therefore give the impression that the experience is without content and of no use. Nothing could be more inaccurate, of course, because aesthetic experience with a work of art is full of content. The trouble is that the unique meaning of the experience is largely nondiscursive, or impossible to translate into words. It is the kind of meaning that can often be absorbed in a trancelike state; yet the nondiscursive knowledge absorbed in those instances contributes to self-determination and to the good life in the same way as the linguistic type of information. It increases the possibilities of being human.

To make the basic value of visual art more apparent, let us

Fig. 3.2
Pierre-Auguste Renoir,
Luncheon of the Boating Party. 1881.
51 × 68 in. Phillips Memorial Gallery,
Washington, D.C. This painting
helps the observer to understand the
particularities of a pleasant occasion.

examine the *Luncheon of the Boating Party* by Pierre August Renoir (Figure 3.2). Years of experience indicate that in this masterpiece the observer finds a pleasing arrangement of line, color, shape, and texture. There is no desire to change it because it seems as appropriate and as natural in its elemental relationships as nature itself. Attracted by its pleasurable structure, the spectator has no difficulty identifying the people, the dog, and the objects that cover the tables. These are the elements of subject matter that help to communicate the content. The fact that there is subject matter, and the fact that it is quite naturalistic, means that the content is relatively easy for most persons to grasp. Part of the content is of the discursive sort that can be put into words, and part is not. It is possible to explain verbally, for example, that fourteen people and a dog are gathered around a table enjoying a luncheon; it is also possible to say that the painting presents blueness, yellowness, redness, treeness, and chairness. But it would be fruitless to try to spell out the specific stance of any individual or the exact relationship that exists among all the parts of the picture. It would be equally impossible to convey linguistically the precise feeling of friendship, sunshine, freshness, and summertime that is found in the painting. Thus Renoir's unique combination of elemental visual forms and relationships constitutes a model of a particular experience of pleasantness that could not be offered through any other medium of expression. The observer who is reached by such material will realize that there are more possibilities for thinking, feeling, and imagining than he would have known if he had not seen the painting. His opportunities for self-determination and self-realization are extended a bit, and thus the good life stands a little closer to being achieved.

An equally worthwhile effect of the art product upon the observer might be an understanding of an experience of unpleasantness. Such an effect is achieved by Honoré Daumier in *La Rue Transnonain, April 15, 1834* (Figure 3.3). The composition is appealing, as it has to be, but the total effect is not. The artist has presented a concept-feeling-image of a particular instance of the gruesome and inhumane treatment some of us give to our

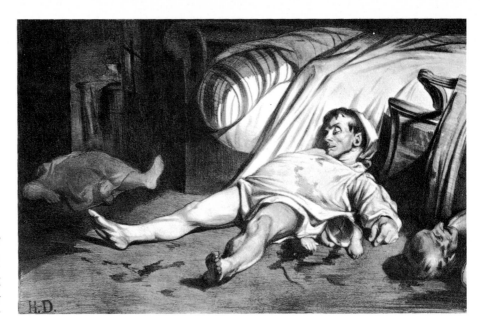

*Fig. 3.3
Honoré Daumier,
La Rue Transnonain, April 15, 1834.
Metropolitan Museum of Art,
New York. From this art object
the observer learns something
about an instance of unpleasantness.*

fellowmen. By doing this, Daumier has extended the range of our intellectual activity to include unpleasant things. He may help us to understand a new point of view about intolerance, blueness, longness, peacefulness, or softness. The possibilities are endless. But the point is that an art product can help us to expand the dimensions of our minds so that we can think, feel, and imagine in ways that may not have occurred to us before. That we can see new possibilities means that we have a greater opportunity to determine our own fate. It increases the will to be and gives us greater freedom. This, in turn, makes it more likely that we can achieve our own potential and thus attain one measure of the good life. Furthermore, mental activity of this kind is the thing that separates us from the lower animals, insects, and machines. The more we engage in it, the more human we become.

Because of the characteristics already mentioned, visual art objects are especially valuable as historical documents. After all, the knowledge we possess of human life prior to the time of written records is knowledge that has been obtained from drawings, paintings, statues, and other visual forms produced by the artists of that day and age. Furthermore, the art object has continued

Pl. 6
Max Abramovitz,
Assembly Hall. 1963.
(University of Illinois Photo.)
Is this object a work of art?
If so, is it a work of
high quality? Why?

to provide valuable information ever since. In the work of Renoir and Daumier, for example, we are presented with the *visual* particularities of manner, dress, attitude, and value that existed in bygone days, and such information simply cannot be obtained from any other source.

Stained-glass windows, mosaics, frescoes, tapestries, statues, painted altarpieces, hymns, chants, and vestments not only provide conceptual information but also contribute to rituals of all kinds. They tend to put the observer in a mood for full participation and acceptance; hence they are often used to advance the cause of religion. The tremendous value of art in such matters is often overlooked until someone eliminates the art, and then there is usually a great protest and a promise to restore it. Apparently, the art work gives the spectator a certain amount of emotional security along with some assistance in fulfilling himself religiously.

Perhaps we could also say that the art product helps the individual attain a degree of emotional security by making it possible for him to identify with other human beings, even if he happens to be in a lonely and isolated place. In other words, a person who has few social contacts is assisted in maintaining his emo-

Fig. 3.5
Harry Breen,
The Four Living Creatures: St. Luke.
1965. Polymer acrylic on ceramic;
ht., 18 in. (Courtesy of the artist).
An example of contemporary
religious art.

tional balance, his sense of reality, or his perspective on life if he exposes himself to books, music, and visual art. They not only cause him to recognize new possibilities for thinking and feeling, but they help him to see that other persons have some of the same ideas, dreams, and problems that he has.

Art products contribute to the attainment of the good life in still another way, by providing excitement. Certainly we are all aware of the mental interest and activity that is generated by such books, plays, and films as *Gone With the Wind*, *The Grapes of Wrath*, *Brave New World*, *A Streetcar Named Desire*, and *The Wizard of Oz*. Hundreds of similar examples could be given, and we could also name innumerable works of visual art that have created excitement in the minds of men. The *Nude Descending a Staircase* by Marcel Duchamp (Figure 3.6) is a prime example because it electrified the country from coast to coast when it appeared in the Armory Show of 1913. It stimulated people not because it was a painting of a nude but because it was so highly abstract and unnaturalistic. And a piece of equally abstract monumental sculpture by Picasso produced a similar reaction when it was exhibited in Chicago in 1967. It seems incredible that such a piece of metal sculpture could evoke so much excitement.

Finally, art objects are valuable because they serve as ornaments in our homes and our communities. Sometimes the ornaments are actually tributes to persons we admire and respect. But the pleasing structure of the art object tends to improve the appearance of our surroundings and makes us "feel good." In the time of Pericles, Athens was probably one of the most artfully ornamented cities in the world; its appearance was a source of pride to the citizens.[4] There can be little doubt that the presence of magnificent statues and buildings contributed to the greatness of the Athenian culture, and there is reason to believe that the art of today could assist our own society in reaching an even higher cultural level.

[4] To get a taste of the Athenian pride, read the famous funeral oration by Pericles, in Thucydides, *The History of the Peloponnesian War* (Sir Richard Livingstone, ed.), Oxford University Press, London, 1943, pp. 109–117.

Secondary values of the art product

Most of the primary values of art have been mentioned. But the fact that the art object is educational and pleasantly organized means that it has certain secondary values. It is economically worthwhile, for example, because its pleasant structure, together with wholesome content, tends to make anything associated with it seem desirable. An attractive box makes cereal and other items more appealing. Thus we have an explanation for the use of art in advertising and industrial design; and we have a clue as to why it is used in hotels, banks, and other institutions that profit from accommodating the public. Works of art make the patron feel comfortable and more favorably inclined toward the products or the services rendered.

Art objects also have value as propaganda because a tasteful, beautiful, and moving statement is almost seductive. It is certainly far more effective in swaying the minds of people than anything dull and unemotional. As a result, nearly all politicians, political parties, governments, and special-interest groups use art to promote their own points of view. This is especially true in Russia and China, where politically motivated art always glorifies the worker and depicts the head of the state as a friend of the working class. Obviously, people who see nothing but models of that kind have a hard time conceiving other points of view.

The history of art in America illustrates quite clearly that the art object also has social value. It acts as a status symbol by suggesting that it's owner is either wealthy or highly cultured. S. N. Behrman, in a most enjoyable book about the art dealer Joseph Duveen, shows how the collection of art became an important social element in the lives of the great tycoons of American business.[5] Here were men who had developed commercial empires and amassed great fortunes; yet they lacked the respect that meant so much to them. They wanted to be known as cultured men and as gentlemen. Art and culture had always been synonymous, so they used their wealth to build some of the largest and finest collections of art in the world. The story is so

[5] S. N. Behrman, *Duveen*, Random House, Inc., New York, 1951.

interesting that it is covered in different ways by several other writers; *The Proud Possessors* by Aline Saarinen,[6] and *The Tastemakers* by Russell Lynes[7] are especially good accounts.

In each of the examples of its secondary value the art product seems worthwhile because it helps someone to realize his potential, to feel emotionally secure, or to feel a certain amount of excitement. But the important thing to note is that such examples are considered to be of secondary value in this text because they might help certain persons to attain the good life at the expense of others. By this we mean that an artful advertisement might sell quantities of inferior if not harmful merchandise, in which case it would aid the seller and hurt the buyer. Or propaganda in the form of art might cause an individual to accept the rule of a dictatorial government only to discover, after it is too late, that his freedom has disappeared. Consequently, the value of the art product must be carefully considered, especially when the worthiness of the product is associated with economic, political, or social goals. But as long as the art object remains a free and highly personal model of the human condition, there should be little doubt of its basic value to man as an aid to the attainment of the good life.

THE VALUE OF THE ART PROCESS

For more than three decades art educators in the public schools have placed greater and greater emphasis upon the value of the art process. Some of them have concluded that the process is even more important than the product, especially for the growth and development of children. Expressing the latter view more effectively than almost anyone else was Viktor Lowenfeld.[8] Through his books, his speeches, and his teaching, he inspired thousands of teachers and gave them a new sense of importance. He did so by giving a perceptive account of the significance of

[6] Aline Saarinen, *The Proud Possessors*, Random House, Inc., New York, 1958.
[7] Russell Lynes, *The Tastemakers*, Harper and Brothers, New York, 1949.
[8] Viktor Lowenfeld, *Creative and Mental Growth*, The Macmillan Company, New York, 1957.

child art and child behavior. He showed that certain characteristics in the art product could provide evidence of the child's growth and development. If changes in the appearance of the product indicated any kind of personality growth, the growth was attributed to the fact that the child had engaged in an art process. And the status of the teacher was given a boost simply by showing that he had a powerful effect upon the growth and development of children.

If there were any weaknesses or errors in Lowenfeld's thinking, they certainly must be excused in view of his remarkable contributions to art education. But it might be worthwhile at this point to question three aspects of his position on the process and the product. First, he had a tendency to speak of the process as a means of facilitating growth, but he offered very few concrete examples of *how* it did so. Instead, he seemed to concentrate upon the product and the evidence that in offered in support of the notion that growth had occurred during the process.

Second, when he did try to show *how* the process aided growth, he inevitably referred to the teacher's stimulation as the major source of information, direction, and emotional support. This is peculiar because the instructor's stimulation is a part of the act of teaching, but it is not a part of the process of drawing or painting. Thus an emphasis upon such stimulation tends to show that teaching is the key to growth and development while suggesting that the art process is of secondary importance. This means that Lowenfeld's argument in favor of the process was actually self-defeating.

The third questionable aspect of his position was a view he shared with many other art educators. In short, he seemed to dismiss the art product as an important part of art education. He did not discuss the values that are obtained from studying art objects, except to indicate that such objects have a diagnostic value; and, strangely enough, he did not seem to see the product as having any functional relationship to the process. In other words, the *act* of creating was the only aspect of art that was worth mentioning as far as Lowenfeld was concerned. But it is

Pl. 7
A crayon drawing of a parade by a thirteen-year-old girl in fifth grade. Is this object a work of art? If so, is it a work of high quality? Why?

Pl. 8
A drawing of a train made with a felt-tipped pen by a five-year-old girl. Is this object a work of art? If so, is it a work of high quality? Why?

very difficult to prove the validity of such a view. Perhaps it would be helpful to show why.

To prove that the art process is the only aspect of art that is important for education and self-realization, we would have to know when a person was actually engaged in the process. Probably, we would agree that an individual is involved in the art process only if he produces a work of art. If the product is not art, we can hardly attribute any growth that might occur to an art process. Thus it is apparent that any teacher must focus his attention on the product if for no other reason than to be sure that his students are engaged in or have been engaged in an art process. Assured of that, the teacher may then proceed to evaluate the process in terms of his student's growth, but how is growth to be ascertained? According to Herbert Read, "Education is the fostering of growth, but apart from physical maturation, growth is only made apparent in expression—audible or visible signs and symbols."[9] If this is a reasonable assumption, it seems clear that we must examine the art product. Dismissing it as unimportant would eliminate one of the primary sources of information about growth. Consequently, the value of the art object to the teacher cannot be dismissed; but what of the student? Does the product have no significance for him?

To understand the importance of the product to a pupil, imagine yourself in the role of a student painting a picture. Your product begins its existence with the first mark placed on the paper or canvas, and the nature of that product changes and develops with each succeeding stroke. Occasionally you stop to observe the paint and paper. You are observing an unfinished product, but it is still a product. It helps you to decide what to do next. If you decide to stop, and eventually you will, it is because your product has told you that you are finished. If the product is supposed to be of no importance to you, you might try going through the process without a product; if you are a musician, you might play a piano with the strings removed, for that would allow you to go through the motions of the process

[9] Herbert Read, *Education Through Art*, Pantheon Books, Inc., New York, 1945, p. 11.

without producing any music; or if you are a painter, you might make all the movements associated with painting without creating a mark. It seems obvious, however, that without any sounds or marks there is no way of deciding what to do next or when to stop. In fact, there is absolutely no evidence that you actually went through the process of making anything. Consequently, it does not seem possible for the art process to be of much value without the product. In fact, you might say that the product is a *vital* part of the process, a part that is just as necessary for children as it is for adults. Therefore, to clear things up, it would be better to avoid saying that the product is of no importance in art education. Instead, it would be far more accurate to say that *both* the process and the product have great educational significance for children and adults. With that idea in mind, let us proceed to a more thorough discussion of the art process and its value to the individual.

Taking a cue from Lowenfeld, we shall try to show that the art process helps the individual grow aesthetically, perceptually, intellectually, emotionally, creatively, and technically. By doing so, however, we do not mean to suggest that the various dimensions of growth are unrelated. They are, on the contrary, very closely related, as we shall attempt to make clear.

Aesthetic or perceptual growth

The term aesthetic is derived from the Greek *aisthesis*, meaning "perception." Hence it is probably not surprising to learn that aesthetic growth is simply one dimension of perceptual growth. To grow perceptually is to become more discerning or more cognizant of the existence, character, or identity of things. The factor that determines the particular nature of perceptual growth is the intention of the perceiver. If he attends to an object or field for the purpose of gathering scientific information, we would say that he is engaged in scientific perception. If he concentrates, however, on an object or field for the purpose of apprehending the full intrinsic being or value that resides in the sensuous aspects of the object or field, we would say that he is engaged in *aesthetic* perception; and we would expect him to grow aesthetically instead of scientifically. The making of visual art facilitates the aesthetic type of perceptual growth because it causes the individual to *practice* aesthetic perception. It causes him to pay attention to the sensuous dimension of experience and to the sensuous aspects of his own visual creations.

Intellectual growth

Intellectual growth presents a problem for discussion simply because there is no completely satisfactory definition of intelligence.[10] Perhaps the best that we can say at this point is that intellectual growth involves an *increase in knowledge* which tends to manifest itself in a higher quality of performance or behavior.

The making of visual art is an aid to intellectual growth because it helps to develop the participant's knowledge of himself and his environment. Perhaps the first and simplest stride in that direction occurs through the use of tools and materials such as pencils, brushes, ink, paint, wood, wire, and paper. As he uses those items, the individual learns their inherent characteristics and how they act in different situations. Knowledge of that kind is simple indeed, but its importance is not reduced in any way by its simplicity. Without it, we cut, burn, and bruise ourselves; we have great difficulty in repairing the kitchen faucet, for example; and we have trouble constructing anything that involves the manipulation of tools and materials. In short, the knowledge that we gain through the use of art materials is the kind of knowledge that is necessary if we are to live safely, independently, and efficiently. But such information is not gained solely from the making of art objects; it can be obtained just as easily through mechanical work, carpentry, and other activities that involve the use of tools and materials.

The art process leads to a more unique kind of intellectual growth, however, because it involves the participant in whatever steps are required to make a tempera painting, a piece of plaster

[10] Lloyd G. Humphreys and Paul L. Boynton, "Intelligence," in the *Encyclopedia of Educational Research* (Walter S. Monroe, ed.), The Macmillan Company, New York, 1950, p. 601.

sculpture, or some other kind of art object. In short, the participant learns artistic procedures by going through artistic procedures. He does not learn the methods of science or business, but he learns the steps that a person must go through to make a certain kind of art object.

The art process contributes to further intellectual growth because it requires concentration on structural organization or composition. By attending to composition, the participant learns to recognize the formal elements that cause a pleasing or displeasing visual arrangement. He learns the effect of lines, shapes, colors, and textures on one another and on the total visual configuration. He also learns to recognize compatibility between form and content.

The art process contributes to still another kind of intellectual growth as it engages the participant in the act of re-forming his concepts in a new medium. By reshaping them, he tends to reinforce them, strengthen them, and refine them in much the same way that a musician builds his concepts of music by singing or playing the music.

As the participant focuses his attention upon the content of his work or upon the concepts and emotions that he intends to symbolize or communicate, he may discover that his concepts are not clear. In that case, he must clarify them or give up the effort to make art. To clarify his concepts, there are two courses of action open to him. The first is trial and error. In other words, he might begin to create form with only a vague notion of the statement he wishes to make, and by trying one thing and then another he discovers in the emerging form the concept or emotion that he wishes to symbolize or communicate.[11]

Another possibility is that a person might begin making a visual form without even a vague concept or intuition of what

[11] Support for this view may be found in the following statement by R. G. Collingwood (*The Principles of Art*, Clarendon Press, Oxford, 1938, p. 111): Until man has expressed his emotion, he does not yet know what emotion it is. The act of expressing it is therefore an exploration of his own emotions. He is trying to find out what these emotions are. There is certainly here a directed process: an effort, that is, directed upon a certain end; but the end is not something foreseen and preconceived, to which appropriate means can be thought out in the light of our knowledge of its special character. (Used by permission of The Clarendon Press, Oxford).

Fig. 3.7
A six-year-old girl learned
about the human figure as she drew
this picture of her mother and father.

he wants to symbolize or communicate. In that case he tries one thing and then another until he develops a concept that he considers worthy of retention or communication. This is a point worth noting, because we do not wish to give the impression that an artist always begins with a preconceived idea of what he is going to do. He may have no idea at all, or he may have a powerful but vague idea, and in both instances he may use trial and error as a way of discovering what he will eventually convey. The result is intellectual growth because a concept has been developed, clarified, or refined.

Sometimes an artist will use trial and error in an effort to develop or clarify a concept, but he will not succeed. In that case he must either give up or try the second method of building concepts and making them clear. The second method is to expose

himself once again to the experience from which his vague concepts and emotions were originally derived. He might look, for example, at something such as a still life, a landscape, or a moving stream of traffic to strengthen or clarify the meaning of the experience for him. If the effort is successful, we may speak of the result as a kind of intellectual growth. And as the artist proceeds to give visual shape to his newly acquired knowledge, his intellectual growth advances even further because his eye and hand movements tend to reinforce the mental image created by the original sensory experience. They contribute to the development of a more highly complex or more highly differentiated concept. But if intellectual growth is one of the results of the foregoing process, what is the more specific nature of the concepts that develop?

Fig. 3.8
Gardner Symons,
Morning Light. Ca. 1929.
Oil on canvas, 40 × 50 in.
Collection, Krannert Art Museum,
University of Illinois, Champaign.
As the artist painted this picture, he developed his concepts of trees, barns, rivers, shadows, hills, color relationships, and other such matters.

In the first half of this chapter it was said that works of art contain nondiscursive as well as discursive information. Naturally, the artist develops and refines concepts of that kind as he attempts to give them tangible form, and *it is through the development of nondiscursive knowledge that the art process makes its most unique contribution to intellectual growth.* Nondiscursive knowledge develops simply because the act of making art forces the individual to concentrate upon the nondiscursive dimension of experience or upon the visual particularities of experience. Hence Renoir grew in a unique intellectual fashion as he painted the *Luncheon of the Boating Party.* He did so because the process forced him to pay attention to the specific qualities of visual form that constitute a particular experience with people, dogs, clothes, food, and other elements of a boating party. Some of that same information can be gained by the spectator as he observes Renoir's work, but no observer of his work can grow as much as Renoir did. Consequently, it is very important for people to engage in the act of making art as well as in the act of appreciating it. It helps them to find out what they really think and what they honestly feel.[12]

Emotional growth

To grow emotionally is to gain a greater understanding of one's own affective life and to develop more security and satisfaction in the living of that life. Emotional growth has a certain relationship to intellectual growth. As an individual learns more about himself and his environment, he enjoys more freedom. He is able to recognize more opportunities for thinking, feeling, and imagining, and such knowledge may serve to reduce frustrations and other emotional difficulties that arise when no encouraging possibilities for the future can be seen. As a person learns more about his own emotions (by giving them form), he is also in a better position to manage them and to live a more secure and satisfying affective life.

[12] For a nice account of art and its contribution to intellectual development, see Harold Taylor, *Art and the Intellect*, Museum of Modern Art, New York, 1960, pp. 16–17.

Another contribution of the art process to emotional growth is that it involves a person in the constructive use of his emotions. Art cannot be produced without emotion because it is one of the essential and distinguishing elements of art. Most of us, unfortunately, are suspicious of emotion; we tend to rule it out of our serious mental activities whenever we can. We want to remain objective. The result, according to Archibald MacLeish, is that our knowledge of facts has become separated from our feeling for facts.[13] He feels that the world crisis of the 1960s is not caused by the Russians, the atom bomb, or the underdeveloped countries, but by the mind of man himself. MacLeish believes that the human mind has developed in such a way that we can do many remarkable things without any real feeling for what we are doing. He suggests that art (poetry in particular) could help us develop a feeling for ourselves and our place in the world. This may be asking more of art than it can deliver all by itself; but certainly the art process does help us to understand our emotions and does emphasize the notion that emotions are constructive, worthwhile, and characteristically human as long as they do not get out of hand. Understandings and attitudes of this kind tend to give an individual greater satisfaction in the affective dimension of life.

A more widely recognized contribution of the art process to emotional growth is its ability to release tension, hostility, or feelings of aggression. Perhaps the clearest example of its helpfulness can be observed in the art activities of children. They can be seen hanging or beating their antagonists in their drawings, pounding them in clay, and slashing them in their paintings. They frequently talk about what they are doing as they do it, and the activity often results in at least a temporary period of relaxation. But this does not mean that the art process has effected a cure for some form of anxiety. It simply helps to relieve it. The success that it has in doing so, however, is based on the fact that tense, hostile, and aggressive acts are carried out in a more socially acceptable fashion on paper and in clay. The same

[13] Archibald MacLeish, "To Face the Real Crisis: Man Himself," in *The New York Times Magazine*, December 25, 1960, p. 5.

acts in linguistic or physical form would probably be repressed.

The art process makes another clear contribution to emotional growth simply because the making of something gives a person a sense of accomplishment. He takes pride in it, and it gives him a feeling of personal worthiness. A similar feeling could be obtained from any constructive process, of course, but the making of art provides a special sense of achievement. It does so not only because it involves the participant in a thoroughly human activity, but also because it gets him into the act of making something that is pleasing or beautiful. Beautiful forms are always more rewarding to make than ordinary or ugly forms.

Anyone who has worked with children will also testify to the fact that youngsters gain some happiness as they use materials to shape their feelings. There is a sense of goodness and well being in the laughs and smiles that accompany their work, and a person does not need to be a psychologist to see it. Perhaps it occurs because the crackling of cellophane, the soft ticklishness of cotton and cloth, the smell of paste, and the magic of crayon resist are pleasing to the senses. Experiences with such ordinary things result in some of the most satisfying and rewarding emotional reactions that life has to offer. When we no longer rejoice at the ooziness of clay, the warmth of drying plaster, and the smell of freshly cut wood, the world will be a sad place in which to live. Unfortunately, it is easy to move in that direction if a person is compelled to pay continuous attention to the practical or academic aspects of life that seem so eminently serious and profound. Thus it is important for the individual to engage in art activities because they bring him close to ordinary things once again and help him "feel good." These feelings of happiness, pride, and personal satisfaction are characteristics that are essential to mental health. Some people believe that such feelings are the most significant benefits to be obtained from the art process, and they consider those feelings to be sufficient justification for engaging in the process.

After reading these comments about the value of the art process for emotional growth and the good life, it would be reasonable to ask why the process was not helpful to a man like

Vincent van Gogh, the great Dutch painter. The answer is that art did help him. To get an idea of how much it helped him, one might read *Lust for Life* by Irving Stone.[14] If it had not been for Van Gogh's artistic activity, he probably would have ended his life long before he did. We must also remember that Van Gogh began painting rather late in life; his personality problems were already firmly established. Furthermore, we are not suggesting that the art process can solve a person's emotional problems. We are merely saying that it can be helpful.

Creative growth

As indicated in the previous chapter, the making of art is one kind of creative activity. A person who repeatedly participates in the art process is drilling himself in creativity, and drill is known to be of help in developing habits and skills. Thus it is reasonable to say that the production of art helps a person to develop the creative habit; but this does not mean that it helps him to become a more creative business man or a more creative scientist. It means that participation in the art process is apt to help a person become a better artist.

Technical growth

To grow technically is to become more skillful or more efficient in the manipulation of tools and materials. The art process fosters such growth, once again, by involving the particpant in the act of using the tools and materials of art. Practice makes perfect. In fact, there is no other way to gain technical proficiency. With the foregoing comment, we conclude our remarks about the contributions of the art process to various forms of human growth. By assuming that the art process does indeed make those contributions, we may conclude that it leads to self-realization, emotional stability, and excitement. And if it does, we may say that it contributes to the good life and that it is valuable to the individual.

79

14 Irving Stone, *Lust for Life*, Random House, Inc., New York, 1939.

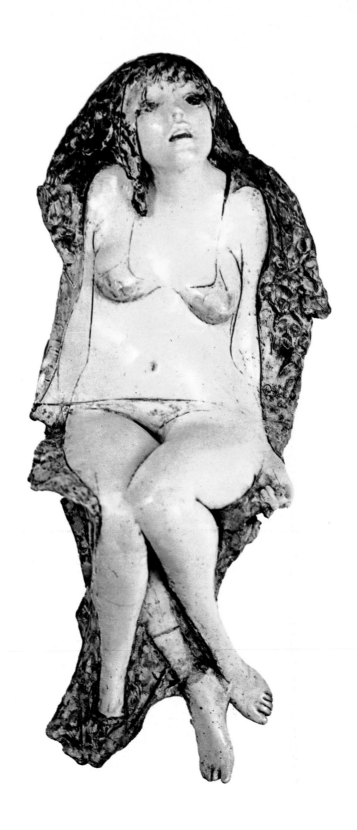

Pl. 9
Frank Gallo, *Love Object*, 1966.
Epoxy resin reinforced with fiber
glass and wood, 57 × 28 × 18 in.
Collection, Krannert Art Museum,
University of Illinois, Champaign.
Is this object a work of art?
If so, is it a work of
high quality? Why?

THE VALUE OF ART TO SOCIETY

So far we have tried to show that both the process and product of art are instrumental in the achievement of the good life; and on that basis we assume that art is valuable to the individual. In a free society, individual growth and development or the condition of the good life is highly valued because of the belief that healthy, intelligent, and emotionally stable persons will make the kinds of decisions that are most beneficial to a free society. Consequently, we may conclude that art is valuable to a free society. But let us hasten to say that individual development does not automatically lead to a better society unless it is accompanied by the voluntary limitation of the self for the good of the community. The 1946 report of the Harvard committee on general education in a free society makes that point quite clear. It reads as follows:[15]

Just as it is wrong to split the human person into separate parts, so would it be wrong to split the individual from society. We must resist the prevalent tendency, or at any rate temptation, to interpret the good life purely in terms of atomic individuals engaged in fulfilling their potentialities. Individualism is often confused with the life of private and selfish interest. The mandate of this committee is to concern itself with "the objectives of education in a free society." It is important to realize that the ideal of a free society involves a twofold value, the value of freedom and that of society. Democracy is a *community* of free men. We are apt sometimes to stress freedom—the power of individual choice and the right to think for oneself—without taking sufficient account of the obligation to cooperate with our fellow men; democracy must represent an adjustment between the values of freedom and social living.

Eighteenth-century liberalism tended to conceive the good life in terms of freedom alone and thought of humanity in pluralistic terms (like matter in Newtonian physics) as an aggregate of independent particles. But a life in which everyone owns his home as his castle and refrains from interfering with others is a community in a negative sense only. Rugged individualism is not sufficient to constitute a democracy; democracy also is fraternity and cooperation for the common good. Josiah Royce defined the good life in terms of loyalty to a shared value. Of course when union is stressed to the exclusion of freedom we fall into totali-

[15] Paul H. Buck and others, *General Education in a Free Society*, Harvard University Press, Cambridge, Massachusetts, 1946, pp. 76–77. (Used by permission of Harvard University Press.)

tarianism; but when freedom is stressed exclusively we fall into chaos. Democracy is the attempt to combine liberty with loyalty, each limiting the other, and also each reinforcing the other.

It is important, however, to limit the idea of the good citizen expressly by the ideal of the good man. By citizenship we do not mean the kind of loyalty which never questions the accepted purposes of society. A society which leaves no place for criticism of its own aims and methods by its component members has no chance to correct its errors and ailments, no chance to advance to new and better forms, and will eventually stagnate, if not die. The quality of alert and aggressive individualism is essential to good citizenship; and the good society consists of individuals who are independent in outlook and think for themselves while also willing to subordinate their individual good to the common good.

The preceding quotation is as relevant today as it was in 1946. As far as art educators are concerned, it means that we must be careful in educating for self-realization, since we are apt to stress individual fulfillment at the expense of social cooperation, which is vital to a democratic society. We must do our best to develop the individual through art and other subjects, but we must also teach the individual that he has an obligation to subordinate his own desires for the sake of the community. To put it differently, we must teach him that freedom is not the license to do anything he pleases for his own self-interest, but it is the freedom to cooperate with his fellowmen for the common good.

SUMMARY

In this chapter, we have tried to show that both the process and product of art have value for the individual and for society. They have value because they both contribute to the attainment of the good life, which is described as the primary goal of human existence.

As we speak of the benefits received from art, it may appear that we have overstated our case. It may sound as if all the world's problems will be solved if we look at art or produce it with seriousness. That is not the view that is intended. We merely wish to show that there are many ways in which art can be of value to man. Furthermore, no one should assume that the full value of art will be received by casual attendance in an art class or by the superficial viewing of art objects in a lecture class. The full benefits will come from *profound involvement* in the making and perceiving of art, and this means we must help our citizens become nonprofessional artists and connoisseurs. That is the function of *art education*. Consequently, teachers of art must try to develop in their students the knowledge, attitudes, and skills that are required in the production and appreciation of art. The characteristics that seem most essential are discussed in the chapter that follows.

QUESTIONS FOR DISCUSSION

1. Censorship of the arts has always been an active subject for debate. Art exhibitions have been closed, books have been banned from school libraries, and films have been kept out of the theaters. What are the arguments for and against censorship?
2. What is the difference between content and subject matter in the visual arts?
3. When arguing the merits of art, why is it important to emphasize the fact that art contributes to the development of nondiscursive knowledge?
4. What is the relationship between creative growth and the other dimensions of growth that were mentioned in this chapter?
5. If a person does not grow aesthetically, how would that affect the other dimensions of growth that have been mentioned in this chapter?
6. Perhaps you believe that art has a value that has not been mentioned in this chapter. What is it? Is it a value that we obtain from the process or product? How do we obtain it?
7. If the observer can learn the values presented in a work of art by studying that work, does the artist who created the work learn any less? Who is likely to learn the most? Why?
8. Are children apt to learn more by making their own works of art or by studying the work of adult artists?
9. If a person devotes quite a bit of time to painting pictures of weeds, what is he likely to learn about weeds? Will he learn the same thing that a scientist learns about weeds?

10. The linguistic development of culturally disadvantaged children is often so meager that they cannot learn in the ordinary school classroom which is linguistically oriented. Could art help such children? How could it put them on the road to linguistic development?

11. In this chapter we discussed the ways in which art contributes to different kinds of human growth. Do you detect any relationships among the various kinds of growth? What are they?

12. Discuss the quotation presented near the end of this chapter. Does it raise an important issue? Why?

13. Search the literature in art education to see if you can find instances in which art was beneficial to emotional growth. Describe those instances.

SUGGESTIONS FOR FURTHER READING

Behrman, S. N.: *Duveen*, Random House, Inc., New York, 1951.
This is an excellent and entertaining book on the life of Joseph Duveen, the great art dealer. It gives us insight into the lives of the great collectors.

Canaday, John: "The Artist as a Social Critic," Portfolio II of the *Metropolitan Seminars in Art* (12 vols.), The Metropolitan Museum of Art, New York.
A very readable account of the artist in his role as a social critic.

Ehlers, Henry and Gordon C. Lee (eds.): "Censorship—by Whom?" *Crucial Issues in Education*, Henry Holt and Company, Inc., New York, 1959, pp. 13–55.
A fine account of the problem of censorship.

Gotshalk, D. W.: *Art and the Social Order*, Dover Publications, Inc., New York, 1962.
Chapters 7, 9, and 10 are especially pertinent because they deal with the value of art. Very readable.

Langer, Susanne: "The Cultural Importance of the Arts," in Michael F. Andrews, ed., *Aesthetic Form and Education*, Syracuse University Press, Syracuse, New York, 1958, pp. 1–8.
Here is a beautiful statement about the value of art as a presentation of feeling.

———: *Philosophy in a New Key*, New American Library, Inc., New York, 1948.
The chapter that deals with discursive and presentational forms is of special significance because it indicates the unique characteristics of visual art. Difficult for the beginner.

Lynes, Russell: *The Tastemakers*, Harper and Brothers, New York, 1954.
This book covers the history of aesthetic taste in America and tells about the individuals who influenced that taste.

Saarinen, Aline: *The Proud Possessors*, Random House, Inc., New York, 1958.
This is another fine book that provides a choice account of the lives of the great American art collectors.

Taylor, Harold: *Art and the Intellect*, Museum of Modern Art, New York, 1960.
Chapter 1 shows how art contributes to the development of the intellect.

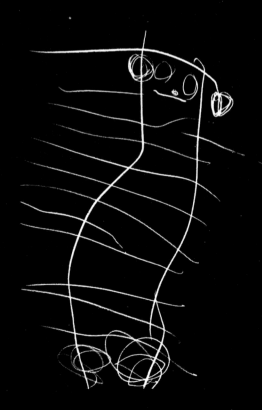

To receive the full value of art, a person must be an artist and a connoisseur. But what does being an artist and a connoisseur mean? What does such a person do, and what are his distinguishing characteristics?

It is quite clear, of course, that the person who produces art is an artist, and the person who exhibits taste or good judgment about art is a connoisseur. The latter may or may not be an artist, but in matters of an aesthetic nature the artist is almost certainly a man of good taste simply because his work demands it. For that reason our discussion will focus upon the nature of the artist and reserve comment on the connoisseur until later.

THE ARTIST AND THE NONARTIST

If concepts and emotions are the content of art, it seems that all human beings possess enough raw material to be called potential artists. They do not become artists, of course, until they produce a work of art, and that raises an interesting question. If a person produces a single object for aesthetic experience, is it reasonable to call him an artist; does it make sense to give him the same designation that is given to a prolific genius like Picasso? The answer is yes, especially if you consider the fact that an artist does not always act as an artist. He does so only when he is actively engaged in the production of art. When he is busy with something else, such as eating or driving an automobile, he is not acting as an artist; yet we sometimes call him one anyway. We always call Picasso by that name, even when he stops to eat, because he acts as an artist most of the time; he is a professional.

By the same token, it is not our custom to speak of the child or the housewife as an artist, especially if she makes only a single work of art. Consequently, we create a false impression. We imply that professionals are the only real artists when in fact *any person is an artist if and when he produces a work of art*. This is a point worth emphasizing, and it will be mentioned again in the chapters that follow. Its immediate importance is that it indicates more clearly who we are talking about when we describe the personality of the artist.

If all human beings are potential artists, and if any one of them can fulfill his potential by making a single work of art, it seems apparent that the artist must have certain characteristics in common with the average man. If that were not the case, a person would have to undergo a complete change in personality as he produces his first work of art, and this is highly improbable.

On the other hand, an artist must be different from a nonartist or the world would certainly contain more art than it does today. Furthermore, the amateur must be different from the professional, and both of them must differ from the connoisseur, or we would not habitually designate them by using separate and distinct terms. With these thoughts in mind, it seems appropriate to discuss the nature of the artist and the connoisseur by answering the following questions:

1. *What are the personality characteristics that the artist and the nonartist have in common?*

2. *What is the difference between the personality of the artist and the personality of the nonartist?*
3. *What is the difference between the mediocre and the master artist?*
4. *What is the difference between the artist and the connoisseur?*
5. *What is the explanation for the artistic personality?*

The answers to these questions are as complex as man himself, but they are of such fundamental importance to art educators that they deserve our most careful attention. Consequently, we shall deal with them one by one.

COMMON PERSONALITY CHARACTERISTICS

If a nonartist can become an artist, it is almost certain that the latter has *many* characteristics in common with other individuals. But the traits that are of major concern to us are the ones that relate to creativity in general and to the making of visual configurations in particular. We know, of course, that the artist and the nonartist are human beings and members of the animal kingdom. But, unlike other animals, they engage in the creation of symbols. *Symbols* are forms that stand for or substitute for something else. They allow us to refer to something, and they also permit us to think about something, even if it is not present. Words, drawings, and musical sounds are examples of symbolic forms.

Symbols are different from *signs*. Signs merely point to or call attention to something in the past, the present, or the future. A cough, for example, is a sign of a cold; it points toward the possible existence of a cold. The lower animals use and rely upon signs all the time. A dog scratches at the door as a signal that he wants to go out, and he returns at the sound of a whistle signifying the presence of food. All animals including man use such signs, but human beings are the only animals that make symbols. Why should we make symbols when other animals do not? Why should this characteristic constitute the most significant difference between human beings and the rest of the animal world?

The need for symbolization

Susanne Langer says that men engage in the unique, human activity of symbolization simply because of the *need* to do so.[1] The lower animals do not have that need. Consequently, they fail to produce symbols. Their activities are based merely upon the satisfaction of the usual biological requirements, and they live highly efficient lives. But by human standards their lives are very uninteresting. If it were not for the need to symbolize, the life of man would be equally dull. He would not produce symbols, and as a result he would not be able to think efficiently, develop his knowledge, communicate with others, or gain control over his environment. That is the importance of making symbolic forms. The need for making them is so basic to human life that we can easily accept it as a fundamental characteristic that the artist and nonartist have in common. If they did not fulfill that need, they would tend to become less human.

The construction of symbols is a matter of changing sensory data into meaningful mental forms such as words and images. Langer calls that process the "symbolic transformation of experience."[2] But it might also be called creativity or the transformation of concepts and emotions into a new form. The termination of that act is a new public form which indicates that creativity or symbolic transformation has actually occurred. The fact that everyone creates or engages in symbolic transformation means that we all have a certain number of the characteristics that contribute to such activity. The most highly creative individuals in any field of endeavor simply have those traits to a greater degree than other people. What are those traits?

Creative traits

Research on creativity has been most intensive since World War II. Investigators have studied the creative product, the process,

[1] Susanne Langer, *Philosophy in a New Key*, New American Library, Inc., New York, 1948, pp. 30–31.
[2] *Ibid.*, p. 35.

the measurement of creativity, and the personality of the creator. In most cases, highly creative individuals were identified by their fellow workers according to their accomplishments. Investigators then tried to find the characteristics that would separate the highly creative people from the rest of the population. One of the most widely publicized studies of that kind was conducted by J. P. Guilford.[3] By using tests and factor analysis (a statistical procedure), Guilford and associates were able to identify certain abilities that seem to separate the more creative from the less creative individuals. In Guilford's judgment the characteristics that distinguish the creative person most clearly are fluency, flexibility, and elaboration.[4] But many art educators assume that those traits are fundamental *requirements* for creativity. Is that a justifiable assumption? Let us examine each of the traits more carefully.

Fluency is the ability to use information with relative ease. It is reflected in an individual's ideational output or mental productivity. Apparently, tests of fluency show that persons identified as highly creative individuals are able to produce numbers of ideas more easily than other people. But that is not especially surprising because the tendency of such persons to generate many ideas is probably one of the reasons for their being identified as creative individuals in the first place.[5] If that is the case, fluency is not an ability that contributes to creativity, but it is an *example* of creative behavior. The extent of that creative behavior or the degree of fluency would seem to depend in part upon the amount of information an individual possesses. If he has a large storehouse of information, he should be able to recognize more possibilities, make more combinations, and produce more ideas.

Furthermore, an individual must be fluent in a medium of some kind. If he possesses a wide assortment of verbal knowledge,

[3] Joy P. Guilford, R. C. Wilson, and P. R. Christiensen, "A Factor-analytic Study of Creative Thinking, II, Administration of Tests and Analysis of Results," *Reports from the Psychological Laboratory*, no. 8, University of California Press, Los Angeles, 1952.

[4] Joy P. Guilford, "Creativity and Our Future," in *Future Implications of Creativity Research*, Los Angeles State College, Pasadena, 1962, pp. 5–32.

[5] A similar view regarding research on creativity is expressed by Ernest van den Haag in "Creativity, Health and Art," *The American Journal of Psychoanalysis*, vol. 23, no. 2, p. 3.

he is apt to be fluent in words. Yet that same individual may fail to produce ideas for art or music because the arts make use of nonverbal information that results in nondiscursive forms. The meaning of this is that a person can be fluent or creative only in those areas for which he possesses the relevant knowledge. Hence *relevant knowledge* is a fundamental requirement for creativity in both art and nonart.

Having dismissed fluency as a factor that is necessary for creativity, we shall turn our attention to flexibility. Apparently, there are at least two kinds. Spontaneous flexibility is the ability to generate *different* kinds of ideas as opposed to ideas that are pretty much alike. The teacher or student who can think of fifteen *different* ways of using a paper clip is more flexible than the person who can think of twenty ways that are all essentially the same. The flexible individual might suggest its use as a fastener, a missile, a shuttle, or a link in a chain. The less flexible person might use it to fasten papers or to hold pieces of cloth together. The last two ideas would both fall in the same category, indicating a lack of flexibility.

Adaptive flexibility is the ability to adapt familiar material to a given problem. It may involve a reinterpretation of the familiar material and may result in a novel solution. A student who readily thinks of a bent wire or a tongue depressor as a shuttle for weaving is flexibly adapting himself to the problem of a broken shuttle.

Both kinds of flexibility are said to lead to a high level of creativity because they generate more possibilities for consideration. But, once again, the desirable flexibility is partly dependent upon a background of appropriate experience and information. A mastery of the French literature of the nineteenth century, for example, is not especially conducive to flexibility in music. A person is much more likely to produce large numbers of ideas in music if he possesses a knowledge of music or information relevant to the making of music. Consequently, it seems appropriate to repeat the notion that *relevant knowledge* is one of the basic requirements for creativity or symbolic transformation. The fact that a creative person scores higher than other

Pl. 10
Then the happy lion went
into the cobblestone street . . .
Illustration by Roger Duvoisin
for *The Happy Lion*
by Louise Fatio (McGraw-Hill Book
Company, New York, 1957). Is this
object a work of art? If so, is it
a work of high quality? Why?

persons on measures of fluency and flexibility does not mean that such traits are necessarily required for creativity. But, as we have already suggested, it may mean that fluency and flexibility are the characteristics that cause such persons to be identified as creative individuals in the first place. In other words, fluency and flexibility may be instances of creativity rather than traits that contribute to such behavior; this is the view that is taken in this text.

The third factor or ability that Guilford considers fundamental in creative behavior is the ability to elaborate or to make a number of additions to a body of information until a complex, detailed, or refined product is achieved. In general, the comments that have been made about fluency and flexibility also apply to elaboration. It is simply an instance of creativity, and one of the fundamental requirements for this is relevant knowledge.

But there are other characteristics in addition to pertinent information that a person is said to possess if he is creative either in art or in nonart. Anne Roe suggests that creative individuals have a willingness to work hard and long.[6] Drevdahl found them to be more self-sufficient, more introverted, and more radical than less creative people.[7] Rogers indicates that creative people are less rigid and more tolerant of ambiguity,[8] and Maslow says that they are more open to experience and that they rely upon internal standards for evaluation.[9] After repeating some of the traits already mentioned, Crutchfield describes creative people as being individualistic, strongly motivated, and free from excessive impulse control.[10] Guilford says that creative individuals observe and remember; they are more likely to have aesthetic and intel-

[6] Anne Roe, *The Making of a Scientist*, Dodd, Mead and Company, Inc., New York, 1953. The same idea appears in Anne Roe, "The Personality of Artists," *Educational and Psychological Measurement*, vol. 6, pp. 501–408, 1946.

[7] John E. Drevdahl, "Factors of Importance for Creativity," *Journal of Clinical Psychology*, vol. 12, pp. 21–26, 1956.

[8] Carl R. Rogers, "Toward a Theory of Creativity," *Review of General Semantics*, vol. 11, pp. 249–260, 1954.

[9] A. H. Maslow, "Creativity in Self-actualizing People," in H. Anderson (ed.), *Creativity and Its Cultivation*, Harper and Row Publishers, Inc., New York, 1959, pp. 55–68.

[10] R. Crutchfield, "The Creative Process", in *Conference on the Creative Person*, University of California, Institute of Personality Assessment and Research, Berkeley, 1967, chap. 6.

lectual interests; and they are likely to possess more feminine interests or attitudes than the average male (the latter does not mean that creative men look or act effeminate).[11]

By examining the foregoing characteristics, we can see that many of them might be described as *attitudes*, and it is not especially surprising to find that attitudes affect creativity. After all, a person might possess a large amount of knowledge pertinent to creativity in mathematics, but he is not apt to create within that discipline unless he is interested in mathematics, confident that he can do the work, tolerant of the various forms that might develop, and willing to work hard and long at the task. Interest, self-confidence, tolerance of form, and willingness to work hard are attitudes. The literature on creativity seems to indicate that they are four of the most essential dispositions in the creative personality. In certain instances, other attitudes also might be conducive to creative behavior, but the four that have been listed seem to be of fundamental importance. Let us hasten to say, however, that the four aforementioned attitudes must be *relevant to a specific dimension of experience if creativity is to occur there.* In other words, self-confidence in mathematics is one of the necessary attitudes for creativity in that subject, but it is not essential for creative behavior in animal husbandry. If we want to develop creativity in animal husbandry, we must help people to become confident of themselves in that kind of work.

So far we have determined that both the artist and the nonartist must possess relevant knowledge and relevant attitudes if they are to create or make symbols. But there is at least one other characteristic that is fundamentally important, and that is *skill.* Skill is technical proficiency or facility with the tools and materials of a particular domain of creativity. Technical proficiency in writing, for example, is the ability to manipulate words, punctuation, pencils, typewriters, and the other tools of the craft. Although a potential writer may have the proper knowledge and attitude for writing, a lack of skill with the tools and materials of the medium may keep him from becoming a writer. A similar

[11] Guilford, *op. cit.*, pp. 5–32.

kind of failure might occur in other dimensions of creative experience if a person does not possess the appropriate skills. Hence it may be concluded that *relevant skill is one of the fundamental requirements for creativity in both art and nonart.*

The artist and the nonartist both have a need for creativity or symbolic transformation, and they both create to fulfill that need. Hence both must possess the knowledge, attitudes, and skills that are relevant to one or more of the domains of creative experience. Obviously, the artist possesses all the characteristics appropriate for the making of art, whereas the nonartist does not. If art educators wish to make the latter into an artist, they must help him to develop the traits that are conducive to the creation of art. Those characteristics will be discussed as we proceed with an account of the differences between the personality of the artist and that of the nonartist.

DIFFERENT PERSONALITY CHARACTERISTICS RELEVANT TO ART

The characteristics that distinguish artists from nonartists are the same factors that make it possible for an individual to produce art rather than nonart. To find out what these traits are, we must first identify the differences between artistic and nonartistic forms of creativity. There are two ways in which they differ. To begin with, art is always pleasing in its organizational structure, while nonart may or may not be pleasing. A configuration is apt to have such appeal if it simulates the elemental formal relationships found in nature or conforms to the principles of perceptual organization. And it is also likely to please if its form is appropriate for the content that is being conveyed.

The second difference between art and nonart is a difference of intention. The art object is created primarily for aesthetic experience, whereas the nonart object may or may not be made for that purpose.

Because we are primarily interested in visual art and artists, it is also necessary to repeat what has been said about the differ-

Pl. 11
Self-portrait in tempera by
a child in kindergarten. Is this
object a work of art? If so, is it a
work of high quality? Why?

ence between visual art and other forms of aesthetic discourse. The major difference is that visual art is presentational while the other forms are not (Chapter 3). This means that it offers all its content simultaneously, a feat that can be accomplished only by iconic or pictorial symbols. Much of the information or knowledge that is embodied in such configurations is of a particular visual nature. Hence it is nondiscursive; it is the kind of knowledge that resides initially in mental images.

If visual art is pleasing in structure, intended for aesthetic experience, and the embodiment of information that resides in mental imagery, the artist must have the knowledge, attitudes, and skills that will permit him to give art those marks of distinction. What knowledge, attitudes, and skills are actually necessary, and what factors contribute to their development?

Knowledge

There are five kinds of information that seem most essential for the creation of art. Perhaps the first and most fundamental is a knowledge of life or, to put it more correctly, a knowledge of the aesthetic dimension of life.

Knowledge of the aesthetic dimension of life. On the basis of what has been said about the unique features of visual art, we may conclude that an artist is one who knows enough about life (the eventual content and subject matter of his work) to have something to say or a point of view to present through visual forms. To have something to say visually is to know or to conceptualize the discursive and nondiscursive elements of experience that can be embodied in iconic or pictorial forms. The discursive aspects of such knowledge can be retained, of course, in the form of words, or rudimentary images, but the nondiscursive elements are obtained and retained *solely* in the form of mental images. We cannot, for example, describe verbally the exact relationship between the specific qualities of color, line, texture, shape, and volume that produce a particular quality of clownness. For that reason, we cannot keep that information in our minds in the form of words. We must retain it in the form of mental images, and it seems fitting to speak of such images as *visual concepts* or concepts of the aesthetic dimension of experience. The visual artist is a person who possesses those concepts, which the nonartist may or may not have. Both individuals, however, may have the elementary discursive knowledge that is retained in words or in simple images. Both may know, for example, that a cat has four legs, two ears, two eyes, a mouth, and a tail; but the weakness of such information is that a dog fits the same description. Hence it is the *particular* visual nature and relationship of the parts of a cat that are important to know in making an artistic symbol of a cat, and it is that information which the artist possesses in the form of a mental image or visual concept.

To make the foregoing point even clearer, we might say that an artist must know the verbally indescribable particularities of cats if he is to make and judge a symbol that presents cattishness. If he does not know cats in that way, he may inadvertently produce a configuration that is strongly canine or erroneously judge a doggish symbol to be a presentation of cattishness. But the need to know something about cats to make or criticize a symbol of a cat does not necessarily mean that the artist must know as much about the animal as a veterinarian or a longtime cat fancier. The amount of knowledge that he must possess depends upon the kind and the quantity of information about cattishness that needs to be conveyed in order to satisfy the purposes of the symbol.

As long as we are discussing the importance of a knowledge of life (content and subject matter), it seems appropriate to say a few words about intelligence. The relationship between intelligence and art ability has been a subject of extensive debate for many years. Probably one explanation for continued attention to the topic is that ideas about intelligence have varied considerably since the concept was originated. In fact, we seem to have no completely satisfactory definition of intelligence.[12] Perhaps the

[12] Lloyd G. Humphreys and Paul L. Boynton, "Intelligence," in *Encyclopedia of Educational Research* (Walter S. Monroe, ed.), The Macmillan Company, New York, 1950, p. 601.

THE NATURE OF THE ARTIST
AND THE CONNOISSEUR

most acceptable thing that we can say about it is that it is a mental quality that manifests itself in performance or behavior. The degree of intelligence is indicated by the quality of a person's total performance. The trouble is that performance is ordinarily measured either by achievement tests or by the so-called "intelligence tests." No doubt those tests do measure certain mental functions, but, from an artist's point or view, they certainly fail to estimate all the productive functions within the universe of mental activity. They measure discursive concepts and discursive thinking, but little of anything else. On top of that, they emphasize an ability that J. P. Guilford calls "convergent" thinking and neglect the "divergent" type.[13] Convergent thought is the kind that moves methodically toward a single, "correct" point of termination. Divergent thought moves in several directions, seeking alternate possibilities for success.

Discursive concepts and convergent thinking definitely contribute to creativity, even in art. After all, there are elements in art that can be identified and named; they are the discursive elements. There is also a kind of thinking that ultimately converges on one suitable configuration or visual image. If there were no such convergence, there would be no art object. Thus it is important that artists do not reject this mental function as foreign to creative activity in art. It is absolutely essential.

On the other hand, there are no answers in art that can be labeled true or false. Works of art are simply more or less appropriate for the state of being that they present. For that reason, divergent thinking is widely employed. The artist often considers several alternative configurations before he converges on the one that seems most suitable. Since intelligence tests and achievement tests do not measure that kind of thinking, it is quite understandable that there should appear to be only a moderate relationship between measured intelligence and art ability.

It is even more understandable if one considers the fact that tests of mental ability do not deal with matters of an aesthetic nature or with nonverbal concepts or imagination. The reason

[13] Joy P. Guilford, "Creative Abilities in the Arts," *Psychological Review*, vol. 64, no. 2, pp. 110–118, March, 1957.

Pl. 12
Computer circuitry. (Courtesy
of J. Paul Kirouac.) Is this
object a work of art? If so, is it
a work of high quality? Why?

Pl. 13
Tadasky, *Untitled*. 1965.
Oil on canvas, 47 × 47 in.
Collection, Krannert Art Museum,
University of Illinois, Champaign.
Is this object a work of art?
If so, is it a work of
high quality? Why?

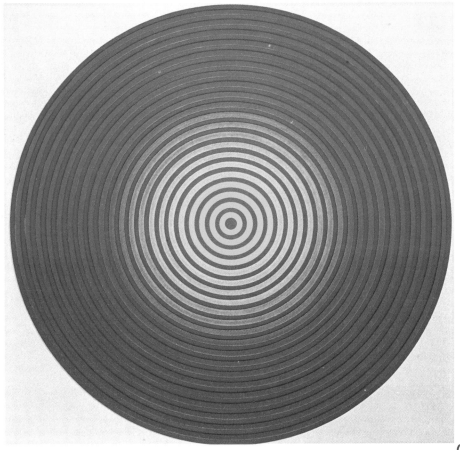

for this is that most concepts are of a kind that are more accurately symbolized by words and combinations of words. This means that language is definitely our most efficient vehicle for thinking about life and dealing with it. Consequently, our tests are verbally oriented.

But there is another kind of mental material that is conceptual, although it can not be transformed into words. It is the highly specific visual information that resides in images. It is the kind of knowledge possessed by artists, but not by nonartists. Performance that makes use of such visual concepts is not measured by our tests of mental ability. Hence it is not surprising that the results of those tests do not correlate very highly with success in art.

Probably it would be reasonable to say that intelligence or mental capabilities of a *broad* nature are necessary in an artist, but a predominance of verbal ability is not. Nondiscursive knowledge or the quality that Norman Meier calls "aesthetic intelligence" is more apt to be responsible for effective performance in art.[14]

Knowledge of composition. Chapter 2 indicated that judgments of structural arrangement should be based upon a standard that is agreeable to most persons. The criterion that was proposed is a triadic one, or a measure in three parts. It was suggested that composition be judged according to: (1) the extent to which it agrees with the perceptual characteristics of a "good gestalt" or a "good form"; (2) the degree to which it simulates elemental shapes and relationships found in nature; and (3) the extent to which the form is compatible with the intended content.

If it is reasonable for an observer or connoisseur to judge composition on the basis of the above standard, it seems equally reasonable for the artist to arrange artistic structures according to the same criterion. When we say, therefore, that the artist has a knowledge of composition, we mean that he is aware of the standard that we have outlined. To know or to be aware of

[14] Norman C. Meier, *Art in Human Affairs*, McGraw-Hill Book Company, New York, 1942, p. 132.

it, however, does not necessarily mean that the artist understands it in a way that permits him to discuss it. His knowledge or awareness of the standard may amount to no more than a heightened sensitivity to it. But to what aspect of experience is a person sensitive if he knows the above criterion? What is a good gestalt? What are the elemental shapes and proportions in nature? And what is compatibility between form and content in composition.

The notion of a good form or good gestalt comes rather obviously from the gestalt psychologists, beginning with Wertheimer,[15] Koffka,[16] and Kohler.[17] *Simply stated, a good gestalt is a percept that is as meaningful, complete, and simple as the conditions of the stimulus field will allow.* It is the result of a dynamic or active perceptual struggle toward order and equilibrium. This struggle is seen as evidence of forces operating within the nervous system that tend to unify and simplify the stimulus field in much the same way as the physical forces of the universe tend to seek order and equalibrium. Such a theory suggests the extension of cosmic order into all activities in the universe, and it is based upon demonstrations of perceptual phenomena developed by the gestalt psychologists. The demonstrations show quite clearly how we organize or structure the visual field in the act of perception.[18] Although some psychologists may not accept the idea of a cosmic cause behind the organizing nature of perception, it is difficult to find fault with the demonstrated facts of visual organization. And the facts indicate that we do tend to perceive as meaningfully, completely, and simply as the stimulus field will allow. In other words, the act of perception naturally leads toward the good form or good gestalt.

Demonstrations seem to show that the good form, good

[15] Max Wertheimer, ''Laws of Organization in Perceptual Forms,'' in Willis Ellis (ed.), *A Source Book of Gestalt Psychology*, Harcourt, Brace and Company, Inc., New York, 1939, pp. 71–88.
[16] Kurt Koffka, *Principles of Gestalt Psychology*, Harcourt, Brace and Company, Inc., New York, 1935.
[17] Wolfgang Kohler, *Gestalt Psychology*, Harcourt, Brace and Company, Inc., New York, 1935.
[18] Nearly any book on gestalt psychology will explain those demonstrations.

gestalt, good figure, or good percept possesses the following characteristics:[19]

1. *It is an organized, distinguishable form in which previously disconnected units become connected. In other words, it is a unitary whole.*
2. *It possesses figure-ground relationships. By this we mean that it is not a chaos of color, texture, and motion, but it consists in distinguishable shapes or figures against a background.*
3. *It is clearly articulated or clearly put together.*
4. *It tends to impress itself upon the observer, to persist, and to recur. A circle is the simplest example of a form that satisfies such a condition.*
5. *It possesses cohesion and resists disintegration into parts through analysis or fusion with another form.*
6. *It is a state of visual equilibrium or closure. In other words, it is the stable realization of form that was previously open, tentative, suggestive, or confusingly complex. It is, for example, a percept of a circle that has resulted from a nearly circular series of dots.*
7. *It is dynamic just as the act of perception is dynamic.*
8. *It tends to persist, and to recur when the same stimulus reappears.*
9. *Its shape, size, and color tend to remain constant.*
10. *It tends towards symmetry, balance, and proportion.*
11. *Units that are similar in color, size, and shape tend to be combined in more clearly articulated forms. Units in proximity also tend to be combined in forms that are clearly discernible.*
12. *It is very meaningful and easily understood.*
13. *It tends to predominate over weaker, less clear, or less meaningful forms.*
14. *It exists independently of its constituent elements. It is the relationship among the elements that determines the form and not the particular qualities of the elements.*

If a person knows or is sensitive to the foregoing characteristics of a good perceptual form, he will be able to create visual compositions that are similar to the good figure or good gestalt. Thus he will be able to make a visual structure that is easy and pleasant to perceive. Such an arrangement can be created by an

[19] These characteristics of good perceptual form are derived from the fourteen laws of perceptual organization that Boring considers to be the major principles obtained from investigations by gestalt psychologists. For further information, see Edwin G. Boring, *Sensation and Perception in the History of Experimental Psychology*, Appleton-Century-Crofts, Inc., New York, 1942, pp. 253–255.

artist because he possesses the proper knowledge or sensitivity. The nonartist, however, lacks the necessary sensitivity to good form or to visual dynamics. Consequently, his visual symbols are irritating and hard to comprehend because they are constructed in a way that makes perceptual organization difficult.

In addition to knowing the dynamics of a good gestalt, the artist knows the elemental shapes and relationships that exist in nature. To put it differently, he is familiar with the natural order of things. To possess such information is to be aware of natural shapes, such as the snowflake, the teardrop, the seed, the crystal, the egg, the skeleton of an animal, or the honeycomb. It is also a matter of recognizing the natural proportions that exist in trees, animals, and plants. By using that information to build a visual composition that displays some of the same fundamental shapes and relationships, the artist is able to evoke a pleasurable response in the observer.

We are confident that adherence to the standard of natural order in composition will produce a pleasurable reaction because the arrangement of nature seems perfect, appropriate, and satisfying. No one questions the correctness of a tree form or the shape of a flower. Probably, there is satisfaction with such things because the forms of natural objects are the results of the natural forces that created them and reflect the order and stability of those forces. The perfection of nature is something to which people are exposed from birth. They become so thoroughly conditioned to it, however, that most of them fail to perceive and to conceive the elemental forms and structural relationships that seem so pleasurable to them. Hence they are unable to simulate these conditions in their own visual symbols, which means that the composition of their work lacks the aesthetic orderliness or correctness that is so common in the world of nature and so necessary in art.

Finally, the ability to create a pleasing composition is dependent upon more than a sensitivity to perceptual dynamics and a knowledge of the structural characteristics of nature. It is dependent upon a knowledge of the relationship between form and its meaning. Nonartists usually lack such understanding. When they attend a circus, for example, they may see that the great white horses are strong and unruly and that the beautiful riders and the large crowd are sources of excitement. But they probably do not develop a knowledge of the movements, shapes, colors, textures, and linear attitudes that produce the qualities of horsiness and strength. They do not perceive and grow to know the visual cues to gracefulness in the rider; and they probably miss the visual contribution to the quality of largeness in the crowd. Consequently, they are not able to create visual symbols of the circus in which the form and the intended meaning are properly matched. And when such a mismatch occurs, the symbol contradicts itself; it is not pleasurable.

An artist such as Toulouse-Lautrec, on the other hand, is able to create a circus painting that not only reveals horsiness to us but is also nicely composed (*Cirque Fernando: The Equestrienne*; Figure 4.1). If he had not been able to see and conceive the specific lines, movements, colors, and textures that were the source of horsey qualities, he might have given the horse a few cowlike qualities that would have made the entire composition irritating.

From these comments it is possible to see that a knowledge of composition is closely associated with a knowledge of the aesthetic dimension of life. And a knowledge of composition, as we have described it, is similar to a knowledge of the old principles of composition that have been used in the teaching of art for many years.[20] In brief, the old principles indicate that a composition should have unity, variety, balance, harmony, rhythm, repetition, and one or two other characteristics. Without much effort, we can see the close relationship between a good gestalt, the natural order of nature, and a configuration arranged according to the old principles of composition. Consequently, it seems reasonable to say that the artist's knowledge of composition might involve an understanding of one or all of the things that have been suggested.

[20] See, for example, Denman Ross, *A Theory of Pure Design*, Houghton Mifflin and Company, Boston, 1907.

THE NATURE OF THE ARTIST
AND THE CONNOISSEUR

Pl. 14
Honeybee on a cantaloupe
blossom. (Photograph by Elbert R.
Jaycox, University of Illinois,
Urbana.) Is this object a work
of art? If so, is it a work of
high quality? Why?

Knowledge of procedures. Giving an attractive pictorial structure to one's knowledge of life requires that a person know at least one method of making visual symbols. Obviously, the artist has that knowledge, which the nonartist may or may not have. In other words, the artist knows the steps that are taken to create a watercolor painting, a plaster figure, or some other art object. He knows which tools and materials are necessary for the task, and he knows how to use them. Without that information, his knowledge of composition and of the aesthetic dimension of life would be relatively useless in making a work of art. He would be unable to select or use the most appropriate medium for his purpose, and he would be unable to judge either the quality of his own craftsmanship or that of others.

Knowledge of art history. Knowledge of art history includes information about specific works of art, about artists, and about the sequential development of art as a form of visual symbolization. Information of that kind is not absolutely necessary for the creation of art, but most professional artists do possess a broad background of art historical information. Consequently, it seems safe to say that the nonprofessional's knowledge of art history is likely to surpass that of the average nonartist. Such knowledge helps the artist to understand the place of art in human history, and it helps him to judge the relative significance of his own work. It gives him an understanding of what has been done and what remains to be done. It also serves as a source of ideas about content, composition, and procedure.

If a person does not have a knowledge of art history, or if he does not pay attention to what he knows about it, he might judge a piece of work that appears spontaneous or loose as the most creative form of visual symbolization.[21] Examined with the perspective that history provides, however, such a judgment seems clearly in error because it reduces practically all the art of the past to a low level of creativity. Thus it is clear that art history

[21] Robert Burkhart, *Spontaneous and Deliberate Ways of Learning*, International Textbook Company, Scranton, Pennsylvania, 1962. Burkhart tends to value "spontaneous" symbols very highly.

provides us with the perspective that is so helpful in judging originality, craftsmanship, and other important characteristics of art works.

Knowledge of aesthetics. The fifth and last kind of information that is relevant to the making of art is a knowledge of aesthetics or a knowledge of the nature of art, the value of art, and the nature of aesthetic experience. The artist must know the meaning of aesthetic experience because art is created primarily for that kind of occurrence; but knowing such a thing does not necessarily involve an understanding of the term "aesthetic experience," nor does it necessarily imply an ability to explain the experience verbally. A person who knows the meaning of aesthetic experience may know it in the sense that he has engaged in it; and, by the same token, he may know the nature of art simply because he understands that it is made primarily for the purpose of being perceived. The nonartist, on the other hand, may or may not have a knowledge of aesthetics.

Attitudes

On the basis of what we have said about creativity, it is reasonable to conclude that there are four primary attitudes that a person who creates art is likely to possess. Perhaps the most fundamental attitudinal requirement is an interest in the aesthetic dimension of experience.

Interest in the aesthetic dimension of experience. An attitude of interest may be defined as one aspect of readiness or as a mental set. A set is "a temporary condition of an organism, facilitating a certain more or less specific type of activity or response...."[22] For some time we have known that mental sets or attitudes determine an individual's choice of objects to perceive. Allport says "they also result in a greater attentive clearness or vividness of those objects."[23] This strongly

[22] James Drever, *A Dictionary of Psychology*, Penguin Books, London, 1952.

suggests that artistically relevant knowledge could be the result of a set to perceive the appropriate things. After all, there are many aspects of experience that a person might perceive and grow to know. But if he develops a broad background of knowledge especially suited to the making of art, it seems reasonable to conclude that his perception is directed by an interest, a purpose, or a mental set of some kind. Consequently, we shall assume that an artist is set and ready to perceive the discursive and nondiscursive elements of experience, the elemental shapes and proportions in nature, and the relationship between the form and the meaning of experience. We shall also assume that an artist is set or ready to attend to the dynamics of perception and to information of a procedural, art-historical, and aesthetic nature.

From what has been said it seems clear that if an artist possesses knowledge relevant to art, he must have an interest in the sources from which that knowledge is gained, namely, aesthetic experience. It seems equally clear that he must also have an interest in aesthetic experience simply because art is created primarily for that activity; it is one of the basic focuses of such activity. Interest, however, may involve no more than a mere awareness that there are things to be perceived and things to be made for perception. It would appear, however, that the artist's interest extends far beyond mere awareness. It may even involve a *commitment* to the making and viewing of art if the interest in aesthetic experience is deep or profound.

The nonprofessional artist need not be interested to the point of deep commitment, but he must be sufficiently concerned with the aesthetic dimension of life to feel that art is worthwhile or important. Without that feeling, a person is apt to lack the dedication and the perseverance that is required in making art. After all, the creation of art often involves discouragement, failure, and criticism that must be overcome. Also, the forceful and beautiful presentation of concepts and emotions demands

[23] Floyd H. Allport, *Theories of Perception and the Concept of Structure*, John Wiley and Sons, Inc., New York, 1955, p. 65.

that the artist spend a large amount of time developing his skill. For those reasons, he must be prepared to enter into his work to the fullest possible extent, but he cannot do that without sufficient interest in the outcome or without the belief that the effort and the result are worthwhile.

A nonartist may not be interested in aesthetic experience. Or he may be interested to the degree that he values the making and viewing of art very highly; but his lack of skill may keep him from creating art. If it is only a lack of skill that holds him back, he might make an excellent connoisseur. Without an interest in aesthetic experience, however, he is not apt to be either an artist or a connoisseur.

Self-confidence in art. If a person has an interest in making or appraising art but doubts his own ability to make it or judge it, he is not likely to engage in that kind of work. By the same token, a person genuinely moved by the experience of life may have all the requirements for artistic expression, but he will probably neither write nor paint if he feels he has no capability as a writer or painter. If he does produce while lacking confidence in himself, his work is not apt to be stirring or persuasive, but is likely to appear hesitant, unsure, and weak.

Clearly, an artist has confidence in his ability to create artistic things, which a nonartist usually does not; however, this does not mean that the artist is always *fully* confident of himself. He has moments of self-doubt, just as other persons do, and those moments frequently lead to concentrated efforts at self-improvement. But if self-doubt prevails over long periods of time, his chances of success will be doomed. For that reason, self-confidence in art generally prevails in the person who acts as an artist.

Tolerance of style in art. An attitude of tolerance toward the various styles or forms that art might take is not absolutely essential for the production of art, but it certainly is helpful. If a person is tolerant of style, he enjoys more freedom in presenting his own concepts and emotions. He is able to say more because

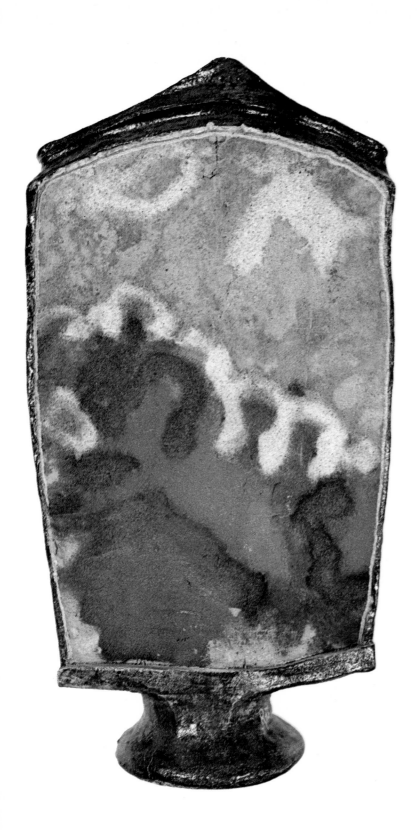

Pl. 15
Jerry Rothman, *Sky Pot*.
Ca. 1963. Stoneware, 26 × 14½ in.
Collection, Krannert Art Museum,
University of Illinois, Champaign.
Is this object a work of art?
If so, is it a work of
high quality? Why?

he does not feel a need to limit himself to one way of constructing visual configurations. In short, the person endowed with this tolerance is less inhibited.

Not all artists are tolerant of style. In fact, some of them are very intolerant. But it is quite clear that the artists who feel free to change their style are the ones who enjoy the widest range of expression. Picasso is an excellent example. His obvious tolerance of form has allowed him to change his style many times and has permitted him to present a wider variety of concepts and emotions for perception.

The average nonartist usually lacks tolerance, and for him such an attitude is especially restricting because it often means that he tolerates the very form which he lacks the skill to produce or that he does not accept the style which he can create; hence he does not produce art.

Willingness to work hard at art. An artist is willing to struggle at the task of making art, and a nonartist is usually not. Probably the acceptance of hard work grows out of a strong interest in art as well as confidence in one's ability to produce it. But there are persons who appear both interested and confident, and yet they do not create any art. Their problem is apt to be one of laziness; and if that is the case, they must learn to value work, or they are not likely to become artists. After all, art is not play. It is a kind of work that requires concentration and practice. Practice is necessary for the development of skill, and skill is essential if a person is to give a pleasing visual shape to his concepts and emotions.

Skill

Skill is technical proficiency. It is the ability to manipulate the tools and materials of a given domain of creativity so that the aims of that domain are achieved. Skill in art is, of course, the ability to use brushes, paint, pencils, papers, and other such items to make a pleasing configuration primarily for aesthetic experience. Skill is also the ability to attain that goal while making the observer understand the discursive and nondiscursive concepts and emotions that were intended for presentation. Naturally the artist has that skill, and the nonartist usually does not. Having such skill, however, does not necessarily mean that the artist can handle *all* the tools and materials of art efficiently. The creation of art requires skill with only one medium of visual expression; but if the artist happens to have skill in a variety of media, his freedom to present a broad range of concepts and emotions is obviously increased.

In art, as in other areas of creativity, skill is developed through practice in the manipulation of appropriate tools and materials. But a person is apt to practice with the tools and materials of art only if he possesses knowledge and attitudes that are relevant to the making of art. If he lacks those characteristics, he will either practice aimlessly or give up.

DIFFERENCES BETWEEN THE MEDIOCRE AND THE MASTER ARTIST

The differences between the average and the master artist are simply differences of degree. For one thing, the master probably knows more about composition than the average artist, or, to put it differently, he is probably more sensitive to organizational structure. In fact, his greater allover sensitivity to life results in an abundance of mental materials. Perhaps one could say that the master is more intelligent aesthetically than the average artist. At least he possesses more nondiscursive knowledge, more procedural knowledge, and a deeper awareness of aesthetic experience. If he did not, young artists would not come to him for advice and instruction.

Of course, it is probably true that average or high overall intelligence is unnecessary for the occasional production of art, but great art is unlikely to appear in the absence of at least average intelligence. Why?

An intelligent individual, possessing highly differentiated concepts, can recognize more avenues for action and can exercise better judgment in selecting the one to pursue than an individual of lesser intelligence. As a consequence, he is able to enjoy more freedom, including freedom of expression. More possibilities occur to him; he has more to say and is aware of more ways of saying it. The less intelligent person is capable of producing art forms that embody concepts and emotions, but the work is likely to be shallow, repetitive, derived, limited in content and subject matter, and devoid of the minutiae of sensitive perception.

In addition to average overall intelligence, the master artist possesses an unusual amount of skill. This is something he develops as a result of more than average hard work and practice. The strong motivation for hard work comes in part from heightened sensitivity or greater knowledge. Without an unusual awareness of life there would be no purpose in creating the artistc kinds of symbols that require so much skill.

A greater degree of self-confidence and interest in art also contribute to the development of skill because they provide the attitude that one can and should attain the perfection that great art demands. Dissatisfaction with things as they are and doubt about one's own work also tends to encourage skillfulness, but self-assurance always prevails. Success in anything depends upon it. A baseball player who goes into a batting slump must believe that he can overcome it and go on to win. If he lacks faith in himself, he will not be a great baseball player. To get an idea of the confidence that a master artist can have in himself, the reader should not miss the autobiography of Benvenuto Cellini, one of the great craftsman of the Renaissance.[24]

An ordinary artist usually produces art that adheres rather closely to the standards of taste that prevail in the environment. The great masters are often innovators. They are independent and self-assertive people who do not conform to fashionable forms and content. They seem to have a kind of inner direction that is not affected by most environmental reactions and opin-

[24] Benvenuto Cellini, *The Autobiography of Benvenuto Cellini*, Modern Library, Inc., New York, 1927.

ions. Why they are able to maintain their individuality in an environment that values behavior of a different kind is hard to determine. Perhaps it comes from a more pressing need for symbolization and self-realization. If some people possess unusually strong biological needs, such as the need for sleep, why would it not be possible for some individuals, such as master artists, to have atypical needs for symbolization? The idea is interesting to contemplate.

DIFFERENCES BETWEEN THE ARTIST AND THE CONNOISSEUR

The artist and the connoisseur have many characteristics in common. They both possess the same artistically relevant knowledge because they both make judgments about content, composition, procedure, contemporary work in relation to art of the past, and the value of an object as the focus of aesthetic experience. Probably the artist knows more about artistic procedures because he experiences them regularly, but, the connoisseur is apt to know more about art history, because he uses it in making comparisons and in justifying decisions. The connoisseur may appear to have a better understanding of aesthetics, but that is simply because a connoisseur often *talks* about art and the artist quietly *makes* it.

Actually both are probably equal or nearly equal in their understanding of the nature of art, the value of art, and the nature of aesthetic experience, but their understanding reveals itself in different ways. If one of them does know more about art, it is probably the artist, because he experiences the act of making it, whereas the connoisseur is forced to guess about such acts.

When it comes to attitudes relevant to art, the artist and the connoisseur are similar, but not quite the same. Both are interested in art, at least to the degree that they consider it worthwhile, or they would not devote their time and energy to making it and criticizing it. Both are confident of themselves in art, but the artist is usually certain that he can create it, whereas the connoisseur is likely to feel that he cannot. The latter is more apt to feel confident that he can make responsible judgments or that he can write or talk about art in an interesting and authoritative manner.

Tolerance of style in art is helpful to many artists, but it is a necessity for the connoisseur. Without it, his mind would be closed to certain forms of art, and he would be unable to appreciate whatever they have to offer.

The artist and the connoisseur both have a willingness to work hard at art, but the one is willing to struggle with its creation and the other is well disposed toward the difficult task of assessing and criticizing.

Finally, both are skilled. The artist is technically proficient with brushes, paints, and other artistic tools, and he is also skillful at viewing and judging the images he makes. In other words, he is proficient as a connoisseur *and* as an artist. The connoisseur, however, is not skilled as an artist or we would call him one. He is skilled at the task of viewing objects for aesthetic experience and estimating their quality.

AN EXPLANATION FOR THE ARTISTIC PERSONALITY

Having described the similarities and differences between the artist and the nonartist, we proceeded to show that the difference between the average and master artist is simply one of degree and suggested that the artist is a connoisseur as well as a creator of art. Consequently, an explanation for the ordinary artistic personality should also help us to account for the personality of the master artist and the master connoisseur.

An explanation for the artistic personality is an attempt to account for the existence of the knowledge, attitudes, and skills that are relevant to the production of art. It seems that there are two major personality determinants: the organismic and the environmental.

Organismic determinants

The organismic determinants of the artistic personality are the ones that reside within the human organism. A person's physical or mental condition, for example, is such a determinant. If he is handicapped in a way that adversely affects the handling of tools and materials, he may not be able to develop the necessary skill. And if his handicap happens to interfere with perception in any way, he is also apt to lack the knowledge that is needed. Color blindness, for example, might make it very difficult for an individual to know the meaningful qualities that are present in aesthetic experience, and it might keep him from managing those qualities effectively in his work. In other words, the inability to see red would probably prevent an understanding of the warmth and vitality that we associate with red, and it would probably prohibit the effective management of that meaning in a visual symbol. It might result in a disturbing relationship between form and content, and it might destroy balance, unity, and other qualities essential for pleasurable composition.[25]

Visual acuity that is poor and uncorrected is another factor that hinders the accumulation of relevant knowledge as well as the development of skill. If a person cannot see nuances of visual form, he is apt to miss the information that such elements provide in an aesthetic experience. This means that he will not have the broad background of knowledge about life that tends to increase the artist's freedom of expression. It also means that he will have trouble composing his own visual symbols because the pleasurable arrangement of them often hinges upon nuances of color, shape, proportion, texture, and other elements of a similar nature.

Like other physical defects, however, poor visual acuity may hinder the development of an artistic personality, but it does not always *prevent* it. Many physical defects can be corrected, or

---

[25] Color blindness does not rule out entirely the possibility of making art. Painting in color, although possible, would be difficult, but drawing, sculpture, or monochromatic painting and print making would be much easier. For an account of the problems encountered by a color-blind painter, see R. W. Pickford, "The Influence of Color Vision Defects on Painting," *British Journal of Aesthetics*, vol. 5, no, 3, pp. 211–226, 1965.

they can be overcome, as Lowenfeld's work with the blind has so clearly demonstrated.[26] Fortunately, the same may be said of certain mental or emotional disturbances. They certainly hinder the formation of an artistic personality, but some of them can be cured or corrected.[27] If they cannot be overcome, however, they may prevent the development of knowledge, attitudes, and skills that are essential for art.

Emotional conditions and needs affect the development of the artistic personality simply because they influence the formation of relevant attitudes, including mental sets or interests. The emotional condition or need that accompanies hunger, for example, is a condition that sets or prepares the individual to perceive food. Or if a person is extremely frightened by dogs, he is apt to see dogs much more readily than someone who is unaffected by them. There are many such needs and emotional states that could create interest or induce perceptual sets. But it seems doubtful that many of those anxiety-laden determinants would result in a set to perceive the aesthetic dimension of experience. It seems equally doubtful that they would evoke attentiveness to other sources of artistically relevant information. After all, the hungry, tired, anxious, or frightened individual is more apt to develop a set that would cause him to ignore the aesthetic dimension of life and attend to other things.

Probably the attitude or mental set that leads most satisfactorily to the sources of appropriate artistic knowledge is an attitude that grows out of a need for symbolization, recognition, acceptance, or self-realization. In other words, a person is likely to pay attention to artistically relevant information and to be interested in making and criticizing art simply because such actities satisfy the need to communicate with others, to achieve an identity, to be respected and loved, and to feel a sense of completeness as a human being.[28] All individuals have such needs, but

[26] Viktor Lowenfeld, *The Nature of Creative Activity*, Routledge and Kegan, Paul, Ltd., London, 1939.
[27] For an account of mental disturbances and their effects upon the artist, see Lawrence J. Hatterer, M.D., *The Artist in Society: Problems and Treatment of the Creative Personality*, Grove Press, Inc., New York, 1965.
[28] *Ibid.*, pp. 25–26.

whether they actually develop an aesthetic or artistic interest or set to fulfill those needs probably depends upon their constitutional makeup (their heredity) or their environment. What do we know about the effect of heredity on the development of interest in the aesthetic?

Although it is quite possible that a person could inherit a neurophysical structure that leads to the satisfaction of basic needs through an instinctive interest in attending to the aesthetic and in making objects for aesthetic experience, there is no research that offers absolute proof of such inheritance. Perhaps Lowenfeld came the closest to such proof in his study of the perceptual and creative differences that are evident among both the blind and the nonblind.[29] He concluded that most persons tend to be either visual or nonvisual (haptic), and he reported the belief that the trait is inherited. The visually minded person makes greater use of his eyes, and he is much more likely to see the details in his environment. The haptic, on the other hand, is much more subjective, and he pays far less attention to the "look" of things. He places a greater emphasis upon tactile and proprioceptive sensations; unlike the visual person, he does not visualize tactile sensations.

It is interesting to note that a later study by W. Grey Walter tends to confirm the existence of visual and nonvisual persons. Walter found that visually minded persons have few if any alpha rhythms when their eyes are open (as measured by an encephalograph) and that nonvisual persons have persistent alpha activity that is hard to block with mental effort. The latter tend toward auditory, kinesthetic, or tactile perceptions rather than visual ones, which is completely consistent with Lowenfeld's findings.[30] Walter points out that "evidence already available, both statistical and experimental, strongly suggests that the alpha rhythm characters are inborn and probably hereditary."[31]

[29] Lowenfeld, *op. cit.*
[30] Viktor Lowenfeld, *Creative and Mental Growth*, 3d ed., The Macmillan Company, 1957, pp. 262–263.
[31] W. Grey Walter, *The Living Brain*, W. W. Norton and Company, Inc., New York, 1953, pp. 214–218.

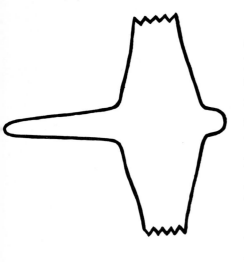

Fig. 4.2
Birds raised in captivity
see this form as friendly if it is
moved to the left, and they see it as
threatening if it is moved to the right.
(Redrawn from N. Tinbergen.)

If Lowenfeld and Walter are correct, it is quite possible that approximately one-fourth of the population may inherit a neurophysical structure that makes it extremely difficult for them to attend to visual experiences, whereas the other three-fourths may inherit structures that instinctively lead to intensive visual perception. Following this line of reasoning, it seems quite unlikely that a nonvisual, or haptic, person could acquire knowledge that is relevant to art and make art consistently. Even if he could gather the relevant information through his nonvisual senses, he would still have to look at his product if he is to control the visual meanings that it exhibits. And it would seem that the visual attentiveness for doing so would be missing in the haptic individual.

The idea of instinct as a determinant of perceptual behavior is not very popular today. Nevertheless, Hilgard[32] has pointed out that newborn babies prefer sugar to quinine and moderate rather than hot or cold temperatures, and Tinbergen[33] has found that birds raised in captivity see the form in Figure 4.2 as either friendly or threatening, depending on the direction in which it is made to move. If it moves to the left, the birds apparently see it as a friend. It if moves to the right, they see it as a foe. This suggests the possibility that certain human beings could attend to the nuances of form instinctively. They might inherit the neurophysical structure that leads to interest in the aesthetic. But, as we said before, there is no absolute proof for such an assertion. There seems to be far more evidence to indicate that the environment plays a major role in determining the mental sets or interests that human beings will develop to satisfy their needs. We shall discuss the role of the environment in a moment, but, first, let us give further attention to the inheritance of organismic personality determinants.

In 1942, after a ten-year study of artists, Norman Meier reported what he believed to be the six basic components in ar-

[32] Ernest R. Hilgard, "The Role of Learning in Perception," in Robert R. Blake and Glen V. Ramsey (eds.), *Perception: An Approach to Personality*, The Ronald Press Company, New York, 1951, p. 96.
[33] N. Tinbergen, "Social Releasers and the Experimental Method Required for Their Study," *Wilson Bulletin*, vol. 6, no. 1, March, 1948.

tistic aptitude: manual skill or craftsman ability, energy output and perseveration in its discharge, general and aesthetic intelligence, perceptual facility, creative imagination, and aesthetic judgment.[34] Although these components have different names, they are exactly the same as many of the artistically relevant characteristics mentioned earlier in this chapter. The point, however, is that Meier considers heredity to have an effect upon the first four components in his list. The artists he studied usually had a craftsman of some sort in their background, and this (among other things) led him to suggest that artists might receive a kind of stock inheritance from their ancestors. But the evidence in support of artistically favorable inherited traits does not constitute absolute proof, although it is strongly suggestive. There seems to be more evidence in support of environmental influences. Consequently, we shall now turn our attention toward the role of the environment.

Environmental determinants

The artistically relevant information that an artist possesses is obtained largely from the environment. To substantiate this notion, think of a person looking at a furry, green-eyed, yellow cat. His percept will include that cat with its appropriate qualities of greenness, yellowness, and furriness. The qualities he perceives and grows to know are assumed to be in the cat rather than in the observer because the observer's perceptual apparatus is not green, yellow, or furry. More support for this assumption is supplied by other observers who testify that they see the same things, and it is unlikely that several persons could by coincidence consistently see the same qualities. Furthermore, the person who sees a cat can make additional checks on the accuracy of his vision through the use of other senses. He can feel the furriness of the cat as well as see it. Thus it seems reasonable to conclude that what an artist knows about life is partly determined by the surface qualities of the environment.

[34] Norman C. Meier, *Art in Human Affairs*, McGraw-Hill Book Company, Inc., New York, 1942, pp. 120–169.

The important question, however, is why the artist happens to see and learn things that are relevant to art whereas other persons perceive and learn things that are not. And why does the artist develop the required attitudes and skills when other persons do not? Apparently the answer is that each of us is influenced by our social and cultural environment as well as by our visual environment. How does the sociocultural climate help in the development of an artistic personality?

For many years art educators have known about the helpful and harmful effects of the environment upon the formation of attitudes relevant to art. They know that people can do and say things that make other people lose interest in art as well as the confidence to produce art. Teachers know that their own behavior can influence a student's tolerance of form and his willingness to work hard. In other words, they know that artistically relevant attitudes can be learned from the environment simply because they have witnessed such learning in real-life situations.

McFee offers another good illustration of how the ordinary environment can create an attitude of interest in the aesthetic when she discusses the children from the nomadic tribes of Northern Siberia.[35] She explains that reindeer are an extremely important part of the environment for those youngsters because these animals are essential to the livelihood of the people. Consequently, the children perceive the animals very keenly and draw them with great skill. This seems to indicate that the values of the culture tend to influence what we see and, ultimately, what we know. The values of the people in Northern Siberia are apparently of the sort that cause them to pay attention to the appearance or to the aesthetic aspects of their reindeer. Hence they are able to learn the things that facilitate the drawing of such animals.

In a four-year study of Oberlin College students, Ikeda also found that the environment was definitely effective in developing interest, activity, and knowledge in art.[36] He discovered that

---

[35] June K. McFee, *Preparation for Art*, Wadsworth Publishing Co., Inc., San Francisco, 1961, pp. 85–86.

[36] Kiyoshi Ikeda, "Extra-classroom Factors and Formal Instruction in Art and Music: A Case Study," *The School Review*, vol. 72, no. 3, pp. 319–351, 1964.

Pl. 16
John Deere tractor.
(Photo courtesy of Deere and Co.)
Is this object a work of art?
If so, is it a work of
high quality? Why?

growth in interest and knowledge was facilitated by exposure to students and staff members who already were committed to the arts. To illustrate how such growth occurs, Ikeda presented the following statement by a student:[37]

> Whenever we come back to the co-op after a musical recital, we usually sit around the table over coffee and discuss the performance and the performer(s). The conservatory students usually lead the discussion in evaluating specific parts of the performance. They even take out their instruments to indicate the strength and weakness of the performance. I actually learn a great deal about the technical elements and criteria by simply listening to the discussion around the table.
>
> In taking courses in the conservatory, I have established a number of friendships with some of the "con" students. Both in the dorms and before and after classes and performances we usually spend a great deal of time talking about the performance of other students or visiting artists. And then we get the judgment of the theory instructor (in this case) too. In this way, it certainly gets exciting to become sensitized to music. In art, similar things happen to make me more aware of what is involved.

Hence it is clear that informal social groups or subcultures can cause an individual to focus attention on art and develop a knowledge of art. But Ikeda also found that the same characteristics could be developed in the formal classroom. In fact, an interest in the visual arts seemed to grow most rapidly after exposure to an art course, and interest seemed to be reinforced by the institutional arrangements for living and dining and by the college requirements for graduation. Thus it appears that students build artistic personality characteristics if they are in a sociocultural environment that values such characteristics and encourages their development.

To develop the attributes of an artistic personality, however, a person need not be influenced by a large number of people in his environment. One individual is enough to provide the influence, if he is highly respected. Theo van Gogh was such a person. He was so thoroughly admired and respected by his brother Vincent that he was able to give his brother confidence, a willingness to work hard, and an interest in perceiving certain

[37] *Ibid.*, p. 341.

unique aspects of experience. He managed to do this at a time when the rest of the environment was almost hostile to Vincent. Hence we may say that Theo van Gogh was partly responsible for building the personality of Vincent van Gogh, one of the most artistic personalities of all time.

It is quite obvious to a teacher, of course, that one individual can cause groups of students to perceive and learn certain things that exist in the environment. But we would be on firmer ground in declaring that sociocultural influences aid the development of aesthetic interests and aesthetic knowledge if we could draw upon the findings of controlled research. Fortunately, we are able to do so.

Eleanor Gibson, in a review of the research on perceptual learning, has concluded that such learning is not only possible but that certain aspects of it may be improved with practice and with the reinforcement of correct responses.[38] And, a more recent empirical investigation by Salome shows that training aimed at getting fifth-grade children to perceive visual cues located along contour lines will increase the amount of visual information that they use in their drawings.[39] The person who offered the training was, of course, a part of the cultural environment that surrounded those fifth-grade children, and the visual cues along the contour lines were aesthetic elements. Thus it is clear that aesthetic form will be perceived and learned if the culture or subculture places an importance upon it. On the other hand, the mental set or the readiness to perceive such form will not develop if the environment places its greatest value on the observation of other things. Unfortunately that is probably the normal situation in a large portion of the world, because "getting ahead" physically, socially, and financially is one of the most highly valued conditions. People attend to materialistic matters more than to cultural ones because materialism helps them get ahead more rapidly. They pay attention to money, property, food,

[38] Eleanor J. Gibson, "Improvement in Perceptual Judgments as a Function of Controlled Practice or Training," *Psychological Bulletin*, vol. 50, pp. 401–431, 1953.
[39] Richard A. Salome, "The Effects of Perceptual Training Upon the Two-dimensional Drawings of Children," *Studies in Art Education*, vol. 7, no. 1, pp. 18–33, 1965.

Pl. 17
Garfield Seibert,
Old Bickel Quarry. 1954.
Oil on canvas mounted on board,
18 × 24 in. Collection,
Krannert Art Museum,
University of Illinois, Champaign.
Is this object a work of art?
If so, is it a work of
high quality? Why?

practical facts, objects that increase efficiency, and other such items, but they are not prepared to see the patterns of color formed by the movement of dresses and automobiles against a blue-black sky. If large numbers of people are to see such things, to obtain the knowledge relevant to art, the values of certain segments of the sociocultural environment will have to change.

SUMMARY

This chapter has tried to show that all persons have a need for symbolic transformation or creativity, and it has suggested that they satisfy that need by making symbols of many different kinds. In each case the fundamental requirements for creativity are relevant knowledge, attitudes, and skills. Hence we may say that artists and nonartists have those general characteristics in common. But the difference between them is that the artist possesses all the appropriate characteristics for the making of art and the nonartist does not. The master artist simply possesses those traits to a greater degree than the amateur; the master connoisseur has attributes that are similar but not quite the same.

Finally, it has been suggested that the artist's unique personality traits might be explained by certain organismic and environmental determinants. Various conditions of body and mind might aid or inhibit the formation of required attitudes and ultimately affect the knowledge and skill that is needed for creativity in art. It is possible that some of those organismic conditions could be the result of stock inheritance, but it is certain that some of them could also be influenced by the environment.

In general, the contemporary environment does not value aesthetic experience. Consequently, most people do not have an interest in making objects for aesthetic experience, nor do they have an interest in viewing them. Lacking that fundamental attitude, they do not attend to the sources from which artistically relevant knowledge is obtained, and they do not practice visual symbolization enough to develop artistic skill. If these conditions are to be overcome, teachers of art must do all they can to teach their students the value of aesthetic experience.

If teachers can get students sufficiently interested in making and viewing visual configurations, the act of making and viewing will itself provide many of the requirements essential to the making of art. In other words, it is important to remember (from Chapter 3) that the characteristics necessary for art may not exist in their most fully developed state prior to the making of a visual symbol. They grow and develop during the process of creation. This means, for example, that a person's knowledge of procedure will increase as he participates in the procedure; his knowledge of the aesthetic dimension of life will grow as he struggles to give it form in his work.

QUESTIONS FOR DISCUSSION

1. If a teacher is successful in developing artistic personalities, nonartists will turn into artists. Is the change apt to be permanent? What evidence would indicate the permanency of change?

2. Find out what is known about the organizational nature of visual perception. How do the principles of perceptual organization relate to the old principles of artistic composition?

3. Read several accounts of research on creativity. How many of the studies were devoted to artists? How did the investigators determine who the creative people were? Are the answers to these questions important? Why?

4. Can you think of a way of measuring the fluency of ideas that are relevant to art? How would you do it?

5. Would it be feasible to try to develop fluency of a general nature in people? Is that the idea behind general education? How good would general education have to be to produce individuals who are highly creative in a variety of media?

6. Some people believe that the artist is highly creative because he is neurotic or psychotic. The view in this text is that the artist is highly creative because he is *not* neurotic or psychotic. See if you can find evidence in the literature to support each of these views. How do you stand on the matter?

7. Much of the research on perception tends to explain why people perceive things differently. But what would happen if we did not see essentially the same things?

8. Examine the art program of your institution. Does it provide for the development of the five types of artistically relevant knowledge? Can you discover what it does provide?

9. Talk to one or two artists. What are the requirements for being an artist in their opinion? How do their views compare with the views in this text?

10. Examples have been given of how the environment influences the development of an artistic personality. See if you can think of other examples from real-life experience. See if you can get examples from research reports.

SUGGESTIONS FOR FURTHER READING

Allport, Floyd H.: *Theories of Perception and the Concept of Structure*, John Wiley and Sons, Inc., New York, 1955.
This is an excellent summary of the work on perception. A discussion of the six broad classes of perceptual phenomena can be found in Chapter 3.

Arnheim, Rudolf: *Art and Visual Perception*, University of California Press, Berkeley, 1954.
A good account of the dynamics of perceptual organization.

Brittain, W. Lambert: *Creativity and Art Education*, National Art Education Association, Washington, D. C.
A booklet devoted entirely to creativity in art.

Cellini, Benvenuto: *The Autobiography of Benvenuto Cellini*, Modern Library, Inc., New York, 1927.
A classic example of a self-confident, self-assertive, and independent artist.

Eisner, Elliot: *Think with Me about Creativity*, F. A. Owen Publishing Company, Dansville, New York, 1964.
A booklet on creativity written especially for classroom teachers.

Golann, Stuart E.: "Psychological Study of Creativity," *Psychological Bulletin*, vol. 60, no. 6, pp. 548–565, 1963.
A recent summary of research on creativity.

Guilford, J. P.: "Creative Abilities in the Arts," *Psychological Review*, vol. 64, no. 2, pp. 110–118, 1957.
The influential work of this prominent psychologist is applied to the arts. Very readable.

Hatterer, Lawrence J.: *The Artist in Society: Problems and Treatment of the Creative Personality*, Grove Press, Inc., New York, 1965.
A book that deals with the personality of the artist.

Langer, Susanne: *Philosophy in a New Key*, New American Library, Inc., New York, 1948.
A magnificent book that belongs in the library of every art educator. Not easy for the beginner.

Lowenfeld, Viktor: *The Nature of Creative Activity*, Routledge and Kegan Paul, Ltd., London, 1939.
This book gives a full account of a great art educator's early work with the blind. It forms the basis for the now famous Creative and Mental Growth. *The haptic and visual tendencies are fully explored in this book. Very readable.*

Meier, Norman C.: *Art in Human Affairs*, McGraw-Hill Book Company, New York, 1942.
Chapter 4 gives a fine account of the nature of creative expression and the nature of the artist.

Roe, Anne: "The Personality of Artists," *Educational and Psychological Measurement*, vol. 6, pp. 401–408, 1946.
An account of the characteristics that exist in the personality of the artist.

Shahn, Ben: *The Shape of Content*, Vintage Books, New York, 1960.
The section on the education of the artist is especially pertinent to the material in this chapter.

Sorokin, Pitirim A.: *The Crisis of Our Age*, E. P. Dutton and Co., Inc., New York, 1941.
A well-known sociologist presents his view of the effect of culture on the fine arts.

Chapter 5

THE DEVELOPMENT OF THE CHILD AS ARTIST AND CONNOISSEUR

Art educators often speak of the child as an artist. They assume, correctly enough, that youngsters are capable of producing art of a quality that is appropriate to their stage of growth and development. But the mere fact that a child's drawing is visual does not automatically make that drawing a work of art. To receive that designation, it must be pleasing in composition and must exist primarily for aesthetic experience. After all, art must have the same identifying characteristics no matter who produces it. This means that aesthetic educators are wrong when they refer to all graphic childhood symbols as works of art. They are wrong because children, like grownups, do not always produce forms that possess the qualities peculiar to art.

Children will normally create visual configurations whether they are trained to do so or not, because the making of symbols is a basic human need. The fulfillment of such a need is so important, however, that it should be encouraged in school. The teacher's job is to assist his students in obtaining the highest possible value from the fulfillment of that need, and he does it *135* by helping them to become artists. Consequently, he must be able to tell the difference between art and nonart. If he cannot do so, his value as an educator is limited, at best, to the encouragement of creative activity of the ordinary, nonartistic kind. To help avoid such a situation, some help in identifying child art will be offered at the end of this chapter.

In addition to knowing the difference between art and nonart, the teacher must know the normal developmental characteristics of visual symbolization. Unfortunately there is a tendency to criticize the concept of developmental stages and to minimize its importance to the teacher. It is generally argued that children do not conform to the neat patterns of growth that writers have suggested. Uniformity of growth by age levels is considered unrealistic because a unique constellation of physiological, psychological, and sociological forces is acting upon each child and causing him to develop in his own peculiar way. Furthermore, there is a feeling that a sequence of stages tends to obscure the smooth, continuous development that actually exists from birth.

On the other hand, we all know that people change between birth and death. They are infants, then children, then adolescents, and finally they become adults. All people who live long enough go through this sequence of growth and development. We know that the rate of progress varies from one individual to another, but it is common enough so that we can make a reasonable estimate of the ages in which human beings pass through the various phases of mental and physical development. Similarly, years of study by different investigators all over the world have shown us that children's drawings change gradually and continuously as children mature. The changes accumulate, and at certain times they result in drawings that appear significantly different from earlier drawings. When this occurs, we say that the child has reached another stage of symbolic development. We speak of stages simply because it is a convenient way of indicating that major changes have taken place. Most persons pass through the stages at rates that are sufficiently similar to permit a reasonably accurate prediction of human development. We can estimate that between the ages of four and seven most individuals will be in a certain stage of symbolic development, and in most cases we will be correct. The fact that investigators have associated chronological ages with each stage does not mean that they consider the developmental timetable to be inflexible or to be exactly the same for each individual. The ages are simply meant to be helpful approximations. Writers have made this point quite clear, and any other interpretation is a misinterpretation. Surely, it would be a shame to eliminate a useful concept from art education just because of such misunderstandings.

A knowledge of the developmental stages in visual symbolization and the approximate ages at which they occur is useful to a teacher because it means that he will know what to expect and when to expect it. Without this kind of information, the teacher might have difficulty in selecting appropriate educational experiences for his students; he might provide materials that are not suitable for the kind of drawing and painting that children do; he might ask students to do things that are either too easy or too hard for their stage of mental and physical development; and, very likely, he would not be able to tell whether changes in their creative work had occurred because of natural maturation or because of his teaching. Consequently, this chapter will offer both a verbal and a pictorial description of the developmental stages in visual symbolization. Most of the explanations for that development appear in Chapter 6.

THE CHARACTERISTICS OF GRAPHIC DEVELOPMENT

An interest in the development of children's graphic symbols is anything but new. In 1885 and 1886, Ebenezer Cooke, made the first recorded examination of children's drawings.[1] He described what he could detect as four stages of symbolic development. The first stage was said to occur between the ages of two and

[1] Ebenezer Cooke, "Our Art Teaching and Child Nature," *Journal of Education*, London, vol. 8, no. 198, pp. 12–15, 1886.

five, when youngsters were busy acquiring knowledge about the things around them. Their drawings were simply the results of muscular movements ending in scribbles. The second stage gave evidence of imagination and of greater mental control over linear movements. The drawings were representational, but according to Cooke there seemed to be little attention given to the accuracy of representation. Eyes, legs, whiskers, and tails were drawn without any apparent knowledge of the number or relationship of such parts. Cooke reported that in the third stage there was a better or, apparently, a more natural relationship of parts. He observed that the drawings were not copied from nature, but were drawn from memory or imagination. Unfortunately, the fourth stage was not described very thoroughly, but Cooke seemed to feel that it occured somewhere between the ages of four and nine. At that point the children were able to copy from nature and to produce drawings that reflected a careful analysis of things they saw.

Ebenezer Cooke was a teacher of English, and his observations were not especially accurate. But, he should receive credit for being the first to write about children's drawings. In the years that followed, additional information obtained from observation and research was provided by Ricci (1887), Perez (1888), Barnes (1893), Herrick (1893), Baldwin (1894), O'Shea (1894), Sully (1896), Maitland (1895), Lukens (1896), Brown (1897), Shinn (1897), Götze (1898), Clark (1902), Levenstein (1905), Kerschensteiner (1905), Stern (1910), Luquet (1913), Rouma (1913), Krötzsch (1917), Burt (1921), Wulff (1927), Eng (1931), Griffiths (1935), Lowenfeld (1947), Kellogg (1955), Lark-Horovitz (1959), and Eisner (1967). This is not a complete list of the persons who have contributed to our knowledge of sequential stages in visual symbolization, but it is offered here to indicate that an interest in the graphic work of children has persisted since 1885. Much of that attention must be attributed to a growing interest in psychology and to the systematic study of children.

A careful survey of all the research will indicate that there is general agreement on the sequence and the visual appearance of developing symbols, but that there is disagreement on the number of developmental stages and about the causes for them. Sir Cyril Burt,[2] for example, suggests that there are seven stages, one of which is called the stage of repression; yet, Viktor Lowenfeld[3] contends that there are only six stages because, in his estimation, a repressive phase is not inevitable. Most of the disagreements about the number of stages, however, seem to occur simply because graphic development is gradual, smooth, and continuous. One author may describe a certain configuration as being characteristic of a stage of development, while another writer may consider that arrangement to be an example of nothing more than a transitional phase.

In the present text the descriptive information given by preceding investigators will be offered again because of its fundamental accuracy, but the number of *major* developmental stages will be reduced to three—the smallest number of stages suggested by any investigator except Dale Harris.[4] The reason for this reduction is the belief that there are only three outstanding changes in the development of visual symbols, and they reflect the number of significantly different functions that visual symbolization seems to serve in the course of human growth.

The reader who is familar with child development in drawing will also notice that new names have been given to the stages to indicate their nature more clearly and more accurately. Two of the stages have been divided into substages because minor but obvious changes can be observed within those developmental periods and because the information is apt to be helpful to teachers. The following paragraphs describe symbolic development.

The scribbling stage (age two to four)

During this phase of development, visual symbolization gives the child an opportunity to satisfy his interest in the muscular sensa-

---

[2] Sir Cyril Burt, *Mental and Scholastic Tests*, P. S. King and Son, Ltd., London, 1921, pp. 317–327.

[3] Viktor Lowenfeld, *Creative and Mental Growth*, The Macmillan Company, New York, 1947.

[4] Dale Harris, *Children's Drawings as Measures of Intellectual Maturity*, Harcourt, Brace and World, Inc., New York, 1963, pp. 229–290.

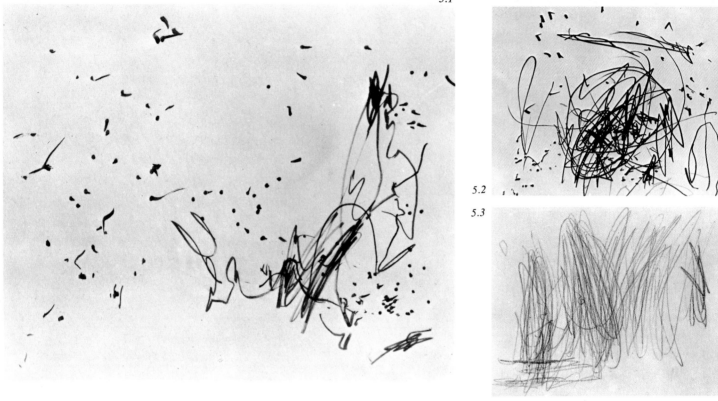

5.2

5.3

Fig. 5.1
*An uncontrolled scribble
made by a two-year-old child.
Most of the marks were made by
hitting the paper with
a felt-tipped pen.*

Fig. 5.2
*An uncontrolled scribble
made by a child at the age of two
years six months. Notice that the
drawing instrument is kept in contact
with the paper for longer periods
of time, making lines that move
in a variety of directions.*

Fig. 5.3
*A longitudinal scribble made
by a three-year-old in the substage
of controlled scribbling.*

tions of mark making. And it produces the satisfaction that comes from seeing that marks can be made, controlled, and eventually ordered in a way that suggests "thingness."

The substage of uncontrolled scribbling. A one-year-old child given a crayon will probably put it in his mouth because that is one of the crude but effective methods of exploration that he uses to discover the nature of things in his world. When he is about eighteen months or two years old, he will stop chewing on the crayon long enough to make marks on paper. This signals the beginning of symbolic development. The marks usually result from the child's attempted imitation of movements that have been made by someone else. Most of the marks are dots or short lines that come from hitting the paper with the crayon (Figure 5.1).

As time goes by, the child gradually will stop biting the crayon and hitting the paper. He will keep the crayon in contact with the drawing surface for longer periods of time, producing lines that move in a variety of directions (Figure 5.2). The haphazard or disorganized appearance of the markings during this early period have caused investigators to call it the *substage of uncontrolled scribbling.* The lines lack order or consistent directionality because the child does not possess sufficient motor control to master his own movements. His primary interest lies in the manipulation of materials and in the kinesthetic sensations that accompany it. His attention span is very short, and he is easily distracted.

The substage of controlled scribbling. Gradually the child develops more eye-hand coordination and passes into the second phase of the scribbling stage that we shall call the *substage of controlled scribbling.* He begins to repeat movements over and over again, producing longitudinal and circular scribbles (Figures 5.3, 5.4). Lowenfeld believes that the child makes the longitudinal marks first and then proceeds to make circular ones.[5] But, in this author's experience, both types of scribbles appear at about the same time. In fact, it is quite common to find both types in a single drawing, as seen in Figure 5.5. The first controlled markings are made with large movements of the whole arm, and because of the leverlike structure of the human arm, it is natural that they should be longitudinal and circular. As the child matures physically, he is able to do more with his wrist and fingers. Consequently, many small scribbles that are separate from one another emerge in his work. They appear as loops, whirls, or other circular forms and are repeated again and again (Figure 5.6).

The naming of scribbling substage. After the child has scribbled for quite some time, he enters the final phase of scribbling which we shall call the *naming of scribbling substage.* During that time the child continues to make all kinds of marks and combinations of marks. Rhoda Kellogg, in a careful study of 100,000 children's drawings, found that youngsters make about twenty

5.4

5.5

Fig. 5.4
A circular scribble made with finger paint in nursery school. It is highly satisfying to the child to be able to repeat lines again and again.

Fig. 5.5
A mixture of longitudinal and circular scribbles by a three-year-old child.

[5] Lowenfeld, *op. cit.*, pp. 87–89.

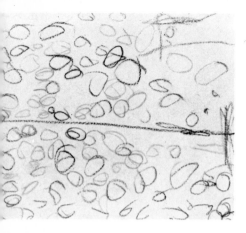

different basic scribbles and that several diagrams, combinations, and aggregates are made from those basic forms.[6] None of the forms bear any clearly recognizable association with visual reality, but the child begins to give them a name near the end of the scribbling period. In Figure 5.7, we see a drawing from this substage by a child who was three years old. He made several longitudinal scribbles with a paintbrush and called the product a bird; the name was given after the work had been completed, which is usually the case at the beginning of this substage. Later, the child may declare his intentions first and then proceed to draw. Whenever naming occurs, however, we can be sure that the child is thinking in terms of concrete objects or events and that he is beginning to use his imagination. From that point on, his drawings will show a greater relationship to visual reality and less relationship to mere kinesthetic activity, but that does not mean that the child will discontinue scribbling, for he will keep on doing it for a long time. Even adults scribble once in a while, usually when they are tired or daydreaming. But the child will produce purely meaningless scribbles with less and less frequency.

It is interesting to note that the work of individual children can often be recognized at the earliest stages of symbolic development. The fact that their work has certain characteristics in common does not mean that individuality is missing. Different children will apply different pressure to the drawing instrument, and their work will possess various degrees of boldness or daintiness. Sometimes one configuration will be simple while other arrangements will be highly intricate. Qualities of neatness, muddiness, clearness, softness, and tightness are other common qualities that can often be associated with certain children. Occasionally a child will paint the whole paper a solid color, or he may paint beyond the paper onto the floor or table. On the other hand, a few strokes in the corner of a sheet may be enough to satisfy him. Still other children may seem to have a compulsion

[6] Rhoda Kellogg, *What Children Scribble and Why*, San Francisco, 1955, p. 4. (Available from 570 Union St., San Francisco, California.)

Pl. 18
A drawing made with
felt-tipped pen and crayon by a girl
aged two years eight months.
From the substage of
uncontrolled scribbling.

Pl. 19
A finger painting by a girl aged
three years five months. From the
substage of controlled scribbling.

Pl. 20
A tempera painting by a girl
aged four years ten months. From the
naming of scribbling substage.

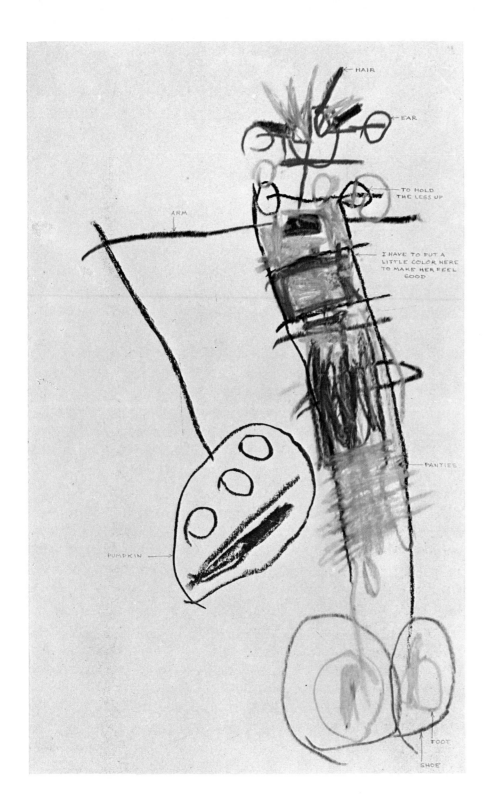

HAIR

EAR

TO HOLD
THE LEGS UP

ARM

I HAVE TO PUT A
LITTLE COLOR HERE
TO MAKE HER FEEL
GOOD

PANTIES

PUMPKIN

FOOT

SHOE

Pl. 21
**A crayon drawing by a girl
aged four years seven months. From
the emerging figurative substage.**

145

for filling in corners or some other portion of the paper. The point is that individual youngsters will produce work that looks unique even at the scribbling level. Their developmental progress will seem more rapid if they use pencils or crayons instead of paint, but that is because paint is more difficult to manipulate and the brushes have wider tips.

When children work with clay, their early productions follow the same pattern as their drawings. They begin by pushing, pounding, and breaking the clay for the sheer enjoyment of tactile and kinesthetic sensations. It is roughly equivalent to uncontrolled scribbling and occurs at about the same time. Later, when the child has sufficient motor control to scribble with consistent directionality, he will also roll his clay into balls and snakelike shapes. Still later he will call his three-dimensional forms by name just as he does his drawings.

The scribbling child also works with a variety of paper, cloth, sticks, yarn, and other materials to make arrangements or constructions of one kind or another. The earliest activity is merely a manipulation of materials, but eventually it becomes more controlled and the child begins to name his product. Again, the same pattern of growth that we found in drawing, painting, and clay work is evident.

A teacher who works with children below the first-grade level should expect to find that many of his students scribble. He should realize that scribbling is a natural part of their development and that it should not be criticized. In other words, he should treat his students as scribbling children and not as older children or as adults. Suggestions about how to treat such youngsters are given in Chapters 7 and 9.

The scribbler as a connoisseur. When we describe the child's development as a connoisseur, we give an account of his responses to works of art. Describing those responses is not a simple matter because reactions vary considerably, according to individual differences and environmental conditions. Probably the best we can do is to offer a general account of the child's development, with the understanding that there are exceptions to the pattern. The description will apply to youngsters who have had little or no education in the appreciation of art, and it must be understood that education can affect the pattern. The *degree* to which education can influence development has not, however, been demonstrated experimentally.

When faced with visual objects, scribbling children respond readily to elemental formal qualities, composition, and subject matter. They are attracted by and seem to prefer vivid colors, strong contrasts, and textures that they can feel with their fingers. They also seem to prefer balance to imbalance, and clarity to obscurity, but they usually indicate a preference only when the differences are quite apparent.

Scribbling children respond most readily, however, to subject matter. Although their attention span in looking at art is relatively short, they usually look for a longer time at pictures that contain recognizable objects. They frequently have a hard time explaining why a picture or statue appeals to them, but when they do explain, they usually say that they like the colors, that the picture looks real, or that the objects in it remind them of something.

The figurative stage (age three to twelve)

During this stage of development visual symbolization serves the child by helping him to understand the concrete objects and events in his experience. He also uses it to give particular visual information to other persons, and much of the information presented in that way cannot be transmitted through other forms of communication.

The early figurative substage (age three to seven). Children in this phase of development may be encountered in nursery school, kindergarten, and first grade. Occasionally, but not very often, you see them in second grade. The child enters this substage of symbolic development when his graphic images display their first relationship to visual reality. In other words, the beginning of this period is indicated by drawings that resemble things

we experience in our environment. Almost all investigators have said that the first and most common object to be drawn and recognized is the human figure. It emerges almost imperceptibly from the scribbling stage because the earliest figures are made from various combinations of the basic scribbles. In Figure 5. 8 we see one of the child's first attempts at drawing a man. A circle forms the head or body, and longitudinal marks are added for legs and hair. Together the elements represent the child's concept of human beings in general. When he draws a figure that we recognize as a human being, we can be sure that he knows at least as much about a man as his drawing reveals. He may know more, but he does not know less or he would not be able to make the figure. Consequently, drawings are a good indication of intellectual maturity up to the age of ten.

During the early figurative substage the child's motor development continues to improve and his perceptual activity increases. Each new experience stimulates him and provides him with more information about the things he encounters. Thus his concepts change and develop. They gradually become more differentiated, and so do his drawings. In fact, his visual creations tend to change or mature more rapidly during this phase of symbolic development than they do at any other time. He might draw a house one way today, another way tomorrow, and still another way the next day. Evidence from the Goodenough Draw-a-Man Test[7] and from the Harris revision of that test[8] indicates that the child's symbol for a man *continues* to change steadily between the ages of five and ten; and there is no reason to believe that symbols for other objects should develop any differently. But the *rate* of change definitely *slows down* after the child gets beyond the age of seven or beyond the early figurative substage. If, however, a child is highly stimulated for a period of time, it is possible that his drawings will show unusually rapid growth during that period, no matter when it occurs.[9]

While he is in the early figurative substage, the child often includes more than one object in his drawings and arranges those objects in a way that is highly characteristic of this developmental period. He places them all over the paper with no meaningful relationship among them. By this we mean that the objects are not arranged in the familiar way that we experience them. Figure 5.9 is a good example of this. The human figures float in the sky together with dishes, string, and a witch's house. Some things appear right-side up, and others are upside down. If you watch the child and listen to him as he works, you will notice that his attention is riveted on one item at a time. He works intently on that item until he finishes it, and then he seems to eliminate it from his mind and begin on another object. As he does so, he moves the paper in any way that will allow him to

[7] Florence L. Goodenough, *Measurement of Intelligence by Drawings*, World Book Company, New York, 1926, pp. 26–34.

[8] Dale B. Harris, *Children's Drawings as Measures of Intellectual Maturity*, Harcourt, Brace and World, Inc., New York, 1963, pp. 141–147.

[9] Support for this statement can be found in Elizabeth R. Dublin, "The Effect of Training on the Tempo of Development of Graphic Representation in Preschool Children," *Journal of Experimental Education*, vol. 15, pp. 166–173, 1946.

reach a space that has not been filled. This partially accounts for the fact that things often appear upside-down or sideways in his drawings. It is also evident that the child is not thinking of complex ideas or of relationships among things. He does not seem concerned with the organization of his world, but he is thinking primarily of concrete objects in relative isolation. He seems to be trying to come to grips with those objects or to understand them one by one; he thinks of a girl and then of a tree, but he does not think of a girl *under* a tree.

To say that drawings from this substage are meaninglessly arranged does not mean that the objects represented are unrelated to each other. Sometimes they are definitely related, and it commonly happens when they are part of a theme; for example, the people in Figure 5.10 are all members of the same family, and all the objects in Figure 5.11 belong in a rodeo. Consequently, they are related to each other, although their spatial organization is meaningless.

Visual symbols in this phase of development possess still other distinctive characteristics. All kinds of things will be drawn with evident exaggerations of size. Sometimes a head will be larger than a tree or a child will be larger than a house. The elements of line, color, and texture that make up the symbols may bear little or no resemblance to the same elements in the object that is being symbolized. A woman may be painted purple, and her dog may be colored green. Her arms and legs are likely to be made of straight lines that lack the shapeliness of the real things. In other words, the drawings are not highly naturalistic. Their resemblance to visual reality is enough to signify a general class of objects, but not much more. This is, of course, the child's only purpose. His symbol for a man simply says that this is an instance of a class of objects called men. As the child matures, his drawings will look more and more like the things we see, but the relationship during this substage is not very great.

Visual symbols in three dimensions continue to develop in a way that is parallel to the development of the child's drawings just as they did during the scribbling stage. Constructions made with clay and other materials begin to resemble things that we

Fig. 5.10
*Although the figures in
this drawing are meaninglessly
arranged, they are not unrelated: all
are members of the same family.*

Fig. 5.11
*The child who made this
drawing was in kindergarten. It is an
excellent example of work from the
substage of emerging figurativism.
The cowboy, cowboy's father,
and cow belong in a rodeo.*

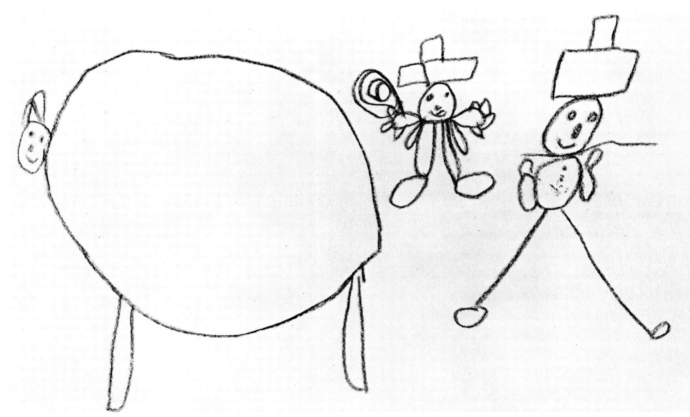

experience from day to day. The resemblance is sometimes more difficult to make out in these materials than it is in drawing, but it can be seen rather clearly in a good many instances. Much of the three dimensional work, however, is not meant to be representational; it is simply meant to be interesting and decorative.

During this period of development the child gives little or no conscious thought to aesthetic problems. Things appear in his creations and are arranged in a certain way because that is the way he feels it should be done. You might say that he works intuitively. At any rate, he becomes absorbed in his work at this time, and he can remain at it for a long time.

The mid-figurative substage (age six to ten). Drawings in this stage of development are found most frequently in kindergarten and in the first, second, third, and fourth grades. But it is important for the teacher to know that such drawings are apt to appear anywhere from nursery school to junior high school; it is the only phase of visual symbolization that can be seen at so many different age levels.

During this period the child's visual symbols continue their trend toward greater differentiation as they become more elaborate. But the most significant change from the previous substage of development can be seen in the arrangement of symbols within the drawing. The placement of one item with respect to another is now obviously intentional and meaningful. Things that touch the ground in visual reality are now made to stand on a line that signifies ground in the drawing; this line has been called a *base line*. It may be drawn by the child, or it may be the line formed by the bottom edge of the paper. Incidently, it is now clear that the child's drawing has a bottom and a top. The orientation of objects within the picture is such that the ground is toward the bottom and the sky toward the top. Figures 5.12 through 5.15, which were made by one child during the early months of this stage, illustrate the new organization of elements quite clearly.

The base line in Figure 5.12 appears near the middle of the drawing, and a child and some flowers are standing on it.

At the top of the picture is a scribble representing the sky, and several boxes appear in the middle. Perhaps it would be more accurate to speak of the drawing as being in a transitional period between this substage and the previous one because the ground and the boxes seem to be floating.

In Figure 5.13, however, we observe a drawing that is clearly in the midfigurative substage, because the symbol of the little girl is standing firmly on a groundline and is no longer hanging in midair. Notice also the greater complexity of the figure as compared to the last one and to the drawings of human beings in the previous substage. This trend toward greater complexity can be seen in the symbols for most objects that are commonly experienced. But if an object is not encountered very often, the child will probably create a simple symbol that reflects his meager concept of the object. In Figure 5.14, for example, we can see a tiger standing on the bottom of his cage beneath a peaceful sky. Because the child's contacts with tigers have been limited, she does not have a complex mental image of the animal. Consequently, she assumes that the tiger has a face similar to that of a man, so she gives the tiger a simple human face. Animals of most kinds are commonly drawn with human faces during this phase of symbolic development.

Figure 5.15 shows a train with its caboose at the left and its engine and a man at the right. Smoke appears over the engine, and a sun, which is so common in children's drawings, shines brightly at the left. Although a band of color that signifies the sky is not present in Figures 5.13 and 5.15, it is equally as evident in this substage as the sun. In fact, a sky does appear in Figures 5.12 and 5.14, and when it exists, it does not extend down to the ground but remains as a stripe across the top of the paper. The child is simply saying, in a very effective manner, that the ground is below and the sky is above. Besides, the sky color and ground color do not interfere with the drawing of trees, houses, and other objects if those colors are kept near the top and bottom of the paper. Consequently, there is absolutely no reason for criticizing the child when he makes a sky that does not touch the ground. He is making a statement that is

Fig. 5.14
A tiger in a cage. Because the five-year-old artist had only limited experience with tigers, she did not have an accurate concept of the animal. That accounts for the smiling, human face.

Fig. 5.15
A five-year-old made this drawing of a train. The base line and the shining sun are typical of the mid-figurative substage.

THE DEVELOPMENT OF THE CHILD AS ARTIST AND CONNOISSEUR

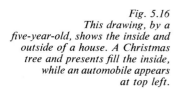

Fig. 5.16
This drawing, by a
five-year-old, shows the inside and
outside of a house. A Christmas
tree and presents fill the inside,
while an automobile appears
at top left.

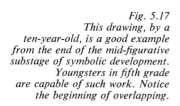

Fig. 5.17
This drawing, by a
ten-year-old, is a good example
from the end of the mid-figurative
substage of symbolic development.
Youngsters in fifth grade
are capable of such work. Notice
the beginning of overlapping.

so logical and powerful that no artist would ever question it.

Although the child's graphic and three-dimensional symbols become more complex or more detailed during this period, they still lack a high degree of naturalism. Figures 5.16 and 5.17 are examples of work from the early and late portions of this substage respectively. The second drawing has almost reached the next phase of development because of the slight illusion of depth that has been created by overlapping. The truck covers a portion of the telephone pole, and the pole does not show through the truck. Nevertheless, the depth is still quite shallow because of the continuing use of the base line and the lack of depth-producing elements other than overlapping. Drawings can be said to remain in this phase of development as long as a base line is evident and the illusion of depth is minimal.

By comparing Figures 5.16 and 5.17 one can obtain a good idea of the development that takes place within a single substage. The first drawing was produced by a kindergarten girl at the age of five, and the second picture was made by a fifth-grade girl at the age of ten. Obviously, the drawing of the human figure becomes more naturalistic as children mature, but it still does not bear a close resemblance to visual reality at the end

of the mid-figurative substage. It remains flat and stiff, rather than round and flexible. The same is true for the symbol of any object. In Figure 5.16 a top view of an automobile appears at the left. Without being told, the observer would find it hard to identify the symbol as an automobile. The truck in Figure 5.17, on the other hand, is clearly distinguishable, but it still remains far from the appearance of visual reality. The sizes, shapes, proportions, colors, and textures of objects are not made to look as we see them, although they are developing in that direction. Color, especially, begins to approach visual reality during this substage; the sky becomes blue, the grass becomes green, and people are less likely to be made purple. From an artist's point of view, of course, there is no reason that nature should be imitated, and we do not intend to make such a suggestion. We are merely describing the development that normally occurs during this substage.

Lowenfeld's description of this phase of symbolic development calls attention to other characteristics that cause the child's drawing to look different from visual reality.[10] He speaks of

Pl. 23
The elephant at the zoo, made with a felt-tipped pen by a girl aged eight years ten months. From the mid-figurative substage.

[10] Lowenfeld, *op. cit.*, pp. 132–181.

Fig. 5.18
An x-ray drawing by
a five-year-old. It shows a mother
with two babies inside.

Fig. 5.19
A ten-year-old boy
produced this picture about riding
on a crowded bus. It shows the
inside and the outside of the
bus. Clearly, the inside was
important to the child.

158

x-ray drawings, combinations of plan and elevation in a single sketch, time-space pictures, and exaggerations and omissions of important parts as if they were peculiar to this particular substage of development. Actually, these characteristics can be seen in drawings at all levels of development except the scribbling stage, but they appear most frequently during the early figurative and mid-figurative substages. Perhaps it would be helpful to describe those characteristics more fully.

During the early figurative substage, x-ray drawings are fairly common. They are drawings that present the inside and the outside of something all at the same time. The inside and the outside of a baby carriage, a car, a house, or some other familiar object might be shown. Figure 5.18, for example, presents a five-year-old's version of a mother with two babies inside her. Such drawings are likely to emerge if the child happens to be especially interested in the interior of something at the time that he is drawing. The picture in Figure 5.19 was made following a stimulating discussion about riding on crowded buses. It was produced by a ten-year-old boy, and it is a good example of an x-ray picture from the end of the mid-figurative substage. Figure 5.16 presents still another typical example of x-ray drawing from the very beginning of the mid-figurative period. It shows a five-year-old's conception of a house with a Christmas tree and presents on the inside. An automobile, the top view of which appears on the left, is drawn so that the seats are visible. It is not unusual to see x-ray drawings such as these in all the grades of the elementary school.

Another characteristic that is frequently seen in children's drawings is the combination of plan and elevation in one picture. This means that one often sees a drawing that reveals the tops and the sides of objects all at the same time. Once again Figure 5.16 provides a good example from the beginning of the mid-figurative substage. The house and the child have been drawn in a front view, which is sometimes called an elevation, and the automobile at the left has been drawn in a top or plan view. Another illustration of this characteristic can be seen in Figure 5.20. From the end of the mid-figurative substage, it

Pl. 24
A lion, in tempera,
by a boy aged six. From the
mid-figurative substage.

Pl. 25
A barbecue, in tempera,
by a girl aged six. From the
mid-figurative substage.

Pl. 26
A drawing of animals
made with a felt-tipped pen by
a boy aged seven. From the
mid-figurative substage.

THE DEVELOPMENT OF THE CHILD
AS ARTIST AND CONNOISSEUR

shows an automobile standing on one of three baselines, with a house standing on another and a bicycle on the third. We see all three objects from a side view, but the road, which is supposed to go into the distance, has been drawn as if it were parallel to the picture plane. Consequently, the road and the vehicles on it are seen from a top view. In Figure 5.21 we see more of this characteristic, but this time it is from the next stage of development, which we shall call the *late figurative substage*. The bedposts, the picture on the wall, the dresser, the legs of the small table and stool, and the bottom of the water glass have been drawn in a side view; yet, the sleeping figure, the pillow and the bed coverings, the top of the water glass, the rug, and the top of the table and stool have been drawn in a top or three-quarter view. Hence it is clear that combinations of plan and elevation are not confined to one phase of development. It is also interesting to note that Figure 5.21 was produced by a nine-year-old girl in fourth grade, while Figure 5.20 was created by a ten-year-old boy in fifth grade. This shows that the chronological ages associated with periods of development are merely helpful estimates that can be wrong for any individual.

Sometimes a child will make a picture containing several events that normally occur in a sequence or at different points in time. He might draw the same man hitting a baseball, running around second base, and sliding into third all in the same sketch. Again, this can be seen at any stage of symbolic development except the scribbling stage, and it is quite common in adult murals and cartoons.

Still another characteristic that keeps children's drawings from looking highly naturalistic is the exaggeration or omission of parts that seem important. All the children's drawings that we have discussed up to now show some form of exaggeration; and if we were to examine the works of master artists, we would always find a distortion of visual reality that might be called exaggeration. In general, however, the degree of exaggeration or distortion tends to decrease as the child gets older, and, by the end of the late figurative substage, the exaggeration in most drawings is minimal. The same is true of body parts, which are

Fig. 5.20
*A mixture of plan and
elevation is evident in this picture
from the end of the mid-figurative
substage of artistic development.*

Fig. 5.21
*This drawing, by a girl
in fourth grade, contains a mixture
of plan and elevation, or top
and side views.*

THE DEVELOPMENT OF THE CHILD
AS ARTIST AND CONNOISSEUR

Pl. 27
A warship, in tempera,
by a boy aged eight. From the
mid-figurative substage.

Pl. 28
Renee and her watch,
in crayon, by a girl aged eight.
From the mid-figurative substage.

Fig. 5.22
The double base line seen in
this drawing is often used to produce
a feeling of depth, or the idea of
rows of objects. It is the work
of a seven-year-old girl.

readily omitted in the first drawings that children make, as we can see in Figure 5.8, where a human being appears with a head, two legs, two eyes, and some hair. But such omissions become rare as the child reaches the late figurative substage.

The four characteristics just discussed are regularly seen at this mid-figurative level of symbolic development; but, as has been said, they may be observed at other stages. There are, however, two characteristics of visual symbolization that are peculiar to this mid-figurative period. One is the double base line, which can be seen in Figure 5.22. To create a feeling of depth in her picture and to keep the people from floating in air, this seven-year-old girl placed her symbols for objects on two base lines. The same technique is used in Figure 5.20, where it also serves to provide a depth and a spatial organization closer to that which we find in visual reality. Because both the multiple and single base line produce essentially the same kind of spatial organization, they are not found in other stages of development. In fact, it should be emphasized that the base line is the most outstanding characteristic of the mid-figurative level.

The second characteristic peculiar to this substage of development is evident in Figure 5.23. Lowenfeld calls it "folding

Fig. 5.23
This is an example of
"folding over," which is often used
to show things seen on the sides
of a street or table.

Faith

over."[11] Multiple base lines are apparent, with the house standing on one, the trees on a second, and the horse on a third. But, unlike the people in Figure 5.22, the objects in this drawing are not all right side up, although each of them stands on a base line. If the drawing could be folded on each of the base lines, the idea the child is trying to get across would be quite evident. Folding over is often employed when the child is trying to show the things that can be seen on each side of a street, a sidewalk, a table, or a football field. As he draws, he turns the paper around or walks around it; he does not draw the objects upside down at any time.

Up to this point in the child's symbolic development, he produces his drawing and his three-dimensional work almost entirely from memory images. Only on rare occasions does he look at an object as he draws it. When he does look, it may have little or no effect on his work or may bring about a remarkable change, depending upon the intensity of his looking. To illustrate the change that can take place, we might compare the drawings in Figures 5.22 and 5.24.

Both drawings were produced by a seven-year-old girl, but the drawing in Figure 5.24 was made while she was looking at her father who was sitting on a sofa. The other drawing was based on memory images. It is clear that observation of the object being drawn has influenced the child's symbolization, and brought it closer to visual reality. It is also interesting to note that the girl's subsequent drawings did not possess this high degree of naturalism except when she was actually looking at the object she was drawing. When she drew from memory, her drawings continued to look like the work in Figure 5.22. She is now ten hears old, and her drawings produced from memory are much more highly detailed or differentiated than they were. In fact, they have moved much closer to the symbolic form we see in Figure 5.24. The reasons for this and for the other characteristics of symbolic development will be discussed in the next chapter.

[11] *Ibid.*, p. 146.

The late figurative substage (age nine to twelve). Drawings from this phase of development are found most frequently in grades five, six, and seven. They may appear as early as the third grade, but this does not happen very often. Beyond the seventh grade, however, it is not unusual to see drawings that exhibit this level of development. The reason for this is that most children give up serious drawing at about the age of eleven or twelve to pursue symbolization in another medium, usually speech or writing. As a consequence, their visual symbols do not develop much beyond the point where they stopped their active drawing. If they were to resume serious drawing, their work would probably continue to develop. But the fact that most people do not continue accounts for the occasional appearance of late figurative drawings, even at the college level.

Perhaps the most significant difference between this substage of development and the previous one is that the base line has now disappeared and perspective has replaced it. Instead of standing everything on a base line, the child places objects on a plane that represents the ground and appears to extend back into the picture. This gives the objects a position in pictorial space that is more closely related to their position in the world as we see it. In addition to the use of a plane, the child makes distant objects smaller than those in the foreground. He also makes the things that are closest to him overlap the things that are far away, and he does so without allowing the distant objects

Fig. 5.25
During the late figurative substage of artistic development, the base line is replaced by a plane and objects in the distance are reduced in size. This drawing was made by a child in fifth grade.

Fig. 5.26
A typical drawing from the fifth grade. The emergence of a plane and the use of overlapping indicate that the child is in the late figurative substage of symbolic development.

169

Fig. 5.27
An example of the use of
linear perspective by a boy in
fifth grade. The drawing is
remarkably naturalistic.

Fig. 5.28
This unusual view of a
crowded bus was made by a girl
in fifth grade. Note the use
of linear perspective.

170

to show through the closer ones. Figures 5.25 and 5.26 are typical examples of these characteristics from the work of fifth-grade children.

Sometimes youngsters in this substage of symbolic development will make use of *linear* perspective, but it is not quite as common as the use of overlapping and the reduction in size of distant objects. Linear perspective is an illusion of depth that is produced through the special treatment of parallel lines. Everyone knows that the edges of a road are parallel, but when we look at the road as it moves into the distance, we see that the edges appear to converge. If an individual represents a road by making lines converge on paper, the road will appear to have parallel sides and will move convincingly into the distance. When he does this, he is using linear perspective. In Figures 5.27 and 5.28 we see drawings by a boy and girl in the fifth grade. Both of them have used linear perspective as well as other means of producing depth. The boy who drew the picture of the trucks possessed an unusual amount of information about vehicles of all kinds, as his drawing clearly reveals. His father happened to be a truck driver, but, nevertheless, his drawings contain far more detail than one would normally expect to find in the work of a fifth-grade child drawing from memory. He used linear perspective in each of the vehicles, down to the smallest crank and headlight.

The girl who drew the interior of the bus used linear perspective in the seats, which is not ordinarily done. Besides, her picture is unusual because of the view it affords the observer and because it reveals only the interior and not the exterior of the bus. Out of approximately 200 drawings of crowded buses from nine different schools, this was the only picture devoted exclusively to the inside of the bus, and it was the only one to provide a view from above. It is important to recognize that such evidence of individuality can be found in different forms throughout the whole developmental process. Children may have certain traits in common and may produce symbols that have essentially the same characteristics; but they will still reveal their individual differences.

*Fig. 5.29
Youngsters in the late
figurative substage of artistic
development normally identify
themselves with members of their
own sex and with activities
associated with that sex. These
members of a band were made
by a girl in fourth grade.*

In addition to a different spatial organization, the drawings of the late figurative period reveal a greater degree of visual realism in each individual object. Take the human figure for instance. Most drawings now depict the figure with a head, a torso, legs, arms, hair, eyes, nose, ears, feet, hands, and fingers. Many of them even contain details of the eyes, ears, nose, and other body parts. The percentage of drawings that contain these various parts can be obtained, for each age level between five and ten, from the statistics of the Harris revision of the Goodenough Draw-a-Man Test.[12]

It is during the late figurative period that children begin to show pronounced differences between the sexes in their drawings. They suggested a difference much earlier, of course, by putting dresses on the women and trousers on the men. But now the women are given long wavy hair, breasts, and prominent lips, while the men are given short hair, broad shoulders, and muscles.

Children also begin to identifiy themselves with the occupational roles that members of their sex usually assume. Girls identify themselves with majorettes, nurses, mothers, movie stars, and even teachers. Boys consider the possibility of becoming baseball players, firemen, policemen, soldiers, and pilots. Occupations that require distinctive uniforms of any kind seem to be especially popular. At any rate, the child cannot symbolize such persons to his satisfaction unless he gives his drawings a sufficient degree of realism. His figures must look like men and women, and they must be specific kinds of men and women. In Figure 5.29 we see two female members of the band drawn by a fourth-grade girl. The long hair, the lips, the body contour, necks, elbows, and knees are all characteristic of this substage of development. The distinctive uniforms also are associated with this period. Other highly descriptive forms of dress can be seen in Figure 5.30, which shows a girl and a boy drawn in clothing suitable for tennis.

The replacement of the base line by a plane, the greater detail that identifies the sexes more clearly, and the characteri-

[12] Harris, *op. cit.*, pp. 141–147.

Pl. 29
Riding on the school bus, made
with a felt-tipped pen and crayon by a
girl aged seven years four months.
From the beginning of the
late figurative substage.

Fig. 5.30
During the late figurative substage, the sexes are clearly differentiated by body contour, hair, lips, and clothing. In general, figures are highly naturalistic. This painting is by a girl in sixth grade.

zation of special people all contribute to a greater realism in the graphic productions of this developmental period. Adding to this general effect is the fact that the sky is no longer signified by a stripe of blue at the top of the page. All the outdoor drawings that have been used to illustrate this substage of development show that the blue of the sky has been brought down to the earth and to the things that rest upon the earth. This trend toward greater and greater realism has been observed from the early stages of symbolic transformation. For some children, this trend will continue, but for others it will not. Some youngsters will change to a more abstract way of expressing themselves with visual symbols, but most of them will stop active drawing. They will draw and paint only when requested to do so by teachers or by other authorities. Consequently, the differences between the visual symbols of individual children will tend to increase. An indication of how wide these differences can become will be given as we discuss the next stage of development.

The connoisseur in the figurative stage. During the early figurative substage, the child continues to react to works of art in the way that he reacted as a scribbler, but he becomes a bit more sensitive to the details in recognizable objects. He notices the way an eye or a hand is made, and he gives a better account of the information that a picture might provide. He detects it, however, only if it is clearly revealed, as it is in the illustrations for children's books. In such instances he may see tears on a child's face and say that the picture looks unhappy. But if the tears are absent, the child is apt to say that the painting appears cheerful, and he is likely to explain that it looks that way because the colors are happy or because the rocks, the trees, and grass look nice. In other words, the child who is just beginning to draw recognizable figures is not especially good at detecting meaning in visual art, unless the meaning is simple and clear.

Probably the most authoritative account of children's responses to art is given by C. W. Valentine, who concludes that there are about four different kinds of reactions that can be observed at any stage of development.[13] He calls the four responses the associative, the subjective, the character, and the objective types. The *associative* type is the most common, and it is exemplified by the person who says that a painting reminds him of blood, of his grandfather's farm, or of a junk heap. The *subjective* type of response is one in which the respondent tells how the painting makes him feel. He might say, for example, that it makes him feel restful, angry, warm, or excited. Much less common is the *character* type of reaction in which the observer speaks of an art object or any of its elements as being feminine, aggressive, brash, or demure. In that case, the appreciator indicates that he perceives character in the visual form. The *objective* type of response, on the other hand, is one in which the respondent speaks of color as color or line as line. He may say that the red is too orange to be a good red, or he may say that the texture is too much the same in all parts of the painting.

[13] C. W. Valentine, *The Experimental Psychology of Beauty*, Methuen and Co., Ltd., London, 1962, p. 419.

Pl. 30
Flamingos, made with
a felt-tipped pen by a boy aged
nine. From the beginning of the
late figurative substage.

Pl. 31
Sledding, in tempera,
by a boy aged ten. From the
late figurative substage.

Such responses may be heard from youngsters in any stage of development, but you rarely hear a child make either the character or the objective type of response during the early figurative substage. Young children are much more likely to make the associative type of response or, occasionally, the subjective type.

During the mid-figurative substage, children continue to show a growing interest in and preference for naturalistic art, and they display great admiration for persons who can make a horse that looks like a horse. Their comments suggest that they see more details in works of art, and the details seem to be of greater interest to them than the picture as a whole. Although they rarely reveal any conscious appreciation of structural organization or formal elements (an objective response), they are more sensitive to such things than they were in the early figurative stage. They tend to prefer balance to imbalance, harmony to disharmony, clarity to obscurity, complexity to simplicity, and technical proficiency to poor craftsmanship.

In the mid-figurative stage, children notice that different styles of drawing and painting exist, and they are sensitive enough to recognize the work of individual artists. They are able to identify youngsters in their own classes by their work, and they often show admiration for the one who can draw most naturalistically. In other words, their tolerance of different styles tends to become less and less as they grow older.

Between six and ten years of age, children also begin to develop an awareness of the different uses of art in their everyday lives. They become aware of advertisements, illustrations in books, and decorations in homes and business establishments. Some children begin to think of themselves as future artists and show an interest in the various kinds of artistic occupations.

By the time they reach the late figurative substage most youngsters are firmly committed to naturalistic art. In fact, they struggle so hard to achieve naturalism in their own work that they occasionally neglect structural organization. The result is often a picture that is close to visual reality in certain respects but not very pleasing to perceive. The emphasis seems to be on the presentation of information, not on the beauty of it.

The children respond to the work of others in the same way. They scorn the lack of naturalism and attend to details rather than to the object as a whole. This description, like all the others we have made, applies to youngsters who have had no formal schooling in art appreciation. Such persons usually reject the visual arts during the late figurative substage and turn their attention to other things. With the proper aesthetic education, however, youngsters of the same age have been known to look at art and talk about it attentively and intelligently for at least an hour at a time. Their responses are still predominantly associative and subjective, but the number of character and objective responses tend to increase with age and with aesthetic education.

The stage of artistic decision (age eleven and beyond). During the figurative stage of development, visual symbolization served the individual by helping him to understand the concrete objects and events in his life, and it allowed him to present his own concepts and emotions for inspection by others. In this stage of development, however, visual symbolization helps a young person to understand abstract concepts as well as concrete ones. And, more importantly perhaps, it serves as a way of changing or affecting the cultural environment as well as a way of adjusting to it. Because he uses his visual symbols in such a way, the young adolescent changes the character of his symbols in very important ways. Let us examine these changes more carefully.

Youngsters who pass through this stage of development are usually encountered in grades six through ten. They do not all reach this stage of course, but if they do, it is usually during the junior high school years.

The most outstanding feature of the period can be noticed in the subject matter and the content of the child's work. Girls draw endless numbers of pretty female figures with ruby lips and flowing curves. They draw brides, horses, movie stars, and unusually handsome men. It is not uncommon to find a princess or an exotic temptress in a dreamworld of castles, knights, tigers, unicorns, jungles, and faraway places. Such pictures ap-

Pl. 32
An imaginative crayon drawing
produced by a boy in fourth grade.
From the late figurative substage.

Pl. 33
Leaders of the band, in crayon,
by a girl in fifth grade. From the
late figurative substage.

pear in corners of notebooks and on scraps of paper as well as in regular classwork. In fact, such drawings can often be found in notebooks when it would appear from the child's classwork that she had never drawn a human figure in her life.

Muscular men engaged in adventurous activities are commonly the subjects of boy's drawings. The picturing of heroic deeds and thrilling exploits with danger existing in all directions is something that appeals to junior high school boys. Both girls and boys produce drawings that contain elements of fantasy or things from the dreamworld, which was not the case in earlier stages.

At this level one can also observe pictures that portray horror, humor, biting criticism, or attitudes about anything from love to politics. Figures 5.31 and 5.32 are the productions of a bright seventh-grade boy who had an interest in political cartooning. Each week he made a large cartoon that was placed under the clock in the art room. His drawings covered a wide variety of topics, and they reveal a new, critical approach to ideas that was not present in previous stages of development. Figure 5.31, drawn in March of 1952, shows Senator Robert A. Taft speaking from a platform. The crowd in front of him is beginning to drift away toward the likenesses of General MacArthur and General Eisenhower. Such perceptive comments on the political scene would not appear in the figurative stage.

Figure 5.32 is a sports cartoon. It shows the Cleveland Indians giving the New York Yankees a difficult time on the way to the American League pennant. It reveals an awareness of what is going on outside the local community and shows that the youngster knows how to suggest a battle for the pennant without drawing a picture of people playing baseball. His ability to manage abstract concepts is clearly evident. In many of his other cartoons he demonstrated an understanding of greed, aloofness, contagious diseases, graft, peace, political alliances, and many other complex ideas. Such understandings begin to appear during this phase of growth.

Drawings from the previous stage of development were highly conceptual. They dealt with concrete objects and events

Fig. 5.31
A watercolor painting by
a boy in seventh grade. During the
stage of artistic decision, young people
begin to deal with abstract concepts
in their art and try to
influence the observer.

Fig. 5.32
In this watercolor painting
a boy in seventh grade tried to show
that the Cleveland Indians were
fighting the New York Yankees for
the American League pennant.
A younger child normally would
not try to depict such
a difficult idea.

and were produced from memory most of the time. Very little abstract thought was evident. Notions of love, hate, intolerance, justice, and ideas about the national economy were rarely, if ever, seen. If they were, they were almost always subordinate to the matter-of-fact description of things. In this stage of development, however, the drawings are no less conceptual, but they begin to deal with ideas of an abstract nature instead of mere descriptive facts. An understanding of emotion is also evident in their drawings, and the children employ a variety of means for objectifying it. Exaggeration of sizes is no longer the only method at their disposal, for they begin to use colors, lines, textures, and shading very expressively. In Figures 5.33 and 5.34 we see two paintings that depict girls who have been through a difficult and unhappy day. The color is dreary and unpleasant; the line and color that provide the facial expressions are depressing, and the texture gives a sense of the day's confusion. These are not accidents, for the students who produced the paintings were conscious of what they were doing. They made a determined effort to match the proper symbolic elements with their concepts of a given event, and they tried to produce a structural arrangement that would be pleasing. To do so, they had to make artistic decisions. It is for that reason that we have called this period the *stage of artistic decision.*

During the previous stages of development the child worked in a much more intuitive manner as he came to grips with the discursive and nondiscursive elements of experience in his drawings. But now the child is conscious, even self-conscious, about what he does. He purposely tries to create an object that will cause the observer to understand the more complex and more abstract concepts that he is presenting. Consequently, he has to pay more attention to the nuances of shape, color, texture, line, and direction. A more sophisticated handling of materials and a greater degree of perceptual or aesthetic sensitivity is required.

Figures 5.35 and 5.36 give an indication of how far the child has progressed in that direction. Both pictures reveal a loose, free-flowing quality that seems to be in keeping with the subject matter and content of the work. Pictures are no longer painted

5.35

Fig. 5.33
A girl after a hard and
tiring day. A chalk drawing by a
student in junior high school.

Fig. 5.34
This chalk drawing by a
junior high school student depicts a
girl who is tired and unhappy.

Fig. 5.35
In seventh grade, young
people occasionally depart from
naturalism to create special effects.
Notice the looseness of this drawing
and the willingness to merely suggest
rather than delineate objects.

Fig. 5.36
This drawing presents a
view from an airplane window. It was
produced by a student in seventh grade.

5.36

THE DEVELOPMENT OF THE CHILD
AS ARTIST AND CONNOISSEUR

with flat areas of color only, but shading is widely used. Color areas are broken up, and forms are suggested with a few appropriate strokes. Although some children may simplify their symbols until they look highly abstract, other youngsters may continue with more detail and develop a very naturalistic style. As a result, various styles or techniques can be observed that one might associate with impressionism, expressionism, surrealism, classical realism, constructivism, or some other well-known manner of expression. Considering the extent to which children enjoy shocking their teachers with pictures that suggest worldliness, it might be said that even dadaism can be found in the junior high school.

The fact that the beginnings of different artistic styles can be observed does not mean that the work of junior high school children is typically free and uninhibited. On the contrary, the very consciousness of self and of others that accompanies the introduction of abstract ideas is sometimes the thing that causes children to rely on crutches of one kind or another. It is not unusual, for example, to see pictures for which youngsters have insisted upon using rulers, compasses, or drawings from magazines. These children are the ones who have lost or are losing confidence in their own ability to express themselves with visual symbols. They are becoming aware of the finished product as a work of art or as a very revealing human statement. At this point they make a decision about continuing with visual symbolization. If they can accept what they find out about themselves in their work and if they see any value in continuing, they will do so. But if they detect weaknesses in themselves and if no value is apparent, they probably will produce drawings only for the sake of satisfying requirements. The fact that youngsters develop at different rates and that some of them abandon visual symbolization during these last two stages of development means that a wide gap often exists between stages of graphic development in the junior high school. Extremely broad differences in development need not exist, of course, if art education from the kindergarten onward is adequate. A good art program would help to keep many students from giving up their visual symbolization, and it also would help the slow students to build their concepts of space more rapidly.

The connoisseur in the stage of artistic decision. If a young person reaches the stage of artistic decision in his own creative work, it means that he is more aware of art as a projection of his own concepts and emotions, and he tries consciously to affect others in a particular way by manipulating the elements of art like a serious artist. When that happens, it usually indicates that the individual is capable of responding with equal sensitivity to the work of others. He is able to enjoy a more complete or more profound aesthetic experience. Hence, it is not unusual to find junior high school students who have a sincere interest in visual art. They are likely to give responses of the character and objective types much more frequently than they did before, and they are able to carry on an attentive conversation about art for a considerable length of time. They are much more likely than younger children to see the pleasantness, the sadness, the freshness, or the calmness in works of art. Unlike their younger brothers and sisters, they can see sadness in something, even if tears and frowns are not depicted.

They tend to favor naturalistic art, but they are capable of appreciating other forms. In fact, many youngsters begin to develop new preferences and new styles of their own. Some of them begin to feel the aura of culture that seems to surround the arts and would like to be in it. They would like to know what is going on in the world that is avant-garde, and they feel that art will provide some of that information. Consequently, they give it careful attention during their more serious moments.

Beyond the age of eleven, young people also are concerned about philosophical matters. They think more and more about the relative values of things and begin to wonder about the purpose of their own lives. Consequently, they show an interest in the value of art to the individual and to society, and their comments are apt to be very sharp and perceptive.

The youngsters who do not reach the stage of artistic decision in their creative work are apt to be slower in developing

Pl. 34
Still life with model, in gouache,
by a girl in sixth grade. From the
stage of artistic decision.

an appreciation for visual art, probably because they have already decided that they are incapable or that art is not very important. Changing such an attitude often takes a considerable length of time.

THE ART AND NONART OF CHILDREN

At the beginning of this chapter, we said that children will produce visual symbols whether they are trained in art or not. In general, they will follow the course of development that we have described. As they do so, they may or may not produce art. If they do not, they will still receive a certain amount of value from the making of visual symbols; but if they do produce art, the value that they receive will be significantly greater. They will tend to become more human because the art process causes them to concentrate upon their more humanistic qualities and forces them to use those qualities. They will come closer to the full realization of the self and closer to the good life because art causes them to learn about themselves and their environment, and it helps them to become more eloquent. If that is so, it is important for the teacher to know if his students are actually producing art. How can he tell?

First he must try to determine the child's intent; he must decide if the object that was created was primarily for aesthetic experience. If it was not made chiefly for attentive perception, it is not art. Hence we may say that the scribbles made by young children are not forms of art because the children create them primarily for the satisfaction they get from muscular activity and eye-hand coordination. When youngsters reach the stage of artistic decision, however, they may produce visual symbols that are not unlike the scribbles of a four-year-old. Such symbols could be works of art because youngsters who are beyond the scribbling stage do not ordinarily make things for the sake of enjoying muscular sensations. They usually make their visual symbols for the purpose of having them studied perceptually. Although most visual creations produced after the scribbling stage are intended for aesthetic experience, there are a few exceptions. If a child creates a model store in the classroom, he does it to make his role as a grocer or as a customer more plausible. He does not make the store chiefly for attentive perception. By the same token he does not always make a model village in a sandbox for the purpose of contemplating its appearance. He often makes it so that he can play in it with automobiles and toy men.

Sometimes a child will produce a visual configuration primarily to satisfy the demands of the teacher. In that case he might do it hastily and unattentively, and he might behave as if he does not care whether it is seen or not. The result is usually an example of nonart simply because the child's intent was not to produce an object for aesthetic experience.

A second thing for the teacher to determine is whether the structural organization of the object is pleasing to the senses. If it is irritating or uncomfortable, the work is not art. Figure 5.37, for example, is a drawing of a horse by a youngster in the first grade. The horse is the only figure in the picture, and it has been placed so far to the left that the picture as a whole does not balance. Furthermore, the relationship of the horse to the vacant space around it is such that the drawing looks unfinished. These are disturbing characteristics, and they place the drawing in the category of nonart.

If the child produces a visual symbol that looks dirty or messy to the point of being disagreeable or repulsive, we also may say that it is nonart. Such work often appears when children use a medium for the first time because they lack the practice that is necessary for proper control.

If the teacher looks at a visual configuration and finds it so disturbing that he is impelled to turn it sideways or upside down, he may also consider it to be nonart. He may come to the same conclusion if the arrangement of the object is such that he cannot tolerate it without changing it.

There are other structural characteristics that might cause a teacher to be irritated by a visual symbol and to classify it as nonart, but the making of such a judgment is frequently very

Fig. 5.37
This is an example of
nonart produced by a child in first
grade. The composition is irritating
because it is unfinished
and unbalanced.

difficult. It is difficult because there is a very fine line between art of low quality and nonart. Both forms could conceivably irritate the observer. When faced with such forms, however, it really does not make much difference if the teacher calls them art or nonart. The need for improvement is clear, and the teacher must do something to bring it about.

SUMMARY

The purpose of this chapter is to show how children develop as artists and connoisseurs. We have described the development by stages and substages because the appearance of a child's work does change significantly through the years, and the change can be associated in a general way with age and grade level. The ages that have been attached to each of the stages and substages are merely estimates and are not supposed to indicate that development is mechanical or subject to abrupt changes.

Pl. 35
A political cartoon,
in watercolor, by a boy in seventh grade.
From the stage of artistic decision.

In fact, the ages for the different stages have been made to overlap so that a smooth, continuous development would be implied.

The description of the child's graphic work is more extensive than the account of his sculptural work and his appreciative responses simply because we know more about his graphic development. Perhaps future research will provide us with information to fill the gaps. At any rate, the descriptive material offered in this chapter should give the teacher a notion of what to expect at any level in the elementary school. It should help him to realize that visual symbols from more than one stage of development are apt to be found in any class; it should also help him to see that much of the growth will occur without instruction. Consequently, he will need to become quite familiar with the work of individual children if he expects to find any evidence of his own influence.

The effect that the teacher can have upon his students is truly remarkable. He can help the children to present concepts and emotions of greater and greater complexity; he can help them to produce better or more pleasing compositions; and he can assist them in becoming more technically proficient. He can also do a lot to help youngsters appreciate art and its place in human history. In fact, the things that a teacher can do to develop connoisseurs have been grossly neglected.

If the instructor is to assist his students in their artistic development, however, he must be familiar with the explanations for that development. Chapter 6 is devoted to those explanations.

QUESTIONS FOR DISCUSSION

1. Rudolph Arnheim offers an account of the child's development in drawing that is different from the one offered in this text. How does growth proceed according to Arnheim?
2. By reading the work of previous writers on the subject of child art, a person develops a great respect for them. What did James Sully, for example, have to say about children's drawings? Or what did Earl Barnes, Louise Maitland, and Betty Lark-Horovitz have to say?

3. See if you can find some drawings or paintings by a chimpanzee. Compare them with the works of children. How are they similar? How are they different? How do you explain it?

4. Occasionally, a junior high school child will produce drawings that are in the mid-figurative substage. If you can find such a child, describe his other behavior.

5. Compare some ancient Egyptian paintings with the work of youngsters in the mid-figurative substage. How are they similar? How are they different? How do you explain it?

6. Show a painting or a reproduction to a few children from each grade in the public school. Ask them (individually and in private) what they see in the painting, and record their responses. How do the results compare from grade to grade?

7. Collect some drawings and paintings from each of the grades in the public school. Do they seem to show a development similar to the one described in this chapter? If there are exceptions, what could account for them?

8. Other writers call the stages of development by different names. What are some of those names?

SUGGESTIONS FOR FURTHER READING

Arnheim, Rudolph: *Art and Visual Perception*, University of California Press, Berkeley, 1954.
As far as child art is concerned, the chapter entitled "Growth" is especially important. It tends to present the gestalt view of development.

Bland, Jane: *Art of the Young Child*, Museum of Modern Art, New York, 1957.
A magnificent little book about the art of preschool children. Written by an experienced and sensitive teacher. It covers three-dimensional as well as two-dimensional work.

Burt, Sir Cyril: *Mental and Scholastic Tests*, P. S. King and Son, Ltd., London, 1921, pp. 317–327.
By reading this portion of Burt's book, it is possible to see how far we had progressed in our knowledge of child art by 1921.

Eng, Helga: *The Psychology of Children's Drawings*, Routledge and Kegan Paul, Ltd., London, 1931.
As far as this writer knows, this is the only extensive account of the drawing of a single child over a period of several years. A highly significant book.

Gesell, Arnold, and Frances L. Ilg: *The Child from Five to Ten*, Harper and Brothers, New York, 1946.
A milestone in the study of child development. It gives a fine description of the child's growth in visual symbolization. It is written by child development experts, not by artists.

Griffiths, Ruth: *A Study of Imagination in Early Childhood*, Routledge and Kegan Paul, Ltd., London, 1935.
An old but wonderful book. It gives the reader the notion that we have learned very little since 1935 about development in art.

Kellogg, Rhoda: *What Children Scribble and Why*, San Francisco, 1955. (Available from 570 Union St., San Francisco, California).
This is probably the most comprehensive book in existence on the subject of scribbling.

Lark-Horovitz, Betty, Hilda Lewis, and Marc Luca: *Understanding Children's Art for Better Teaching*, Charles E. Merrill Books, Inc., Columbus, Ohio, 1967.
A comprehensive book on child development in art.

Lowenfeld, Viktor: *Creative and Mental Growth*, The Macmillan Company, New York, 1947.
This book presents one of the most recent and most popular accounts of artistic development in children.

Chapter 6
EXPLANATIONS FOR ARTISTIC GROWTH IN CHILDREN

From the foregoing description of visual symbolic development it is clear that several significant changes take place between the first uncontrolled productions of the young child and the highly sophisticated work of the young adult. But why do those changes occur? Why do children draw as they do? Is it simply because of a growing ability to coordinate the hand and the eye, or is it more than that? These are questions that have concerned observers of child behavior since the days of Ebenezer Cooke. What are the answers?

Since 1885 a number of explanations have been given for the nature of visual symbolic development. To summarize them, it can be said that children draw as they do because of (1) their physical condition; (2) their perceptual development and the medium that they use to make symbols; (3) their conceptual development; (4) their emotional condition; (5) their environment.[1]

[1] Clearly, the last explanation in the list has to do with the environmental determinants of the artistic personality, while the other explanations have to do with the organismic determinants (see Chapter 4).

Writers who offer one explanation frequently do not agree with persons who advocate another. But this author's view is that there is an element of truth in each of the explanations. To justify that view, we shall discuss the explanations one at a time.

THE EFFECT OF PHYSICAL CONDITION

As we compare the work of children in the nursery school or kindergarten with the work of youngsters in the junior high school, we see that the latter produce drawings and paintings that are much more detailed and more subtly organized than the productions of the younger children. Obviously, part of the difference is caused by physical growth or an increase in motor control. The four-year-old who has trouble buttoning his coat and tying his shoes is clearly incapable of building a model airplane or making a complex drawing that requires fine coordination. He makes curved lines, circles, ovals, and other simple figures partly because they can be made without complete control of the small muscles. Lauretta Bender,[2] Rudolph Arnheim,[3] and others attribute the circular and longitudinal direction of such early marks to the leverlike construction of the arm, hand, and fingers.

If physical development or motor control does affect the making of visual symbols, it would seem that the symbols should become more complex or more highly differentiated as the child grows older, and that is exactly what happens. Hence it appears that physical development is at least partially responsible for the appearance and the development of child art.

Although experts on child development agree that motor control does have an effect upon visual symbolization, they carefully point out that it does not offer a full explanation for the appearance of visual symbols. For example, in 1926, Florence

[2] Lauretta Bender, "Gestalt Principles in the Sidewalk Drawings and Games of Children," *Journal of Genetic Psychology*, vol. 41, pp. 192–210, 1932.
[3] Rudolph Arnheim, *Art and Visual Perception*, University of California Press, Berkeley, 1954, pp. 136–137.

Goodenough said that the number of fingers in the drawing of a hand could hardly be explained by technical difficulty because it is just as easy to draw five fingers as it is to draw four or six.[4] In 1956, Jean Piaget, the Swiss psychologist, echoed the same idea when he said that the absence of a high degree of motor control does not explain why a child should draw a human face with the mouth placed above the nose.[5] Placing the features in their natural positions would require no more control than placing them in unnatural positions. Consequently, factors in addition to motor control must influence symbolization.

To make the point even stronger, we might take a cue from Arnheim and ask a child in the substage of emerging figurativism to copy a realistic drawing of a human ear. He is likely to make two concentric circles or something similar, and we might logically ascribe this action to a lack of sufficient motor control. Although that may be a partial explanation, Arnheim has effectively pointed out that other factors must be involved.[6] To prove it, Arnheim suggests that an adult place a pencil in his mouth or between his toes and attempt to copy the same realistic ear. By holding the pencil in such a way the adult tends to reduce his control of the drawing instrument approximately to the child's level. Nevertheless, the adult drawing is not likely to consist in two concentric circles. According to Arnheim, it will probably come closer to resembling the pictured ear. Motor skills are therefore not completely responsible for the shapes of visual symbols. Other influences will be discussed in a moment. But, first, are there any aspects of physical condition other than motor control that might account for the character of visual symbols?

The answer is yes. Youngsters with partial sight, for example, usually produce drawings and paintings that are not as highly detailed as the creations by children with normal sight.[7] Proba-

[4] Florence Goodenough, *Measurement of Intelligence by Drawings*, World Book Company, New York, 1926, pp. 76–77.
[5] Jean Piaget and Barbel Inhelder, *The Child's Conception of Space*, Routledge and Kegan Paul, Ltd., London, 1956, p. 47.
[6] Arnheim, *op. cit.*, p. 127.
[7] For evidence of this, see Viktor Lowenfeld, *The Nature of Creative Activity*, Routledge and Kegan Paul, Ltd., London, 1939.

bly, the lack of adequate vision makes it difficult to develop the differentiated visual concept that is necessary for a detailed drawing, and the same visual deficiency makes it hard to draw and paint details even if a person can imagine them in his mind. This means that youngsters with partial sight usually produce visual symbols that are not as advanced developmentally as drawings by children with normal sight.

Brain damage of certain kinds also has been shown to affect drawing. Lauretta Bender, among others, has indicated that youngsters with brain damage have difficulty in reproducing certain linear shapes and patterns, and this difficulty sometimes reveals itself in drawings that are severely distorted.[8] At this point, we do not know much more about the effects of brain damage on visual symbolization.[9] But we do know that such a defect might reduce a youngster's motor control or might affect his ability to perceive, remember, imagine, conceive, judge, or reason. And any lessening of those abilities might result in a drawing or a three-dimensional configuration that is simpler or more distorted than the work by youngsters who do not suffer from brain damage.

Another aspect of the physical condition that influences the character of visual symbols is handedness. Several persons, such as Jensen,[10] have studied the orientation of pictorial figures on the drawing surface, and the results show that most youngsters draw figures that are oriented toward the left. As children grow older, the number of them that face their configurations toward the left tends to decline, but the majority still face their figures in that direction. This strongly suggests but does not prove that handedness has an influence on drawing. It is suggestive simply because most youngsters are right-handed.

Still another aspect of physical condition that is related to artistic development is sex. After a careful examination of research,

[8] Lauretta Bender, *Child Psychiatric Techniques*, Charles C. Thomas, Publisher, Springfield, Illinois, 1952, pp. 78–89.

[9] For a summary of some of the research, see I. P. Howard and W. B. Templeton, *Human Spatial Orientation*, John Wiley and Sons, Inc., London, 1966, pp. 332–333.

[10] B. T. Jensen, "Left-right Orientation in Profile Drawing," *American Journal of Psychology*, vol. 65, pp. 80–83, 1952.

especially the results from the Harris revision of the Good-enough Draw-a-Man Test, Harris concludes that girls in Western cultures are better at drawing the human figure than are boys.[11] To do "better" on the Goodenough test and on the Harris revision of that test is to make a figure drawing that is more highly differentiated and more naturalistically constructed. As you might expect, boys do better in certain respects and girls do better in others. But according to Harris, girls are about one-half to one full year ahead of boys on the overall task of drawing the human figure. Whether the difference is caused by physical condition, psychological disposition, or environment is not clear, but the fact is that there is a positive correlation between sex and success on the Goodenough test.

A summing-up

From the foregoing accounts, it is obvious that physical condition does have an influence upon artistic development, but it is equally apparent that other influential factors exist. Perceptual development, for example, has been identified as one of those factors. Some persons may consider perceptual development to be a special dimension of the physical condition, but it seems quite clear that perception is also a psychological phenomenon. Consequently, it seems reasonable to discuss it separately, and it is to that factor we now turn.

THE EFFECT OF PERCEPTUAL DEVELOPMENT AND THE MEDIUM OF EXPRESSION

Probably more study has been devoted to perception than to any other topic in the field of psychology. It has received so much attention because it is widely recognized as a factor that influences all kinds of behavior, including the creation of art. As

[11] Dale Harris, *Children's Drawings as Measures of Intellectual Maturity*, Harcourt, Brace and World, Inc., New York, 1963, p. 226.

a result of all the research, many theories have developed which attempt to explain perception. Some of them seem to have more relevance than others to art and art education. In this author's opinion, gestalt theory, cell-assembly theory, Piaget theory, sensoritonic theory, set theory, directive-state theory, and hypothesis theory are especially pertinent. Consequently, each of these explanations of perception will be discussed in the paragraphs that follow.

Gestalt theory

According to the gestalt point of view as it is so thoroughly developed in the writings of Rudolph Arnheim, children draw as they do because they draw what they see or perceive.[12] Arnheim does not agree with the so-called "intellectualist theory" that children draw what they know because it suggests to him that abstract thinking governs the symbols that youngsters produce. He maintains that the knowledge required to make visual symbols is provided largely by the perceptual image and not by abstract thought. In fact, he says, "nothing but our particular one-sided tradition suggests that concepts are formed only by the intellect."[13] For that reason he speaks quite frequently of *perceptual concepts.* Apparently he believes that percepts are visual concepts and that drawing is based upon those percepts.

The gestalt view is that the earliest of those percepts are not filled with detail, but, instead, are highly generalized, and consist in the overall structural features of things. In other words, a young child's first percepts do not contain all the details of a tree, but they reveal the verticality of the trunk and the general roundness of the combined limbs and leaves. As the child matures, his perceptual concepts become differentiated or more highly detailed. And if his drawings are based upon those percepts, they should undergo the same change, which is exactly what happens. The child's symbolic representations begin as gen-

200

ART, ARTISTS,
AND CONNOISSEURS

[12] Arnheim, *op. cit.*, p. 131.
[13] *Ibid.*, p. 134.

eralities and gradually become more complex as time goes by. Hence the facts of artistic development seem to support the gestalt notion that youngsters draw what they see.

But careful observation of graphic work at any stage of development indicates that people actually draw *less* than what they see. Arnheim recognizes the fact and offers an explanation. He contends that representation is not the replication of an object (for that would involve its reproduction in the same medium), but that it is the production of a structural equivalent in another medium. The *medium* (and the youngster's ability to manipulate it) restricts the child to the making of forms that are less complicated than the perceptual image. That is, the medium in which an image is reproduced may require simplification of the percept to a very basic equivalent structure simply to make the image clear. Thus, a child might make a fly much larger and much simpler than the one he sees because his crayon will not allow him to make smaller or more intricate details. If he were to make a crayon drawing of a small fly and include the details, he might lose the essential structure of the fly and, consequently, its meaning.

In response to Arnheim's valuable comment about the influence of the medium on the size and the simplicity of child art, we might add that it also affects the color, texture, technical quality, and developmental level of the work. If red and blue are the only colors available, the child is not apt to paint a green tree. If the paste is lumpy and dry, the technical quality of a collage is likely to suffer. And if the child is given new and unfamiliar art materials, the developmental level of the product is apt to drop for a while until the youngster gains experience with the medium. Perhaps there are other effects that the medium might have, but the reason for mentioning it here is to show that it does have an important influence on child art.

Arnheim also claims that the major difference between an artist and a nonartist is that the former is able to develop *representational concepts* or concepts of the form that a perceived object must take if it is to be represented by the characteristics of another medium.[14] In other words, the artist is a person who can conceive the shape that a three-dimensional apple must assume if it is to be represented with paint on a two-dimensional surface. But such a view indicates that Arnheim is somewhat inconsistent. He rejects the notion that children draw what they know; yet he contends that artists make use of representational concepts.

Apparently, Arnheim feels that children can be artists, for he mentions their ability to represent the three-dimensional roundness of a human head by constructing a two-dimensional circle. But he is careful to point out that the *earliest* circles that youngsters make do not represent roundness. Their meaning is explained by the gestalt theory that there is a perceptual preference for the simplicity of round shape, plus the fact that body structure lends itself most readily to circular movements. Having made a few of those rudimentary circles, the child recognizes the quality of "thingness" in them, and he repeats them again and again with the great satisfaction that comes from making "something." Consequently, the early circles do not stand for roundness, but represent the quality of "thingness."

Gradually the child realizes that he can use his circular shapes to represent objects of all kinds. In such representations he follows a procedure that Arnheim calls "the law of differentiation."[15] This means that a perceived object is rendered in the simplest possible way until the perceptual image indicates differences in size, shape, and direction that require a more complex symbol. Thus the child makes his first human being in the simplest possible way that the structure of the object and his perception of it will allow. This means that he adds vertical and horizontal appendages to the original circle. The legs are added as simple circles or lines placed in a vertical position, and the arms are similarly drawn in a horizontal position. The parts of the total configuration are therefore perpendicular to one another and symmetrical, as we see in Figure 6.1a. The total image takes the form of a good gestalt because it is the simplest and clearest

[14] *Ibid.*, p. 133.
[15] *Ibid.*, p. 140.

two-dimensional shape that one can invent as the structural equivalent of a three-dimensional man.

It is interesting to note that Lowenfeld describes the man in Figure 6.1a as a head with two legs and two arms, but Arnheim disagrees.[16][17] The latter feels that the circle represents the head and body as a whole. Lowenfeld suggests that the child drew a head with legs and arms because those particular body parts seemed most important at the time the child was drawing. Arnheim, on the other hand, believes that the youngster's symbol is the result of rudimentary perception, the limitation of the medium, and the child's ability to manipulate the medium. Although the arguments are different, both are feasible and lead their authors to the same conclusions. They indicate that the child should not be criticized for the apparent omission of a body.

In Arnheim's view the child continues to use circular shapes and vertical and horizontal lines in a perpendicular relationship to one another until he becomes perceptually aware of the frequent obliqueness of arms and legs in walking and running. When that occurs, the perpendicular relationships in his earlier drawings do not please him, and he begins to draw arms and legs in an oblique direction (Figure 6.1c). Finally, the child produces a fusion of the parts of an object in a contour drawing that gives a feeling of wholeness and continuity to the object (Figure 6.1d).

From Arnheim's account it is difficult to tell when the circle stops representing "thingness" and starts to mean roundness. Presumably, this would occur as the child begins to include a variety of shapes and directions in his work, for the presence of a square in his drawing would indicate that he perceives a difference between squareness and roundness. It would show that perceptual concepts had grown beyond the stage of "thingness."

Finally, it is important to point out that chimpanzees[18] and children seem to have a natural tendency to organize their visual

Fig. 6.1 (a, b, c, d)
These are adult copies of children's drawings. They illustrate phases of child development in drawing.

---

[16] Viktor Lowenfeld, *Creative and Mental Growth*, 3d ed., The Macmillan Company, New York, 1957, pp. 108–109.
[17] Arnheim, *op. cit.*, pp. 157–158.
[18] Desmond Morris, *The Biology of Art*, Alfred A. Knopf, Inc., New York, 1962.

creations in a simple but pleasurable way. The explanation for that tendency might be found in the writings of gestalt psychologists, such as Arnheim, who indicate that there is an organizing action in perception itself. The idea is that there are cortical forces within the neurophysical structure that cause us to seek balance, simplicity, closure, and clarity in our perception. If that is true, it seems reasonable that we should make symbols that satisfy our inherent perceptual desires. And if certain youngsters, especially older ones, do not produce pleasurable configurations easily, it is probably because they no longer act like little children or monkeys. In other words, they are probably so deeply concerned with the presentation of concepts and emotions that they no longer pay attention to inherent perceptual desires or to the organization of the total visual form.

Although gestalt theory does help to explain the developing nature of child art, it has an important weakness. It fails to explain how perceptual growth occurs. It indicates that an adult's percept is more highly differentiated than a child's percept, but it does not tell us how the details are acquired. Two theories of perception that do explain growth, however, are those of Donald O. Hebb and Jean Piaget.

Cell-assembly theory

The theory offered by Hebb is called the cell-assembly theory.[19] He agrees with the gestalt notion that early percepts (or primitively unified figures against a background) are the result of an innate neuropsychological mechanism. But, unlike gestalt theorists, Hebb contends that the identification of those figures as triangles, squares, circles, or anything else is *gradually learned*. He comes to that conclusion on the basis of his own work and after studying the pertinent research, especially the work of Senden.[20]

Senden compiled information about congenitally blind individuals who had been given sight by a surgical operation for

[19] Donald O. Hebb, *The Organization of Behavior*, John Wiley and Sons, Inc., New York, 1949.
[20] M. Von Senden, *Space and Sight*, The Free Press, Glencoe, Illinois, 1960.

cataracts. Such persons clearly experienced the same perceptual phenomena that occur in babies at the initial occurrence of human vision, but they were in the unique position of being able to talk and to describe what they saw. In the beginning they were able to perceive primitive unity or figure-ground separation, but they could not perceive identity. In other words, they could see the unity or the "thingness" in forms presented to them, but they could not identify the forms or describe them as triangles, squares, spheres, or cubes. The ability to identify or classify forms took a long time to develop. In fact, the shortest time it took to approximate normal perception was a month, and the best patients had to go through a painstaking search for corners if they were to distinguish a triangle from a circle. Sometimes they could manage to identify forms after repeated experiences with them, but the patients frequently had a hard time remembering the differences between the forms. In some instances, the patients who had learned to identify shapes could no longer recognize them if the form or its setting was slightly changed. An egg, a potato, and a sugar cube, for example, were seen repeatedly until they could be named, but those same objects could not be recognized under colored light. Color actually seems to be the dominating influence in identifying forms during the earliest stage of perceptual development. After that, an individual appears to pay separate attention to each part of a figure, such as the corners, in his endeavor to recognize form; and, finally, he is able to perceive the whole as a whole.

According to Hebb, it is the visual exploration of a figure *through many separate fixations on its parts* that causes perceptual learning to take place. Each fixation activates a certain number of nerve cells in the cortex forming a simple percept or a simple cell assembly. As the eye moves from one fixation point to another, several cell assembly systems develop, and with time they facilitate each other. In other words, they tend to develop contacts with each other through electrochemical action, and the result is a more complex percept or a compound of cell assemblies. When the compound of simple percepts is formed, the individual has reached the point at which he can identify the object of his attention. But, as Senden's research indicates, the individual may not be able to identify the object if it is presented in a different setting. To be able to do so, the individual would have to engage in more perceptual activity. And by viewing the object in different settings or from different angles a perceptual pattern eventually develops that has constancy; or to put it differently, the perceptual exploration of an object from a variety of viewpoints finally reaches the stage where it produces the same neural activity or pattern no matter where the observer happens to be when he views the object. When this occurs, it seems fitting to speak of the constant mental pattern as a *concept* because it is not directly controlled by the individual's sensory experience of the moment.

The formation of a conceptual image or the development of a state of perceptual constancy would seem to require considerable time because it necessitates a large amount of perceptual activity from a variety of vantage points. If that is so, we have another explanation (in addition to a lack of motor control) for the child's inability to draw recognizable objects before the age of three or four. He is able to perceive and identify objects, but he has not engaged in enough perceptual activity to have acquired perceptual constancies or visual concepts. And without a stable notion of an object he can not draw the object.

Furthermore, it would seem from what has been said that the first perceptual constancies or visual concepts are rudimentary in nature and that further perceptual activity gradually brings about the development of a more highly differentiated compound of cell assemblies or a more complex mental image. This, in turn, should permit a gradual increase in the naturalistic quality of children's drawings; and, of course, a slow but steady increase in naturalism does occur. The earliest drawings are very rudimentary, but they gradually become more complex.

According to Hebb, the early formation of interfacilitated cell assemblies (perceptual constancies or visual concepts), or early learning, should be much slower and more difficult than later learning. The reason for saying so is that later perception should benefit from the vast network of earlier cell assemblies.

Electrochemical contacts among cell assemblies should occur in much larger numbers and activate a larger neural network. If that actually does occur, adult perception should result in either immediate or rapid recognition of objects, and it should lead to speedy conceptualization. The fact that recognition and conceptualization do occur more rapidly with age is an indication that Hebb may be correct.

As soon as perceptual constancies or visual concepts develop, however, the individual may think that he perceives something that he actually does not see. According to Hebb, it is possible for this to occur because a limited view of an object can activate a network of cell assemblies developed previously from a variety of vantage points. Hence the image that comes to mind is one that is more highly differentiated than the view immediately available to perception. This tends to explain why the drawings of children often contain elements that, at the moment, cannot be perceived. The youngsters simply draw what they know as well as what they see.

Having reached this point, it is interesting to note that Hebb speaks of child art as being affected by *conceptual* activity, and Arnheim reluctantly agrees after insisting that children draw what they see rather than what they know. Hence the work of Hebb and Arnheim leads us to the conclusion that child art is based upon concepts and that it is affected by concept development; but *perceptual* activity or perceptual development affects child art because it determines the nature of the concept and the speed with which the concept grows.

Piaget's theory

Like Senden, Hebb, and others, Jean Piaget found that perception is learned. But he also discovered that there are three major stages in perceptual development and that children pass through those stages during the first two years of their lives.[21] At the

---

[21] Piaget sometimes subdivides the three stages into six substages. See, for example, Piaget and Inhelder, *op. cit.*, pp. 3–43.

very beginning (from birth to four or five months), the child does not coordinate vision and grasping, and he does not perceive the permanence of solid objects nor the constancy of shape and size. In other words, he does not perceive a bottle as the same bottle when it is turned around, and he fails to perceive a nearby object as being the same size when it is far away. The spatial relationships that he does detect, however, are *topological* in nature. This means that he can see the proximity, separation, and serial order of objects, and it also means that he can see things enclosed by other things, plus the continuity of a line or surface. It is interesting to note that topoligical spatial relationships were also the first visual elements to be perceived by Senden's congenitally blind patients after the removal of their cataracts.

During the second stage of perceptual development (from five months to a year) the child learns to coordinate vision with grasping, and his movements are controlled by vision. As a result, he can explore objects much more systematically. He can finger them, pass tham from hand to hand, and move his eyes around them. This increase in visual and tactile exploration helps him to learn the permanence of solid objects as well as the constancy of shape and size, and it helps him to see *Euclidean* and *projective* spatial relationships. To see Euclidean relationships is to see straight lines, angles, circles, and other geometric figures as well as proportions. And to see projective relationships is to see things in perspective.

The third stage of perceptual development lasts from about the age of one to the age of two. During that time the child engages in further systematic sensory exploration. But in addition to learning the shapes and dimensions of single objects, he begins to learn the relationships among those objects. He internalizes and coordinates his sensory impressions and actions, and the result (near the end of the third stage of perceptual development) is a mental or conceptual image.

At no time up to the age of two or thereabouts does the child draw, and Piaget attributes that deficiency to the lack of a mental image or a visual concept. Unlike Arnheim, Piaget does not believe that children draw what they see, because they do not draw Euclidean or projective spatial relationships until they are seven to nine years old; yet they are able to perceive those relationships by the time they are two years old.

For the gestalt psychologists, perceptual movement occurs in response to the percept, but it does not seem to be of vital importance. For Hebb, on the other hand, effective perception is more apt to occur with movement than without it. After all, perceptual movement does bring about more sensory fixations, more cell assemblies, and more opportunity for the formation of perceptual constancies and visual concepts. Piaget's ideas on the matter are much more like those of Hebb, but Piaget tends to place even more importance upon perceptual activity. He believes that even the good gestalt develops as a result of perceptual movement and suggests that the percept and perceptual activity are equally important and interdependent.[22] Perceptual activity contributes to the development of both the percept and the concept of space.

In summary we might say that Piaget gives us a more detailed theory of developmental stages in perception and indicates the vital importance of perceptual movement in the formation of percepts and concepts. He also agrees with the notion that child art is dependent upon the existence of concepts, but, unlike Arnheim, he does not consider the percept to be a concept. Percepts and perceptual activity are fundamentally important to child art, however, because they affect the nature of the concept and the speed with which it develops.

Sensoritonic theory

The theory of perception offered by Werner and Wapner is often referred to as the sensoritonic theory or the organismic theory.[23] They maintain that perception is not determined solely

[22] *Ibid.*, p. 10.
[23] Heinz Werner and Seymor Wapner, "Toward a General Theory of Perception," *Psychological Review*, vol. 59, pp. 325–338, 1952.

by environmental stimulation and by distance receptors such as the eyes and the ears. In fact, there seems to be a substantial body of evidence indicating that visual and auditory percepts are at least partially determined by changes in body posture and muscle tonus.

Apparently, proprioceptive impulses reach the cortex and make contact with sensory impulses from the exteroceptors (eyes, ears, skin, etc.), resulting in a sensoritonic whole. If this is so, it might explain why certain individuals have difficulty drawing a particular experience, or it might indicate why their drawings are highly individualistic. During the experience that is being drawn, they might have been in a sensoritonic state that caused them to perceive the event incompletely or differently from other children.

Werner also indicates that animals, primitives, and children use a *physiognomic* mode of perception.[24] By that he means that a child's perceptual experience with an object is made up of both the factual attributes of the object and the youngsters inner motor-affective needs and impulses. The motor-affective condition of the child tends to impress itself on the outside world and shape it. Hence a child perceives things as being dynamic rather than static. He might see a triangle as being cruel or sharp rather than as a three-cornered object with certain specific dimensions. And as he grows older, he tends to separate himself more fully from the observed object and begins to see it more matter-of-factly.

If the idea of physiognomic perception is correct, it might help to explain why a child draws an automobile with circular scribbles for wheels or a human being with a greatly enlarged head. The child might perceive the wheels as spinning, and he might draw them as circular scribbles to show the spinning. His affective condition might cause him to perceive the head of a particular person as being highly significant. As a result, he might draw the person with a large head.

[24] Heinz Werner, *Comparative Psychology of Mental Development*, International Universities Press, Inc., New York, 1957, pp. 59–103.

Set theory, directive-state theory, and hypothesis theory

Like the sensoritonic theory of perception, set theory is highly organismic in nature.[25] It emphasizes the effect of the individual's total physiological state upon perception. In other words, a "set" is a sensorimotor state of readiness for action, and a "perceptual set" is a readiness to perceive. It involves a continuous supply of messages from the muscles and viscera to the central nervous system and a continuous feedback from the central nervous system to the muscles. This circular activity prepares the organism for perception and sustains it. When outside stimulation occurs, it provides energy that raises the activity of the neuromuscular network to the threshold of perception.

Apparently certain sets may inhibit other sets. Hence they may determine what is to be perceived, the speed of perception, and the vividness of the percept. The theory raises the possibility that a person could inherit a neuromuscular structure or set that would cause him to perceive and draw certain things more easily than other things.

Like the previous theories that have been mentioned, set theory tends to place the responsibility for perception upon structural factors, such as the stimulus, the receptors, the nerves, the cortex, and the muscles. The *directive-state theory or motivation theory*, on the other hand, stresses the importance of behavioral characteristics in determining perception. The advocates of the directive-state theory, such as Bruner and Postman, contend that structural factors determine the extent to which needs, attitudes, values, past experiences, and other such behavioral factors can influence perception.[26] The directive-state theory is mentioned together with the set theory because it is possible to think of needs, attitudes, and values as "behavioral sets." The supporting research, for example, seems to indicate that a given attitude or value can constitute a set, or a kind of readiness to perceive cer-

[25] For a summary of set theory, see Floyd Allport, *Theories of Perception and the Concept of Structure*, John Wiley and Sons, Inc., New York, 1955, pp. 240–241.
[26] Jerome Bruner and L. Postman, "Perception, Cognition, and Behavior," in J. S. Bruner and J. Krech (eds.), *Perception and Personality: A Symposium*, Duke University Press, Durham, North Carolina, 1955.

tain things and to perceive them in a particular way (e.g., a rich and a poor subject perceive the size of a coin differently).

The directive-state theory of perception has made important contributions to our understanding of perception, but it has received a number of significant criticisms. In an effort to eliminate the elements that prompted criticism, Bruner and Postman reformulated the theory.[27] The new view, called the *hypothesis theory*, postulates that perception and other cognitive processes represent hypotheses that are usually unconscious and require "answers" in the form of further experience. The experience either confirms or rejects the hypotheses. If it confirms them or fulfills their expectations, the hypotheses come into consciousness as percepts. If experience does not confirm the hypotheses, the percepts do not develop, and other hypotheses must be tried.

Again, we mention hypothesis theory here because a hypothesis is equivalent to a set. The hypothesis, or set, develops as a result of past experience and depends upon environmental situations as well as motivational and cognitive factors. Hence we may say that the hypothesis theory adds a new element to the list of factors that seem to affect perception; that new element is the environment. The set theory, the directive-state theory, and the hypothesis theory all have one thing in common however: they postulate the existence of a set (or a hypothesis, which is equivalent to a set) or a state of readiness that influences what is perceived, the speed of perception, and the vividness of the percept. If the theories all have an element of truth in them, and it seems that they do, we might conclude that children draw differently and develop at different rates because their perceptual sets are different. They might inherit neurophysiological or structural sets, and they might develop behavioral or motivational sets as a result of certain needs, attitudes, values, and past experiences with the environment. Some of those sets might cause a child to see things that are relevant to art, and some might do just the opposite.

[27] Leo Postman, "Toward a General Theory of Cognition," in J. H. Rohrer and M. S. Sherif (eds.), *Social Psychology at the Crossroads*, Harper and Brothers, New York, 1951.

A summing-up

It seems quite clear from Arnheim's comments that the medium of expression is partially responsible for the character of child art. The effect of perception seems equally clear, but conclusions about it must remain tentative. The reason for the hesitancy is that the study of perception is still going on, and it probably will be quite a while before a full explanation of perceptual phenomena is available. Art educators must therefore rely upon existing theories as they search for the factors that affect child art. We have tried to indicate what some of the most pertinent theories imply. Briefly, they suggest that perception is learned and that it is affected by both the personality of the individual and his neurophysiological structure. Hence we might say that perception is organismic. But that is not altogether correct because personality is partially determined by the environment. As a result, it seems reasonable to say that perception is a function of the interaction between the total organism and its environment.

Child art is affected by perception because it is through perception that the individual gathers the basic mental materials for thinking, feeling, and expressing himself. If that is so, we may conclude that child art is affected by the neurophysiological state of the organism, its personality, and its environment. Parents and teachers are prominent parts of the environment; therefore it is clear that they are apt to influence the character of child art. The pages that follow discuss that influence together with other determinants of artistic development.

THE EFFECT OF CONCEPT DEVELOPMENT

Children may not perceive exactly the same things that adults perceive, but their perception is close enough to the adult view so that both groups can live very efficient lives without being aware of any differences. Consequently, the adult usually wonders why the young child should make drawings that are so unnaturalistic. Why should the child make a man with a circle and four

EXPLANATIONS FOR ARTISTIC
GROWTH IN CHILDREN

straight lines when he can see that a man is much more complex? It is understood, of course, that his motor control is not equal to that of an adult, but he is fully capable of placing body parts in their natural locations. Why does he fail to do it?

The oldest and most persistent explanation of why children draw as they do is that they draw what they know rather than what they see. This is the opposite of the gestalt view, but observers of children have come to this conclusion because they know that *child artists rarely look at the object that is being drawn*. And if that is so, youngsters must rely upon concepts of things that they have retained in memory. Memories are usually less complete than the original sensory experience because human beings do not engage in enough perceptual activity to retain all the details of all their experiences. Following this reasoning, observers conclude that children's pictures are naturally much simpler than perceptual images because their work is commonly based on memory. This means that pictures drawn from retained concepts or memories will be less naturalistic than drawings of objects that are made while looking at those objects. Evidence in support of this point of view can be seen in the work of the seven-year-old girl who drew her father as he sat on a sofa (Figure 5.24). She looked at him intently as she drew, and the result is much more naturalistic than the drawing of children that she made a few days later from memory (Figure 5.22).

Another example in support of this explanation can be found in Figures 6.2 and 6.3. Both pictures were produced by the same five-year-old girl, and both are pictures of her father. The first drawing was made while looking at him occasionally, and the second was made a few hours later from memory. Clearly the first drawing was affected by the child's observation as she worked. It contains eyeglasses and a shirt, both of which are omitted in the second drawing. For most observers the greater simplicity of the second drawing is explained by a deterioration of the concept in memory.

Drawing an object from memory, so that it can be recognized, obviously means that the artist has been exposed to the object in the past. Without previous experience with it or without information about it, he would not possess the mental materials that it takes to make a recognizable object. This explains why many children are unable to draw certain things. They simply do not know anything about them.

By the same token, a brief experience, a small amount of information, or erroneous information might permit the formation of a concept, but the concept probably would bear little or no resemblance to visual reality. According to this view the most naturalistic drawings from memory would come from those youngsters who have had the longest firsthand experience with the object being drawn. This partially accounts for the fact that most junior high school children draw more naturalistically than first-graders. They have had more experience with the things they draw, and the concepts upon which they base their drawings are therefore more highly differentiated.

Fig. 6.2
"My father" was drawn by a five-year-old girl while looking at her father. Notice the number of details as compared with Fig. 6.3.

Fig. 6.3
"My father" by the same five-year-old girl who produced the drawing in Fig. 6.2 But this drawing was made from memory about two hours after the drawing in Fig. 6.2.

EXPLANATIONS FOR ARTISTIC
GROWTH IN CHILDREN

Although the preceding views come from years of working with children and adolescents rather than from experimental research, it is interesting to note that research has produced the same conclusions. Many investigators have contributed to the idea that concept development has a pronounced effect on children's drawings; one of the earliest and most influential of those investigators was Florence Goodenough.

Goodenough believed that perceptual images and eye-hand coordination did not fully explain the nature of children's drawings.[28] She felt that concept development and cognition were strongly responsible for the graphic configurations that youngsters make, and she believed that the richness of the concept is dependent upon the ability to analyze the things we see and to detect their essential elements and the relationships between those elements. She also believed that concepts of objects grow as experiences with those objects become more extensive. It therefore follows that children's drawings based on concepts will become more highly differentiated with age, experience, and more careful visual analysis.

On the basis of that view, Goodenough created the famous Draw-a-Man Test that has enjoyed years of successful use as a nonverbal measure of intelligence in children. As the title implies, the test requires the drawing of a man. It is scored according to the number of elements included in the figure, the way they are drawn, and their relative location. Years of experience with the test has shown that it measures conceptual or intellectual factors much more successfully than it measures aesthetic or personality factors.[29] Thus, we do have some rather substantial emperical evidence to indicate that concept development has an effect upon visual symbolization.

In a magnificent book, *Children's Drawings as Measures of Intellectual Maturity*, Dale Harris presents a revision of the Goodenough test together with a wealth of information about it.[30] Along with that information, he provides the most extensive

[28] Goodenough, *op. cit.*, pp. 73–75.
[29] Harris, *op. cit.*, p. 36.
[30] *Ibid.*, pp. 68–154, 239–329.

review and summary of research and theory pertaining to children's drawings that has ever been made. The work is a classic and belongs in the library of every art educator. The coverage of research is so extensive, however, that the details cannot possibly be reproduced in a textbook of this kind. The reader is therefore urged to consult the Harris book for further information.

As a result of his research and his careful survey of the literature, Harris affirms the Goodenough idea and concludes that concepts and cognition have a more pronounced effect than other influential factors on the nature of children's drawings. Concepts affect the amount of content or the degree of its complexity; they affect the spatial arrangement of details within depicted objects as well as the spatial relationships among those objects. Concepts determine the concrete or abstract nature of the content, and in this author's opinion they also affect the design or compositional quality of child art. We make this suggestion because we believe that rudimentary concepts and a limited number of concepts necessitate the repetition of form, and the repetition of form contributes to compositional unity. As the child grows older, his concepts increase in number and in complexity, and he is likely to make drawings or works of art that reflect the breadth and depth of his conceptual development. Consequently, he is not apt to repeat shapes, colors, and textures unless he makes a conscious effort to do so, and a lack of repetition is likely to reduce the compositional unity of his work.

When we explain the nature of artistic development in children by saying that they draw what they know rather than what they see, it seems to make sense. But it is probably difficult for many persons to accept the idea that youngsters who draw the mouth above the nose do so because they do not know or remember the true relationship of those elements. Nevertheless, that seems to be the case. Perhaps it would help to point out that a youngster who draws in that manner is very young. He would be in the beginning of the early figurative substage, and his drawing of the figure would hardly be recognizable as a representational image. Some of the most convincing evidence that such drawings are related to conceptual development comes from

EXPLANATIONS FOR ARTISTIC
GROWTH IN CHILDREN

the research of Jean Piaget, but comments about his work have been largely neglected in the literature of art education. We would therefore be negligent if we did not cover his views as thoroughly as possible. As we do so, the reader is asked to pay special attention to the relationship between the stages of artistic development (Chapter 5) and the stages of conceptual development.

The development of the child's concept of space

According to Piaget, the infant does not perceive the same thing as the adult.[31] In fact, Piaget has postulated that infants pass through three successive developmental stages in their *perception* of spatial relationships. We reported that development in our account of perception and its effect upon child art. But Piaget also makes a clear distinction between perceptual images and mental representations or mental images. And he shows that the mental images follow the same pattern of development as perception, but they do so *after* perception has occurred. As we describe the development of mental or representational images, however, we shall refer to them as *conceptual images* or *visual concepts*, because they are not directly controlled by the sensory experience of the moment. With that introduction, we shall proceed to the stages of conceptual development as Piaget has described them.

The sensorimotor period (from birth to age two). This period involves a perceptual and motor adjustment to the world, but it does not involve drawing or symbolic manipulation of any kind. It is the period during which the infant learns to perceive the topological, Euclidean, and projective spatial relationships that have already been described. The increase in perceptual movement that occurs during this period is the factor that contributes to perceptual development and to the formation of a mental image

[31] Much of this report of Piaget's research appeared for the first time in "The Research of Jean Piaget and Its Implications for Art Education in the Elementary School," *Studies in Art Education*, vol. 7, no. 2, pp. 33–42, 1966. (Reprinted with the permission of the National Art Education Association.)

or a visual concept. The emergence of a conceptual image signals the beginning of the second period of development.

The concrete operations period (age two to eleven). According to Piaget, the child has been able to perceive topological and Euclidean spatial relationships and coordinated perspective up to this point, but the lack of a mental image that he can retain prevents him from drawing and from thinking intelligently. As he acquires representational or conceptual images during the concrete operations period, he is able to draw concrete objects and events, and he is able to think about them. But it is evident that changes in thinking and drawing occur within this period of development. Consequently, the period is divided into three substages.

The first of the substages within the concrete operations period is called the *preparatory* or *preoperational substage*, and it extends from about the age of two to the age of four. This is the time when the child makes his first unorganized attempts at symbolic representation (scribbles). Piaget asked children between two and seven years of age to copy a few simple circles, triangles, squares, crosses, and other geometric and nongeometric figures. Up to the age of three the youngsters were unable to do anything but scribble. Between three and four, however, they were able to indicate the open or closed quality of the forms being copied, and they could make irregular circles as well as shapes that enclose other shapes. Triangles, squares, crosses, and other Euclidean forms were drawn as circular figures. This means that the earliest aspects of form they could conceive and draw were the topological aspects. We also find this to be true in spontaneous drawing. Children follow their earliest controlled scribbles with loops, whirls, and irregular circular forms, but they do not begin making Euclidean shapes until a little later. They make drawings of men by attaching four lines to an irregular circle, and sometimes they put other circles inside a large one to represent eyes and other facial features. But when the child attempts a complicated human being at this stage, it is clear that his concepts of topological relationships are not *fully* developed, because he may place the mouth over the nose or draw the ears detached from the body. Although his visual concept of proximity, separation, and enclosure is well formed, his mental image of order and continuity is still poor. Thus he cannot retain in his mind the correct sequence of mouth and nose along a vertical axis, nor can he imagine a man wearing a hat to be a continuous unit. Consequently, he draws the hat above the figure but not on it.

The second substage within the concrete operations period is the stage of *intuitive thought*, and it lasts from the age of four to the age of seven. During the previous substage the early drawings of a man display a rudimentary concept of topological spatial relationships because parts of the body are frequently scattered over a sheet of paper. Between the ages of four and seven, however, the topological relationships within the human figure are more clearly understood and are drawn convincingly, whereas the forms that contain Euclidean relationships are just beginning to emerge. This means that the child is beginning to make straight lines, squares, triangles, houses, and tables in his drawings. He makes these simple geometric forms by interrupting the rhythmical movements used in making topological forms. Therefore the earliest triangles might have slightly curved sides and angles of imperfect inclination. Such figures and collections of figures are assembled intuitively, without thoughtful organization. They are like the figures that are produced during the emerging figurative substage of artistic development.

By the age of six or seven, however, the child's perceptual activity and his drawing have been extensive enough so that he develops a more coordinated mental image of the world. This signals his arrival at the next substage of the concrete operations period.

The third substage of the concrete operations period, called the *concrete operations substage*, lasts from about the age of seven to the age of eleven. Perhaps it would help, at this point, to give the meaning of the term "operation." To Piaget, an operation may be defined as a perceptual action, a perceptual movement, or a perceptual decentration, which can return to its starting point and be integrated with other actions also possessing this feature of reversibility (reversibility is the ability to retrace action to its starting point). A concrete operation is therefore the coordination and the internalization of perceptual actions that have been made on a concrete object. It is the perceptual abstraction of parts of objects and their coordination into meaningful wholes. To become fully coordinated and internalized as an accurate concept of a concrete object, the perceptual actions that we perform on that object must be reversible. The reversibility implies one or more stable points of reference, such as a starting point, and a person must have a stable perceptual reference point if he is to achieve a full understanding of the world from his perceptions. If he does not have a reference point, he merely receives a number of unrelated perceptual images.

The concrete operations substage is the period during which the child achieves reversibility in his actions. Thus for the first time he is able to imagine the relationships *between* concrete objects and organize those objects meaningfully in his drawings. Piaget's description of this substage of conceptual development is especially important for public school teachers because the stage is one that covers the years spent in the elementary school. The child's progress in perceptual exploration during this period yields the kind of organizational or spatial synthesis that we see in pictures from the stage of symbolic development, which we have called the mid-figurative substage. He begins to draw objects in a more natural relationship to each other because he is drawing what he conceives rather than what he perceives. The child, according to Piaget, perceives such meaningful relationships during the first two years of life. Consequently, if he were drawing his percepts, his work would have been spatially organized for quite some time. Describing his present work as a kind of *visual* realism would therefore be inaccurate, and it would be more correct to speak of it as *conceptual* realism.

The topological relationships within single objects in the child's drawing are well developed, and the same kind of relationships are maintained throughout the total picture. In other words, the spatial relationships within the symbol for a house are topologically well developed, and that same house is placed on a base line in proximity to other houses and to trees, yet separate from them. The houses may be placed on the base line in an order that is correct and continuous, and some of them may show occupants enclosed in the rooms. Thus the child's total pictorial organization is topological.

Although Euclidean shapes appear as the triangles, rectangles, and squares in houses and other such objects during this period, there are many Euclidean and projective relationships that do not exist in the child's work until the age of eight or nine. The proportions of objects are apt to be different from visual reality, for example, and there is likely to be no perspective or depth in the drawings. Lacking a coordinated perspective, a single drawing may contain a number of irreconcilable views of an object. You might see three sides of a cubical house or its top and front all at the same time. In other words, things are drawn without any attention to the angle from which they are viewed.

Piaget developed a series of tasks for children that demonstrate how they develop toward a fully coordinated concept of Euclidean and projective relationships. In one experiment he placed matchsticks with Plasticine bases on square, oblong, and round tables: "The child was told that each matchstick represented a telegraph pole and that each must be arranged to form a perfectly straight line running along a straight road. To start with, the first and last posts were placed in position, and both were equidistant from the edge of the table."[32] In most cases, children under four years of age were incapable of making a straight line. Between four and seven they could make straight lines parallel to the edge of the table. But it was not until the children were seven years old that they could make a truly straight line (the shortest distance) between two points. They were able to do this by sighting along a line that projects through the two end poles. According to Piaget, younger children are not able to make the straight line because they cannot distinguish between the various possible views of the matchsticks and thus relate the placement of the matchsticks to their own positions in space.

[32] Piaget and Inhelder, *op. cit.*, p. 156.

In another experiment he placed a child and a doll in positions that would cause them to view the same object from different angles. He asked the child to draw or construct his view of the object and to select from a number of prepared pictures the view that he saw. The prepared drawings eliminated any effects in his own drawings that might have been caused by motor ability. Piaget also asked the child to draw and to select pictures of the view the doll would get of the object. Apparently, the children who participated in this experiment were able to see and to say that things look different from the doll's viewpoint. They also seemed to know that things look smaller as they become more distant. But those same children drew and selected pictures for the doll's view that were the same as the pictures they drew and selected for their own view. During this same period, the children drew pictures without perspective even though they could see and say that objects appear smaller in the distance and that railroad tracks appear to converge in the distance.

In Piaget's words:[33]

The explanation for these difficulties must be sought in the basic difference between perception and representation of perspective. To see an object with a given perspective is to view it from a particular viewpoint, but it is not necessary to be consciously aware of this viewpoint in order to perceive the object accurately. On the other hand, to represent this object in perspective by means of a mental image or a drawing necessitates a conscious awareness of the percipient's viewpoint, together with the transformations induced in the perceptual object by this viewpoint. Thus, in contrast to perception, representation of perspective implies operational, or at least conscious, coordination between object and subject; or in other words, a recognition of the fact that they both occupy the same projective space extending beyond the object and including the observer himself . . .

It is apparent from the foregoing explanation and from his explanations of other phenomena that Piaget considers characteristics such as single and double base lines, folding over, and mixtures of plan and elevation to be caused by the creator's lack of a conscious awareness of his own viewpoint. Not until the

[33] Piaget and Inhelder, op. cit., p. 178. (Used by permission of Humanities Press, Inc., New York, and Routledge and Kegan Paul, Ltd., London.)

child reaches the age of nine, or thereabouts, does he develop the conscious awareness of his own point of view that allows him to draw what he sees and to give his work a single perspective. To develop such a personal perspective, an individual must not only be aware of other points of view, but he must be able to coordinate his visual knowledge of them. When a child uses either a combination of plan and elevation or "folding over" in his work, he is not aware of the highly unique quality of his own view of things. He knows that there are different things to see in a given object, but he is unable to coordinate the different views in such a way that he understands his own unique relationship to the object, and that is a highly egocentric attitude. It is interesting to note that both Piaget and Lowenfeld attribute "folding over" to the egocentricity of the child, but Piaget goes a step further when he connects most other graphic characteristics to the same basic cause.

Piaget has shown experimentally that a child cannot accurately conceive a cross-sectional drawing until he reaches the age of nine. For that reason, the x-ray drawings he makes are not truly cross-sectional, but are merely topological concepts of enclosure. A real sectional drawing is made from a recognized point of view, whereas x-ray drawings are often a jumble of several points of view. The child stops making such drawings about the age of nine because he has become conscious of his own perceptual position and recognizes the impossibility of his earlier x-ray views. Subsequent to the age of nine, the child conceivably might make a drawing that resembles an x-ray picture, but it is likely to be much more of a true cross section.

During the mid-figurative substage of artistic development, the base line is a prominent element in the child's visual symbols, and it is common to see objects placed on the base line and perpendicular to it. This seems reasonable enough, but chimneys on houses and objects on a mountainside remain perpendicular to the line that forms the surface of the roof or the mountain. Children who draw such things would probably feel that the chimneys or trees were tilted if they were drawn in a vertical position. The reason for this, according to Piaget, is that the child, prior to the age of nine, does not establish a vertical and horizontal frame of reference that is outside the object he is drawing. Suppose, for example, that we replicate one of Piaget's experiments by partially filling a jar with water and capping it. Then we ask a child of six or seven to draw the jar and its water as if it were lying on its side. Chances are that the child will draw the water line parallel to the bottom of the jar. His frame of reference is the jar itself, and he assumes that the water will have the same relationship to the jar in any position that the jar happens to take. Not until he is about nine years of age will he use a table, the floor, or the ground as a reference to determine the position of the water.

Thus between the ages of nine and eleven (or during the late figurative substage of artistic development), the child's visual symbolization becomes more highly naturalistic than it has ever been before. This is because the child's concept of spatial relationships is more accurate than it has ever been in the past. Distortions of reality are rare, but when they do occur, they are apt to mean that the child is approaching a higher level of conceptual development.

The formal operations period (age eleven to fifteen). Between the ages of two and eleven, the child becomes increasingly capable of conceiving concrete objects and of thinking about them. The spatial relationships within them and among them become clearer to the child, allowing him to draw objects more naturalistically and more accurately in relationship to one another. But his thinking and his visual symbols are usually confined to concrete objects and events. There is little or no evidence of abstract ideas either in his thinking or in his creative productions. By the age of eleven, however, the child begins to think philosophically. He entertains ideas that go beyond references to matter-of-fact objects and relationships, and he is able to follow an argument while disregarding its concrete content. Piaget does not discuss the child's artistic symbols from this period of development, but it would seem that a youngster who can think abstractly would put some of those abstract notions into his visual creations. And that is exactly what happens. His creations frequently deal with love, hate, strength, peacefulness, and other abstract concepts, and they occasionally depart from the naturalistic style of representation. When they do depart from that style, it is the first time that we have a right to speak of them, logically, as abstract works of art because it is the first time that the child *consciously* departs from naturalism.

A summing-up

Art educators know that children rarely if ever draw while they are in the act of perceiving. It therefore makes sense to conclude that youngsters base their visual creations upon concepts rather than percepts. Dale Harris, one of the world's foremost authorities on childrens drawings, has shown that research tends to confirm the idea that concept development is the most direct and influential factor affecting child art.

Like Goodenough, Harris, and many other authorities on children's drawings, Piaget has found that the nature of child art is largely dependent upon the growth and development of visual concepts, especially the concepts of space. And we must admit that there is a remarkable parallel between the stages of artistic development and the stages of concept development.

If child art is influenced strongly by concept development, there is plenty of justification for saying that we do the child no good by criticizing the shape of the visual forms that he produces. If we wish him to change the shape of his work, we must change his concepts first. As we do that, we must pay attention to the fact that his ability to form concepts will change as he grows and matures. In preschool or kindergarten classes the child will have difficulty conceiving the relationships among objects, but he will have much less trouble visualizing single objects. In the elementary school he will be able to entertain concepts that deal with concrete objects and events, but he will not be able to manage abstract ideas. Among other things, this means that the teaching of aesthetics must be limited to that which can be taught without involving high-level abstractions.

Piaget does not say so, but his work also seems to suggest that we might improve the child's concept of space by causing him to engage in selected and intensive perceptual movement. This seems especially important for young or visually inexperienced children, such as the culturally disadvantaged. As they grow older and become more visually sophisticated, the amount of perceptual movement required for concept formation will probably decrease, but a certain amount of perceptual activity always will contribute to the clearness and efficiency of visual concepts. Hence it is important, from an educational standpoint, for teachers to encourage perceptual activity.

There are a number of things that a teacher might do to get his students to look at the world more carefully, but one of the best things he could do would be to have them draw their environment. Drawing from nature not only requires a large amount of intensive eye movement but reinforces that activity. It engages the child in the act of physically tracing out or reproducing his eye movements with his fingers.

Within the drawing domain there are many different kinds of exercises that teachers might devise for children, but many of them are not being used. One activity that is employed, however, is contour drawing. Such an exercise requires the artist to keep his eyes on the object being drawn but not on his paper. He moves his eyes slowly around the contour of the object and moves his drawing instrument accordingly. The objective, of course, is to make a drawing that looks like the perceived object, and to do so without looking at the drawing requires intensive perceptual concentration. It also demands conscious and sensitive coordination between the hand and the eye. Such an activity is most suitable for youngsters in the upper elementary and secondary schools. But a teacher at any level might have his students draw objects from several different vantage points. He might have them handle objects before they draw them, or he might have them look at something and draw it in midair with their fingers. He might have them use a grease pencil and trace around objects they can see through a window, or he might have them draw an object several times in the course of a semester.

As the teacher engages his students in drawing as an aid to concept development, it probably would help to have them use pointed instruments rather than blunt ones. It probably would be wise to have them use pencils, skinny crayons, ballpoint pens, and felt-tipped pens rather than big brushes and fat crayons because large instruments will not permit the making of details. Consequently, they make it more difficult to develop highly differentiated concepts.

It is also important for the art teacher to consider the probable stage of the child's concept development and let it influence the amount and the complexity of the things that he asks the youngster to perceive and to draw. A very young child or a child who has had no experience with the objects to be seen will probably develop a clearer concept and have an easier time drawing if the amount of the new visual experience is kept to a minimum. As the child matures conceptually and gets a lot of perceptual activity behind him, the teacher might increase the complexity of the things that he causes the youngster to perceive. In other words, he might ask first-graders to draw an automobile while sixth-graders might be asked to draw the traffic at a local intersection.

In each of the foregoing suggestions we have recommended that children draw from the environment if they are to develop accurate and complex concepts of their surroundings. Experience has shown that the drawing of an object from memory may result in a slight distortion of the object. And as subsequent drawings of that object are made from memory, they tend to become more distorted in the direction that was taken in the first drawing. This suggests that accurate concepts of the world are more apt to develop if we ask children to draw more frequently from nature and less often from memory.

At this point, it seems fitting to say that accurate concepts of spatial relationships are not absolutely necessary for the creation of art, but they do give the artist more freedom of expression. If he has a detailed concept of a horse, he is free to draw it, but if he lacks such a concept, his freedom to draw a naturalistic horse is restricted. Such a restriction, in a visually oriented society, is apt to discourage children from drawing because it prevents them from making the naturalistic configurations that are so highly valued. Consequently, the growth of an individual's concept of space is important not only for the development of rational abilities but for the continuation of drawing beyond the childhood years. Intensive perceptual investigation of the environment will help, but it must begin early in the child's life. Thus drawing must begin early in life.

Finally, we should like to call attention to the fact that there seems to be circularity in the process of perceiving, conceiving, and drawing. Percepts and perceptual movements lead to concepts; concepts permit drawing; drawing requires careful perception and is itself a kind of perceptual activity; such activity leads to the formation of concepts which permit more drawing; and so on. But the circularity of the process should not lead to the belief that we have been wrong in saying that drawing contributes to concept development. After all, concepts permit thinking, and we all know that thinking leads to the formation of more concepts.

Although the physical, perceptual, and conceptual aspects of development seem to explain certain characteristics in child art, they do not account for everything. They fail to explain, for example, why a child in the mid-figurative substage of artistic development should produce a drawing in which some people are normally proportioned and others are not. They do not indicate why some symbols are bold and others are delicate, and they do not explain fully why children draw certain highly familiar objects rather than others. We must turn elsewhere for an explanation of such phenomena.

THE EFFECT OF EMOTIONAL CONDITION

For a number of years psychologists have sought evidence of affective traits in the form and content of graphic symbols. The hypothesis behind their work is that emotions will affect the process of manipulating materials by projecting themselves into the activity. This is certainly a plausible idea. After all, personality projection in the Rorschach and the Thematic Apperception tests has been generally accepted. Furthermore, graphic work allows the individual the additional freedom of creating his own symbols. And without being restricted to a set of given forms, he should be able to project his feelings more fully.

Although many persons have claimed success in correlating affective traits with graphic symbols, the results have been anything but impressive. In a highly comprehensive review of the pertinent research, Harris says that "children as well as adults intentionally adapt lines and color in drawings to indicate moods, states, or affect. It is not possible, however, from the available evidence, to state that there is a language of line, form, or color particularly expressive of affect."[34] In other words, there is no conclusive evidence at this time that links specific emotional states to specific graphic forms or content.

Because affective traits project themselves into the act of visual symbolization in so many different ways, we cannot predict the form that they will take in the final product. And if we cannot do that, we obviously cannot diagnose an individual's emotional condition merely by looking at his visual creations. But we can show that affective conditions influence the art of both children and adults if we discuss a few of the instances in which they seem to have had an influence in the past.

A child who is angry at his teacher might draw pictures of the instructor in some sort of a punishing situation. For example, he might show the teacher being hanged. In that case, while his emotional condition causes him to choose the subject for his picture, his concept of the instructor allows him to make the necessary identifying characteristics. Those characteristics, of course, could also be affected by emotion. Thus the head of the teacher might be exaggerated in keeping with its importance, and the features on the face might be selected for their effect as indicators of emotion. Scars, long teeth, bloodshot eyes, and other features might therefore appear as a part of the teacher's face. The fact that the child drew them indicates that he could

230

ART, ARTISTS,
AND CONNOISSEURS

[34] Harris, *op. cit.*, p. 67.

conceive such things, but it does not mean that he believes the teacher has those characteristics. The child uses such grotesque elements simply to indicate how he feels toward the teacher. But the important point is that the resulting drawing is a *combination* of concept and emotion, and it is difficult, if not impossible, to separate the effects of the two determinants.

In the case of Vincent van Gogh, an adult artist, we may not be able to detect his personal emotional problems in his work, but we can perceive certain affective reactions he must have had to the matter-of-fact aspects of his environment. In Plate 36, his portrait of an old peasant from the south of France, we observe in the peasant a feeling of ruggedness that seems appropriate for a man who works close to the earth. And we also perceive a strength and vitality in him that must have been felt and conceptualized by Van Gogh. If they were not, we would have to attribute the close relationship between the portrait and the recognized qualities of French peasants to accidental events, and that is difficult to do.

It should be noted that we are suggesting that Van Gogh not only *felt* the ruggedness and vitality of the peasant but that he was able to *conceive* it. His affective reaction, in other words, impinged on perception, participated in shaping the concept, and appeared in his work. How did it appear?

The artist conveyed his feeling for the character of the peasant by selecting a peasant as subject matter rather than a bird or some other object. He then manipulated lines, colors, shapes, and textures to produce warmth, rugged strength, and vitality. He used strong, intense yellows, blues, and reds to give life and energy, and clear, vigorous brushstrokes for added vitality.

The adult artist can adjust such elements of form in an infinite number of ways to communicate the emotion he feels. As we look at his work, we may understand the feelings that he has tried to transmit, but it may not be easy for us to detect how he does it. This is because the adult artist is able to create subtle nuances of line, color, shape, and texture, and he is able to make use of a large storehouse of conceptual information. In other words, he has an infinite number of formal combinations at his disposal.

231

Pl. 36
Vincent van Gogh, *Old Peasant*
(*Patience Escalier*). 1888.
27¾ × 22¾ in. Collection of
Mrs. Chester Beatty, London.

The child artist, on the other hand, is not as well developed conceptually, and he does not possess the degree of motor control that is essential for the subtle manipulation of form. As a result, he is unable to reveal concepts of emotion in his work except by the simplest of means. He includes concrete objects or parts of objects if they contribute to the general emotional concept that he wishes to express. As an illustration we might use the work of a child who wishes to create the idea of happiness. Chances are that he will draw a picture of the human figure with a smiling mouth. Unhappiness might be depicted with the same figure, a frowning mouth, and tears. In both of these instances the emotional content is conceptual, and takes the form of recognizable subject matter, a characteristic to be expected in the work of children under eleven years of age. The reason for this is that children in the elementary school are in the concrete operations stage of conceptual development. They think in concrete terms, so they draw in concrete terms. They reveal what they know about their feelings by including appropriate objects and by altering those objects in the simplest and most direct manner.

Sometimes children change the form of an object such as the human figure by drawing it in movement. If enough figures are drawn in positions of movement, a strong feeling of action or excitement is created. By drawing the wheels of an automobile as a circular scribble, a youngster is able to produce the feeling of speed and of spinning.

By manipulating the size of an object it is possible to express the feeling of its significance. Figure 6.4 is a picture drawn by a first-grade girl when a group of adults visited her class. The visitors, shown sitting on chairs, are all about the same size. The figure that is much larger than the others is the one that represents the child herself. We cannot attribute the differences in size entirely to concept development, for the child knew that she was not larger than the adults, but as the visitors were watching her, she felt quite important. As a result, she made herself larger than the other figures to reveal that feeling of importance.

Another example of the use of exaggeration to communicate affective traits can be found in Figure 6.5. The large head represents a teacher, and the small figures are her students. Again, the difference in size cannot be caused entirely by concept development. It is brought about by the teacher's importance in the child's mind.

We should point out, however, that opinions differ on the cause of exaggerated sizes in a youngster's visual symbols. Arnheim, for example, tends to minimize the idea that emotions are responsible for the enlargement of symbols.[35] He feels that exaggerations in size may be produced simply because the child needs more room to include all the facial features. Arnheim also suggests that enlargements could result if the child begins drawing on a large scale and then discovers that there is not enough room to draw the remaining objects to the same scale.

A teacher who observes children closely knows that exaggerations in size are frequently caused by the situations that Arnheim has indicated. But look at Figures 6.4 and 6.5 again. If Arnheim is right, why should the child in Figure 6.4 and the teacher in Figure 6.5 be made larger to include facial features when the other people in the pictures are not enlarged? It would seem that the emotional significance of the enlarged person to the child offers a reasonable explanation.

Perhaps the children who made the pictures in Figures 6.4 and 6.5 started with the parts that seem exaggerated. They may have been forced to make the remaining elements in the picture smaller because of a lack of space. But anyone who observes children closely will notice that they rarely begin their drawings with the least significant element in the picture. Ordinarily they start with the part that seems most important to them, and so do adults. After all, it is an unusual artist who begins a full-length portrait by starting with the shoelaces. Consequently, the importance that a child feels for an object may account for its exaggerated size in many instances.

By the time the child reaches the age of nine or ten, however, the size relationships in his drawings are much more naturalistic. He discontinues exaggeration at that point because his conceptual

[35] Arnheim, *op. cit.*, pp. 155–157.

Fig. 6.4
In this drawing by a girl in
first grade the exaggerated size of
one figure is undoubtedly caused by
the feeling of importance that
the child artist attached to that
figure. In this instance
the enlarged figure is
the child artist herself.

Fig. 6.5
The large head in this
picture represents a teacher, and the
small figures are her students.
Without doubt, the exaggerated
size of the head is a reflection of
the importance of the teacher in the
mind of the child artist.

development will not allow him to accept unnaturalistic forms; they seem illogical.

After the age of eleven or twelve, the adolescent may begin to exaggerate sizes once again, but if he does, it is usually by design. He is conscious of what he is doing, and he does it to achieve a special effect, whereas the youngster of elementary school age is much more intuitive in his expression.

Differences between elementary and secondary school children are also apparent in the use of color. The younger child rarely uses color to express his concepts of emotion. In fact, he is not consciously aware of the relationship between color and emotion. He begins, in the earliest stage of symbolic transformation, with an arbitrary use of color, and as he grows older, his concept of color in the environment tends to grow. As a result, his color becomes more naturalistic; the grass is green, the sky is blue, and human beings are less likely to be painted purple. Instead of painting everything with flat, unmodulated hues, the youngster in the late conceptual stage of symbolic development begins to model or shade his work.

When the child reaches the stage of artistic decision, however, he uses color to express his concepts of emotion. He recognizes the meaning that color possesses, and he uses it effectively. He might use reds, oranges, and yellows to convey a feeling of warmth, or he might use hues that suggest happiness, sickness, freshness, or death. From this point on it becomes increasingly difficult for the layman to detect how the child artist communicates feeling through his work because the youngster has reached a stage of intellectual and emotional maturity that allows him to make infinite combinations of formal elements.

A summing-up

From the foregoing account we may conclude that children draw as they do partly because they project emotions into their work. This does not mean that we are capable of discerning the artist's psychological state by looking at his visual symbols, but it means that the artist can create in us an understanding of feelings or emotions that he conceives and wishes to communicate. He does it through a judicious selection of subject matter and a careful manipulation of formal elements. Because children are conceptually, emotionally, and physically less mature than adults, they are unable to reveal emotions in a complex and profound manner. They communicate their feelings in a very general way by including or omitting certain things, by exaggerating the size of objects, by drawing objects in positions of movement, and by making traces of bodily movement in their work. Not until they reach the age of eleven or twelve do they begin to use *color* to express concepts of emotion, and by that time they have matured sufficiently so that it is difficult to tell their work from the work of an adult.

So far we have discussed the effects of physical, perceptual, and conceptual growth upon child art, and we have shown that the medium of expression and the emotional condition of the child influence the shape of his visual symbols. It seems clear that such factors are *directly* responsible for the characteristics that exist in child art. But what is it that causes the child to use a particular medium, conceive a certain object rather than another, or develop one affective trait instead of another? What is it that causes a child to express some of his ideas and ignore others? What causes him to draw certain objects, and why does he choose to include or omit various parts of those objects? No doubt the environment is one of the causative factors.

THE EFFECT OF ENVIRONMENT

According to Lowenfeld, children draw certain objects rather than others because *they draw the things that are most important to them, the things that actively stimulate them at the time they are drawing.*[36] They might draw human beings at one time and trucks at another because their attention happens to be focused on human beings and trucks at those particular moments. Simi-

[36] Lowenfeld, *op. cit.*, p. 82.

larly, they might omit certain objects or parts of objects if those elements do not capture their attention during the act of symbolization. Thus a child might omit ears or legs in a picture about blowing his nose. Ears and legs are not involved in the activity of nose blowing, and for that reason they are not apt to enter the child's thoughts as he draws. But what is it that causes a person to think of a human being, a truck, an arm, or a foot while he is drawing. What causes him to perceive such things with attentiveness in the first place? Or to put it differently, what causes a person to develop a perceptual set or a readiness to perceive certain things?

As we indicated while discussing the effect of perception on child art, it seems possible that an individual could inherit a neurophysical structure that leads him to perceive certain things rather than other things. But experience, as well as the bulk of research, points more strongly toward a different determinant. The factor that seems most influential in arousing a person's interest, developing his perceptual set, directing his attention, and provoking his behavior (including visual symbolization) is the factor that we call *stimulation*. And there is a constant flow of such excitation from the environment; part of it is natural and part is cultural. Let us examine the effect of the natural environment on child art.

Natural stimulation

Trees, clouds, animals, and other elements of nature constitute what we shall call natural stimuli, and their effect upon children is well known. The falling of the year's first snow or the coming of colored leaves in October is sure to capture the attention of youngsters and cause them to include snow and colorful trees in their drawings. Children who live in Panama or the Congo, however, would not be expected to draw snow or colorful autumn leaves. Like children elsewhere in the world, they would draw and paint the things that they experience in their own environment. In that way nature exerts her influence on visual symbolization. But despite the fact that nature often arouses our attention and moves us to self-expression, it probably is not as stimulating as the culture in which we live. For that reason we turn our attention to cultural stimulation.

Cultural stimulation

When we speak of the culture in which an individual lives, we are referring to the traditions, values, and mores of a given group as well as to the institutions, structure, and methods of organization in that group. By living in the United States each of us is exposed to the American culture. We contribute to it and are affected by it. In time we develop many habits, values, and attitudes that are similar to those possessed by our fellow Americans. And the same process of enculturation occurs in other countries all over the world. The effect of that enculturation on child art can be shown by citing a few examples.

In Bali, for instance, the adult artists produce visual symbols that conform as closely as possible to the art forms of the past.[37] They do so simply because that has been the traditional function of the Balinese artist. Probably his lack of individuality in art has become traditional because art in Bali is one of the primary means of passing cultural values from one generation to the next. If the art were to change in any appreciable way, it would not permit the transmission of traditional values.

Because art in Bali is used as a means of cultural maintenance, children are exposed to it from infancy, especially to the wajang puppet shows, which they see from eight to ten times a year. The puppet shows introduce the children to stylized figures that represent demons, witches, and other characters that have an important place in the Balinese tradition. Consequently, when children are asked to draw, they commonly produce the stylized figures from the wajang puppet shows. The figures are intricate, active, spontaneously organized into a composition, and decisive in their linear quality.

[37] This account of art in Bali is based on the writing of Jane Belo, author of "Balinese Children's Drawing," in Margaret Mead and Martha Wolfenstein (eds.), *Childhood in Contemporary Cultures*, University of Chicago Press, Chicago, 1955, pp. 52–69.

According to Jane Belo, Balinese children draw like children in other cultures until they reach the age of four or five. Then they adopt the culturally accepted techniques and subject matter. If they do attempt to draw anything different, they often have trouble because they do not have an acceptable model upon which they can base their work. Thus it is clear that the subject matter and the style of child art in Bali is strongly influenced by the cultural environment. It causes the children to perceive certain things intently and to think of those things during the act of drawing.

Another example of cultural influence can be found in the work of French children. According to Martha Wolfenstein, who reviewed an exhibition of child art from France, the work is highly controlled, detailed, and patterned.[38] It seems to lack energetic human action, and there is also an absence of wide vistas and expanses of sky. Wolfenstein recognized her sample of child art as a highly select one that might not accurately represent the child art of France. But many art educators have observed the work of French children under different conditions, and they also have noted its high degree of control. Wolfenstein suggests that such qualities are the result of strong restraints placed on the energetic outward drives of children. In her view, childhood in France is not a time for fun; it is a time for diligence and sobriety. Freedom and pleasure are more apparent in adult behavior and in adult art. Hence we have another indication of cultural influence on the art of children. In the case of French children, it causes them to control themselves in thought and action as they make their paintings, and their paintings reflect a certain amount of that control.

In examining the effect of environment on Japanese children's art, Helen Merritt concludes that the remarkable vitality and variety in the work can be explained by the rich respect for art that is demonstrated by the Japanese people.[39] Adults consider art to be a natural means of expression for everyone, and

[38] Martha Wolfenstein, "French Children's Paintings," in *ibid.*, pp. 300–305.
[39] Helen Merritt, *Guiding Free Expression in Children's Art*, Holt, Rinehart and Winston Inc., New York, 1964, pp. 21–23.

they freely produce it. Consequently, the children are surrounded by artistic activity and by tasteful visual arrangements from birth onward. They are conditioned to perceive the aesthetic dimension of experience, and their high level of sensitivity reveals itself in art work that has a considerable degree of differentiation.

Still another example of the effect of culture on child art is offered by June McFee.[40] She explains that the Zia Indians of New Mexico expect boys to draw and paint animal pictures on walls and to paint ceremonial masks and other objects, but they expect girls to make geometric designs on pottery. As a result, the boys perceive things with more care and draw them in greater detail than the girls do. The culture therefore influences the things that youngsters perceive and conceive, and it affects the extent of their development in art.

From the foregoing comments it is clear that the culture of a country or of a tribe can have an effect upon the art of children. In most countries, however, there are within the national culture many subcultures, each of which can influence child art. The family, the neighborhood, and the school classroom are examples of social units that are often described as subcultures. Hence the family, the neighborhood, the classroom, and other social units can and do affect child art. How do they do it?

One way that a subculture can influence child art is by providing verbal, auditory, tactile, and other types of stimuli that are interesting and attract attention. In the absence of such stimuli the child frequently loses interest in visual symbolization because the concepts that constitute the content of visual expression are drastically reduced. Sometimes, a child who has been given materials for graphic activity will finish his drawing very quickly and move on to another kind of work. He may look around the room, daydream, bother other children, or he may refuse to draw altogether and ask to do something else. The child's lack of interest in symbolization is obvious in such instances, and his graphic work will show it. It is likely to be extremely simple, with few details and little additional evidence of

[40] June K. McFee, *Preparation for Art*, Wadsworth Publishing Company, Inc., San Francisco, 1961, pp. 84–97.

personal involvement. Lowenfeld has called such drawings "pure objective reports."[41] An example of one such drawing is seen in Figure 6.6. It is a visual cliché, produced by a girl in the first grade to satisfy the teacher's request for a drawing. Beyond the simple request there was no provocative stimulation preceding the work. Naturally the youngster had nothing to say, so she created a stereotyped symbol that has little or no meaning or importance for her. When such a lack of stimulation becomes a frequent occurrence, the child finds no value in visual symbolization. Before long he will stop drawing and give his attention to other matters; and he will not continue to develop artistically.

As you might expect, the more stimulating experiences are the ones that are likely to occupy the child's attention and provoke the creation of a highly expressive symbolic image. Such an impressive stimulation can take many forms. It can be kinesthetic, auditory, olfactory, tactile, visual, or a combination of these

[41] Lowenfeld, *op. cit.*, p. 52.

forms. An example of kinesthetic and tactile stimulations and their effect on children's drawings can be found in the research of Sina Mott.[42]

Mott asked twenty-four children between the ages of fifty-one and seventy-two months to draw two pictures a day for ten days. Following that, they did no drawing at all for six weeks. Then they resumed the drawing of two pictures a day for five days.

For their first drawing each day, Mott merely asked them to draw the best picture of a man that they could. Then she asked them to turn over their papers and stand up. Each child listened to the teacher and followed her suggested activity.

On the first day the teacher said, "This is my head, I nod it," and the children repeated the words and nodded their heads. After that, they sat down and drew another picture of a man. On succeeding days the teacher followed the same procedure, but she concentrated on other body parts. All drawings were scored according to the Goodenough scale, which showed that each child included more body parts in his drawings after he had engaged in muscular activity.

Mott's work shows that kinesthetic and tactile stimulation can have a positive and direct effect upon the making of visual symbols; it can cause certain parts of objects to be included and drawn in detail. Similar evidence comes from the work of Mc-Vitty[43] and Lansing,[44] who provided other forms of cultural stimulation. In each case the motivation served to focus the child's attention on a given experience. It helped him to develop a clearer concept of that experience, to develop an emotional reaction to it, and to refresh his memory if the experience occurred in the past. This is the function of the cultural stimulation that a parent or teacher provides. Without some form of cultural excitation,

---

[42] Sina M. Mott, "Muscular Activity an Aid in Concept Formation," *Child Development*, vol. 16, pp. 98–108, March–June, 1945.
[43] Lawrence McVitty, "An Experimental Study in Various Methods in Art Motivations at the Fifth Grade Level," *Research in Art Education*, Seventh Yearbook of the National Art Education Association, Kutztown Publishing Co., Kutztown, Pennsylvania, 1956, pp. 74–83.
[44] Kenneth Lansing, "The Effect of Class Size and Room Size upon the Creative Drawings of Fifth Grade Children," *Research in Art Education*, Ninth Yearbook of the National Art Education Association, Kutztown Publishing Co., Kutztown, Pennsylvania, 1959, pp. 70–74.

the child has little or nothing to say that would require artistic expression.

Yet exciting experiences do not always lead to the creation of visual symbols. This is because excitement or stimulation can be either encouraging or discouraging. Destructive criticism and ridicule of the child's creative productions are thoroughly stimulating, to say the least, but they also are discouraging and often lead to forms of behavior other than visual symbolization. They might easily cause the child to lose confidence in his own graphic expression, or they might make it so distasteful that he abandons it for other, less anxious activities.

If there is a continual lack of excitement or a constant flow of moving but discouraging stimulation, the child may give up his graphic expression. If he continues to draw and paint despite such experiences, his work is not apt to mature, but is likely to remain below the developmental level that would be expected for a child of his age. This is one of the explanations for the immature symbolization that we often find in secondary schools and colleges.

Another way in which the subculture can influence child art is through the art materials that it provides. If it offers tools and materials that are too difficult for the child to manage, he is apt to become frustrated or lose confidence in his ability to make visual symbols, and he is likely to stop creating visual forms. Or if he does continue, his symbols probably will be immature or unpleasant in their appearance.

If the family or the classroom teacher offers the child nothing but red paint, his art work obviously will be red. When he is given a pencil, his work will be more detailed than it will be if he is given a 1-inch brush. And if he is encouraged to fill the space on his paper, the space is more likely to be filled than it is if the encouragement is lacking. Hence the cultural environment can affect the structural organization of visual creations.

Finally, it is important to mention the fact that the habits, attitudes, and values in any given subculture can affect child art. In a well-known study by Thelma Alper, for example, children from middle-class homes did not engage in finger-painting as quickly or as easily as youngsters from lower-class homes.[45] The implication is that the greater middle-class emphasis on cleanliness has an effect on the child's willingness to participate freely in activities that seem dirty. If this is so, the child from a middle-class home is not likely to work easily with such materials as clay, papier-mâché, and chalk; and if he does not work freely with certain materials, the visual symbols that he makes with those materials are likely to remain immature.

A Summing-up.

Clearly, the natural and cultural environment can influence child art, and it can do so in ways that we have not mentioned. But to indicate all the possible effects of the natural and cultural environment would require the writing of another book. Hence we are satisfied to say that the natural environment influences child art because it is the source of much artistically relevant knowledge. And the cultural environment (habits, attitudes, values) helps to determine the nature of child art because it possesses the power to shape the personality or the emotional condition by influencing habits, attitudes, and values; thus it is able to stimulate and direct attention and to aid or abet the formation of artistically appropriate knowledge, and by affecting habits, attitudes, and values, it encourages or discourages the development of relevant skills.

SUMMARY

This chapter has tried to show that there is a certain amount of truth in each of the traditional explanations for artistic development in children. Understandably, experts tend to agree that physical condition and the medium of expression both have an effect upon child art. But when it comes to perception

[45] Thelma Alper, Howard Blanc, and Barbara Adams, "Reactions of Middle and Lower Class Children to Finger Paints as a Function of Class Differences in Child-Training Practice," *Journal of Abnormal and Social Psychology*, vol. 51, pp. 439–448, 1955.

as a determinant, authorities disagree about the directness of its influence. The bulk of experience and research seems to indicate, however, that perception affects child art simply because it determines the nature of a person's concepts and the speed with which they develop. In other words, concepts appear to have a more direct influence on child art, but artistically relevant concepts are largely dependent upon perception for their existence and their characteristic qualities.

Although it is not fully understood, perception seems to have two primary determinants, both of which are highly complex: the first is the total organismic state of the individual perceiver; the second is the environment. The total organismic state is the singular combination of a person's neurophysiological structure and his personality; the environment is partly natural and partly cultural.

The teacher is an important part of the child's cultural environment. Consequently, the teacher is in a position to shape the personality, to direct perception, to promote the formation of relevant concepts, and to affect the nature of child art. He must take that responsibility seriously and do what he can to build the appropriate knowledge, attitudes, and skills. Before he can do that, however, he needs to formulate his objectives very clearly, and he needs to base those objectives upon the nature of art, artists, and the known facts about artistic development in children. We proceed with that task in the chapter that follows.

QUESTIONS FOR DISCUSSION

1. We have said that emotional condition has an effect on child art. What is the relationship of emotional condition to physiognomic perception?
2. Color blindness is an aspect of the physical condition. What effect could it have on child art? Be specific.

3. Try Arnheim's suggestion. Put a pencil in your mouth and copy a drawing of a human ear. Then ask a four or five-year-old child to copy the same ear. Are there any differences between the drawings? What are they? What causes them?

4. Examine the visual symbols that were produced by blind students under the direction of Viktor Lowenfeld (see *The Nature of Creative Activity*, Routledge and Kegan Paul, Ltd., London, 1939). Were any of those children totally blind before the age of five? What effect is blindness before the age of five likely to have on child art? (See Berthold Lowenfeld, *Our Blind Children*, Charles C Thomas, Springfield, Illinois, 1956, p. 158).

5. If a person is culturally disadvantaged, what does that mean? Would it have any effect on his art? If so, in what way?

6. We refer to Balinese children in this chapter. Are they culturally disadvantaged? Why?

7. If we accept Hebb's cell-assembly theory of perception, what effect could brain damage have on concept development? Would it have the same effect regardless of the portion of the brain that was damaged?

8. Watch a left-handed child draw. Does he face his figures towards the left or the right? How does a right-handed child orient his figures? Why do they do it?

9. Take a look at the Goodenough Draw-a-Man Test. If this test were administered to children in different cultures, why would it be unwise to compare the results from the two groups?

10. Find a young child who draws a human figure as a circle with arms and legs attached. Ask him if the circle is a head or a body. Does the result confirm Lowenfeld's view or Arnheim's view?

11. At what age can a child first copy a drawing of a square? Can he conceive a square before that age? Can he perceive it before that age?

12. The gestalt psychologists claim that children draw as they do because they draw what they perceive. Do monkeys perceive in essentially the same way as human beings? If so, why does monkey art fail to develop in the same way as child art?

13. If different subcultures possess different habits, attitudes, and values, what effect would this have on the teaching of art in the public schools?

14. Think of several ways to encourage active, intensive perception in children. Try them. Do they work? Do they cause any change in the children's drawings?

15, We do not recommend that a teacher diagnose children's problems by looking at their drawings. Why?

16. June McFee speaks of art as a means of maintaining culture (see *Preparation for Art*, Wadsworth Publishing Company, Inc., San Francisco, 1961). To what extent is it also a vehicle for cultural change?

SUGGESTIONS FOR FURTHER READING

Allport, Gordon: *Theories of Perception and the Concept of Structure*, John Wiley and Sons, Inc., New York, 1955.
A highly respected summary of the theories of perception. Technical and difficult for the nonpsychologist.

Arnheim, Rudolph: *Art and Visual Perception*, University of California Press Berkeley, 1954.
This book presents the gestalt view of art and its relationship to visual perception.

Ball, John, and Francis C. Byrnes (eds.): *Research, Principles and Practices in Visual Communication*, a publication of the American Association of Land-Grant Colleges and State Universities, The National Art Education Association, Washington, D. C. 1960.
This booklet provides a concise account of perceptual organization and its practical application in visual communication. It also offers a brief summary of the various theories of perception.

Goodenough, Florence: *Measurement of Intelligence by Drawings*, World Book Company, New York, 1926.
An account of the effect of concept development on child art by one of the early authorities on the subject.

Harris, Dale: *Children's Drawings as Measures of Intellectual Maturity*, Harcourt, Brace and World, Inc., New York, 1963.
The most comprehensive account of research on children's drawings ever assembled. The things that influence such drawings are examined thoroughly.

Lorenz, Konrad: *On Aggression*, Harcourt, Brace and World, Inc., New York, 1966.
A magnificent book by a famous ethologist. It contains many references to animals and insects that attend to certain visual configurations instinctively. The implications of this book are tremendous.

Lowenfeld, Viktor: *Creative and Mental Growth*, The Macmillan Company, New York, 1957.
In this book, a highly sensitive observer and a gifted teacher offers a point of view about the determinants of child art. A very practical book.

Lowenfeld, Viktor: *The Nature of Creative Activity*, Routledge and Kegan Paul, Ltd., London, 1939.
In this book the art of blind children leads the author to discoveries about the art of normal children and the factors that affect it.

McFee, June K.: *Preparation for Art*, Wadsworth Publishing Company Inc., San Francisco, 1961.
A popular textbook on art education that discusses many of the factors affecting children's drawings. It offers a perception-delineation theory of child art.

Mead, Margaret, and Martha Wolfenstein (eds.): *Childhood in Contemporary Cultures*, University of Chicago Press, Chicago, 1955.
This book examines the effect of culture upon child-rearing practices. Chapter 4 covers the effect of culture on Balinese child art, and chapter 8 covers its effect on the paintings produced by French children.

Piaget, Jean, and Barbel Inhelder: *The Child's Conception of Space*, Humanities Press, Inc., New York, 1956.
An important book on one aspect of concept development by one of the world's leading authorities. Intimately related to the child's artistic development.

Read, Herbert: *Education through Art*, Pantheon Books, Inc., New York, 1958.
In this book, a famous philosopher and critic examines the factors that shape child art. He postulates the existence of certain personality types and suggests their influence on art.

Schaefer-Simmern, Henry: *The Unfolding of Artistic Activity*, University of California Press, Berkeley, 1950.
This book presents a theory of artistic development based on a gestalt point of view.

Smith, I. Macfarlane: *Spatial Ability: Its Educational and Social Significance*, Robert K. Knapp, San Diego, California, 1964.
The research dealing with spatial abilities is covered thoroughly in this book.

Sorokin, Pitirim A.: *The Crisis of Our Age*, E. P. Dutton and Co., Inc., New York, 1941.
An interesting examination of the effect of culture on the various dimensions of social life. Chapter 2 covers the effect of culture on the fine arts.

Von Senden, M.: *Space and Sight,* The Free Press, Glencoe, Illinois, 1960.
An English translation of a highly significant book on perception written in 1932.

Werner, Heinz: *Comparative Psychology of Mental Development*, International Universities Press, Inc., New York, 1957.
Physiognomic perception is explored in this book.

ART EDUCATION Part II

Chapter 7
FORMULATING OBJECTIVES AND BUILDING A CURRICULUM FOR THE PUBLIC SCHOOL

The idea that art has value for the individual and for society was developed in Chapter 3. Now it is important to explain that *art should be taught*, because the absence of such an explanation might lead to the belief that the value of art can be obtained most satisfactorily by attempting artistic activity without any guidance.

Naturally it is not reasonable to contend that art *must* be taught if people are to become artists and connoisseurs, because a number of highly successful painters, sculptors, and critics have received no training at all. Yet it does make sense to argue that art *should* be taught simply because teaching speeds the learning that is to occur and reduces the chance that a person will spend valuable time on something that is not art and not invested with artistic values. After all, the production and appreciation of art should not be left to chance or to the self-education of aesthetically unsophisticated individuals if art activities really have a unique value for all human beings.

Making and appraising art *are* valuable activities for *all*   253 persons because they make a significant contribution to the attainment of the good life. Art is unusually helpful in that respect because it is one of the primary modes of discourse, and it deals with the kind of nondiscursive knowledge that can not be offered through any other form of communication. It deals with the specific visual information that resides in pictorial or iconic images. Without that information the individual is less free. He lacks one of the most fundamental kinds of knowledge, and this deficiency severely limits his chance of self-realization. If the individual fails to realize his potential in that way, he becomes less human than we should expect him to be. When that happens, the quality of the culture is bound to deteriorate. We say this because we believe that *the greatness of a culture is indicated most clearly by the level of discourse used by the average man and not by the communicative efforts of a few professional artists*. If so, it seems imperative that art be *taught* to everyone.

Therefore, assuming that the value of art definitely justifies the teaching of art, why must it be taught in the public schools? Could it not be taught just as well by some other agency? If it could, one less demand for instructional time would be made on the public school.

Obviously art can be taught elsewhere, and it is supposedly being taught outside the public school at the present time. Instruction is offered by the Boy Scouts, the Girl Scouts, the YMCA, 4-H clubs, museums, churches, PTA enrichment programs, and various municipal youth organizations. Without a doubt the museums do the best job because they are able to limit enrollment and employ qualified teachers. The Girl Scouts also have succeeded in producing excellent films and other teaching materials. But, in general, the offerings in art outside the public school are not beneficial. The major difficulty is that the sponsoring organizations are not financially equipped to hire competent teachers and to provide adequate equipment and supplies. The customary volunteer teachers are to be admired, and, in many ways, they offer a lot to children. But they are usually aesthetically untrained parents whose knowledge of art and art education is not sufficient for the job. In fact, it is not uncommon for Sunday school teachers, den mothers, recreation leaders, and other conscientious, service-minded persons to offer instruction that is actually detrimental to the production of art and diametrically opposed to everything that an artist would recommend for the teaching of his subject. Giving an activity the name of art does not automatically make it art. Thus professional art educators often have their work undone, or they have to break firmly established habits that lead to nonart before they can make much progress in teaching their subject.

Furthermore, most organizations outside the public school require dues, fees, or payments that many families cannot afford. Sometimes the classes are not conveniently located, or they are offered in places that are socially out-of-bounds for certain youngsters. Perhaps there are other reasons that prevent attendance, but the point is that not all children receive art instruction when art classes are offered apart from the public school.

Consequently, the public school is the most logical place to teach art to children. The schools are financially capable of hiring competent teachers; they can provide the necessary equipment and supplies; and they have professionally trained administrators, supervisors, and consultants who can see to it that the quality of instruction remains high. And even more important is the fact that *instruction in the public school reaches all the youngsters in America.*

If we hope to teach art in the public school, however, we must be sure that the subject will make a unique contribution to the attainment of educational goals. This is an important consideration because the value of a subject to the individual does not necessarily guarantee that it will lead to the attainment of educational objectives. Religion provides a good example. Religion is valuable to a great many people, but the teaching of it would not lead to goals that are considered proper for public educational institutions. Religious instruction is more appropriately a function of the family and the church. We must therefore be sure that the teaching of art will lead to the attainment of educational objectives. What are the goals of education in America?

THE AIMS OF EDUCATION IN AMERICA

Several attempts have been made to formulate the goals of education in America, and in each instance the resultant objectives reflected the dominant values of the age. In Colonial times, people felt that they could teach their children everything that was essential, except the fundamental processes of reading, writing, and arithmetic. Consequently, the aims of formal education centered on the development of ability in those fundamental processes. By 1918, however, the purposes of education had grown considerably. In that year the Commission on Reorganization of Secondary Education[1] issued a document that was perhaps the most influential statement of educational objectives up to that time. It presented goals that have become known as the seven cardinal principles of education: health, command of the fundamental processes, worthy home membership, vocational competence, effective citizenship, worthy use of leisure, and ethical character. Without a doubt the writers of that document were influenced by the unhappy experiences of World War I because the statement reveals an awareness of the fact that more must be required of the educated individual than a command of the fundamental processes. He must be able to keep himself healthy and be able to adjust to his society and contribute to it. He must understand that his responsibilities extend beyond himself and include his duty as a member of a family and as a citizen of the United States.

The limitations of the 1918 objectives, however, are at least three in number. The aims are presented in such general terms that they could mean different things to different people; they do not indicate how the educated person should differ from the uneducated person; and they do not show that a democratic society expects anything different from its educational system than an undemocratic society. Consequently, new goals were almost certain to be formulated. And, sure enough, in 1938, another statement of educational objectives was constructed by

**ART
EDUCATION** [1] U.S. Bureau of Education, *Cardinal Principles of Secondary Education*, Bulletin no. 38, 1918.

the Educational Policies Commission of the National Education Association. The report states: "The general end of education in America at the present time is the fullest possible development of the individual within the framework of our present industrialized democratic society. The attainment of this end is to be observed in individual behavior or conduct."[2]

Unlike previous statements of objectives, the report of 1938 indicates the types of *behavior* to be expected of the *educated* individual, the *educated* member of the family and community, the *educated* producer and consumer, and the *educated* citizen. A complete list of the objectives is reproduced below:[3]

The objectives of self-realization

The Inquiring Mind. The educated person has an appetite for learning.

Speech. The educated person can speak the mother tongue clearly.

Reading. The educated person reads the mother tongue efficiently.

Writing. The educated person writes the mother tongue effectively.

Number. The educated person solves his problems of counting and calculating.

Sight and Hearing. The educated person is skilled in listening and observing.

Health Knowledge. The educated person understands the basic facts concerning health and disease.

Health Habits. The educated person protects his own health and that of his dependents.

Public Health. The educated person works to improve the health of the community.

Recreation. The educated person is participant and spectator in many sports and other pastimes.

Intellectual Interests. The educated person has mental resources for the use of leisure.

Esthetic Interests. The educated person appreciates beauty.

Character. The educated person gives responsible direction to his own life.

---

[2] Educational Policies Commission, *The Purposes of Education in American Democracy*, National Education Association, Washington, D.C., 1938, p. 41.
[3] *Ibid.*, pp. 50, 72, 90, 108. (Used by permission of the National Education Association).

The objectives of human relationships

Respect for Humanity. The educated person puts human relationships first.

Friendship. The educated person enjoys a rich, sincere, and varied social life.

Cooperation. The educated person can work and play with others.

Courtesy. The educated person observes the amenities of social behavior.

Appreciation of the Home. The educated person appreciates the family as a social institution.

Conservation of the Home. The educated person conserves family ideals.

Homemaking. The educated person is skilled in homemaking.

Democracy in the Home. The educated person maintains democratic family relationships.

The objectives of economic efficiency

Work. The educated producer knows the satisfaction of good workmanship.

Occupational Information. The educated producer understands the requirements and opportunities for various jobs.

Occupational Choice. The educated producer has selected his occupation.

Occupational Efficiency. The educated producer succeeds in his chosen vocation.

Occupational Adjustment. The educated producer maintains and improves his efficiency.

Occupational Appreciation. The educated producer appreciates the social value of his work.

Personal Economics. The educated consumer plans the economics of his own life.

Consumer Judgment. The educated consumer develops standards for guiding his expenditures.

Efficiency in Buying. The educated consumer is an informed and skillful buyer.

Consumer Protection. The educated consumer takes appropriate measures to safeguard his interests.

The objectives of civic responsibility

Social Justice. The educated citizen is sensitive to the disparities of human circumstance.

Social Activity. The educated citizen acts to correct unsatisfactory conditions.

Social Understanding. The educated citizen seeks to understand social structures and social processes.

Critical Judgment. The educated citizen has defenses against propaganda.

Tolerance. The educated citizen respects honest differences of opinion.

Conservation. The educated citizen has a regard for the nation's resources.

Social Applications of Science. The educated citizen measures scientific advance by its contribution to the general welfare.

World Citizenship. The educated citizen is a cooperating member of the world community.

Law Observance. The educated citizen respects the law.

Economic Literacy. The educated citizen is economically literate.

Political Citizenship. The educated citizen accepts his civic duties.

Devotion to Democracy. The educated citizen acts upon an unswerving loyalty to democratic ideals.

The foregoing statement of educational objectives is an improvement upon previous announcements because it lists the specific characteristics found in educated persons in a democratic society. Yet it continues to have some of the same weaknesses attributed to previous statements of objectives. It emphasizes the qualities that should exist in the educated *adult*, but it does not mention the degree to which *children* in the various grades should be expected to develop those qualities. In addition, it does not relate objectives to the areas of subject matter that make up the instructional program in the public school; or to put it differently, the objectives do not tell the teacher how an educated child should behave in art or any other subject at each of the different grade levels. Consequently, a much more specific formulation of goals is needed if teachers are to know what to do in their classrooms. Such objectives will be presented later in this chapter. But, first, let us continue with more information about the attempts that have been made to formulate educational aims.

Despite their weaknesses the statements of 1918 and 1938 have served a useful purpose as general guides for curriculum

FORMULATING OBJECTIVES AND
BUILDING A CURRICULUM

development. In 1961, however, another Educational Policies Commission[4] reexamined these objectives and concluded that they were good but impossible to attain. It has become clear, for example, that the schools do not have the time or the energy to provide all the activities that are necessary to achieve the old objectives.

For that reason the commission believed that it must decide which of the goals were most imperative for us to achieve. It concluded that the central purpose of American education should be the development of rational powers, the powers of thought. The thinking behind that conclusion is that freedom is the primary goal of American society; a free society is dependent upon the individual's freedom of mind; and a free mind is one that has a rational understanding of man, his surroundings, and the relationship between them.

In the words of the commission, ". . . individual strength springs from a thinking, aware mind, a mind that possesses the capacity to achieve aesthetic sensitivity and moral responsibility, an enlightened mind. These qualities occur in a wide diversity of patterns in different individuals. It is the contention of this essay that central to all of them, nurturing them and being nurtured by them, are the rational powers of man."[5]

Later on, the commission says, ". . . the society which best develops the rational potentials of its people, along with their intuitive and aesthetic capabilities, will have the best chance of flourishing in the future. To help every person develop those powers is therefore a profoundly important objective and one which increases in importance with the passage of time. By pursuing this objective, the school can enhance spiritual and aesthetic values and the other cardinal purposes which it has traditionally served and must continue to serve."[6]

Another important statement by the commission reads as follows: ". . . there is a highly creative aspect in processes of

---

[4] Educational Policies Commission, *The Central Purpose of American Education*, National Education Association, Washington, D.C., 1961.
[5] *Ibid.*, p. 4.
[6] *Ibid.*, p. 11.

thought. All the higher mental processes involve more than simple awareness of facts; they depend also on the ability to conceive what might be as well as what is, to construct mental images in new and original ways. Experiences in literature and the arts may well make a larger contribution to those abilities than studies usually assumed to develop abstract thinking."[7]

The foregoing statements by the Educational Policies Commission of 1961 clearly indicate the importance that has been assigned to the development of rational powers. The ability to think has become a more important goal than the memorization of facts, for it is likely to be more helpful in solving contemporary problems and in overcoming the unpredictable difficulties of the future.

But we cannot think effectively about a given subject without a fund of relevant knowledge. The commission does not say what kind of knowledge should serve as the raw material for thought, but it does suggest two bases for making that decision: "One is the potential of the knowledge for the development of rational powers; the other is the relative importance of the knowledge in the life of the pupil and of society."[8] Does the knowledge associated with the production and appreciation of art satisfy these requirements? Apparently, the commission thinks so, for it mentions aesthetic capabilities time after time as worthy objectives for American education. Never before have aesthetic powers received such emphasis, and never before have they been so closely associated with rational abilities by a prominent educational group outside the field of art. This is highly significant. It means that influential persons are beginning to recognize the value of art as both an end in itself and as a means to rational power. But many laymen and school administrators will have to be convinced that art actually contributes to the goals of education. Consequently, it is fitting that we turn our attention to the value of art in education.

[7] *Ibid.*, p. 18.
[8] *Ibid.*, p. 19.

ART AND THE AIMS OF EDUCATION

In Chapter 3 a special effort was made to indicate the value of art to the individual and to society, but the present task is to point out its more specific value in the attainment of educational objectives. Naturally, art will not help us to achieve each of the goals listed by the Educational Policies Commissions of 1938 and 1961, but it can help us to reach some of them. We shall mention, first, its most apparent contributions to self-realization, human relationships, economic efficiency, and civic responsibility, and then we shall discuss art as a builder of rational power.

Self-realization

Sight and hearing. *Art helps the individual to become skilled in sight because it forces him to look more attentively than usual at his environment and at his work. In short, it helps him to become more perceptive by causing him to practice intensive perception.*

Recreation. *Art involves its creator in an activity that can serve as recreation during his leisure hours. It causes him to become a participant in the production and appreciation of art.*

Intellectual interests. *As we mentioned in Chapter 3, the art process and product help the individual to develop his mental resources. Art makes a* unique *contribution to intellectual development because it causes the individual to become aware of both discursive and nondiscursive information. The nondiscursive knowledge obtained from visual art is not obtainable from any other source. Furthermore, the art product provides its information instantaneously; it does not make knowledge available in sequential form over a period of time. Thus it offers the individual a* unique *point of view.*

Aesthetic interests. *Because art is inherently aesthetic, it involves the individual in the recognition, production, and appreciation of the aesthetic.*

Character. *Like all forms of expression, art helps the individual to give responsible direction to his own life because it provides some of the knowledge that it takes to make responsible decisions. Art is a model of the human condition; it provides possibilities for thinking, feeling and imagining. By making those alternatives available, it gives the individual a wider choice in what he wants to become. Thus it provides him with the freedom of mind that is so necessary for the full development of character.*

Human relationships

Respect for humanity. *As we mentioned in Chapters 2 and 3, art is a humanistic activity. As an individual produces or appreciates it, he exercises and becomes aware of those qualities within himself that identify him as a human being. By developing a greater awareness of his own strengths and weaknesses as a human animal, he comes to respect the human qualities in others. Art places a high value upon individuality. It fosters individuality and, consequently, causes its creator to respect uniqueness in others.*

Cooperation. *Before anyone can cooperate effectively with others, he must understand himself. The production of art brings about a greater understanding of the self through extensive concentration on one's own concepts and emotions. If a person does not have a clear understanding of himself, he cannot express himself clearly.*

Homemaking. *Art develops aesthetic capability. Such sensitivity and skill is useful in arranging and decorating the home.*

Economic efficiency

Work. *Art is work of a very high quality and requires the total involvement of the personality. By engaging in artistic production or appreciation the individual comes to know the satisfaction of good workmanship.*

Occupational information. *Many persons wish to be professional artists. Involvement with art helps them to understand the requirements and opportunities of the profession.*

Occupational efficiency. *An individual who wants to be an artist will stand a greater chance of succeeding in his chosen vocation if he engages in art activities while in school; he will become more efficient.*

Occupational appreciation. *To appreciate the social value of work in art, one must engage in its production or a study of its production. Art education provides this opportunity.*

Consumer judgment. *Because the production and appreciation of art require aesthetic sensitivity, it equips the individual with the standards of good taste for guiding his expenditures.*

Efficiency in buying. *As the producer and appreciator of art develops aesthetic standards, he becomes a more informed and skillful buyer. He is able to select items that have an appropriate appearance.*

Civic responsibility

Social justice. *Art requires sensitive observation, and sometimes that observation is aimed at the social scene. When it is, the creator and the appreciator become very much aware of the disparities of human circumstance. The chance that such awareness will develop through art is extremely good because the content of works of art is always some aspect of the human condition.*

Social activity. *Social activity is not always a matter of participating in civic groups. A writer, a playwright, or a painter who calls attention to unsatisfactory social conditions through his work is engaging in social activity. In fact, artists of all kinds frequently take the lead in such matters. Perhaps it is their unusual sensitivity to life that causes them to develop the conviction and the drive that produce eloquence.*

Social understanding. *The person who engages in artistic activity is always trying to comprehend the world around him, for his experience with the environment forms the content of his work. Because social structures and social processes are a vital part of his environment, the artistically involved person often grows to understand them.*

Critical judgment. *Art can be an extremely effective form of propaganda because of its pleasurable and its emotional qualities. Therefore, who would be more aware of propaganda and its damaging effects than the student of art? He may have a better defense against propaganda than anyone.*

Tolerance. *As we have already pointed out, art causes a person to be aware of his own strengths and weaknesses and of social justice. Such awareness is essential for the understanding and tolerance of others.*

If we accept the foregoing comments as accurate statements, it seems clear that art makes a significant contribution to the attainment of American educational objectives as they were formulated in 1938. But what can be said about the value of art in developing *rational power?*

*Fig. 7.2
Robert Gwathmey,
Southern Community. 1950.
Oil on canvas, 30 × 38 ⅛ in.
Collection, Krannert Art Museum,
University of Illinois, Champaign.
When art deals with the social scene,
the artist often becomes aware of
the disparities in human circumstances.*

Rational power

Again and again we have emphasized the idea that making and appreciating art are important ways of building conceptual, intellectual, or rational dimensions of mind. Involvement in art causes a person to perceive the visual aspects of life with intense, active perception of a kind that tends to build mental images of a conceptual nature. Visual images are partly discursive and partly nondiscursive, but it is the nondiscursive portion of that visual knowledge which is the unique contribution of artistic activity. Without information of that kind a person is less human than he might be; he is less intelligent, less free, and less able to realize his potential.

Perhaps we could also say that art is important to the rational activities of men because it helps them to learn about tools and

Fig. 7.3
Mitchell Siporin, Night Club.
1948. Pen and ink on white paper,
22 × 29 ⅝ in. When an artist deals
with the social scene, he grows
in his understanding of it.

materials and because it keeps thought within human bounds. By keeping thought within human bounds we mean that art tempers reason with feeling. When rationality ignores feeling or occurs in its absence, we are likely to reach conclusions that are highly accurate, but they may be so mechanistically rational that human beings cannot live with them. Therefore, in summary, we may say that art helps us to reach our educational goals. With that thought in mind, let us proceed to a discussion of the general aim of art education.

THE GENERAL AIM OF ART EDUCATION

It has been shown that art has value for the individual and for society, and the need for teaching it in the public schools has been demonstrated. Fortunately, we have also seen that it contributes to the attainment of educational objectives and that its contributions are in certain respects unique; for that reason it has a legitimate place in the school curriculum.

To reach educational objectives through art, however, a person must make and appreciate art. Thus the major aim of art education is the production of artists and connoisseurs of art. It seems incredible that we should have to emphasize an objective that seems so obvious, but art educators are fond of saying that the aim of art education is *not* the development of artists. This is nonsense. If art educators justify their subject by stressing the value of the art *process*, they must admit that one of their objectives is the production of artists. After all, a person is not engaged in an art process unless he produces art; and if he produces art, he is an artist.

By the same token, art instructors cannot logically justify their subject simply by pointing to the value of the art *product*. They must admit that they aim to develop connoisseurs. The reason for this is that the full value of an art object cannot be realized if people are incapable of making critical judgments about form and content. In other words, the art teacher must develop a competent sense of taste in his students if he intends to have them grow toward the good life in the presence of art objects.

Furthermore, the development of artists and critics of art is not apt to help in achieving some of the aims of education, as it has been claimed, unless the relationship between art learnings and other aspects of life is made absolutely clear. For example, instruction leading to the development of "picturers" and connoisseurs will not necessarily lead to better consumer purchases or to beautification of the home and community. This is because a transfer of training is not likely to occur without consciously striving for it. Transfer is apt to take place only if the principles of making and appreciating art are shown to apply in an important way to the objects and events of daily life as well as to the products and processes of the fine arts. Can this application be made?

The answer is yes. The principles of artistic organization, of design, or of composition can be applied to the way we dress, the way we landscape our yards, the way we talk, and the way we live our lives. One of the commonly known principles of artistic organization, for example, is that similar elements placed in proximity will be seen as a group rather than as single elements. Applied to daily living, this might mean that similar shrubs planted close to each other will be seen as a cluster of shrubbery and not as separate plants.

Another well-known principle of artistic composition is that a visual configuration must balance if it is to look and feel right or comfortable to human beings. As far as daily living is concerned, this might mean that we must avoid excesses of all kinds if we are to live the good life, a life that is to be judged as appropriate for the human animal.

But it may also be said that proximity, balance, and other principles of artistic organization have been applied to objects and events outside the fine arts for many years; so why should we make such a fuss over the transfer of those principles from art to life. The answer is that the principles of art have *not* been applied often enough or strongly enough to prevent the growth of man-made ugliness in our landscape and in our daily lives.

And when information about composition has been applied, it usually has been at a low level of competence and taste. Consequently, popular art, city planning, architecture, furniture, and many other man-made products present forms and values that are far less human than the spirit of man should permit. But to improve the aesthetic dimensions of life, we need to do more than produce designers and artists of greater competence. We need to produce competent judges of art and of *life* who will demand higher levels of expression from designers and artists. Then we shall have forms and models of the human condition that are suitable for men who think and feel at a level that is more than a step above the lower animals.

With these thoughts in mind, we may say that *the values of the art process and product can be attained and that the aims of education can be achieved by producing artists and connoisseurs of art and of life.* The next question that we must face is what subject matter to include in the art curriculum so that instruction may have its full effect in producing such individuals.

THE ART CURRICULUM

Ordinarily the education of the professional artist at the post-high school level is fostered through instruction in drawing, painting, print making, sculpture, or crafts. By working in one or more of those areas, the preprofessional college student develops the knowledge and skill that is needed to give pleasing aesthetic form to concepts and emotions. But he also needs a different kind of knowledge that will provide additional assistance in making competent judgments about visual symbols; this is usually provided through instruction in art history and aesthetics.

The professional connoisseur commonly receives a broad schooling at the collegiate level in art history and aesthetics, and he is often required to do studio work as well. The studio experience is included because it is felt that a full appreciation of art cannot be obtained without a first-hand knowledge of the problems encountered in creating objects for aesthetic experience.

But the amount of instruction that the critic must have in the productive aspects of art has never been determined.

When it comes to the education of artists and appraisers in the public school, it is important to remember that the objective is *not* the full development of specialists or professionals. The aim is to produce limners and critics with a knowledge and skill in art that is sufficiently broad and fundamental to permit a sensible interpretation of life and a learned judgment of life. The goal is the development of individuals with enough knowledge, skill, and taste to interpret or communicate the meanings of human experience through visual models; this means that those individuals will have enough taste to select the meanings of life that are most appropriate. They must also be able to judge the efficiency of the visual models that are meant to communicate those concepts and emotions. In addition, the goal of public schooling is the development of persons who can apply their artistic skill and taste to the problems of everyday existence that fall outside the arts. But if such individuals are nonspecialists, how should their education differ from that of a preprofessional artist or a preprofessional connoisseur?

The answer to the question hinges upon the nature of the professional in art. Fundamentally he is no different from the artist-housewife or the appreciator-mechanic. He simply acts as an artist and as a connoisseur more often and more effectively because it is his vocation and he is expected to act that way. If he differs from the nonprofessional, and he certainly does, it is merely a difference of degree, as indicated in Chapter 4. He is more sensitive to the dynamics of perception and to the elemental relationships in nature; he is more skillful; he has a better memory for visual forms; he is more self-confident; and he believes more strongly in the value of art and in the application of its principles to life situations.

If the difference between the professional and the nonprofessional artist and critic is simply one of degree, it seems reasonable to say that their education need not differ in any fundamental sense but merely in extent. In other words, the art instruction available to both the preprofessional and the nonprofessional

FORMULATING OBJECTIVES AND
BUILDING A CURRICULUM

would cover the same areas of content and skill, but the prospective specialist would select one or more of those areas for advanced study and practice. This experience with concentrated or delimited study would lead him to become a painter, a sculptor, an art historian, a critic, or a person with some other special talent in art. The youngster in the public school, by contrast, would be given instruction in the knowledge and skill basic to all the areas of specialization that are open to the prospective professional. He would receive training in drawing, painting, print making, sculpture, crafts, art history, and aesthetics. But the broad nature of the content would not allow him to qualify as a specialist. It would simply provide him with the knowledge and experience necessary for further work in art should he wish to continue. If he does, his training would give him a basis for making wise decisions about an area of specialization. If he chooses to remain a nonprofessional artist and connoisseur, the program of study would provide him with the knowledge and skill for enjoying the good life.

The current thinking in education, however, indicates that the full and efficient attainment of our goal to develop artists and appreciators is not destined to occur simply by offering instruction in the various dimensions of art. The reason for this is that the available bits of information related to drawing, painting, print making, sculpture, crafts, art history, and aesthetics are so numerous and so different in their relative importance that a teacher might easily present the least essential fragments of knowledge to his students. How shall we decide what is most important for the student to know about art as we teach the various dimensions of the subject?

Several criteria have been used by curriculum workers in selecting subject matter or content for instruction. Smith, Stanley, and Shores have listed five of the criteria for curriculum development that have been used alone or in combination in recent years.[9]

[9] B. O. Smith, W. O. Stanley, and J. H. Shores, *Fundamentals of Curriculum Development*, rev. ed., World Book Company, New York, 1957.

These five measures are presented below in question form:

1. *Is the subject matter significant to an organized field of knowledge?*
2. *Does the subject matter stand the test of survival?*
3. *Is the subject matter useful?*
4. *Is the subject matter interesting to the learner?*
5. *Does the subject matter contribute to the growth and development of a democratic society?*

Although contemporary educators use most of these criteria regularly, the current emphasis happens to be on the first one in the list. Educators maintain that the most significant thing for youngsters to know and the most important thing to teach is the structure of knowledge within each of the subjects in the curriculum. This means that it is most important to develop an understanding of the fundamental elements that give a subject its unique character. If the student is able to grasp those elements, his understanding will permit him to see relationships among the various fragments of knowledge within a given subject and will also allow him to see how the information in that subject is related to other branches of knowledge.

Jerome Bruner tells us that an understanding of structure will make the content of a subject more comprehensible, easier to remember, easier to apply to life situations, and less distant from the advanced knowledge in the field.[10] In other words, the rudiments of a subject are not only significant to an organized field of knowledge, but they have probably stood the test of survival and are more useful than other bits of information. If they are more useful, more comprehensible, and easier to remember, there is real hope that they can be made interesting to school children. Therefore, assuming that the rudiments of a discipline satisfy the criteria for selecting instructional content, what are the basic elements that constitute the structure of knowledge in art?

[10] Jerome Bruner, *The Process of Education*, Harvard University Press, Cambridge, 1963, pp. 23–26.

The structure of knowledge in art (the cognitive domain)

Five types of knowledge are basic to the production and appreciation of art. They were mentioned in Chapter 4 when we were discussing the nature of the artist and of the connoisseur. The first type of essential information is a *knowledge of life*, especially a knowledge of the aesthetic dimension of experience. If a person did not have that knowledge or imagery, he would have little or nothing to say about art and would be unable to make or judge artistic symbols.

The second type of knowledge that is basic to art is a *knowledge of composition*. A person must know what constitutes a pleasurable composition, or he will be unable to decide if his own work or the work of others is well organized.

A third type of essential information is a *knowledge of procedures*. Obviously, an artist must know how art objects are made, or he will be unable to make them or judge them adequately.

Information about *art history* is also basic to the making and appreciating of art. It gives the individual a perspective that helps him to make competent judgments about his own work and the work of others. Lacking such knowledge a person might make the mistake of thinking that a contemporary fur-lined teacup is a new and unique work of art.

The fifth type of information that is vital to the making or judging of art is a knowledge of aesthetics or knowledge of the *nature of art, the value of art, and the nature of aesthetic experience*. It is this type of understanding that allows a person to decide if visual symbols are actually works of art and helps him to estimate the relative value of the symbols that qualify as art objects. The artist need not reveal his understanding verbally, but it must appear in his work. A similar statement may be made about the connoisseur. He need not demonstrate his understanding of aesthetics in words, but he must show good taste in his judgments. There are many instances, however, when a connoisseur is called upon to justify his decisions, and on such occasions he must verbally disclose his aesthetic knowledge. For that reason, it is highly recommended that teachers strive for student verbalization of aesthetic knowledge.

If the foregoing types of knowledge are fundamental to the making and appreciating of art, we should ask ourselves if that knowledge must be developed through instruction in *each* of the dimensions of art (drawing, painting, print making, sculpture, crafts, art history, and aesthetics). After all, we cannot afford to pad a curriculum with instruction that is unnecessary.

The answer is that each dimension of art *must* be taught. Instruction in the productive dimensions, such as drawing and painting, provides the student with a knowledge of life as well as a knowledge of composition and procedures. The teaching of art history gives the student information about artists, art objects, and sequences of artistic production, and instruction in aesthetics provides information about the nature of art, the value of art, and the nature of aesthetic experience. Naturally, information about aesthetics is offered during the teaching of the productive dimensions of art, but much more information may be given if occasional class sessions are devoted exclusively to aesthetics. Hence we may say, in summary, that the elimination of instruction in any of the above dimensions of art would deprive the future artist and connoisseur of knowledge that is necessary for his full development.

But a person who shows that he is skilled and cultured in the visual arts is a person who has more than an *intellectual* acquaintance with the subject. He also possesses certain highly essential interests, attitudes, appreciations, values, and emotional sets or biases. Consequently, we must develop the most fundamental of those affective characteristics if we hope to build skilled draftsmen and learned appraisers in the visual arts. What is the basic structure of attitudes and values that a person must have if he is to succeed in the arts?

The structure of attitudes in art (the affective domain)

The four attitudes fundamental to the making and appreciating of art were mentioned in Chapter 4, but a brief repetition of them seems to be in order. The first of those necessary attitudes is an *interest in the aesthetic dimension of experience.* An interest, a set, or a bias in that direction is required if the individual is to perceive the shape of experience, the meaning of experience, and the relationship between them. If such things are not perceived, they cannot be included in visual symbols, and they cannot be appreciated.

The second attitude that is required is *confidence in one's ability to make and evaluate works of art.* Without self-confidence in such matters, a person is unlikely to engage in those activities.

The third attitude that is necessary is an *open-mindedness toward the different forms or styles that art might take.* This is especially important for the connoisseur because he cannot hope to appreciate a given aesthetic object if his mind is closed to the form, style, shape, or technique that constitutes that particular work of art. In some respects the artist would also be hampered by a lack of open-mindedness because it would limit the number of things that he could say with visual symbols.

The fourth necessary attitude is a *willingness to work hard and to persevere* until the task of creating or assessing is over. Hard work is especially vital to the development of skill in arranging art materials so that they present the meaning of experience in a pleasing aesthetic form.

The reference to skill indicates that creativity in art requires more than knowledge and attitude. What fundamental skills must a person have to be an artist?

The structure of skill in art (the psychomotor domain)

There is not much that can be said about skill in art. It is simply a matter of having sufficient eye-hand coordination to manipulate the many tools and materials of art efficiently. It is not absolutely necessary to be able to operate all the tools and materials associated with art, but such versatility is bound to increase the opportunities for expression.

Adapting the structure of art to the learner

Having listed the fundamental types of knowledge, attitude, and skill that are needed by the artist and connoisseur, it would be reasonable to ask if it is *possible* to teach or to develop those characteristics at *all* levels of the educational system. According to authorities, such as Bruner, "the foundations of any subject may be taught to anybody at any age in some form."[11] This is an idea that has been expressed by certain educators for more than two decades. It means, for example, that in teaching concepts of aesthetics the teacher could begin during the child's early years to offer him a rough notion of the nature of art; and during the course of the child's schooling, the teacher could gradually build upon that concept until the youngster has acquired a more complex idea of art. Similar examples could easily be drawn from other subject matter areas. For that reason contemporary educators are likely to agree that it is *possible* for the fundamental nature of content, attitude, and skill in art education to remain the same from kindergarten through high school, as long as it continues to become more complex. But these same educators are apt to disagree about the wisdom of developing *all* the rudiments of a subject at *all* levels of the educational program even if it is possible. Such a disagreement clearly exists on the question of teaching drawing, painting, print making, sculpture, crafts, art history, and aesthetics in each of the grades from kindergarten through high school. The position that a person takes in this argument depends upon how he views the purpose of elementary and secondary education, the nature of the specialist in art, and the nature of the child.

Broudy, Smith, and Burnett take the view that a mass society requires an elementary and secondary education that is both *general* and *common*.[12] This means they would remove from the curriculum any instruction that tends to be specialized or vocational in nature. Consequently, they would favor the elimination

---

[11] *Ibid.*, p. 12.
[12] Harry Broudy, B. O. Smith, and J. R. Burnett, *Democracy and Excellence in America Secondary Education*, Rand McNally and Company, Chicago, 1964.

of training in artistic performance from the secondary school because, in their opinion, it is vocational. Furthermore, they would remove such instruction from the regular secondary curriculum and place it in the extra curricular program because they believe that "for people without talent, such training rapidly reaches the point of diminishing returns, except perhaps on a hobby basis."[13] In its place, they would offer six years of value education or aesthetic education, by which they mean an education aimed at changing the student's values in the direction of those that are held by experts in aesthetics or by connoisseurs of life. To bring this about, instruction would focus on a highly select and limited number of recognized artistic masterpieces or exemplars. The study of such exemplars is recommended because aesthetic objects of high quality tend to invite inspection and to present accepted standards of value at the same time. Theoretically, this study would lead to a higher level of taste in art and in life.

Most art educators would heartily support the idea of value education through the study of exemplars in art, music, literature, and other modes of aesthetic discourse because they realize that training in art appreciation, art history, and aesthetics has been badly neglected. In fact, art educators have been so concerned about this neglect that they have been trying to create humanities programs in the public schools for a number of years. Consequently, any disagreement with Broudy and his colleagues exists because of their suggestion to remove artistic performance courses from the secondary curriculum and place them in the extracurricular program. Such action would mean eliminating the creative aspects of art from the lives of most children because few people ever participate in extracurricular programs other than sports. What are the arguments *against* the omission of art from the program?

To begin, Broudy, Smith, and Burnett make a mistake when they classify the teaching of such things as drawing and painting as a form of specialized or vocational instruction. Vocational

[13] *Ibid.*, p. 228.

education tends to emphasize the kind of information that can be replicated or applied "on the job." To a certain extent, of course, art education does involve the development of procedural knowledge and motor skill that can be used on the job in the same way as they were learned in class. But, like all the expressive arts, the process of drawing and painting leads to the assimilation of additional knowledge, attitudes, and values that are more correctly described as elements of general education; that is, such learnings are useful for interpreting life in general. They help us to perceive, understand, and feel life situations. They are the discursive and nondiscursive elements of experience that artists *must* come to know if they are to give them form in their art. They are concepts about the self and the environment that range from a knowledge of particular shapes, colors, and textures to a knowledge of peacefulness and how it reveals itself in things we see. They are the kinds of learnings that make a human life worth living and possible to understand. And they are the things that must be stressed in the teaching of drawing or painting, for they are the content, or the heart and soul, of all art. By contrast, the procedures and skills that a student learns are the grammatical aspects of the subject.

Obviously people who advocate the elimination of the productive aspects of art from the secondary school are not familiar with the process of making visual art. They seem to think that the only things to learn from the process are the tricks of manipulating a brush or a pencil, and they apparently believe that teaching art is simply a matter of telling or showing students how to perform a variety of those tricks. They simply fail to understand that the values so highly admirer in art objects are values that are placed there by the artist. And to do so, the artist has to study those values so that he can give them a shape that will be understood. Sometimes he actually discovers new concepts in the act of shaping old ones; but the point is that the artist learns about the values that are presented in his work. In fact, it is fairly obvious that the person who makes art learns more about its content than the man who looks at it, and the artist has the advantage of learning technical skills as well. Consequently, it does *not* makes sense to suggest, as Broudy does, that a general education can be obtained by looking at art and talking about it, but only a vocational or specialized education can be obtained by making it.

Those who would remove productive art from the secondary school would probably argue that great works of art present values that are more important and more profound than the values children learn as they give them shape in their art. Hence the opponents of drawing and painting would probably contend that it is more profitable, educationally, for children to *study* great works of art than it is for them to *make* mediocre works of art.

It is quite possible, of course, that artistic masterpieces *might* present values of greater significance simply because the masterpieces were produced by adults. But the history of art shows very clearly that great works of art do not necessarily deal with topics that are more complex or more profound than the topics handled by children. Compare, for example, the painting by Giotto in Figure 7.4 with the drawing by a junior high school student in Figure 7.5. Both works deal with the same topic, and one is about as important and profound as the other. If there is a difference, it is probably a difference in composition or technique. In other words, it is not *necessarily* the importance of the content that separates a masterpiece from a piece of child art.

On the other hand, it is definitely important for youngsters to study exemplars of great art because masterpieces often do present ways of thinking and feeling that might not be encountered in the making of child art. But the question is whether a high school student should be required to study the values of Giotto, Rembrandt, and other masters for six whole years without being required to develop and present his own values for inspection. After all, most of us know that a high school student is usually interested and concerned about *contemporary* life; and in a short time he will be helping to shape the values of his society. For that reason it seems very important to help young people discover what they really think and what they honestly feel about life as

they find it. And what could be a better way of discovering the self and the environment than making art? It not only causes them to learn about life, but it helps them to present their ideas with clarity, grace, and eloquence.

The argument that art training rapidly reaches a point of diminishing returns for people without talent is not valid and indicates that the persons offering the argument have not taught art. Those of us who teach art to elementary school teachers know that great improvement can and does occur if the instructor is interested in teaching everyone and is willing to put forth a little effort. The same may be said of art instruction in the elementary and secondary schools. If teaching *appears* to reach a point of diminishing returns, it is usually because the teacher is not willing to exert the effort that is required to help the slower students.

Another disagreement with Broudy and with other persons who share his views is a disagreement about the nature of the

Fig. 7.5
The content of this
drawing, by a girl in seventh grade,
is not much different from
the content of Fig. 7.4.

artist. He seems to consider any artist to be a professional, a person with capabilities that are sufficient to permit employment even if they are not used for that purpose. But the fact is that an individual can be an artist without reaching a professional level of competence. To become an artist, all a person has to do is produce a single work of art, and that hardly means that his capabilities are of a professional caliber. Probably his work would fall at the lower end of the art continuum and receive a rating of not-so-good. To be classified as a professional, however, his work would have to be good enough to fall near the superior end of the continuum. Yet the art instruction offered in the public school is not intended to raise the student's creative abilities to the superior level; it is given for the simple purpose of lifting visual expression to the artistic but nonprofessional plane.

Broudy, Smith, and Burnett would permit the teaching of drawing, painting, and the other productive dimensions of art in the elementary school, but art instruction is basically the same no matter where it is offered. Its purpose is to make artists out of nonartists. Consequently, it seems strange that anyone would omit art from the secondary curriculum because he considers it to be too highly specialized and then condone its presence in the elementary school. After all, the elementary school certainly is not the place for specialized or vocational education.

Still another criticism to be leveled at the Broudy proposal is that six years of value education could be viewed as specialized instruction, too, if one chooses to look at it that way. It could lead to the production of professional critics who replicate or apply their classroom learnings in life siuations just as they learned them in school. Actually, value education is as general as education is apt to become, but the point is that a person can view it as special education if he decides to look at certain characteristics and ignore others.

If we drop instruction in artistic performance from the secondary curriculum and replace it with six years of value education, we may, indeed, develop a nation of connoisseurs or critics of art and of life. Having more connoisseurs is highly desirable, but it seems equally desirable to help our people to become capable nonprofessional writers, poets, musicians, dancers, and artists. After all, why should we bother to develop learned critics of life if we do not train people so that they can *create* a better life when they recognize the need for it. To leave such creative matters entirely to professionals is to place enormous responsibility in the hands of very few people. It is already too apparent that we are producing a nation of spectators and passive picture watchers who can hiss, boo, cheer, and applaud at appropriate times. Learned spectators and judges are important, of course, but their importance will certainly diminish if we are left with no one who can play the game, no one who can paint the picture, and no one who can write the tune.

Furthermore, automation may enrich the average man with leisure in the next fifteen or twenty years. The hard work he now considers to be highly moral, manly, and vigorous is apt to disappear. What will take its place? What will be as rewarding and as valuable as work? Will the individual be satisfied to act as a passive spectator? Will it be good for him to spend his time criticizing life and the products of life? Will he help himself and society by writing critical essays on other men's paintings, the paintings from the days prior to automation and educated connoisseurs? Or would it be better for him to write, paint, and make music? In short, would it be better to criticize society or to create a better one? It is important to do both, is it not?

Finally, Broudy and his colleagues propose to drop art from the curriculum precisely at the point when youngsters begin consciously to act as artists. As Piaget has shown, children do not begin to think abstractly or to consider a variety of possibilities for solutions to problems until they reach the stage of formal operations (age eleven). As a result, they are not apt to present abstract ideas or emotions in their visual symbols, and they are not likely to ponder the numerous visual possibilities for presenting concepts and emotions until they reach the age of eleven or twelve. Youngsters under the age of twelve are capable of acting as artists, but they tend to do so intuitively. They are primarily concerned with the concrete content of their work and not with abstractions, with pleasing aesthetic qualities, or with the many ways of altering formal elements to communicate content. Consequently, elementary school children do not become sufficiently involved with the fine points of art at the conscious level to build a background of understanding appropriate for connoisseurs. By the same token, they do not progress far enough in art to make wise decisions about a specialization in the subject, if they should wish to continue. Thus it seems unwise to eliminate art from the secondary school program.

Recommendations. Obviously, the curricular recommendations to be made here will be different from those of Broudy, Smith, and Burnett, but only with regard to their suggestions about courses in artistic performance at the secondary level.

To begin, it is recommended that the structure of knowledge, attitude, and skill be developed in the elementary school through instruction in drawing, painting, print making, sculpture, crafts, art history, and aesthetics. It is suggested that all dimensions of the subject be taught in all the elementary grades because:

1. *The potential artist (professional or nonprofessional) needs a full understanding of the structure of art if he is to have the freedom to express a wide range of concepts and emotions.*

2. *The potential connoisseur (professional or nonprofessional) needs a broad background in the fundamentals of performance and appreciation if he is to make competent judgments about art and life.*

3. *A student who wishes to become a professional artist must have a broad background in the fundamentals of performance if he is to make wise decisions about an area of artistic specialization beyond high school.*

4. *A broad range of activities are necessary to give the elementary school program the variety that it must have to interest and challenge children for long periods of time.*

5. *Children are interested in all dimensions of art, and they are capable of learning about each of those areas if the content is adapted to their level of growth and development.*

6. *An individual learns more about himself and his environment by working with a number of different materials.*

7. *Young children use art as one of their primary ways of learning about themselves and about their environment.*

As far as the secondary school is concerned, it is recommended that students receive aesthetic education or value education through the study of exemplars from all the arts. This is the excellent suggestion made by Broudy, Smith, and Burnett. But, it is recommended, in addition, that students receive studio instruction in the creative aspects of art. Many activities may be pursued under the headings of drawing, painting, print making, sculpture, and crafts, but they should not include such semi-professionalized offerings as advertising design, dress design, industrial design, or cartooning. Instruction of such a specialized nature should not be included in the secondary school curriculum because it does not provide the general education that seems so appropriate for the common schools.

Furthermore, advertising design and other professionalized fields related to art do not provide the best vehicle for the teaching of art because they must take into consideration values that are not always in the best interest of art. In fact, there are some persons who might say that dress design and industrial design are not art activities because dresses and automobiles are not made primarily for aesthetic experience. And, in addition, most teachers are not equipped with training, experience, or classroom facilities to provide adequate professional training, even if it were desirable. After all, it is a constant chore for the public school teacher to stay abreast of the technical advancements in commercial art. If he falls behind, his students may have to unlearn what they were taught in the public school when they get to college.

The amount of aesthetic or value education and the amount of creative art education that is necessary and reasonable for the secondary school must still be determined. But it seems clear that six full years of art education at the secondary level will be required if we are to do a decent job of training nonprofessional artists and connoisseurs. Assuming that matters of scheduling and matters of balance are solved most satisfactorily in practice, let us turn our attention back to the question of the objectives of art education.

THE SPECIFIC AIMS OF ART EDUCATION

We may accept the notion that the major goal of art education is the development of artists and connoisseurs who have the appropriate knowledge, attitudes, and skills, and we may agree upon the basic curriculum most suitable for attaining that overall objective. But we still face the difficult task of stating our objective in a way that will be most helpful to the teacher in the public school. The task is difficult because objectives may be stated with different degrees of specificity, and we must try to articulate our goals in such a way that they are neither too general nor too detailed. The objectives of the Educational Policies Commissions are examples of aims that are too general to be of much help to a teacher except as a rough guide. The same is true of our suggestion that the teacher produce artists and connoisseurs. The idea is simply too broad to give the educator any notion of the *knowledge*, *attitudes*, and *skills* that he should foster at any particular grade level. On the other hand, an objective is too specific if it tells the teacher that youngsters should be able to paint pictures of their families, their classrooms, and their homes during their fourth and fifth weeks in the second grade. Goals as detailed as that should be determined by the teacher and his students.

Another difficulty that we face as we state our aims in a useful manner is that there are different levels of knowing and understanding, there are different levels of valuing, and there are different levels of psychomotor attainment. To make this clear, let us consider two examples.

On previous pages we listed the structure of knowledge, attitude, and skill that must be learned if students are to become artists and connoisseurs. We said that it is necessary to help students to *know* art history. But there is a big difference between knowing the terminology and specific facts associated with art history and knowing the theories and generalizations that are encompassed by the subject. In like manner, it is one thing to understand a subject well enough to translate readings into your own words and another thing to understand it well enough to analyze and evaluate your readings.

We also said that teachers must cause children to develop an *interest* in art. But there is a vast difference between interest that is mere awareness and interest that amounts to a commitment. If you are aware of something, you are simply conscious of it, but if you are committed to it, you seek it out and become involved in it.

From these examples we can see that the objectives of knowledge, attitude, and skill can be stated in ways that call for different levels of learning. These levels have been thoroughly described in two excellent handbooks, each of which is called *Taxonomy of Educational Objectives: The Classification of Educational Goals.*[14][15] The first handbook deals with the cognitive domain (knowing and understanding), and the second covers the affective domain (attitudes and values). Anyone interested in formulating objectives should consult these books so that he can see the importance of writing objectives in a way that makes the desired level of learning sufficiently clear. Two brief outlines of the taxonomies mentioned above are presented below to give the reader a notion of the levels of knowledge and attitude that people can attain. The lowest level of attainment appears at the top of each list, and the highest level appears at the bottom.

As we try to list the objectives of art education in a useful manner, it is obvious that we must make them appropriately specific and clear enough so that the teacher can tell what level of knowledge, attitude, and skill he is to achieve in his students. We must also make sure that our objectives are suitable for the child's level of physical, mental, and emotional development. We know that his physical development proceeds gradually from a state of awkwardness in kindergarten to a state of grace and coordination in high school. We know that his mental growth progresses from a preoccupation with concrete objects and events to an interest in abstract ideas and concepts. We know that the

[14] Benjamin Bloom (ed.), *Taxonomy of Educational Objectives, Handbook I: Cognitive Domain*, David McKay Company, Inc., New York, 1956.
[15] D. R. Krathwohl, B. S. Bloom, and B. M. Masia, *Taxonomy of Educational Objectives, Handbook II: Affective Domain*, David McKay Company, Inc., New York, 1964.

THE COGNITIVE DOMAIN (KNOWING AND UNDERSTANDING)[16]

KNOWLEDGE

Knowledge of specifics ∨

    Knowledge ot terminology
    Knowledge of specific facts

Knowledge of ways and means of dealing with specifics

    Knowledge of conventions
    Knowledge of trends and sequences
    Knowledge of classifications and categories
    Knowledge of criteria
    Knowledge of methodology

Knowledge of the universals and abstractions in a field

    Knowledge of principles and generalizations
    Knowledge of theories and structures

INTELLECTUAL ABILITIES AND SKILLS

Comprehension

    Translation
    Interpretation
    Extrapolation

Application

Analysis

    Analysis of elements
    Analysis of relationships
    Analysis of organizational principles

Synthesis

    Production of unique communication
    Production of a plan, or proposed set of operations
    Derivation of a set of abstract relations

Evaluation

    Judgments in terms of internal evidence
    Judgments in terms of external evidence

[16] Bloom, *op. cit.*, pp. 201–207. (Used by permission of David McKay Company, Inc.) `

THE AFFECTIVE DOMAIN (ATTITUDES AND VALUES)[17]

RECEIVING (ATTENDING)	Awareness Willingness to receive Controlled or selected attention
RESPONDING	Acquiescence in responding Willingness to respond Satisfaction in response
VALUING	Acceptance of a value Preference for value Commitment
ORGANIZATION	Conceptualization of a value Organization of a value system
CHARACTERIZATION BY A VALUE OR VALUE COMPLEX	Generalized set Characterization

very young child is highly egocentric and dependent and that he becomes more socially conscious and more independent as he grows older. And we know that his artistic development proceeds through the stages described in Chapter 5.

If we take all these difficulties or considerations into account, it is clear that we must specify the behavior to be expected of a child artist and child critic at as many levels of the educational system as we can. This is necessary because the kind of behavior we expect from the child artist and critic is sure to change as he grows and develops. Major changes in growth and development do not occur rapidly, however, as we have learned from our

[17] Krathwohl, Bloom, and Masia, *op. cit.*, pp. 176-185. (Used by permission of David McKay Company, Inc.).

study of symbolic development. For that reason we shall not attempt to list the aims of art education for each grade in the public school. Instead, we shall outline the specific behavior to be attained at the major points of change in symbolic development. This fixes our attention on the child as *enters* the first, fourth, seventh, and tenth grades. And as we list the goals for those grade levels, we will also indicate what kind of growth is revealed by the attainment of each objective. In other words, the information in parentheses (at the end of each objective) indicates what kind of knowledge, attitude, or skill is revealed by the behavior described. Such information should be helpful to the teacher when he wishes to evaluate the student's progress in art. Additional help with evaluation is provided in Chapter 10.

Nursery school and kindergarten

1. On entering the first grade the educated child is able to behave like an artist:

> (a) By *making his own understandable symbols for his concepts*. He should be able to represent rudimentary concepts of the ordinary objects, events, or qualities that are most familiar to him. Symbols for man, house, tree, redness, or greenness are examples. (This indicates a *knowledge of life* or a conceptual imagery that is necessary as content in art.)

> (b) By *communicating his emotional reaction* to qualities, objects, events, or parts of objects and events through the exaggeration, omission, or inclusion of visual symbols for those items. In other words, he is able to show such things as happiness, unhappiness, or the importance of certain things by changing the shape or direction of lines or by exaggerating, omitting, or including things. A big head, for example, might indicate the importance of the head, and tears might suggest sadness. (This indicates a knowledge of or sensitivity to the emotional dimension of life. A *knowledge of life* is necessary as content in art.)

(c) By *producing a configuration* that appears to have a relationship to the area of experience that the child *intended*. In other words, the child's symbol for a cow should appear to have *some* relationship to a cow. (This is a sign that the child possesses a *knowledge of life* and the *skill* to give it form.)

(d) By *arranging his visual symbols so that the organizational structure or composition is pleasing*. Perhaps the most that can be expected at this point is a balanced composition that seems to require no major organizational changes. The configuration should appear to be finished or complete. (If the basic arrangement is pleasing to the spectator, the child possesses a *knowledge or awareness of composition* that is necessary for art.)

(e) By *producing symbols in which the technique or the manipulation of materials is pleasing and unobtrusive*. The tools and materials that a youngster in the preprimary grades should be able to use efficiently are listed in Chapter 9. Probably the most that can be expected at this point is that the child's work not appear so dirty, messy, or uncontrolled that it is *especially* displeasing. (If the child can do this, while accomplishing the other things on this list, he posesses the *knowledge of procedures* and the *skill* that are required in art. It also may indicate a sensitivity to composition.)

(f) By *giving proper care to the tools and materials he uses*; by gathering the necessary items and returning them to their proper places; and by following a procedure that is in keeping with the nature of the tools and materials that he is using. (These behaviors indicate that the youngster has a *knowledge of procedure* that is conducive to art.)

(g) By *achieving the foregoing results independently*, without inhibition and without constant help from anyone. (If he can do this, it indicates that his *attitude* toward art is one of *interest* and *confidence*.)

(h) By *displaying satisfaction with his own visual symbols.* (Doing this is a sign that his *attitude* is one of *interest* and *confidence*.)

(i) By *working intently at the foregoing tasks for at least twenty to thirty minutes.* (Doing this is evidence that his *attitude* is one of *interest, confidence,* and *willingness to work hard.*)

(j) By *doing the things that are expected of a connoisseur.*

2. On entering the first grade, the educated child is able to behave like a connoisseur of art and of life:

(a) By *recognizing* and *naming* the *formal elements* in art and in the rest of the visual environment. The formal elements are color, texture, line, shape, and volume. Thus the child should recognize and name such things as the primary and secondary colors, plus black, white, and gray; rough and smooth textures; long, short, wide, and thin lines. He should recognize the difference between a shape and a color, and he should recognize large and small volumes. (This reveals a *knowledge of life* and a *knowledge of compositional elements.*)

(b) By *recognizing an especially displeasing visual composition.* (This shows a *knowledge of composition.*)

(c) By *recognizing* and *naming* the *tools* and *materials* he uses in visual symbolization. (This shows a *knowledge of procedure.*)

(d) By *describing* the various *procedures* he has encountered for making visual art. (This reveals a *knowledge of procedures* as well as *skill* in verbalization.)

(e) By *responding verbally and enthusiastically to the meanings* or expressive qualities that exist in the "look" of common objects, including visual symbols and works of art of all kinds. In other words, the child should be able to show that he sees happiness, coldness, men, dogs, blue, red, etc. Probably the most that we can expect is that he will perceive meanings that take a concrete form. This means that he is likely to see unhappiness if a person is pictured with tears in his eyes, but the child is not apt to see unhappiness if it is represented in an abstract manner. Furthermore, the child's responses to art are likely to be associative or subjective in nature (see page 175). (This indicates *interest* in the aesthetic, shows *self-confidence*, and reveals a *knowledge of life*.)

(f) By *responding (recognizing and describing) verbally and enthusiastically to the formal qualities (color, texture, line, shape, volume) in a variety of common objects,* including visual symbols and works of art of all kinds. (This indicates *interest* in the aesthetic and shows *self-confidence*.)

(g) By *recognizing and accepting a variety of styles in art.* (This shows an *attitude of interest* as well as *tolerance toward style*, and it reveals a *knowledge of aesthetics*.)

(h) By *talking about the nature of art, the value of art, and the job of the artist*. This will be done at a very elementary level, but the information should be accurate. The child might say, for example, that art is drawing, painting, or making pictures; it is good because it helps us to see and understand things; and the artist is a person who makes pictures. (This indicates a *knowledge of aesthetics* and shows *verbal skill*.)

(i) By *behaving independently* in the ways that have been indicated, without inhibition and without constant help from anyone. (This shows an *attitude of interest and confidence*.)

(j) By *displaying satisfaction with his own comments or judgments* about visual configurations of all kinds, including works of art. (This is a sign that his *attitude* toward the aesthetic is one of *interest and confidence*.)

(k) By *engaging in the foregoing verbal tasks for at least ten to twenty minutes*. (This indicates an *attitude of interest, confidence*, and a *willingness to work hard*.)

(l) By *using a basic vocabulary* that permits the foregoing discussions, and by doing so with relative ease. (This indicates a full range of artistic *knowledge* as well as *skill* as a connoisseur.)

The primary grades

Teachers in the primary grades also should read the objectives for nursery school and kindergarten. It will help them to see the similarities and differences between grade-level objectives and it will be helpful in evaluation. Further assistance with evaluation is offered in Chapter 10.

1. On entering the fourth grade, the educated child is able to behave like an artist:

(a) By *making his own understandable symbols for his concepts*. He should be able to represent concepts of the ordinary objects, events, or qualities that are most familiar to him. And each individual symbol (tree, house, man) should be more detailed than it was in the preprimary grades. This does not mean that we should expect highly naturalistic art from the child, but it means that his work should be more naturalistic than it was in the preprimary grades. Furthermore, we should expect to see a more naturalistic spatial organization. By this, we mean that a child should be able to show elemental relationships of proximity,

295

separation, and enclosure similar to those that exist in visual reality. He should be able to show the continuity of an unbroken line and he should be able to show the order or sequence in which things naturally appear. For example, he should be able to show eyes enclosed in a face, but close to the nose and separate from it; he should be able to show the eyes, nose, and mouth in their natural order from top to bottom; and he should be able to show the continuity of a ground line. A greater understanding of the spatial relationship *among* objects should also be revealed, but we should not expect the representation of complex or highly naturalistic relationships. The most we can expect is that objects will be related to each other through placement on a base line.

The characteristics mentioned above are to be expected in drawing, but the child is not likely to proceed *quite* so far if he uses big brushes, paper, wood, or other materials that are more difficult to manage or more difficult to shape into detailed configurations.

The above objective should *not* lead the teacher to believe that he should teach a child to draw naturalistically or to draw objects on a base line. It simply means that if the teacher does his job in developing the child's knowledge of life, visual configurations of the kind we have described will naturally follow. (If the child produces work of the kind we have described, it indicates a *knowledge of life* and a *knowledge of natural composition*.)

(b) By *producing a total visual configuration that occasionally includes symbols for several objects*. In other words, it would be realistic to expect the child to make symbols for more things than he did in the preprimary grades. (This indicates a growing *knowledge of life*, and it shows *skill*.)

(c) By *communicating his emotional reaction* to qualities, objects, events, or parts of objects and events through the exaggeration, omission, or inclusion of visual symbols for those items. In other words he is able to show such things as happiness, sadness, or the importance of certain things by changing the shape or direction of lines or by exaggerating, omitting, or including things. A big head, for example, might indicate the importance of the head, while tears might suggest sadness. (This indicates a *knowledge of* or a *sensitivity to the emotional dimension of life*.)

(d) By *producing a configuration that appears to have a relationship* to the area of experience that the child *intended*. In other words, the child's symbol for a cow or a street should appear to have *some* relationship to a cow or a street. (This is a sign that the child possesses a *knowledge of life* and the *skill* to give it form.)

(e) By *arranging his visual symbols so that the organizational structure or composition is pleasing.* This means that the composition should balance; it should contain pleasant proportional relationships similar to those found in nature; it should have unity and variety; and it should seem finished or complete. Ordinarily, the child will produce such symbols intuitively. If he does not, the teacher should try to give assistance in the manner suggested in Chapters 8 and 9. The child also should be expected to produce pleasurable arrangements when he organizes a bulletin board, a science corner, or some other display. But pleasurable compositions are not to be expected on all occasions, especially if the child is confronted with a wholly new task, new tools, or new materials.

The classroom teacher who is unfamiliar with composition may judge it by asking himself if the configuration is interesting and pleasing in its arrangement (not its content). If it seems that something should be changed to make it less disturbing, the objective has not been reached. (Behavior of this kind is an indication of a *knowledge* or *awareness of composition*.)

(f) By *producing symbols in which the technique or the manipulation of materials is pleasing and unobtrusive.* The tools and materials that a youngster in the primary grades should be able to use efficiently are listed in Chapter 9. The child's work should not appear dirty, messy, uncontrolled, unfinished, or strained. If it is three-dimensional, it should not appear weak, unstable, or poorly constructed. In other words, the craftsmanship should not be irritating. (This is a sign that the child possesses a *knowledge of procedures* and *skill* in managing tools and materials. It also may indicate a sensitivity to composition.)

(g) By *giving the proper care to tools and materials*; by gathering the necessary items and returning them to their proper places; and by following a procedure that is in keeping with the nature of the tools and materials that he is using. (This shows that the youngster has a *knowledge of procedure* that is conducive to art.)

(h) By *using formal elements (colors, textures, lines, shapes, volumes) that are a little more complex* than those used in the preprimary grades. This means that the child should be able to mix colors, produce different textures, make different kinds of lines and shapes, and construct volumes of different sizes and contours. (This shows *skill*, a *knowledge of life,* and a *knowledge of procedures.*)

(i) By *achieving the foregoing results independently*, without inhibition and without constant help from anyone. (This signals an *attitude* of *interest* and *confidence* toward art.)

(j) By *occasionally making art, when he is not required to do so.* (This indicates an *attitude of interest, confidence,* and *willingness to work* or to *practice.*)

(k) By *displaying satisfaction* with his own visual symbols. (This is a sign that his *attitude* is one of *interest* and *confidence.*)

(l) By *working intently* at the foregoing tasks for *at least thirty to forty-five minutes*. (This is evidence that his *attitude* is one of *interest, confidence,* and *willingness to work hard*.)

(m) By *doing the things that are expected of a connoisseur*.

2. On entering the fourth grade the educated child is able to behave like a connoisseur of art and of life:

(a) By *recognizing and naming the formal elements* in art and in the rest of the visual environment. The formal elements are color, texture, line, shape, and volume. Thus, the child should recognize and name such things as the primary, secondary, and intermediate colors, and he should be able to describe how they are made. He should be able to detect and name different textures (rough, smooth, shiny, dull, etc.), lines (long, short, wide, light, dark, gentle, bold, etc.), shapes (circles, triangles, squares, free, animal, etc.), and volumes (large, small, cube, cone, sphere, etc.). (This reveals a *knowledge of life* and a *knowledge of compositional elements*.)

(b) By *recognizing an especially displeasing visual composition* of any kind, including an unusually *displeasing* aspect of the *environment*. (This indicates a *knowledge of composition*.)

(c) By *recognizing* and *naming* the *tools* and *materials* he uses in visual symbolization. (This shows a *knowledge of procedure*.)

(d) By *describing* the various *procedures* he has encountered for making visual art. (This reveals a *knowledge of procedures* as well as *skill* in verbalization.)

(e) By *responding verbally and enthusiastically to the meanings* or expressive qualities that exist in the "look" of common objects, including visual symbols and works of art of all kinds. In other words, the child should be able to show that he sees happiness, coldness, men, dogs, blue, red, etc. Probably he will see more details than a preprimary child, but, in general, the most that we can expect is that he will see meanings that take a concrete form. This means that he is likely to see unhappiness if a person is pictured with tears in his eyes, but he is not apt to see unhappiness if it is represented in an abstract manner. Furthermore, the child's responses to art are likely to be associative or subjective in nature (see page 175). (This shows an *attitude of interest* in the aesthetic, a *knowledge of life*, and an *attitude of self-confidence*.)

(f) By *responding (recognizing and describing) verbally and enthusiastically to the formal qualities (color, texture, line, shape, volume) in a variety of common objects*, including works of art. (This indicates *interest* in the *aesthetic*, and it shows *confidence*.)

(g) By *recognizing and accepting a variety of styles in art*. (This shows an *attitude of interest* as well as one of *tolerance toward style*, and it reveals a *knowledge of aesthetics*.)

(h) By *discussing the nature of art and the value of art and by offering a point of view about such things in his own words*. He might be expected to say that art is a beautiful way of telling other people what you know, think, or feel. And its value is that it helps us to know things that we would not know if there were no art. A child also might be expected to know that a rock or tree is different from a painting because it does not tell us what a person knows, thinks, or feels. (This kind of behavior indicates a *knowledge of aesthetics* and reveals *verbal skill*.)

(i) By *discussing artists* (what they do, where they work, what kind of people they are, why they do what they do). The information that the child offers should be accurate, of course, and it should indicate some understanding of the old masters as well as contemporary artists. (This is evidence that the child has a *knowledge of aesthetics and of art history* as well as an *attitude of interest* and *verbal skill*.)

(j) By *recognizing and naming the various art forms* (drawing, painting, sculpture, printing, and crafts). (This is a sign that he possesses a *knowledge of procedures* and *aesthetics*.)

(k) By *verbally indicating an understanding that there is a history of art* and that art in the past has taken different forms and served a variety of purposes. He might be expected to know some of the purposes that it served. (This shows a *knowledge of art history and aesthetics*.)

(l) By *behaving independently* in the ways that have been indicated without constant help from anyone. (This shows an *attitude of interest* and *confidence*.)

(m) By *displaying satisfaction with his own comments* or *judgments* about visual configurations of all kinds, including works of art. (This is a sign that his *attitude* toward the aesthetic is one of *interest* and *confidence*.)

(n) By *engaging* in the foregoing *verbal tasks* for at least *twenty to thirty minutes*. (This indicates an *attitude of interest* and *confidence*, and a *willingness to work hard*.)

(o) By *using a basic vocabulary* that permits the foregoing discussions, and by doing so with relative ease. (This indicates a full range of relevant *knowledge* as well as *skill* as a connoisseur.)

The intermediate grades

Teachers in the intermediate grades also should read the objectives for the primary level. It will help them to see the similarities and differences between grade-level objectives and will be helpful in making evaluations. Further assistance with evaluation is offered in Chapter 10.

1. On entering the seventh grade, the educated child is able to behave like an artist:

> (a) By *making his own understandable symbols for his concepts.* He should be able to represent concepts of most of the objects, events, or qualities that are familiar to him. And, each individual symbol (tree, house, man, etc.) should be more detailed or more naturalistic than it was in the primary grades. We should not expect photographic naturalism, of course, but the symbols should be naturalistic enough that parts removed from the whole still retain their meaning (i.e., an arm removed from the figure of a man should still look like an arm). Furthermore, we should expect to see a more naturalistic spatial organization. By this we mean that a child should be able to show relationships of proximity, separation, and enclosure similar to those that exist in visual reality; he should be able to show the continuity of an unbroken line or surface; he should be able to show the order or sequence in which things naturally appear; and he should be able to show depth or perspective.
>
> In other words, the child should be able to present the idea that some things are enclosed by other things, close to other things, and separate from other things. He also should be able to show the sequential order of parts or wholes as they occur in visual reality, such as the order of houses on a street, and he should be able to show the continuity of hat, head, neck, torso, legs, feet, and ground (i.e., the sequence is not broken).
>
> A greater understanding of the proportional relationship among objects also should be evident. By this we mean that less exaggeration should be expected and that the size relationships among objects should closely resemble the relationships found in nature (i.e., heads should be smaller,

not larger, than bodies; people should be smaller than houses; etc.).

In addition, the child should be expected to show depth by overlapping, by varying the size of objects, by manipulating color, and by locating objects on a plane instead of placing them on a base line.

The characteristics mentioned above are to be expected in drawing and painting, but the child is not likely to proceed *quite* so far if he uses big brushes, paper, wood, or other materials (especially unfamiliar ones) that are more difficult to manage or are more difficult to shape into detailed configurations.

The above objective should *not* lead the teacher to believe that he should teach a child to create naturalistic art. It simply means that if the teacher is doing his job in developing the child's knowledge of life, visual configurations of the kind we have described will naturally follow. (If the child produces work of the kind we have described, it indicates a *knowledge of life* and a *knowledge of natural composition*.)

(b) By *producing a total visual configuration that occasionally includes symbols for several objects.* In other words, it would be realistic to expect the child to make symbols for more things than he did in the primary grades, and it is realistic to expect a more complex relationship among those things. (This indicates a growing *knowledge of life* and demonstrates *skill*.)

(c) By *communicating his emotional reaction* to qualities, objects, events, or parts of objects and events through the *exaggeration, omission, inclusion, or detailed treatment* of visual symbols for those items. In other words he is able to show such things as happiness, sadness, terror, or the importance of certain things by manipulating shapes, lines, and colors or by exaggerating, omitting, including, or giving more detail to things. Exaggeration, however, is not to be expected as much as detailed treatment. A detailed truck, for example, is to be expected if the truck is more important than other elements in a picture. (This indicates a *knowledge of* or a *sensitivity to the emotional dimension of life*.)

(d) By *producing a configuration that appears to have a relationship* to the area of experience that the child *intended*. In other words, the child's symbol for a cow or a street should appear to have a rather close relationship to a cow or a street. (This is a sign that the child possesses a *knowledge of life* and the *skill* to give it form.)

(e) By *creating symbols that include the identifying characteristics* of particular persons (doctors, soldiers, football players), trees (pine, maple, willow), trucks, airplanes, and other objects. (This indicates a *knowledge of life*.)

(f) By *arranging his visual symbols so that the organizational structure or composition is pleasing*. This means that the composition should balance; it should contain pleasant proportional relationships similar to those found in nature; it should have unity and variety; and it should seem finished or complete. Ordinarily, the child's intuitive sense of design does not prevail at this stage in his life because other factors capture his attention (i.e., he is interested in presenting information accurately). Consequently, we can expect the child to create pleasing compositions most readily (1) when he gives *conscious* attention to composition, and (2) when he is involved in an artistic activity that does not call for much representation.

The child also should be expected to produce pleasurable arrangements when he organizes a bulletin board, a science corner, or some other display. But pleasurable compositions are not to be expected on all occasions, especially if the child is confronted with a wholly new task, new tools, or new materials.

The classroom teacher who is unfamiliar with composition

may judge it by asking himself if the configuration is interesting and pleasing in its arrangement (not its content). If it seems that something should be changed to make it less disturbing, the objective has not been reached. (Behavior of this kind indicates a *knowledge of composition*.)

(g) By *producing symbols in which the technique or the manipulation of materials is pleasing and unobtrusive*. The tools and materials that a youngster should be able to use are listed in Chapter 9. The child's work should not appear dirty, messy, uncontrolled, unfinished, strained, or over-worked. If it is three-dimensional, it should not appear weak, unstable, or poorly constructed. He should be able to fasten things together that are as difficult to fasten as the parts of a *simple* model airplane. In other words, the craftsmanship should not be irritating. (This is a sign that the child posessesses a *knowledge of procedures* and *skill* in managing tools and materials. It also may indicate a sensitivity to composition.)

(h) By *giving the proper care to tools and materials*; by gathering the necessary items and returning them to their proper places; and by following a procedure that is in keeping with the nature of the tools and materials that he is using. (This shows that the youngster has a *knowledge of procedure*.)

(i) By *using formal elements (colors, textures, lines, shapes, volumes) that are a little more complex* than those used in the primary grades. This means that the child should be able to mix primary, secondary, and intermediate colors; he should be able to mix light, dark, bright, and dull colors; he should produce a wide variety of textures, lines, and shapes; and he should construct volumes of different sizes and contours; and he should be able to fasten the volumes together to make a more complex whole. (This shows *skill*, a *knowledge of life*, and a *knowledge of procedure*.)

(j) By *achieving the foregoing results independently*, without inhibition and without constant help from anyone. (This signals an *attitude* toward art that is one of *interest* and *confidence*.)

(k) By *making art, occasionally, when he is not required to do so*. (This indicates an *attitude of interest, confidence*, and a *willingness to work or to practice*.)

(l) By *displaying satisfaction with his own visual symbols*. (This is a sign that his *attitude* is one of *interest* and *confidence*.)

(m) By *working intently* at the foregoing tasks *for at least forty-five to seventy-five minutes*. (This is evidence of an *attitude of interest, confidence*, and a *willingness to work hard*.)

(n) By *doing the things that are expected of a connoisseur*.

2. On entering the seventh grade, the educated child is able to behave like a connoisseur of art and of life:

(a) By *recognizing and naming the formal elements* in art and in the rest of the visual environment, and by doing so *with fewer errors* than he did in the primary grades. The formal elements are color, texture, line, shape, and volume. Thus the child should recognize and name such things as the primary, secondary, and intermediate colors, and he should be able to describe how they are made. He should be able to detect and name different textures (rough, smooth, shiny, dull, etc.), lines (long, short, wide, light, dark, gentle, bold, etc.), shapes (circles, triangles, squares, diamonds, octagons, free forms, animal forms, etc.), and volumes (large, small, cube, cone, sphere, hemisphere, etc.). The child should also be able to recognize and name the effect that one formal element has on another. In other words, he should see and say that green looks greener on a red background than it does on a green background, and he should detect other such relationships. (This indicates a *knowledge of life* and a *knowledge of composition*.)

(b) By *recognizing and naming the approximate value and intensity of colors* (light, dark, bright, dull). He should also be able to describe how to change the value or intensity of colors. (This shows a *knowledge of life, compositional elements*, and *procedures*.)

(c) By *recognizing a displeasing visual composition* of any kind, *including a displeasing aspect of the environment*, and by describing a way in which that structural organization might be improved. (This indicates a *knowledge of composition* as well as *verbal skill*.)

(d) By *recognizing and naming* the *tools* and *materials* that he uses in visual symbolization. (This shows a knowledge of procedures.)

(e) By *describing the various procedures that he has encountered for making visual art*. (This reveals a *knowledge of procedures* as well as *skill* in verbalization.)

(f) By *responding verbally and enthusiastically to the meanings* or expressive qualities that exist in the "look" of common objects, including visual symbols and works of art. In other words, the child should be able to show that he sees happiness, fatigue, men, cats, blueness, redness, etc. He will see details and subtlties of meaning that youngsters in the primary grades will miss, but, in general, the most that we can expect is that he will see meanings that take a concrete form. This means that he is likely to see depth if it is produced through naturalistic representation, but he is not apt to see it if it is produced in a nonobjective or nonfigurative manner. Furthermore, the child's responses to art are likely to be associative or subjective in nature. But a few of them probably will be of the character or objective type (see page 175). (This shows an *attitude of interest in the aesthetic*, a *knowledge of life*, and an *attitude of self-confidence*.)

(g) By *responding (recognizing and describing) verbally and enthusiastically* to the *formal qualities* (color, texture, line, shape, volume) in a variety of common objects, including works of art. (This indicates *interest in the aesthetic* and shows *confidence*.)

(h) By *recognizing and accepting a variety of styles in art*. (This shows an *attitude of interest* as well as *tolerance toward style*, and it reveals a *knowledge of aesthetics*.)

(i) By *discussing the nature of art and the value of art* and by offering a point of view about such things in his own words. He might be expected to say that art is the shaping of ideas and feelings primarily for the purpose of having them seen or observed. Consequently, art communicates ideas and feelings, and it does so especially well because it is beautifully organized. In fact, the beauty of its structure tends to separate it from other forms of communication. Its value, of course, is that it presents information that can only be presented in visual form.

The child should also be able to explain the value that art has in education, business, social relations, and in the field of propaganda. And he should be able to explain how art differs from rocks, trees, automobiles, and from other instances of nonart. (This kind of behavior indicates a *knowledge of aesthetics* and reveals *verbal skill*.)

(j) By *discussing artists* (what they do, where they work, what kind of people they are, why they do what they do, what the future holds in store for them). The information that the child offers should be accurate, of course, and it should indicate familiarity with a selected group of artists from the past and present. The group might include Giotto, Paolo Uccello, Leonardo da Vinci, Michelangelo, Rembrandt, Daumier, Cézanne, Van Gogh, Kandinsky, Matisse, Braque, and a limited selection of past and present American artists. (This indicates a *knowledge of aesthetics and art history* as well as an *attitude of interest* and *verbal skill.*)

(k) By *recognizing and naming the various art forms* (drawing, painting, sculpture, printing, and crafts). The child also should be able to identify a *few* different kinds of painting (watercolor, oil), sculpture (kinetic, wood, plaster, steel, plastic, etc.), printing (wood block, etching, silk screen), and crafts (pottery, weaving, jewelry, etc.). (This is a sign that he possesses a *knowledge of both procedures and aesthetics.*)

(l) By *recognizing, naming, and discussing the art from the major periods of art history* (primitive, Egyptian, Greek, Roman, Medieval, Renaissance, eighteenth-century European, modern European, American). The child should indicate through his comments that he has a little understanding of the purposes that art served during each of the major historical periods. (This shows a *knowledge of art history and aesthetics.*)

(m) By *revealing verbally that he has an understanding of the function of museums.* (This indicates a *knowledge of art history and aesthetics.*)

(n) By *behaving independently* in the ways that have been indicated, without inhibition, and without constant help from anyone. (This shows an *attitude of interest and confidence.*)

(o) By *displaying satisfaction with his own comments or judgments* about visual configurations of all kinds, including works of art. (This is a sign that he has an *attitude of interest and confidence* toward the aesthetic.)

(p) By *engaging in* the foregoing *verbal tasks* for *at least thirty* to *forty-five minutes*. (This indicates an *attitude of interest*, *confidence*, and *willingness to work hard*.)

(q) By *using a basic vocabulary* that permits the foregoing discussions, and by doing so with relative ease. (This indicates a full range of relevant *knowledge*, as well as *skill as a connoisseur*.)

Junior high school

Teachers in the junior high school also should read the objectives for the intermediate level. It will help them to see the similarities and differences between grade-level objectives, and it will be helpful in evaluation. Further assistance with evaluation is offered in Chapter 10.

1. On entering the tenth grade, the educated adolescent is able to behave like an artist:

(a) By *making his own understandable symbols for his concepts*. He should be able to represent concepts of most of the objects, events, or qualities that are familiar to him. It is reasonable to expect the child to be *able* to make symbols that are more naturalistic than those that were made in the intermediate grades, but it is not reasonable to expect naturalistic art of a more complex nature from all youngsters all the time. It is more appropriate to expect art forms to range from the nonobjective to the highly naturalistic. This is because the student's intentions are likely to involve the expression of ideas of a more abstract nature, and that is likely to result in a wider variety of art forms.

We should expect the student to use his art forms as a means of arousing or influencing the observer and not merely as a means of presenting descriptive information. In other words, the content of his work is apt to be humorous, satirical, shocking, or propagandistic. (Behavior of this kind indicates a *knowledge of life*.)

(b) By *communicating his emotional reaction* to experience through the *conscious* manipulation of many formal elements and the meaningful qualities that they possess. This means that he might use yellow-green to give a feeling of sickliness or blue to produce calmness. He might be expected to shade colors to create eeriness, or he might exaggerate a nose and ears to make a person seem funny. He can be expected to do this much more frequently than he did in the intermediate grades. (This indicates a *knowledge of the emotional dimension of life*.)

(c) By *producing a configuration that appears to have a relationship* to the area of experience that the student *intended*. In other words, his symbols for horses, terror, or kindness should have a close relationship to those things. (This is a sign that the student possesses a *knowledge of life* and the *skill* to give it form.)

(d) By *making symbols that include the identifying characteristics of particular persons* (doctors, soldiers, etc.) *if* he wishes to produce symbols of particular persons. (This indicates a *knowledge of life*.)

(e) By *arranging his visual symbols so that the organizational structure or composition is pleasing*. This means that the composition should balance; it should contain pleasant proportional relationships similar to those found in nature; it should have unity and variety; and it should seem finished. Ordinarily, the student's intuitive sense of design does not prevail at this stage in his life because other factors capture his attention (i.e., he is interested in presenting information accurately and is concerned with the act of influencing the observer). Consequently, we can expect the student to create pleasing compositions most readily: (1) when he gives *conscious* attention to composition, and (2) when he is involved in an artistic activity that does not call for much representation. We can expect the student to approach composition consciously or deliberately at this point because he should begin to realize that he can affect the observer more effectively if he presents his ideas and emotions in a pleasing' structural form.

The child also should be expected to produce pleasurable arrangements when he organizes a bulletin board, makes a poster, plans the clothes that he will wear, builds stage sets, decorates the cafeteria, or plans some other visual configuration. But pleasurable compositions are not to be expected on all occasions, especially if the student is confronted with a wholly new task, new tools, or new materials. (Behavior of this kind indicates a *knowledge of composition.*)

(f) By *producing symbols in which the technique or the manipulation of materials is pleasing and unobtrusive.* The tools and materials that a student should be able to use are listed in Chapter 9. The student's work should not appear dirty, messy, uncontrolled, unfinished, strained, or overworked. If it is three-dimensional, it should not appear weak, unstable, or poorly constructed. He should be able to fasten things together that are as difficult to fasten as the parts of a fairly complex model airplane or a basic dress. In other words, the craftsmanship should not be irritating. (This is a sign that the child possesses a *knowledge of procedures* and *skill* in managing tools and materials. It also might indicate a sensitivity to composition.)

(g) By *giving the proper care to tools and materials*; by gathering the necessary items and returning them to their proper places; and by following a procedure that is in keeping with the nature of the tools and materials that he is using. (This shows that the youngster has a knowledge of procedure.)

(h) By *using formal elements (colors, textures, lines, shapes, volumes) that are more complex* than those used in the intermediate grades, and by adjusting those elements to the content of the symbol. In other words, the child should be able to make a wide range of shades, tints, transparencies, transitions, patterns, details, surfaces, and other such things with his materials, and he should be able to select and use the ones that are most appropriate for what he wants to say. To put it differently, we might say that he should be able to vary the style or the form of his work to suit the content of the work. (This shows *skill*, a *knowledge of life*, a *knowledge of procedures*, and a *tolerance toward style*.)

(i) By *taking advantage of accidents or unexpected developments* that occur during the creative process. In other words, he should be able to meet obstacles and overcome them successfully. An unexpected knothole in a block of wood is such an obstacle. (This indicates *interest, confidence*, and a *knowledge of procedures*.)

(j) By *making symbols that are intrinsically interesting to perceive*; or to put it differently, his work should show an increase in the richness of formal elements, in the combinations of those elements, and in the complexity of the meanings presented. (This is an indication of *total artistic growth*.)

(k) By *making art, occasionally, when he is not required to do so*. (This indicates an attitude of *interest, confidence*, and a *willingness to work* or *to practice*.)

(l) By *achieving the foregoing results independently*, without inhibition and without constant help from anyone. (This signals an *attitude of interest* and *confidence toward art*.)

(m) By *displaying satisfaction* with his own visual symbols. (This is a sign that his *attitude* is one of *interest* and *confidence*.)

(n) By *working intently* at the foregoing tasks *for at least one to two hours*. (This is evidence of an *attitude of interest, confidence,* and *willingness to work hard.*)

(o) By *doing the things that are expected of a connoisseur.*

2. On entering the tenth grade, the educated adolescent is able to behave like a connoisseur of art and of life:

(a) By *recognizing and naming the formal elements in art, and by making it known verbally that he recognizes nuances of form.* By this we mean that the child should indicate that he detects subtle but effective instances of color, texture, line, shape, or volume. He should also reveal through his selections or through his comments that he can detect the effect that one formal element has on another, and he should show that he can perceive the meanings that seem to be inherent in certain formal elements. Hence he should be able to see and say that green looks greener on a red background than it does on a green background. And he should see and say that green possesses a certain freshness, crispness, and coolness while red possesses warmth, vitality, and excitement. Naturally, other formal elements should be understood in the same way. (This indicates a *knowledge of life* and a *knowledge of composition.*)

(b) By *describing the ways to create various meaningful or expressive effects through the alteration of formal elements.* Thus the student should be able to explain how to manipulate formal elements to produce qualities such as peacefulness, coolness, excitement, sickness, sadness, and stability. (This shows verbal *skill* as well as considerable *knowledge of life, composition, procedure, and aesthetics.* And, it reveals an *attitude of interest and confidence.*)

(c) By *recognizing a displeasing visual composition of any kind, including a displeasing aspect of the environment,* and by describing a way in which that structural organization might be improved. (This indicates a *knowledge of composition* as well as *verbal skill*.)

(d) By *showing disgust with the displeasing appearance of the environment*. (This indicates an *attitude of interest in the aesthetic dimension of life*.)

(e) By *recognizing and naming* the *tools* and *materials* that he uses in visual symbolization. (This shows a *knowledge of procedures*.)

(f) By *describing* the various *procedures* that he has encountered for making visual art. (This reveals a *knowledge of procedures* as well as *skill in verbalization*.)

(g) By *responding verbally and enthusiastically to the meanings or expressive qualities* that exist in the "look" of things, including visual symbols and works of art. In other words, the student should be able to show that he sees calmness, movement, excitement, hate, terror, kindness, gentleness, purpleness, etc. He will see details and subtlties of meaning that youngsters in the intermediate grades will miss. In other words, we can expect the student to see meanings that are revealed in abstract as well as concrete form. Hence we can expect him to see happiness even if it is not depicted with smiles and clapping hands; in fact, we can expect him to see it in abstract configurations. By the same token, we can expect him to see depth in a nonfigurative presentation. This means that the number of objective or character responses are much more likely to increase (see page 175). (This shows an *attitude of interest in the aesthetic*, a *knowledge of life*, and an *attitude of self-confidence*.)

(h) By *responding (recognizing and describing) verbally and enthusiastically to the formal qualities* (color, texture, line, shape, volume) that exist in the visual environment, including those that exist in works of art. (This indicates *interest in the aesthetic*, and it shows *confidence*.)

(i) By *discussing the nature of art and the value of art* and by offering a point of view about such things in his own words. The view that he offers might be the one that is presented in this textbook, or it might be another. But the child should be able to offer a reasonable justification for the view that he takes, and he should be able to demonstrate what effect his view will have on the judgment of visual symbols.
The student should be able to explain the value that art has in attaining the good life, and he should be able to explain how art can lead us away from the good life if we are not educated in aesthetics. (This reveals a *knowledge of aesthetics* as well as *verbal skill*.)

(j) By *discussing artists* (what they do, where they work, what kind of people they are, why they do what they do, what the future holds in store for them). The information that the child offers should be accurate, of course, and it should indicate familiarity with a selected group of artists from the past and present. It should include the artists covered in the intermediate grades plus several others, but it seems reasonable for the student to reveal considerable familiarity with modern and contemporary artists, especially American artists. The students familiarity with artists, however, need not go beyond an understanding of those who have made unusually outstanding contributions to art. (This indicates a *knowledge of aesthetics and art history* as well as an *attitude of interest* and *verbal skill*.)

(k) By *showing through discussion a knowledge of the motivating forces in art*. Thus, the student may be expected to say that the making of art is motivated by the desire to communicate, to be admired, and to understand the self and the environment. And, he should recognize such motivating factors to be natural and worthwhile. (This reveals a *knowledge of life and of aesthetics*, and it shows *interest* and *verbal skill*.)

(l) By *recognizing and naming the various art forms* (drawing, painting, printing, sculpture, and crafts). This means that the child should be able to identify most of the different kinds of painting (watercolor, oil, tempera, etc.), sculpture, drawing, printing, and crafts. (This is a sign that he possesses a *knowledge of both procedures and aesthetics*.)

(m) By *recognizing, naming, and discussing the art from the major periods of art history* (primitive, Egyptian, Greek, Roman, medieval, Renaissance, eighteenth-century European, modern European, American). The child should indicate through his comments that he has an understanding of the purposes that art served during each of the major historical periods. He should know a little about the interests and values of the various cultures, the living conditions, and the patrons of the arts. (This shows a *knowledge of art history and aesthetics*.)

(n) By *revealing verbally that he has an understanding of the function of museums, art departments in public schools, art schools, and university art departments*. (This reveals a *knowledge of life and of aesthetics*, and it suggests an *interest in the aesthetic*.)

(o) By *revealing verbally that he has some understanding of the work of art historians and aestheticians*. (This indicates a *knowledge of life, of art history*, and *of aesthetics*.)

(p) By *paying attention to art and to other aspects of the visual environment when he is not required to do so*. (This is a sign of *interest in the aesthetic as* well as *confidence in responding*.)

(q) By *recognizing, naming, accepting, and discussing a variety of styles in art.* (This shows an *attitude* of *interest* as well as one of *tolerance toward style*, and it reveals a *knowledge of aesthetics.*)

(r) By *behaving independently in the ways that have been indicated*, without inhibition and without constant help from anyone. (This shows an *attitude of interest and confidence.*)

(s) By *displaying satisfaction with his own comments or judgments* about visual configurations of all kinds, including works of art. (This is a sign that his *attitude* toward the aesthetic is one of *interest* and *confidence.*)

(t) By *engaging* in the foregoing *verbal tasks* for *at least thirty to sixty minutes.* (This indicates an attitude of *interest, confidence,* and *willingness to work hard.*)

(u) By *using a basic vocabulary* that permits the foregoing discussions, and by doing so with relative ease. (This indicates a full range of relevant *knowledge* as well as *skill as a connoisseur.*)

MEETING ANTICIPATED CRITICISM

Since the writing of Leon Winslow[18] in 1939, statements of specific objectives for art education have been rare. Probably there are several explanations for their disappearance, but one is that art educators have shifted their emphasis from teaching art to teaching the "whole child." They frequently say, "I do not teach art. I teach children." In an important effort to produce creative, cooperative, democratic, and uninhibited youngsters they have forgotten about the subject that is supposed to produce

[18] Winslow, Leon Loyal, *The Integrated School Art Program*, McGraw-Hill Book Company, New York, 1939.

those characteristics. Consequently, their goals have become so highly generalized that they are practically meaningless. For example, it is not uncommon for teachers to say that one of their purposes is to develop creativity in children. But the fact that creativity is on a continuum means that the teacher can point to anything the child does and correctly say that is it creative. If the teacher lacks specific goals in a given subject-matter area, he has no way of knowing whether his pupils are more or less creative than we should expect them to be.

Another explanation for the unfortunate disappearance of specific objectives in art education is that art educators fear that teachers will adhere so rigidly to specific objectives that no help will be given to capable youngsters who might be able to progress beyond the stated goals. They also feel that a typical class in the public school is so heterogeneous that we cannot expect all children in that class to reach a given set of objectives. In other words, some art educators feel that specific goals give education an inflexibility that is totally unrealistic.

But it is not goals that create an inflexible educational program, it is teachers. Persons who do not give attention to objectives or persons who do not know how to use objectives are the elements that need to be eliminated from education, not the standards of achievement. By failing, on the other hand, to state our aims in specific behavioristic terms, we simply create a chaos in which the teacher is left without a clear indication of what he is to accomplish. Knowing that children are to be creative or uninhibited is of no great help to the teacher. After all, what does it mean to be creative in art as opposed to being creative in nonart? Is the behavior of a creative first-grader any different from the behavior of a creative sixth-grader? Does mere sensitivity to the world make the child more creative? If it does, the teacher should be able to see its effect in the child's work. But what does he look for? If mere sensitivity is not enough, what is necessary for creativity in art, and how does it reveal itself?

The objectives listed in this chapter are simply standards that the average child should be able to achieve in art. They are based on the nature of the subject, the nature of the artist, the nature of symbolic development, and the nature of the child as a maker of artistic symbols. No teacher is expected to adhere to these objectives with rigidity. Some children may not be able to keep up with the goals, and some may be able to surpass them. The teacher's job is to help each child progress as far as he is capable of going without "pushing" him or taking him so far that his skills cannot keep pace with his purposes.

QUESTIONS FOR DISCUSSION

1. Review Chapter 3, and ask yourself if the value of art is important enough to justify the teaching of art to all children in the public schools.
2. Discuss the following statement: If art can justifiably be taught to only a limited number of students, it has no place in the curriculum of the public school.
3. Why is it important to state the educational objectives for the country as a whole?
4. Why have the educational objectives for the country as a whole been stated in such general terms?
5. Who should be responsible for framing educational objectives? Why?
6. Select approximately six curriculum guides from as many states. What do they offer the teacher in the way of goals? What do they say about the goals for a third- or sixth-grade teacher?
7. Should goals be stated in terms of projects to be completed? Why?
8. Examine the writings of Belle Boas, Rosabell McDonald, Margaret Mathias, William Whitford, and Leon Winslow. What goals do they offer the teacher? Are these goals consistent with the nature of art, artists, and child art as described in this book?
9. Assume for a moment that there are no specific goals in art education. What would a good teacher do that a poor teacher would not do? What would he try to accomplish?
10. Self-expression is sometimes listed as a goal of art education. Could an individual express himself in a nonartistic way? How would his expression differ from artistic self-expression? How adequate is self-expression as a goal for art education?
11. Examine the levels of knowing and valuing that are presented on pages 289 and 290. Do our objectives provide for a rise in the level of knowing and valuing? Are our expectations realistic?

SUGGESTIONS FOR FURTHER READING

Bloom, Benjamin S. (ed.): *Taxonomy of Educational Objectives*, Handbook I: *Cognitive Domain*, David McKay Company, Inc., New York, 1956.
Chapters 1 and 2 give a good account of the need for objectives in education and the problems connected with their formulation.

Broudy, Harry: *Building a Philosophy of Education*, Prentice-Hall, Inc., New York, 1954.
Chapter 2 is especially pertinent, for it takes up the philosophical problem of aims in education. Beautifully written.

Educational Policies Commission, *The Central Purpose of American Education*, National Education Association, Washington, D.C., 1961.
This document signals a significant development in American education. Short, readable, and especially important for the art educator.

Educational Policies Commission, *The Purposes of Education in American Democracy*, National Education Association, Washington, D.C., 1938.
This is the most thorough account of American educational objectives available. All teachers should be familiar with these goals. Very readable.

Henry, Edith M.: *Evaluation of Children's Growth Through Art Experiences*, The National Art Education Association, Washington, D.C., 1959.
This pamphlet deals with evaluation, but it also gives the teacher an indication of what his goals should be. One of the few attempts to list objectives since the 1930s.

Chapter 8
THE TEACHING OF ART

Teaching is a deliberate effort to get someone to learn something, and it usually involves *showing* and *saying*. Frequently an emphasis is placed upon either showing or saying, depending upon the subject that is being taught. In art education, however, it is common practice to engage in the verbal activity of saying or telling, and it is equally common to offer a nonverbal demonstration of how something is done.

After recording and analyzing about 125 classroom sessions in various academic subjects from grade nine to grade twelve, B. O. Smith concludes that the teacher's *verbal* behavior (saying or telling) may be divided into three kinds of actions: logical, directive, and admonitory. The logical actions may be subdivided into twelve different types:[1] "defining, describing, designating, stating, reporting, substituting, valuating, opining, classifying, comparing and contrasting, conditional inferring, and explain-

[1] B. Othanel Smith, "The Logic of Teaching in the Arts," *Teachers College Record*, vol. 63, no. 3, p. 178, December, 1961.

ing." Obviously, an art teacher engages in logical actions of all those types as he discusses art with his students.

Directive verbal action, on the other hand, is nonlogical. It is employed by a teacher when he tells a youngster to do something instead of describing how to do it. Thus an art teacher exhibits directive verbal behavior when he tells a student to make a plaster cast instead of demonstrating or describing how it is done.

Admonitory actions are also nonlogical. They are the actions that a teacher uses when he wishes to indicate approval or disapproval. Usually they are verbal, but they could be silent, expressive gestures such as smiles, frowns, or scowls. Naturally, the teaching of art involves admonitory behavior of that kind.

If the nonverbal and verbal behaviors described by Smith are the actions that constitute the practice of teaching, it seems clear that improvements in art education are largely dependent upon the teacher's ability to perform those actions effectively. To acquire that ability, a person must learn his subject thoroughly; he must learn the rules for effective verbal and demonstrative behavior, adjust that information to the level of his pupils, and practice the actions of teaching. But teaching, or trying to get someone to learn something, does not guarantee that learning will occur. Israel Scheffler explains the problem when he says that success in teaching "depends on factors outside of one's trying: the universe must cooperate."[2] In other words, getting someone to learn requires more than the act of teaching; it requires a cooperative or a supporting environment. If this is true, the teacher is destined to fail on certain occasions, because he is not able to control everything that surrounds his students. It is possible, however, for him to regulate the appearance of the classroom, its emotional atmosphere, the day-to-day routine, and other dimensions of the immediate environment or subculture. This aspect of his work may be called classroom management. And when we speak of teaching, we usually mean

[2] Israel Scheffler, *The Language of Education*, Charles C. Thomas, Publisher, Springfield, Illinois, 1960, p. 68.

classroom management as well as the acts of showing and telling. With these general comments about the nature of teaching in mind, we shall proceed with recommendations for teaching the structure of knowledge, attitude, and skill in art.

DEVELOPING A KNOWLEDGE OF THE AESTHETIC DIMENSION OF LIFE

To act as an artist, the child must have a desire to make symbols and have something to say; or to put it differently, his knowledge of life must be sufficiently interesting and exciting to deserve expression. Furthermore, his knowledge must include visual concepts, or concepts of the aesthetic dimension of experience if he is to make artistic symbols of a visual nature. Consequently, it is a mistake for the art teacher to assume that a mere request for art will cause a youngster to produce art. The instructor must make a determined effort to sharpen the student's awareness of the aesthetic aspects of life if the necessary images are to form in the youngster's mind. The teacher must also try to inspire or stimulate the child; he must try to arouse ideas and emotions that demand expression. But how does he move his students to the point of eager and eloquent expression?

Direct experience as a form of stimulation

Fortunately, there are many ways of stimulating emotions and visual concepts. One of the most effective methods is to provide youngsters with *direct experiences*. By this we mean that one of the most influential ways of stimulating students is to take them to the furnace room, to the fire station, or to the school kitchen so that they can experience such places directly. By making such visits, or by walking around the school or around the block, the children can look, listen, touch, and smell as they go. They can experience direct contact with trees, puddles, the bright, warm sun, and the smell of spring. They can detect the movement and sounds of people, trucks, cars, and animals.

They can touch the weeds and the leaves; they can look at billboards, dirty pavements, and telephone poles. In fact, there are hundreds of such things to experience in the immediate vicinity of any school.

In the school building itself there are other things that the teacher and his class can experience besides the furnace room and the kitchen. They can look at the gymnasium, the nurse's room, and the principal's office. They can observe a dance, a debate, a basketball game, or an assembly. And in their own classrooms, the teacher can arrange to have them handle, feed, and groom a little chicken, a hamster, or a row of plants. He can ask a student to act as a model for the others to draw, or he can arrange a still life for everyone to paint. In addition, he can have children go through the motions of the activity that they are expected to portray; this means that the teacher might have his students swing in a swing, take the stance of a baseball catcher, or act as if they were skating around the room before they draw such activities. Physical activities are especially helpful to children who are sensitive to muscular sensations.

By making it possible for his students to have direct experiences, the teacher increases the chance that their concepts and emotions will be clear and sharp. This clarity and freshness of idea and feeling makes it easier to draw and to paint. But teachers occasionally ask if the kitchen, the furnace room, and other such places are not too commonplace to provide artistic inspiration. The answer is that great artists such as Cézanne and Chardin have created masterpieces with concepts and emotions that were generated by nothing more sensational than a bowl of apples. Furthermore, a school kitchen or a furnace room is a very exciting place for children to visit. They respond with great enthusiasm to the sight and sound of a giant potato masher, to the heat and smell of a pie-filled oven, or to the chilling cold of a refrigerated room with its frozen sides of beef. They are awed by the flames of the janitor's furnace and are impressed by the complicated pipes that crisscross the room. Thus they return to their art materials with vivid concepts that are ready for shaping in material form.

8.1

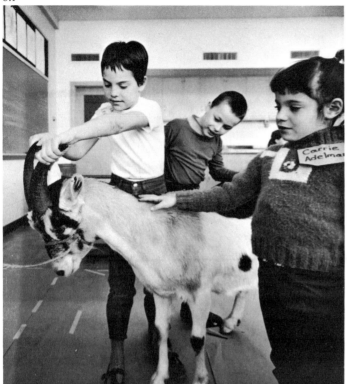

8.2

8.3

Fig. 8.1
Children having a direct
experience with a goat
prior to drawing.

Fig. 8.2
A result of the direct
experience depicted in Fig. 8.1.

Fig. 8.3
This child is going through
the motion of shooting a bow and
arrow before she draws it.

Verbal stimulation

Direct experiences in themselves can provide the mental raw materials that are needed for drawing and painting. But the teacher can enrich concepts and deepen emotional concern to a greater extent if he *talks* with his students while he provides them with a direct experience. By saying and showing he can direct their attention to specific objects, events, and details that otherwise might have been missed. In addition, the teacher can solicit *verbal reactions* from his students, causing them to concentrate more keenly upon the things that they see, hear, touch, taste, and smell. By focusing attention on such things, the students are likely to have a much more meaningful and more clearly defined experience. It is very important, of course, for the teacher to make sure that his students pay particular attention to the *visual* qualities of the environment and to the effects that they create. Intensive *visual* perception is important because it is through such activity that a person develops the mental images that are so necessary for the making of visual art. In other words, it is through intensive perception that a person develops his knowledge of the aesthetic dimension of experience.

It is not possible or desirable, however, to make continuous use of direct experience as a form of stimulation, for anything that is done repeatedly becomes boring. Consequently, the teacher will find it desirable to make use of purely verbal stimulation from time to time. After all, speech is a versatile medium of expression and a powerful influence. By asking questions, telling stories, reading books and poems, and by engaging in other verbal activities, the teacher can arouse the student's interest in the objects and events of contemporary life and create a concern for the ideas and happenings of the past. As he does so, however, he may have a hard time getting students to respond to his comments and questions. Verbal responses are highly desirable because they force the child to concentrate more carefully upon his experience and to learn more about it. What can the teacher do to encourage verbal responses?

Youngsters who do not react verbally are sometimes unsure

of the kind of response that the teacher is seeking. Consequently, it is a good idea for the teacher to give an illustration of the kind of comment that he expects. If he hopes to have youngsters express their reactions to a busy street corner, for example, he might offer one or two of his own reactions, and then ask the children for theirs. By saying and doing the desired things himself, the teacher "breaks the ice" and makes it easier for his students.

The verbal form of stimulation also helps youngsters to recall experiences that they have had with animals, people, and other ordinary things in daily life. To move, persuade, touch, or inspire students with words, however, is to behave as an orator or as an actor. Professional actors make a business of impressing their audiences, and they contend that a person's *manner* of speaking is just as important as *what* he says. This suggests that teachers could be more effective if they would dramatize a few of their verbal presentations. Persons who act and speak professionally, however, know that success also depends upon the ability to select a topic and a manner of speaking that are appropriate for a given audience. This means that a teacher is more apt to have the desired effect upon his students if the selects a subject and a dramatic style that are suitable for his particular group. A clownish presentation, for example, might be useful on certain occasions with youngsters in the primary grades, but it is not a suitable technique in most situations above that level. Older children react more favorably to a sedate form of verbal stimulation.

Although dramatization can have a marked effect in building concepts and emotions for artistic expression, we do not mean to imply that a teacher should always dramatize. If he did, he probably would develop a class that is overstimulated, and no one wants his students to be in a constant state of nervous excitation. The point is that an occasional stimulation of the dramatic type can provide variety in the teaching act, and it can be a powerful spark to creative activity.

When certain teachers are advised to be more dramatic in telling a story, they often say that they cannot behave that way because they feel too silly or too unnatural. This is perfectly understandable, and when a teacher feels that way, he should not try to dramatize. After all, an actor often rejects a role in a play because he feels that the part does not suit his personality or his style of verbal behavior. He is fussy about such things because he knows that poor casting can destroy his effectiveness with an audience. By the same token, the teacher-actor should be fussy about the teaching roles that are available to him. He should select the form of verbal stimulation that seems most natural and comfortable, and he should stick with it. Certainly, the various dramatic techniques he might use, while effective, are less important than a command of the subject, a commitment to the subject, and sincerity. A teacher who speaks sincerely about something he knows and likes is a person who infects others with his enthusiasm.

As we have said, good verbal stimulation helps children to recall their experiences vividly and to relive them in their minds. When offering such stimulation, the teacher is advised to activate as many of the child's senses as he possibly can. By this we mean that the teacher should talk about the sound, the smell, and the tactile qualities of an object or event as well as its appearance. Under those circumstances a youngster who was not especially impressed by the *look* of a certain experience might be able to recall and reassemble a mental image of it because the teacher mentioned familiar *sounds*.

Sometimes a teacher can help a youngster to imagine an event that the child has never witnessed if reference is made to more than one sense experience. It also helps in such cases to compare the unfamiliar event with adventures that the child is known to have had. Let us say, for example, that the teacher wishes to give his students the idea of an encounter with a leopard, an animal that many children have never seen. He could compare the leopard with a cat and discuss their differences in size, weight, color, and strength. He could compare their stalking habits, the sounds that they make, and their degrees of tameness. He could describe the encounter with the leopard in terms of the sounds that were heard, the texture of the ground,

330
ART
EDUCATION

Fig. 8.4
*A teacher stimulating
her class verbally.*

the color of the vegetation, and the heat of the day. Perhaps
he could imitate sounds or make additional comparisons that
would help to build the child's concept of a leopard and move
him to draw it or paint it.

Naturally a stimulation that deals with familiar subject
matter is likely to be more successful than one which involves
strange subject matter. This being the case, a teacher in the United
States will probably have more luck in promoting art activity
if he talks about dogs instead of kangaroos. The child from the
city will develop more artistically helpful visions of the urban
scene than he will of a barnyard or a milking machine. By the
same token, the rural youngster will picture a barn more easily
than he will a suburban country club. Consequently, the easiest
and most successful stimulation is one that deals with life as
the child knows it, with life in his environment. But the things
that a youngster can know about his environment depend upon
the extent of his perceptual experience. Because of this, the

331

**THE TEACHING
OF ART**

next chapter will deal with topics of stimulation that are especially suitable for children at specific stages in their schooling. But, first, let us consider the matter of stimulation in a more general fashion. Is there, for example, any topic that is usually more fitting than another as a verbal incitement to art?

Probably it is correct to say that any subject is appropriate as stimulation for art because the content of art is unrestricted in a democratic society. The point we wish to make, however, is that teachers often select motivational topics that can be handled adequately only by a genius. That is the case when a teacher uses such themes as the meaning of life, America the beautiful, or the hope of mankind to excite his students. In each of these instances the subject is so large that Michelangelo himself would have a hard time doing justice to it. Besides, it is a mistake to think that a sizable topic will naturally lead to art of the same magnitude. This was made especially clear by John Ciardi in a statement about the writing of poetry. He said, "A fool could look at the universe and see nothing . . . , but the most mind, the most intelligence, could look at an amoeba and project the universe from it."[3]

If a person has something new and significant to say about a complex topic such as life, there is a possibility that it could result in a work of art. If it does, we might agree that the finished work is a greater achievement than a product that deals with a less complex subject. But few of us are apt to be so successful in handling topics of overwhelming importance. Certainly we have no reason to expect such miracles from children. Consequently, it seems more sensible to use the ordinary objects and events of everyday life as topics for verbal stimulation. They interest and excite nearly all children, and if Ciardi is right, the gifted youngster will project the universe from them.

Unfortunately we tend to neglect the ordinary aspects of life, especially the little things, the things that make living so fresh and so desirable. As teachers we fail to speak of such

[3] John Ciardi, "The Form is the Experience," *Art Education*, vol. 14, no. 7, October, 1961, p. 17.

objects and events because we are no longer aware of them. Our lives are caught in the race to own things, to have security, to achieve status, to have influence, or to gain control over others. In short, we busy ourselves at getting ahead and overlook the twinkle of morning sunlight in the grass and flowers. Our minds are occupied, and time is short. We neglect the softness of the clouds we observed when we were children. We miss the skip of a happy child, the rainbow of color in an oily puddle, and the look of a lonely dog. We pay no attention to beauty; we take no note of ugliness; we ignore the nuances of life on earth; and we race to the moon. If instructors are to stimulate the formation of concepts and emotions through occasional discussions of the wondrous but ordinary things that occur on this planet, they must become more sensitive than we have described them. They must perceive more than it has been their habit to see, but how can this be done?

Probably the only way for a person to improve his own sensitivity is to make a *special* effort to do so. Teachers are therefore urged to look, listen, and touch with greater attentiveness. Perhaps they could begin by trying to perceive at least one new object or event each day on the way to school. They could try to observe the visual details that are encountered in riding on an elevator, talking in a telephone booth, or swinging in a swing. The important thing is to *practice* being sensitive. Soon the success of their efforts will become clear, especially as they try to verbalize their experiences for their students. Verbalization is extremely important. It not only lets the teacher know how sensitive his experiences have been, but permits him to communicate the meaning of those experiences to others. If a teacher cannot verbalize, he is about as valuable as a painter who cannot paint.

Art materials as stimulation

Artists and persons who work with children know that tools and materials can act as a strong inducement to visual symbolization and as a source of original ideas for creative work. Persons of all ages are fascinated by new and interesting things, but young children are especially eager to explore them and to experiment with them. Children seem to be keen on discovering the nature of their supplies and equipment, and they like to see what they can make them do. In fact, there are many instances in which exciting papers, scrap objects, printing presses, and other items are the only stimuli that are necessary for the making of symbols. Art teachers are therefore acting wisely if they introduce a few new materials in each of the grades. But this does *not* mean that the teacher must "beat the bushes" each year to find new substances, such as bottle caps or old venetian blinds, that could be used to make artistic objects. Treasure hunts of that kind soon lead to the notion that good art and inventive teaching are simply a matter of using odd materials. Naturally, this is not the view that we wish to develop. We agree that scrap materials can be useful and that teachers should be alert to the artistic possibilities that such things provide. But we also believe that a person who starts to symbolize with junk is more than likely to finish with junk. We believe that art objects are more apt to result from the use of materials that have already demonstrated their fitness for making art and their suitability for young people. Consequently, our advice about introducing new materials in each of the grades means that teachers should plan the curriculum so that a few different supplies and pieces of equipment of recognized educational value are presented to the children each year.

Materials act as an incentive to symbol making, but they also stimulate concepts and emotions. Professional artists are probably more aware of this than anyone else. Most of them, if questioned, will probably say that their materials suggest ideas to them as they work, ideas that they did not have when they started to create. A particular combination of colors might suggest a new mood, or the accidental forming of paints on wet paper might give an inkling of subject matter that was unintended but highly satisfactory. Like professional artists, children are notoriously good at taking such leads from their materials. A youngster might begin by making a spot of color that stands for a flower, but by the time he finishes, that same spot of color may have gone through stages when it was a cat, a man, a house, and a birdbath. Children are most likely to respond that way between the naming of scribbling period and the early part of the mid-figurative stage; and again during the high school years, they are apt to let their materials lead them. The whole intervening period, however, is one in which children are more apt to force their materials into a preconceived pattern, for it is during that period that youngsters are likely to be very unhappy if the materials give any resistance to their desires. The art teacher, in such instances, would do well to stress the importance of being sensitive to tools and materials. If he can help children to accept suggestions from such things, he will be doing a lot to develop artists. If he does not help them to respond to materials, many potential artists will not develop.

Audio-visual aids as stimulation

In this day and age few people will argue that audio-visual aids are not stimulating, for almost everyone has experienced the birth of ideas and emotions as a result of exposure to television, films, slides, recordings, and printed reproductions. Such aids have become so good and so plentiful that a teacher can offer his students a vicarious experience with almost any aspect of life, and it will be nearly as good as a direct encounter with the real thing. He can show the daily activities of a beaver in his natural environment; he can present life on a farm; or he can take children to faraway places and back to bygone days. It is especially nice to be able to show children the exemplars of great art without making a trip to the museum—a journey that may be impossible. It is equally nice to show an artist at work or a procedure for working with materials. The possibilities are nearly endless, and by utilizing such resources the teacher provides stimuli of unequaled value to potential artists and connoisseurs.

It is clear, of course, that films, recordings, and other aids do not present life in a way that we can smell, touch, or taste it. They offer only the visual and auditory aspects of existence, and as a consequence they are inferior to direct experience. Yet it is safe to say that in other respects audio-visual aids are *superior* to direct experience as a stimulus to creativity. They allow the teacher to be very selective with the material that is to be seen and heard. He not only can select the subject matter, but he may also find an aid that will focus attention on the elements that are most significant for the effective perception of that subject matter. After all, a fine visual aid may very well be a work of art, and few things are more pointed in their stimulating effect than art.

On the other hand, not all audio-visual aids are works of art, and some of them may provide material for perception that is not conducive to either the creation or appreciation of pleasing artistic form. For that reason the teacher is advised to examine instructional aids carefully and to select only the best ones for use in his classes. The *best* teaching aid is one that helps the instructor to get his students to learn something about the structure of knowledge, attitude, and skill in art; or we might say that a good aid helps to create a pleasing classroom climate that supports learning. The latter *may* be one of the art teacher's best uses for musical recordings.

Music has been used in art classrooms for many years, and as a pleasant background for creative activity, it may be a fine thing. It may have an effect similar to its alleged influence on the production of milk in a dairy barn, but no one knows. Even if it does have such an effect, there is still some question as to whether a contented artist is more desirable than a discontented one. Consequently, a full endorsement of background music as a support for learning must be withheld until its positive influence is more firmly established.

A much more strenuous objection is made, however, to the other ways in which art educators use music as an aid to education. Sometimes they use it to stimulate the formation of a pleasing arrangement in the visual symbol. They seem to assume that children will change musical rhythms into visual form and thereby produce an art object that is harmoniously organized. But there is no evidence that such transformations take place.

In the primary grades, for example, children commonly keep time with the music by beating their papers with crayons or brushes. Beyond that level, youngsters may use colors or lines that simulate the mood or the tempo of the sounds that they hear. In neither of those instances, however, is there any indication that pleasing aesthetic compositions are produced, nor is there any evidence that such exercises will be applied to the organization of drawings and paintings at a later date.

Furthermore, it is important to ask what we are doing to music education when we ask children to search for visual meanings in musical compositions. To do so is to build bad habits of appreciation, because music is not to be pictured any more than pictures are to be whistled. Consequently, a child who is taught to visualize music is a child who may never appreciate music. This possibility should be sufficient to deter any teacher from using music as a stimulus for concept formation in the visual arts.

Helping the youngsters who have problems

Sometimes students are unable to create visual images, their images are nonartistic, or they make them with great difficulty. The explanations for this are numerous and complex, and we shall try to cover each of them as we proceed with this chapter. At this point, however, it seems appropriate to discuss the explanations that relate to a knowledge of life, the knowledge that acts as the content of art.

First of all, a child may have the difficulties we have described because the teacher has provided no stimulation, a practice that is fairly common in the public shools. For example, the teachers give out the art materials, and, without further discussion, ask the children to create anything they wish. Sometimes this is done simply to keep the youngsters busy and out of trouble. At other times it is done because teachers feel they are providing the freedom that art allegedly requires. In either case, art of high quality is not apt to develop, and the aims of education are not likely to be attained, because art and education do not

Fig. 8.5
*Art of low quality
produced by a child in first grade.
It was made by creating marks
arbitrarily and by coloring
the open spaces.*

Fig. 8.6
*Drawn by a six-year-old
child without the benefit of any
stimulation from the teacher.
A visual cliché, or stereotype.*

emerge from a mental vacuum. To produce art, the creator
needs to have concepts and emotions that seem worthy of the
trouble that it takes to express them with elegance; and he is
not apt to have such worthy thoughts unless the teacher stimulates them. Without this generative action, the student may
fail to produce anything or he may make symbols of the kind
seen in Figures 8.5 and 8.6. Both drawings exhibit a minimum
of content, and the content is neither individualistic nor novel.
The symbols are shallow stereotypes, produced on command,
and free from any qualities that identify them as the creations
of the children who made them. They are less than the visual
equivalents of "small talk." They are bad works of art.

To help these children to create something better, the teacher
must offer stimulation. It is not uncommon, however, for teachers
to work very hard at generating concepts and emotions in their
students, only to find that the students are still unable to create
or that they produce the poor artistic work already described.
A possible explanation for such behavior is that the youngsters

339
THE TEACHING
OF ART

lack experience with the topic specified by the teacher. If the stimulation concerned a cow, for example, it is quite possible that certain children may never have experienced a cow; and that means that they lack trustworthy concepts of a cow as well as feelings toward one. Without such knowledge and feeling for content and subject matter, a child is unable to create or is unable to do so with distinction simply because he has nothing to say about cows.

To find out if the child's problem is really caused by a lack of experience with cows or any other subject, the teacher must question the student. If he finds that the child has not experienced a cow, he has three alternatives. The first, and probably the best, is to allow the child to base his art work on another topic. The second alternative is to provide a direct experience with a real cow; but if that appears too difficult, the teacher might try the third possibility, visual aids. Photographs or other reproductions may permit the child to have a vicarious experience with a cow, and films about such animals would be excellent for that purpose. But we recommend most strongly that the child be allowed to work with a new topic because it is not easy to bring cows, reproductions, or films into the classroom on the spur of the moment.

It is best, of course, if the teacher can avoid such problems in the first place. To do so, he must select the subject of his stimulation with care, making sure that it is well-known to his pupils. It is also helpful to work a direct experience or a visual aid into the original stimulation, so that any inexperienced youngsters will get a notion of the topic while experienced persons are freshening their memories.

These comments clearly suggest that a *poor* stimulation by the teacher may be just as responsible for the child's creative problems as a lack of stimulation or a lack of experience. For that reason a teacher must consider the need to improve his inspirational techniques if he is confronted with youngsters who cannot create as expected. He can improve by providing supplementary direct experiences; by saying, telling, or showing in a more efficient or more dramatic way; by selecting topics that are more familiar and about which he can speak with greater sincerity and conviction; and by using better teaching aids.

Naturally the teacher's success in generating knowledge and emotion is limited by the mental and emotional capacities of his students. A retarded child is not capable of understanding the same concepts that are understood by a normal child of the same age, and a typical first-grader cannot grasp the knowledge that is understood by the average sixth-grader. This means that a teacher must give careful attention to the suitability of the concepts he is trying to develop through stimulation; he may have to adjust these concepts to specific students as well as to different grades.

DEVELOPING A KNOWLEDGE OF PROCEDURES

The teacher of art may do such a good job of stimulating his students that they have a detailed knowledge of some aspect of life. Yet they may not create art unless the teacher provides them with information about an appropriate procedure for making art. Procedural information includes advice about the tools, materials, and sequences of action that are required to achieve certain effects in a given artistic activity. Such instruction is appropriate if it is consistent with the growth and development of the students and suitable for the content and subject matter covered in the teacher's stimulation. We shall suggest appropriate artistic procedures for the various levels of the public school in the next chapter. Meanwhile there are some general comments that can be made about the teaching of those procedures.

To begin, it is important for the teacher to go through the same procedure of making art that he expects to teach to his students. If he intends to tell them about the process of forming a papier-mâché mask, he should make a mask beforehand with the same process. By doing so, he becomes aware of the kind and the number of tools and materials that are needed, and he learns the degree of difficulty involved in each step of the procedure. If the work is easy for him, it still may be hard for his students, but anything that is difficult for the teacher is almost certain to be more than children can manage. In either case the teacher who is sensitive to the abilities of his pupils will be able to anticipate the tasks that will give them trouble. He may decide to alter the procedure or to use a new one, but the experience of trying it out gives him the basis for making decisions.

As the instructor tries the process that he intends to teach, he is advised to examine the tools and materials carefully. Although there are no absolute rules in art, it is generally a good idea to use tools and materials in a way that is in accord with their nature. By this we mean that a saw should be used for sawing rather than for hammering; cereal should be used for eating rather than for making durable works of art; paper should not be forced into positions that it does not take with relative ease; and marble should be chiseled into comparatively massive forms instead of lacelike patterns. We say these things realizing that, under certain conditions, a child might be acting creatively if he hammers with a saw or opens a can of paint with a wood chisel. We simply mean to say that such creative actions are inefficient and foolish if hammers and can openers are available or can be made available.

We also realize that a sculptural genius might be able to make an artistically successful doily out of marble. But most of us are not that clever, especially as children. We are more apt to succeed if we use a material that is conducive to doily making. In other words, it is usually wise to use the tools and materials that are by nature or by design the most suitable for the task at hand.

If the teacher tries the procedure that is to be taught beforehand, he will reap still another reward. He will have a finished example that can be used to give his students a general notion of the objects they will be trying to create. This does not mean, however, that the teacher should use the example as a model for the children to imitate. If he did that, he would be encouraging the production of bad art. It is therefore important that the teacher stress the value of originality and the unworthiness of imitation. In addition, copying is reduced if the example is displayed no longer than it takes to give a general idea of the ends that are sought.

When the instructor begins his actual teaching, he might use logical and directive actions; he might show or demonstrate how something is done; or he might use a combination of teaching behaviors. Without a doubt the combination of showing and telling is most effective because it allows the child to both see and hear the procedure. And it is especially helpful to the teacher in pointing out difficulties that the youngsters will encounter and in showing them how to overcome those difficulties.

In addition to showing and telling, it sometimes helps to write the procedure on a chart or chalkboard together with the names of tools and materials that are essential to the process. New words may also be included. This allows the student to check a forgotten step without having to ask the teacher what it was. The disadvantage of the system is that it might encourage students to ignore the instructor's verbalization. But the disadvantages are outweighed as the teacher saves himself the trouble of repeating a dozen times. Besides, written directions need not duplicate verbal comments in every detail. They would probably tend toward plainness and brevity, whereas showing and telling would lend itself to dramatic or elaborate presentation.

When we speak of showing, telling, and writing procedural information, we do not mean to imply that a teacher should offer his students step-by-step directions down to the last stroke of paint or the last dab of paste. Too much information, too much direction, or too much control is just as bad as a laissez-faire approach to teaching. It keeps the child from acting as an artist because it does not allow him to make decisions about aesthetic organization, content, or subject matter. If he fails to act as an artist, he cannot receive the values that the art process has to offer. Consequently, the teaching of procedure should not be carried to extremes, or it may result in overdirection, nonart, and miseducation. It must be confined to the presentation of *general information about a* process, and it must *not* include directions about such things as the number and kind of objects to include in the product; the style of working; the shapes, colors, and textures to be used; or the placement of elements within the composition. This does not mean, however, that the instructor should refrain from discussing such matters with his students as they work, for that is part of his job as a teacher of art. On the other hand, it does mean that such information must not be included in the teaching of procedure because it then has a dictatorial effect, instead of an advisory effect, upon students. The results of this dictatorial effect can be seen in the large number of products that look exactly alike or nearly alike in our public schools. In such instances the teachers have carried the teaching of procedure far beyond its proper limits and have trained their students to act like machines rather than artists.

Sometimes teachers go beyond the limits of procedural instruction because they feel the personal need, the parental desire, or the administrative pressure for products that are neat, naturalistic, clever, or useful. When teachers, parents, and administrators express such desires, they usually have a narrow, misguided view of the nature and the value of art, and they have a profound lack of respect for children as children. Persons of that type are probably the world's most formidable obstacles to art education and the good life, and it takes a strong, well-informed teacher to change their opinions.

When introducing a new procedure, it is probably wise for a teacher not to expect high-quality art from his students. Their lack of familiarity with tools, materials, or sequences frequently means that they will concentrate on the mechanics of creative production at the expense of content or meaning. This is especially true if, in addition to being new, the procedure is complex or the time for working is short. For this reason it is recommended that youngsters be given an opportunity to use a procedure more than once. In fact, they should go through it enough times so that they no longer have to think about it. When the process becomes that automatic, the teacher can expect more and better art from his students.

Taking the above comments into consideration, constantly introducing new procedures in the public schools seems unwise.

If we teach painting today, printing tomorrow, and weaving the next day, the students must continually readjust themselves to new tools, new materials, and new techniques. Under such conditions they have little or no opportunity to develop skill and confidence with any procedure. They do not get to know the struggle that an artist goes through with form and content, and they do not get to know what it means to produce art of high quality. If they are lucky, they may learn to design or to adjust to new situations. But surely art education must offer more than that. It must help students to develop a proficiency in the various modes of visual expression; and, to do so, it must provide repeated instruction in each of the basic art processes (drawing, painting, print making, sculpture, and crafts).

When we say that certain procedures should be repeated for the sake of building competence, we do not mean that a variety of art activities is bad. After all, variety is as important in teaching and learning as it is in art. It stimulates interest and prevents boredom. A variety of art activities helps children to grow intellectually by allowing them to experience new materials. But too much variety or too much change brings chaos to education. It eventually leads to the point where even the teacher is unable to tell if progress is being made. Consequently, the art teacher is advised to maintain a balance between the introduction of new procedures and the repetition of old ones.

Instruction in the basic processes should continue until youngsters have the sequences sufficiently internalized to follow them intuitively, to describe them, to compare them, and to discuss their advantages and disadvantages. The ability to follow procedures and the power to verbalize about them are important characteristics of both the artist and the connoisseur, but verbal ability probably suffers the greatest neglect. Teachers must do what they can to eliminate that weakness.

Finally, it is important to give procedural instruction at the most opportune time, and that time is usually before or immediately after the stimulation of concepts and emotions. In general, it is not a good idea to offer instruction to the whole class once they have begun working because it is disturbing and interrupts the concentration that artistic activity requires. For this reason any necessary help should probably be given individually, unless the whole class appears to have the same problem.

Sometimes children are so thoroughly stimulated that a lengthy lecture on procedure is unwelcome. They want to get started. In fact, the effect of a good stimulation can be ruined by the careless introduction of a new procedure. Unfamiliar materials and processes can frustrate children if the desire to express a particular idea is strong, because new procedures are often difficult to master in a short time.

DEVELOPING A KNOWLEDGE OF COMPOSITION

To know composition is to know the characteristics of pleasurable organization and the various ways of achieving that organization. In Chapter 4 we suggested that a pleasurable arrangement is one that: (1) possesses the properties of a good gestalt; (2) simulates the elemental shapes and relationships found in nature; and (3) displays a shape that is compatible with its intended content. And because of the close relationship between those characteristics and the old, well-known, and widely used principles of artistic composition, it was suggested that a configuration organized according to those principles would also constitute a pleasurable arrangement.

The good gestalt

On the basis of the foregoing comments we *might* propose that the instructor tell his students the properties of a good Gestalt (as they are listed in Chapter 4) and we *might* suggest that he show his pupils how to apply that information to the organization of their visual symbols. Probably there are times when information of that kind would be appropriate in the schooling of a college student or an academically oriented high school student; but it is *not* suitable for most youngsters in the elementary schools and junior high schools. It is too technical and too complicated. In other words, the correct scientific or psychological explanation of a good Gestalt and its implications for art are too complex for use below the high school level. Fortunately, the same compositional information may be presented, justified, and applied in ways that are less dependent upon scientific or psychological language; and for that reason they are easier methods for the teacher to use.

Natural order

It is easier, for example, for the teacher to help his students develop a knowledge of good form by causing them to pay attention to nature. As was indicated in Chapters 2 and 4, the natural organization of nature is infinitely pleasing. Most of us do not feel compelled to change the shape of a flower, a tree, or a dog, and we find the relationships among those natural objects to be fitting and proper. Consequently, it seems reasonable to assume that a youngster will grow to know or to sense the characteristics of good form if he can be made to perceive and conceive the elemental shapes and relationships of nature.

The teacher can assist the child in perceiving and conceiving such things if he points, in one way or another, to elemental natural structures, proportions, and relationships. This means that he might point to the structure of a leaf, a skeleton, a crystal, or a shell, and he might compare its beauty to that of an ugly man-made object. He might point to the proportional relationships that exist within a skeleton, a tree, a flower, or an insect, and he might compare those proportional relationships to the ones that are found in an unpleasant, poorly designed television set, dress, or building. Having proved that natural shape and organization are appealing, the teacher must see that his students apply the information to the judgment and construction of their own visual symbols. Hence he might suggest that they use the proportional relationships they have observed in a tree as they relate visual elements to each other in their drawings. And he might show how other artists have used those proportions in their drawings, paintings, and pieces of sculpture.

Naturally, the extent to which children can conceive shapes and proportional relationships and the degree to which they can apply what they know depends upon their level of development. As a result, the teacher must be careful to introduce the recommended compositional tasks at an appropriate time. If he begins them too soon, his students are very likely to become frustrated and discouraged. Consequently, it is much better for the teacher to be a little *late* in developing and applying concepts of natural organization. Specific suggestions about what to do at the various grade levels are offered in Chapter 9. But at this point it seems fitting to emphasize the importance of *drawing* as a method of getting children to learn the elemental shapes and relationships in nature. The drawing of trees, people, animals, flowers and other natural items causes the child to engage in active, intensive perception, and his finger movements reinforce that perception. According to Hebb and Piaget, active perception leads to the formation of concepts or mental images. Thus it seems reasonable to assume that drawing from nature will lead to a knowledge of natural order; fortunately, it also is an activity that is suitable for any grade in the public school.

Relationship between form and content

Another thing that the teacher can do to help his students develop a knowledge of composition is to assist them in detecting forms that seem to be incompatible with their intended content. This means, for example, that the instructor might point to instances in which the child's desire to present cowness is disrupted by the creation of a shape that has certain horsey qualities. Or he might call attention to the fact that the intent to present happiness is foiled by an abundance of inappropriate blacks, grays, and horizontal lines. Calling attention to the mismatching of form and content is, however, a very delicate task. If it is not handled carefully, the child is apt to lose his self-confidence and his interest in art. Sometimes the best thing for the teacher to do is to avoid comments on the matter and to take the earliest opportunity to expose the child to the content that was unsuccessfully shaped. In other words, he might expose the child to a cow or to an instance of happiness, and he might talk about the identifying characteristics in a cow or the lines, colors, shapes, and textures that produce the look of happiness. Hopefully, then, the child may produce a more pleasing configuration the next time he presents cowness or happiness.

Principles of artistic composition

Still another way of building the student's knowledge of composition is to tell him about the principles of artistic organization and to show him how to apply them. As we make this suggestion, we realize that undoubtedly a few artists will disagree with the old and widely used principles, but we believe that psychological research on perception definitely confirms the accuracy of those principles as guides to good visual form. Assuming their validity, we shall therefore proceed with suggestions for teaching them; however, we do not intend to present all the information that might be offered about the principles of artistic composition. The topic is too complex to be covered in a few pages; and in addition to that, it is not necessary or advisable for the elementary school instructor to teach more than the fundamentals of composition. If he attempts to do more than that, he is apt to spoil the joy of the art experience for children.

Balance. Balance is equality in opposition of any sort; it is a state of equilibrium or stability. Human beings and other animals seek balance both in themselves and in their environment. When they are faced with instances of imbalance, they become frustrated, disturbed, anxious, and unhappy. Thus it is natural for them to want to change or avoid things that seem unstable. They will usually avoid a visual object that lacks equilibrium, or they will try to look at it sideways or change its position. This means that the effectiveness of a visual symbol is apt to be lost if it does not balance. Hence the teacher must help his students to recognize instances of imbalance and to correct them if he wants them to be successful in making and judging works of art. He might compare a visual symbol that is well balanced with one that is not, so that the children will learn the meaning of balance; and he might call attention to instability when it occurs in their work.

As he gives assistance in correcting the defect, he might explain that stability is obtained by making one side of an object equal to the other side in its visual weight and in its capacity to attract attention. Making the sides equal is a matter of adjusting the formal elements of color, texture, line, shape, direction, and volume. If a large shape dominates one side of the child's work, the teacher might suggest that he balance it with: (1) another large shape; (2) several small shapes; (3) a smaller but more exciting shape; or (4) a color, texture, pattern, or linear treatment that demands an equal amount of attention. In other words, balance need not be symmetrical; it might be asymmetrical and therefore much more interesting to perceive.

To illustrate the changes a teacher might suggest, Figure 8.8 shows one of the ways in which a child's original unbalanced drawing in Figure 8.7 might be balanced. The success of the teacher's suggestions, however, are largely based upon his ability to convince the child that visual symbols are more effective when they balance.

Unity. The second fundamental principle of artistic composition is that a configuration must have unity if it is to be pleasurable. Unity is a state of oneness, wholeness, or coherence. Without it, an image tends to break up or disintegrate into unrelated fragments that compete for attention. Such an arrangement is difficult and unpleasant to perceive, and its chaotic state makes it extremely hard to understand. Consequently, the teacher must help his students to recognize disunity and to avoid it in their work if the work is to be artistic and effective. But what advice can the teacher give about creating unity after he has assisted his students in detecting the lack of it?

He might suggest that they repeat colors, textures, lines, shapes, patterns, and other formal elements throughout their work. By using a color or a texture in more than one place, the artist

Fig. 8.7
An unbalanced drawing
produced by a youngster
in third grade.

Fig. 8.8
The drawing from Fig. 8.7
after instruction from the teacher.
The child has succeeded in
achieving balance in her work.

351

**THE TEACHING
OF ART**

makes the various parts of his product relate to one another; or to put it differently, he creates a relationship among the parts of the product by giving them something in common. Children ordinarily are very good at composition because they naturally repeat colors, shapes, and linear qualities. But improvements can be made, as seen in Figures 8.9 and 8.10 showing a child's drawing before and after compositional instruction about unity.

Sometimes disunity occurs because the segments of the whole are placed too far apart to be perceived as portions of the same integrated product. They tend to be seen as units in themselves and compete with one another for attention. This creates the feeling of spottiness, busyness, disorder, chaos, and meaninglessness. The remedy, fortunately, is not very difficult. It requires that the existing segments be placed closer together or that more segments be introduced, so that the open spaces are reduced in size. Figure 8.11 shows a child's drawing in which the parts are too far apart to make a pleasing whole, and Figure 8.12 shows the same drawing after help from the teacher.

Another suggestion that will aid the creation of unified objects is that the product should be made to appear finished or complete. If any part of a configuration seems incomplete or unfinished with respect to another part, the total image will seem to lack something. The unfinished portion will seem unrelated, foreign, and weak. Consequently, the teacher is advised to have his students work long enough so that they complete all portions of their products. If he were to do that and nothing else, the quality of child art in America would improve immensely.

By the time youngsters reach the fifth or sixth grade they are capable of benefiting from another suggestion about composition. They might be told that the unity of their work will improve if they arrange the parts of the product so that the observer's eye will move easily from one place to another in the work. By arranging a path for the eye to follow, the artist tends to tie the parts of his work together, and he is most successful if he can do it without making his plan too apparent. Subtlety of that kind, however, is not easy for a child to achieve. Probably

Fig. 8.11
The parts of this drawing are too far apart to make a pleasing whole. The parts tend to be perceived as separate, unrelated units.

Fig. 8.12
The drawing in Fig. 8.11 after the teacher gave the student instruction concerning unity in composition.

the most that we can expect in the elementary school is the kind of arrangement that appears in Plate 32. Notice how the eye moves from one portion of the work to another without shooting out of the picture.

Variety. If the student tries to produce unity by doing the things that have been recommended, it is possible that he will also produce boredom. The repetition of almost anything has that effect, and, of course, a pleasurable composition is one that does *not* create boredom. Consequently, it is understandable that one of the fundamental principles of artistic composition is that a configuration must have variety if it is to be pleasurable. Variety is diversity; it is a state of existence characterized by differences among its constituent elements. If there is too much variety in a visual symbol, however, the symbol is apt to lose its unity and vice versa. Thus it is important for the teacher to help his students maintain the proper balance between unity and variety. How can he do it?

He might suggest that the child create variety by changing the color or size of shapes as he repeats those shapes for unity, or he might recommend that the youngster use more colors, shapes, textures, linear qualities, and patterns in his work. As he does so, however, he must caution against too much variety.

Work that is uninteresting to perceive may be improved by creating variety in still another way. Proportions may be enhanced, for example, by showing the student that lines, shapes, and volumes are more interesting if they are divided into unequal parts. Divisions that result in matched or uniform parts are comparable to the division that occurs in symmetrically balanced arrangements; both are rather dull to perceive.

Variety and visual interest also may be achieved by making one portion of a configuration dominate the others. Some teachers refer to such dominant areas as "centers of interest." In other words, the eye tends to return to those areas more frequently than to others, and it usually does so because those areas offer a form of contrast that does not occur elsewhere. Sometimes there is more simplicity or more complexity in the dominant section

Fig. 8.13
Sandro Botticelli,
Birth of Venus. Ca. 1478.
68 ⅞ × 85 ½ in. Uffizi Gallery,
Florence.

Fig. 8.14
Jackson Pollock,
November 27, 1950. Oil on canvas.
Whitney Museum of American Art,
New York.

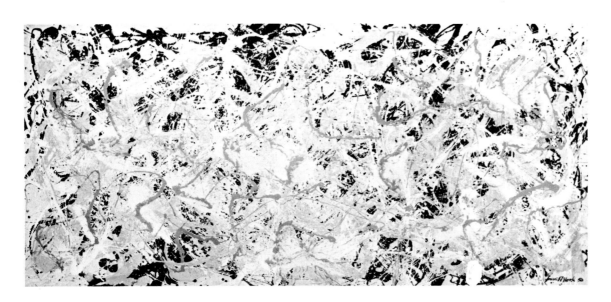

than there is elsewhere, or the area may exhibit more contrast between hues, values, intensities, textures, or directional movements. The painting in Figure 8.13 obviously has a "center of interest," or an area of dominance; but the painting by Jackson Pollock in Figure 8.14 is the same all over and, in this writer's view, is not very interesting to perceive because it lacks variety.

Miscellaneous concerns

Developing a knowledge of composition is partly a matter of getting youngsters to understand the material just mentioned. And, it is also a matter of getting them to learn procedures and to develop skill. If a person does not know the procedure for making art, his knowledge of composition will do him no good. And if he fails to develop skill, his poor craftsmanship will make the composition look bad. Therefore, good structural organization requires that a number of things be done well.

Finally, it is very important for the teacher to remember that children in the elementary school use art primarily as a way of learning about themselves and about their environment. They do not begin to use art to affect other people until they reach the secondary school. As a result, composition is not consciously important to youngsters in the elementary grades. They tend to become aware of its significance only when they begin to realize that composition affects the influence that they can have and the understanding that they can generate in the observer.

The importance that composition has for youngsters in the elementary school is about equal to the importance that it has for a chimpanzee. Good composition feels good and comfortable, while poor organization is disturbing. Consequently, children usually produce pleasing arrangements in the same natural way that a chimpanzee does. They begin to fail in that respect only when naturalistic representation becomes so important to them that it overpowers their natural instinct to act like little monkeys. Usually this begins to occur in the intermediate grades, and it is an indication that the teacher should begin to place a little more emphasis on compositional instruction.

Although young children are normally sensitive to visual organization, or design, some youngsters are more sensitive than others. Thus it is necessary to offer instruction in composition as soon as children enter school if we want them to develop the knowledge of design that is necessary for making pleasurable configurations. Considering the relative unimportance of composition to the child, however, it is wise to offer instruction informally and privately to individual children. And if the instruction seems to have no immediate effect, it is wise not to raise a fuss about it. Strong criticism or formal lessons on composition are almost certain to spoil art for young people and to end in failure. Tactics of that kind were used many years ago, and they were completely unsuccessful. They made children feel inadequate and discouraged because they overemphasized the grammar of art at the expense of its content. In summary, then, we might say that compositional instruction in the elementary school should occur; but it should be offered informally and should be related to the purpose that each child has in making art. It should be a kind of conditioning rather than a formal training.

DEVELOPING A KNOWLEDGE OF ART HISTORY

Teaching art history to children is really a matter of getting them to learn about specific works of art, about artists, and about sequential developments in art. Armed with a knowledge of visual communication and its significance in human history, the student should be able to make competent judgments about the quality and the importance of his own work and the work of others.

Making the teacher's job more difficult is the fact that the history of art covers thousands of years and is concerned with large numbers of persons, objects, and events that have played a part in the visual expressions of men. The accumulated knowledge of art history is, in fact, so great that no teacher could possibly cover it all. This being so, he must be selective about what he teaches, and the most reasonable selection probably would include information about the *major* historical developments in art, the *most* distinguished or representative artists of each period, and the *most* significant of their works.

To understand the distinctive character of art during any historical period, it is helpful to know what life was like at that time. It helps to know something about the living conditions, the politics, the religion, the work, the entertainment, and the daily routine of the people. It also helps to know about the customs, the ideas, and the values that moved people to act as they did. It is most important to know who was buying art.

To make any historical period live for students, it is a good idea to discuss one or two artists who are exemplars of that period. Information about the artist's appearance, his workshop, his home, and his friends is just as important as knowledge of his tools, his creative mannerisms, and his final products. If the artist has an especially interesting or exciting life, so much the better, for it helps to make teaching and learning more enjoyable.

Getting an intimate view of art history through the careful study of a few selected artists is much more effective than a superficial survey of many artists and the thousands of facts associated with them. It gives the student an opportunity to relax and to enjoy what he sees and hears, and it gives him the chance to find out what artists are really like and what contributions they have made to society. This is a matter of vital importance. If students are to grow toward the good life as a result of looking at works of art and appreciating them, they must feel that the artist is someone whose expressions are worth viewing. They must come to feel that artists are honorable, capable, intelligent people who have performed a worthwhile service for society. They must learn that the stereotype of the artist as an odd, antisocial, bohemian anarchist is largely a myth. For the most part, established artists are very much like other members of society. They eat, sleep at night, work in the daytime, raise families, vote, and dress like the rest of us. Naturally, a few of them do not fit this image, but there are always a few people in any profession who appear to be different. There are mathematicians, atomic scientists, plumbers, and college presidents who look and act distinctively; they add interest and excitement to life. Besides, it is not clothes or eating habits that make the man; it is his contributions to our attainment of the good life that really count. It is therefore recommended that teachers emphasize the effects that artists have had on the men and women of their time.

Teaching students that an artist was a social force is not especially interesting, however, unless the instructor is able to show how the artist managed to be influential. In other words, it is important to show examples of his work and to study them carefully. The object is to see and to feel the concepts and emotions that he presents, the manner with which he presents them, and the persuasiveness of the presentation.

If a teacher has no background in art history, he will have to work hard to prepare his lessons. But the overabundance of detailed information in art history makes it unlikely that a busy classroom teacher will take the time to dig out the most significant facts, theories, and works of art. Hence there is a clear need for the kind of assistance that teaching materials can provide. A few good films specially prepared for children can save the teacher a lot of time, and so can a collection of good reproductions, slides, and books that present the essential facts in a condensed form. Until such teaching materials are available, the instructor must do some digging and reorganizing in order to teach art history. With a little persistence, however, he will be able to add information about three or four artists a year to his repertory of art-historical knowledge. At that rate it would not be long before he could speak confidently about the lives and works of fifteen or twenty people.

Probably the most important thing to remember in the teaching of art history is that the subject must be made important to the student. If the teaching amounts to no more than a dry and dreary account of the facts, it is doomed to failure. This being so, the teacher must see that the content of his instruction is exciting as well as relevant to the interests of the child, to the words he uses, to the concepts he can entertain, and to the life he leads. Without this relevance, nothing is important enough to learn; with it, youngsters in the public school can listen and learn for long periods of time.

DEVELOPING A KNOWLEDGE OF AESTHETICS

Gotshalk says that aesthetic experience is "simply intrinsic perception, or attention to an object or field preeminently for the apprehension of the full intrinsic perceptual being and value of the object or field."[4] This is the notion accepted in this text, and it means that an individual is having an aesthetic experience if he gives attention to *any* object or field primarily for the purpose of absorbing whatever meaning exists in the *appearance* of the object or field. Thus it is possible to have an aesthetic experience with a tree, an old tin can, a thumbtack, or any other object or event, including a work of art. It is the teacher's job to get youngsters to learn the nature of that experience, and it is also his business to get them to learn that there is a difference between the aesthetic experience we have with a tree and the one we have with a work of art. If he can do that, he will be helping his pupils to understand the difference between art and nonart.

If he accepts the definition of art offered in this text, he will teach his students that art is a humanistic symbol, a model of the human condition. He will teach them that it presents concepts and emotions in visual form and that we apprehend those concepts and emotions in the total configuration of the art product as we experience it aesthetically. He will also explain that a tree is not a humanistic symbol but a natural object. Consequently, a tree cannot be said to *present* human meanings, although we may see a tree as being sturdy, tranquil, or cold. Such meanings are human, of course, but come entirely from the observer; they cannot be said to have been placed in the tree by someone else.

It may also be said that the observer furnishes the meaning when he views a work of art, but there is an important difference. In art there is a conscious effort on the part of the artist to organize the visual symbol in such a way that the observer will furnish the meaning that the artist desires. This means that an aesthetic experience with a work of art is an experience that involves the

[4] Denman W. Gotshalk, *Art and the Social Order*, Dover Publications, Inc., New York, 1962, p. 3.

transmission of meaning, whereas an aesthetic experience with a tree entails no such sharing.

Because the observer does attribute meaning to the things that he sees, it is extremely important for the art teacher to get children to learn that they must be careful to attach to works of art only those meanings that are justified by the appearance of the art object. In other words, youngsters must be taught to attribute meaning to the art product only if that meaning can be said to reside in the object as it is apprehended. If they are taught to associate a meaning with an object that its visual form does not justify, they are being taught to make judgments that are not based on aesthetic experience. Perhaps an example would be helpful here.

If we teach children that "pop" art (Figure 8.15) is a visual objection to the materialism and the cultural decadence of the 1960s, we are teaching them to associate a meaning with pop art that does not reside in the object itself. Such teachings cause children to place an undeserved value on that particular visual symbol and cause them to miss the values that actually may be realized through an aesthetic experience with the object.

As the teacher tries to get children to perceive the meanings that are intrinsic in a work of art, he faces another danger. If he is not careful, he may cause the children to look at the object

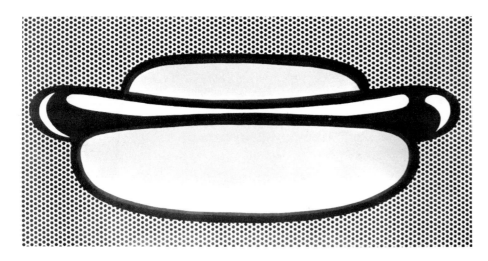

Fig. 8.15
Roy Lichtenstein,
Hot Dog. 1964. Baked enamel,
24 1/4 × 48 in. (Photo by permission
of Benjamin Birillo, New York).

as a scientist looks at a specimen under the microscope. Ordinarily a scientist is interested in seeing the descriptive, factual, or discursive meanings in the specimen, and he does not look for the nondiscursive qualities that might be there. If an individual is taught to perceive a work of art in the same way, he is likely to apprehend nothing but the subject matter, the material with which the object was made, the dimensions of the object, the name of the artist, and other such discursive items. This indicates that he is not having a full aesthetic experience with the work because he is restricting his attention to only a fraction of the meanings that exist in the "look" of the object. Thus he is not in a position to judge the value of the work as a work of art.

Furthermore, aestheticians such as Clive Bell[5] are apt to say that representative or discursive elements are irrelevant in aesthetic experience. Such persons would probably contend that descriptive content ought to be ignored in favor of the more nondiscursive meanings found in the formal relationships within the object. In fact, there are some persons who feel that it is perfectly reasonable for art to have no meaning at all and that we try too hard to find meaning in it.

It is perfectly true, of course, that observers may try too hard to find meanings that are not there, but the content of perception is always meaningful to a greater or lesser degree. Discursive meanings exist in visual configurations, and so do nondiscursive ones. If we ignore either of them, we are not having a complete aesthetic experience because we are not apprehending the full being and value of the perceived object or field. The art teacher must therefore get his pupils to see both the conceptual and the emotional, the discursive and the nondiscursive, if he wants them to have a full aesthetic experience. And they must have such an experience if they are to learn the difference between art and nonart and if they are to judge the value of art with any degree of competence. With these rather esoteric remarks as a background, what can be said about the practical aspects of teaching such things?

[5] Clive Bell, *Art*, Capricorn Books, G. P. Putnam's Sons, New York, 1958.

First of all, getting someone to learn about the things that we have discussed is largely a verbal enterprise, although it does entail the showing of objects of art and nonart. The mere showing of things would not be enough, of course, because it might result in nothing more than an awareness that something is present. Consequently, the teacher's job is to direct attention and to solicit reactions to the item being observed. As a start he might ask his students to tell him what they actually see in the object, making sure that they respond with meanings that could reasonably be said to reside in the object. While doing this he must encourage the children to look for more than the literary meanings that are so easy to find in the subject matter of a work of art. Literary content is important, and it is part of the aesthetic experience with art, but the teacher must get his pupils to see more if there is more to see. In other words, he must get them to see more than the fourteen people and a dog in Renoir's *Luncheon of the Boating Party*. He must get them to see the specific kinds of gaiety, freshness, and friendliness and the particular qualities of color and texture, as well as the relationships among all these things.

Naturally, the teacher will not be able to translate the full content of a work of art into words, nor will his students be able to do so. They might declare that a certain portrait painting presents the idea of man and gloominess, but such meanings are generalizations of a high order. Without a doubt there is much more import in the "look" of the painting, but much of that meaning is locked in the mental image of the work and cannot be framed in words. For that reason the best comment the teacher can make and the best he can expect from his students is a *general* comment about the discursive and nondiscursive meanings that are perceived. In other words, he can call attention to the man, to the gloominess, and to the formal structure of the portrait, but he cannot go much beyond the kind of global comment that misses the more complex content of the picture. In spite of this inability to discuss the full meaning of a work of art, the teacher should still try to get his students to discuss the content of the work because it is the only way that he has of estimating the degree to which the children have experienced an object or event aesthetically. Developing the ability to respond verbally is especially important for the future connoisseur, who will be called upon to justify the value that he attaches to works of art, to architecture, and to other dimensions of life.

As the teacher solicits verbal reactions to the "look" of objects and events, he is advised to offer some of his own responses in a sincere and nondogmatic way. This exchange of reactions will give him an opportunity to project his own interest in the aesthetic and his sincerity about the importance of the aesthetic. It will also give him the chance to introduce fundamental ideas about the nature and value of art in an informal way, and it will permit the use of elementary artistic terms that are new to the students. The informality of such an occasion usually makes the subject matter more appealing to children. But, informal or not, the early introduction of aesthetic knowledge and an artistic vocabulary are essential if the teacher and the student are to have meaningful and efficient conversations about creative work or aesthetic experience. For that reason it is recommended that such instruction begin when the child first enters school. At that point he could be taught the elementary version of the ideas on art and aesthetics that are presented in this book. He could learn that art is a matter of putting our ideas and our emotions into a pleasing form for others to see, and he could come to know that such an activity is valuable because it helps us to learn what other people are thinking and how they feel. He could also learn that we grow and become better persons because other individuals have shared their thoughts and emotions with us through the arts.

The beginning vocabulary presented by the teacher might include such words as subject matter, content, light, dark, bright, balance, watercolor, texture, sculpture, and other terms that are equally as simple. Without a doubt the teacher will find it necessary to repeat his definitions, and he will discover that art and its value must be explained in more than one way. This repetition should not disturb him, because it is through repetition and rephrasing that difficult concepts are made clear; and as the children begin to understand, they will use and respond to the new words and concepts more frequently and more knowingly. This indicates the need to move on to new and more complex ideas and terms.

Although the complexity of the new material should increase with the child's ability to understand, it is still necessary for the elementary school teacher to avoid abstract philosophical content in his instruction. The reason for this is that the child is unable to think in abstract terms until he is about ready to enter the secondary school. At that point, however, the instruction in aesthetics should become more rigorous. The student in the junior high school should begin to learn that there are several theories of art, and he should be able to explain two or three of them and compare them. Having learned the notion of art presented in this text, he might be expected to learn the theories of such persons as Clive Bell and Tolstoy, and he might be expected to support his comments about art and life with logical arguments.

It may appear that teaching such things to children is difficult, but it is not as hard as it may seem. The hardest part the teacher will face is getting the ideas straight in his own mind. When that happens, he will be able to reduce some of the most complex aesthetic notions to a level that the child can understand. The view mastered by the teacher might be the one that is expressed in this book, or it might be another; but it is very important for the teacher to base his instruction on a philosophy that he can *understand* and *accept*. Otherwise he is apt to confuse his students or display a lack of conviction.

Furthermore, the *elementary school* teacher is strongly advised to center his instruction around a *single* point of view about the nature of art. If he tries to teach more than one definition, he is apt to do more harm than good. The reason for this is that youngsters in the elementary school are struggling to understand themselves and their environment, and the task is difficult and time-consuming, even if they are provided with a single valuative framework. After all, they must internalize that framework or philosophical system and live with it for quite a length of time if they are to recognize its utility or its relevance to life. By introducing several new and competing views about the nature of the art, the teacher would interfere with the development of a coherent and meaningful value system and make it difficult for the child to understand. He would add to the noisy, moving, chaos of experience by providing several different perspectives on art before the child has had time to master one of them and give it an adequate test. Without one well-developed standard or point of view, a person is hardly equipped to understand or judge other philosophical positions. Thus the teacher of art is more apt to help his students reach the age of reason (the secondary school) equipped to make logical philosophical decisions if he encourages the internalization of a single definition of art and allows his students to live with it long enough to recognize its relevance to life.

As the instructor discusses art and aesthetics with his students, it is clear that he must have something to show that will serve as a point of reference; the logical items to observe and discuss are the masterpieces that are used in teaching art history. In other words, it makes sense to teach art history and aesthetics at the same time, although this is not ordinarily done. Information about the nature and value of art can be made more understandable if it is considered in the light of history; examined from an aesthetic point of view, the masterpieces of long ago take on a new vitality and a new significance. Such works have passed the test of time, and one can speak of them confidently as great works of art. The conditions that stimulated their creation are often well known, and the effects that they have had upon generations of people are quite clear. But when it comes to contemporary visual expression, it is much more difficult to be sure that it is art of high quality and that it will have a significant effect upon society. The reason for this is that contemporary symbols are often different from previous ones, and it takes a while to fully appreciate them. Nevertheless, children should become familiar with the visual expressions of their own day in order that they may ascertain the spirit of their time and estimate its effects on the future.

It is equally essential for students and teachers to engage in discussions about the aesthetic merits of the child's own creative

Fig. 8.16
Reproductions of masterpieces are used by this teacher as she discusses aesthetics with her students.

Fig. 8.17
It is important for students to discuss the aesthetic merits of their own work as they are doing in this instance.

work. If they did not, it would be impossible to teach the performance aspects of art. But such discussions are bound to be just as difficult as conversations about the contemporary art of professional artists because there has been no time to live with the work and to absorb it. In other words, it will be hard to tell if it is high-quality art and if it has any significant value; but this is the reason for developing a knowledge of aesthetics in students. Such information helps a person to see the difficulties involved in creating and judging visual expression, and it helps him to understand the reasons for the standards of judgment employed by his teacher. It also assists him in formulating his own criteria for measuring aesthetic significance.

In addition to looking at his own work and at masterpieces from art history, it is advisable for the student to look at popular art and at nonart while studying aesthetics. Without making comparisons it would be very difficult for him to learn the nature of fine art and the nature of its superiority over flashing signs, magazine advertisements, calendar decorations, and cereal boxes. It can be hoped that this aesthetic education will lead the child to change his attitudes and values in favor of the fine arts and that perhaps he will even come to like them. To say, however, that it is the teacher's job to get youngsters to like fine art is *not* to say that the teacher's job is to get them to like all *styles* of fine art. On the contrary, it is his business to get children to understand that there are different styles, that the styles have a reason for existing, and that the differences are valuable.

The practical application of aesthetics

During the student's stay in the public schools, it is understood that he will be taught aesthetics as it applies to art and as it relates to life in general. It is our intention that the teacher get children to understand that the art object displays the highest aesthetic quality that man is capable of embodying in the products he produces. According to this view, masterpieces of art constitute a standard by means of which we can judge the aesthetic quality of other man-made objects. And our students can be shown that the high aesthetic quality of art makes it more valuable than nonart in our pursuit of the good life. But it is vitally important to teach our youngsters that *everything* has an aesthetic dimension and that it affects us strongly even if the object or event is not a fine work of art. In other words, teachers should explain that the appearance of our homes, communities, television programs, and automobiles is an aesthetic dimension of life that has a powerful effect upon us even if those objects do not qualify as great works of art. If television, magazine advertisements, books, and other communications media of ordinary quality are pleasing in their appearance, they can be nearly as seductive and convincing as the best art, and if the content of the communication is of a kind that leads us *away* from the good life, it is clearly detrimental to the individual and to society.

Private and public housekeeping also can lead to the degradation of culture. If we discard our garbage in the forests, on the highways, and around our feet, we are acting like dogs discarding their bones; and we create an environmental model that is more animalistic than human, an environment that conditions our children to live as dogs. Surely we must help our students to see that the appearance of ourselves and our surroundings does affect us, and we must teach them the characteristics of a more humanizing private and public appearance.

Architecture, urban planning, and consumer products can also lead us away from the reasonable approximation of paradise if they are not sufficiently human or natural. Buildings and highways, for example, often look as if they were designed and located by computers rather than by men. They lack the comfortable organizational relationships of nature; they lack the warmth and the individual style or accent of the human personality. Their design and construction seems to be affected more strongly by the standardization of materials, tools, and building practices than by the spirit and desire of people who think profoundly and feel with passion. Consequently, the man-made environment is rapidly becoming impersonal, featureless, and uninspiring. Such appearances affect our future generations undesirably because they do not present models of spiritual celebration;

they do not permit our youngsters to see the flowering of a unique personality as it occurs in the work of a Palladio or a Frank Lloyd Wright. In other words, seeing the human products we have described is not apt to inspire anyone to great human accomplishments, and it is not likely to make us feel as comfortable and contented as the sight of a tree, a mountain, or a moving stream. In fact, it is more apt to promote neuroses.

Therefore, to show that a knowledge of aesthetics can and should be applied to the practical aspects of life as well as to art, the teacher must make a special effort to demonstrate the application. He must show how the principles of artistic composition may be applied to community planning, to furniture construction, and to other practical matters. In fact, it would be helpful for him to show that such principles can and should be applied to writing, speaking, singing, and ordinary human relationships as well as to visual creations. He also must indicate that the human meanings embodied in art are meanings that could and should be included in our buildings, parks, national monuments, and other creative products. Probably the same quantity of meaning could not be incorporated in the landscaping of our parks, but the highest human qualities should be included, wherever possible, to create a natural human environment suitable for human beings.

From these comments the reader probably will recognize the suggestion that we should teach our children to make the nonartistic aspects of the man-made environment more artistic. The belief underlying this suggestion is that artistic images are the most humanizing models and that such models are the only ones that will raise the level of a culture to the heights of a great society if such a society is ever to exist.

The child's ability to appreciate the aesthetic

After reading these comments, some people probably will express the doubt that we can help children to learn about the nature of art, the value of art, and the nature of the aesthetic experience. Without a doubt there are persons who wonder if youngsters are *capable* of recognizing the aesthetic and responding to it; if they are not, they are certainly not prepared to understand the nature and the value of art. Fortunately, both research and experience with children have shown that youngsters *do* recognize and respond to the aesthetic aspect of life and of art. Probably the most comprehensive review of the pertinent research is given by C. W. Valentine.[6] In his summary he indicates that children are very much aware of subject matter and strongly influenced by it in forming their preferences for works of art. This is a condition that one might expect, for Piaget has shown us that elementary school children are in a stage of development in which they come to grips with the concrete objects and events in their world. The conceptual meanings of such concrete subject matter are part of the aesthetic dimension of experience; they are present in the "look" of things. Thus children are capable of recognizing and responding to a part of the aesthetic if they see and are influenced by subject matter.

In addition, most experienced teachers will testify that children notice the emotive content in a work of art or in a human event. They see happiness or sadness in a classroom situation or in a painting, and it often causes them to express their likes or dislikes for things. Like the conceptual content of experience, these emotional meanings reside in the "look" of experience and constitute a part of the aesthetic dimension of that experience. Hence we have further indication that children are capable of seeing the aesthetic and responding to it.

Evidence that youngsters can respond to other dimensions of the aesthetic appeared in 1933, when Parmely Daniels, Constance Jasper, Katherine Whorley, and William Walton published the results of experiments conducted under the direction of Norman Meier at the University of Iowa. Daniels found that youngsters of preschool age preferred balance to imbalance in three-dimensional designs.[7] Jasper concluded that some children

---

[6] C. W. Valentine, *The Experimental Psychology of Beauty*, Methuen and Co., Ltd., London, 1962, pp. 119–180.
[7] Parmely Daniels, "Discrimination of Compositional Balance at the Pre-school Level," *Psychological Monographs*, no. 200, pp. 1–11.

could respond to visual rhythms as early as three years of age, and she found that such responses tended to increase with chronological age.[8] Although Whorley did not feel that absolute conclusions could be drawn from her work, she felt that certain youngsters did seem to be sensitive to unity in arrangement when they were between four and seven years of age.[9] And Walton discovered that certain rare children were sensitive to color harmony as early as the fourth year, but she also learned that older children were more sensitive in this respect than the younger ones.[10]

In each of the foregoing experiments it is clear that the youngsters were responding to nonfigurative formal elements. But it is only fair to say that there were children who did not react to those elements, and some of them did not respond sensitively even if they were older than the other children. Apparently young people are affected more readily by conceptual and emotional content and subject matter than by nonfigurative compositional elements. The fact that some youngsters did respond to formal arrangement, however, is evidence that it is possible for children to do so without being taught. This, in turn, suggests that teachers might help larger numbers of students to become sensitive to the structural aspects of aesthetic experience if instructional efforts in that direction are actually made.

Helping youngsters who have problems

In spite of the fact that the teacher is thoroughly familiar with the subject and dedicated to it, children may still have trouble learning aesthetics. Part of their trouble might be caused by a teacher who does not develop the proper attitudes and values in his students as he teaches them the structure of knowledge. We shall consider the development of attitudes and values in a

[8] Constance Jasper, "The Sensitivity of Children of Pre-school Age to Rhythm in Graphic Form," in *ibid.*, pp. 12–25.
[9] Katherine Whorley, "An Experimental Investigation of the Sensitivity of Children to Compositional Unity," in *ibid.*, pp. 26–45.
[10] William Walton, "The Sensitivity of Children and Adults to Color Harmony," in *ibid.*, pp. 51–62.

moment, but, first, there are a few suggestions that can be made about the development of aesthetic knowledge.

As we have said, the teacher must be able to make the essentials of aesthetic knowledge as concrete as possible, at least until the child reaches the secondary school and is capable of handling abstract concepts. If there are aspects of aesthetic knowledge that cannot be made concrete, the instructor should not attempt to teach those elements at the elementary school level, for they will only produce a lot of frustrated, bored, and troublesome youngsters.

Having achieved a degree of concreteness in the teaching of aesthetics, the instructor may still fail to influence his students if he is unable to adjust his vocabulary to their level of understanding. Unfortunately, the ability to do so is developed only through practice. Consequently, it will take a little time for the teacher to learn to talk to children efficiently. It is possible, however, for the teacher to speed his own learning by recording his conversations with children and by studying the playback. Listening to his own questions, explanations, comparisons, and other logical actions helps the teacher to uncover mistakes in a relatively short time.

A tape recording might show the teacher that he does not treat the students' ideas with the proper respect. He may have formed the habit of following their judgmental remarks with the immediate notification that they are wrong, causing some youngsters to refrain from making judgments. Other bad habits may also appear to the teacher in a recording, but the point is that he can help children who are having difficulty with aesthetics by studying his own verbal behavior as objectively as possible.

DEVELOPING INTEREST IN THE AESTHETIC DIMENSION OF EXPERIENCE

The aesthetic dimension of experience is the sensuous aspect of experience, which contains meanings that are both verbal and nonverbal. A person who is interested in the visual aspect of things is an individual who is interested in the form or shape of the things he perceives, in the meanings or values that reside in the image, and in the relationship between the form of the image and its meaning. A person's interest may take the form of a relatively passive *appreciation* or it may consist in active *production*. By this we mean that an interested individual may be one who prefers to "take in" the "look" of experience or one who goes beyond that to the creation of an object that is meant to be experienced visually and aesthetically. The former may be called a *connoisseur*, and the latter an *artist*.

An interest in appreciating or creating the aesthetic may involve no more than a mere *awareness* that there are such things to see and to make, or it may mean that the individual *places a high value* on appreciating or creating. In fact, it is possible for a person to value those activities so highly that he becomes *committed* to them and thoroughly involved with them. This is the highest level of interest in the aesthetic dimension that one can attain, and the student who reaches that level becomes either a dedicated connoisseur or a fairly productive artist.

The aim of art education is to develop an interest in the aesthetic that goes beyond mere awareness. But the most we can reasonably expect to achieve in the elementary school is a limited feeling of worthwhileness in the appreciation and creation of visual configurations. In fact, we are not likely to develop our students to the highest level of commitment much before the senior year in high school. There are at least two reasons for that delay. The first is that youngsters are unable to reason logically and to deal with abstract ideas until they are about eleven years old. This means that some of the values in the aesthetic dimension of life will be difficult if not impossible to explain below the sixth or seventh grade. Also, a more comprehensive understanding of value in the aesthetic aspect of experience must exist before an individual is apt to commit himself to a visual pursuit of the aesthetic or to serious involvement with its creation.

The second reason for saying that commitments to the aesthetic are not likely to be developed before the senior year in high school is that our society does not value the aesthetic dimension of experience. As a result, teachers will have to *change* cultural values as well as develop them, and that takes time as well as tact and understanding. It takes enough time so that students are very likely to be seniors in high school before the teacher can develop in them the kind of devotion to the aesthetic that will cause them to go out and do something about their own appearance, the looks of their homes and communities, and the various modes of visual expression that bombard them every day.

Getting children to have an interest in the aesthetic aspect of life is partly a matter of developing in them a perceptual set or a readiness to perceive the aesthetic. After all, a person must perceive it if he is to appreciate it or give it an artistic form. This point was stressed in Chapter 4 while discussing the nature of the artist, and it was said that a set to perceive aesthetic form is more apt to develop if the culture or subculture places a value on it. But if the culture as a whole does not value the aesthetic, the child will not do so unless a respected individual within one of the subcultures recognizes it as worthwhile. The schoolroom, of course, is such a subculture, and everyone in it is a potential determinant of the values that children will have. Consequently, it is the teacher's job to see that his own behavior clearly reflects the high value that he places on the appreciation and creation of aesthetic form, and it is equally important for him to see that he is respected by his students. Respect is vital because children will rarely accept as their own the values of a person whom they do not admire. But how does the teacher manage to gain the respect of students and become their *model of value*?

Probably there is no completely satisfactory answer to such a question because of the unique relationship between a teacher and each of his students. Yet there are certain teaching behaviours that are generally helpful to an art teacher in winning the admiration of children and building their valuative framework. One of the most important of them is to demonstrate a serious involvement in the production of art. This does not mean that the teacher must paint in competition with professional artists, but it does mean that he should reveal his dedication to creative activity and his satisfaction with it by making art in school or by bringing his finished products to class. High school art teachers have recognized the effectiveness of such activity for a long time, and some of them make a point of requesting studio space when they apply for new jobs. They find that youngsters enjoy "hanging around" when something new is going on and that such persons are usually more than willing to lend the teacher a hand whenever they can. The seriousness and excitement of creative activity tends to rub off on them, and they begin to identify themselves with the teacher's values. In other words, they begin to feel a worthiness in the aesthetic dimension of experience; that same feeling can be generated by elementary school classroom teachers as well as by art teachers. It simply requires the instructor's occasional participation in the art activities that occupy his students.

If the teacher does paint with his pupils, however, he must do it with seriousness and confidence. No student will be favorably impressed by artistic activity if his teacher seems to be playing, killing time, or taking a break from the serious business of life. By the same token, no student will believe the teacher's comments about the value of artistic activity if the instructor constantly speaks of his own lack of ability. After all, a person is not experiencing much that seems worthwhile if he is always complaining about his inability to make a straight line or his lack of success in drawing the human figure.

Still another suggestion for the teacher who creates with his students is that he should do the best he is capable of doing. If he purposely works at the child's level, he is not apt to be genuinely interested in what he is doing and, in that case, is not likely to reveal any dedication to the creation or appreciation of aesthetic objects. Sometimes teachers work at a childish level because they are afraid that work of a more adult nature will discourage their pupils, but that is a mistake. Children are much more inclined to admire the teacher who works in a mature fashion, and they are more likely to feel that there is something worthwhile to which they can aspire. If they become discouraged by such work, it is because the teacher or someone else has lead them to believe that they should be achieving at that level or that the teacher's manner of painting is the one and only correct method.

In addition to doing creative work of his own the teacher can demonstrate a strong interest in the aesthetic by exhibiting his work, by attending art exhibits, by promoting the arts in his school and community, and by discussing art with his students. He can take an active part in trying to improve the appearance of the community and in trying to save its aesthetically significant landmarks. And he also can show his values by keeping up-to-date on current events that have a bearing on the arts at a national or international level.

Still another way for the teacher to demonstrate his interest in appreciating and creating the aesthetic is to see that his art classes do not become a dumping ground for potential dropouts, disciplinary problems, and youngsters looking for an easy course. Nothing can do more to discourage serious high school students from pursuing the aesthetic aspects of life than the feeling that administrators and counselors are using art classes as a baby-sitting service; and it is even more discouraging to feel that the art teacher is too unintelligent to realize what is going on or too unconcerned to do anything about it. Consequently, it is recommended that art teachers must not permit their classes to be used as dumping grounds, even if attempts to do so are clothed in laudatory statements about the therapeutic value of art. After all, anything can be therapeutic if is handled properly. Furthermore, public schools are educational rather than therapeutic institutions. The teachers are not trained to act as therapists; and if they attempt to treat their students as patients, they may damage them unintentionally. In addition, treatment of that kind takes a lot of time, patience, and personal attention. It takes so much time, in fact, that one or two "troubled" students can monopolize a teacher's time and cause him to neglect the youngster's who are capable and serious about learning to appreciate and create aesthetic objects. Situations of that kind are a tragic waste of educational manpower and money because they are not significantly helpful to the troubled students and alienate the capable ones. Thus it is essential that the art teacher try to keep his class from becoming an educational dumping ground. He must raise his standards to a realistic level and not allow them to be lowered.

As art teachers in the secondary school try to maintain realistic educational standards, they may be blocked by administrators and counselors who want to know where the troubled students are to be placed if they are not placed in art, home economics, and industrial arts classes. The administrator frequently asks if the art teacher expects the troubled students to be placed in math classes or physics classes. This is a disturbing response because it indicates that the administrator values other subjects more highly than art, and that should not be the case. Any subject that is sufficiently worthwhile to be offered as a part of the curriculum in the public schools is a subject that deserves to be taught well. The people who pay for the professional instruction of their children in art do not wish to have the content or the teaching of the subject made inferior by turning the art classes into baby-sitting sessions.

When an administrator asks where else he can put troubled students, he also shows that he can see no alternative to the sacrifice of art, except the sacrifice of all subjects. Fortunately, however, there are educators who are beginning to solve the problem of "troubled" students without sacrificing either the youngsters or the subjects. One of their answers is to offer instruction at several different levels in each subject.[11] Most of the troubled students would probably receive instruction at the lowest level, while the more capable persons would get their training in separate, more advanced classes. As the troubled pupils improve and are capable of moving ahead, they are placed in the next most advanced group. This system does not solve the problem completely, but it does ease the teacher's job and allow him to do the most good for all students because it puts those with common abilities and problems together in the same classes. Homogeneous grouping of the kind described above

[11] Harry Broudy, B. O. Smith, and J. R. Burnett, *Democracy and Excellence in American Secondary Education*, Rand McNally and Company, Chicago, 1964, pp. 211–226.

can reduce some of the teacher's difficulties and serve to make him and his aesthetic values more respectable in the eyes of the students, but this does not mean that all the pupils in each class will be the same. In fact, they will all be different, as always, but the differences among them will not be as great. This may also tend to reduce discipline problems, although it certainly will not eliminate them. The question of what to do about discipline is a question that preoccupies almost all young teachers. It is mentioned here because discipline is absolutely essential it the teacher is to be admired by his students; and he must be respected if his aesthetic interests or values are to become the values of his pupils. How does he maintain discipline?

The perfect answer to such a question is almost impossible to give because the achievement of a disciplined class depends upon the particular situation and the characteristics of the individuals involved. Like anyone else, teachers respond to certain acts or events in the ways that they always have responded. If they have always been angered by cheating, they will probably be angry when it occurs in their classrooms. But teachers often are taught to look for the *cause* of the cheating and to eliminate it. This is the ideal thing to do, of course, but situations requiring disciplinary action usually demand an immediate response that does not permit the investigation of causes. This being so, the teacher usually reacts automatically in the way he has always reacted in similar circumstances. Reactions of that kind may not be suitable from the psychological point of view, but the teacher who postpones his response until he can think back to his college days and select the correct reaction is apt to be too late for maximum effectiveness. Consequently, we need to do all we can in our teacher-training institutions to help the future teacher internalize appropriate responses to common disciplinary situations, and the only way this can be done is by giving him more opportunities to work with youngsters under supervised conditions. Until we can provide more supervised teaching opportunities, we must continue to give the traditional suggestions about how to avoid situations that lead to disciplinary problems and a lack of respect.

In the first place, trouble often develops when the teacher has the idea that youngsters should be allowed to do an unlimited amount of talking, singing, and wandering during the art class. Since materials and tools must be obtained and pieces of equipment must be shared, it is reasonable to expect a certain amount of talking and moving about; but it is also sensible to expect the art work of the excessive talkers and movers to be inferior to the work of their quiet and relatively less active classmates. No one can paint seriously while talking or racing around the room, because art requires a maximum of concentration. Thus it is the teacher's obligation to see that children understand the need for quiet and that peace is maintained from the first day of class to the last. It is recommended, moreover, that the teacher remain just as firm during the art class as he does during the rest of the day. It is not a time to be "buddy-buddy" with students, nor is it a time to relax from the rigors of teaching the social studies or the language arts; it is still a time for valuable education through serious activity.

In addition to remaining firm about talking and walking, the teacher is advised to keep the quiet youngsters busy and deeply involved in their work. When children are singing and wandering around, it is clear that they are not engrossed in their art; but youngsters can sometimes be quiet and equally uninvolved. That is usually the case if a child finishes his work quickly and asks to do something else. By looking at the finished product, the teacher can determine if the child should give it further attention. Just how long he should be kept at the task is difficult to determine, but the product should not look as if he completed it in a "jiffy" just to get it over. Unless there is a good reason, the work should reveal sufficient conceptual and emotional elements; it should be pleasantly composed; and the technique should be suitable for the child's developmental level. If it does not display those characteristics, he might be asked to work on it some more. In fact, a little extra hard work from most of our students would help to improve the art work of many American youngsters. As the situation now stands, we seem to promote speed at the expense of quality. And the children who finish with amazing speed are likely to produce inferior art and create discipline problems at the same time, because there is nothing more conducive to horseplay than a child with nothing to do.

The teacher will not always be able to get the early finishers to return to work. After all, some youngsters are able to do outstanding work more quickly than others. Therefore it is wise for the teacher to plan activities that will keep the early finishers busy. Sometimes it helps to keep a file of short art projects available for such purposes. The materials that are needed and the procedure for completing the project might be given in mimeographed form so that the students can look in the file, read the directions, gather the materials, and start on a new activity without demanding special attention from the teacher. Again, it is important to remember that all procedures, materials, and tools should be suitable for the ages of the children. If they are not, there is an excellent opportunity for disciplinary problems to develop from frustrated or bored youngsters.

In addition to being well prepared, the teacher can help to avoid discipline problems by refusing to give instruction or by refusing to permit work until the children are quiet. If he talks over their noise at the beginning of the year, it is quite possible that he will have to continue to do so as long as the youngsters are under his guidance, because a well-developed habit is difficult to change and often results in a breakdown of rapport between the teacher and his students. Thus the old advice about being firm in early encounters with students is good advice. It places the teacher in the position of respect that is necessary if he is to influence the children and get them to value the aesthetic.

Young teachers sometimes exhibit the natural desire to be liked by their students. They feel close to their pupils in age and in spirit, and they make the mistake of trying to win admiration by acting like the youngsters they teach. They use the same slang; they dress in a similar way; and they talk as if their listeners were their equals in artistic competence. Clearly this is a mistake because a teacher cannot act like a student without being treated like one; he cannot speak with authority by relinquishing his authority; and he cannot hope to elevate the culture of his students by displaying himself as a model of value that looks and acts no different from the youngsters themselves. It is for that reason that teachers must act their age and present themselves as friendly authorities who recognize and accept their role as leaders. They must let it be known that schooling is serious but enjoyable work, and they must be willing to assert themselves and scold their pupils firmly if the need arises. This is mentioned because some teachers have developed the notion that children are fragile creatures who will crumble at the slightest criticism. But children are really quite capable of receiving verbal reprimands, and they must receive them if they are to learn the behavior that society expects from them.

Disciplinary action can be avoided, in part, by stimulating the students and giving as many directions about procedure as possible before the work period begins. This eliminates the need to interrupt youngsters after they have become immersed in creative activity. Concentrated effort is essential in art, and interruptions break concentration and make youngsters more susceptible to horseplay. If further instruction must be given after work has begun, it is best to give it quietly and individually to each student. Keeping an eye on the whole class and moving around the room are also helpful, for there is no one more unimpressive in projecting aesthetic interest than the teacher who sits at his desk while his students draw and paint. His apparent lack of interest tends to encourage undesirable behavior; but if he walks around the room and discusses each student's aims in relation to the emerging art object, he will project a more favorable image and enjoy a more favorable response. In some cases, however, it is not even necessary to speak, for a smile or a pat on the back is worth a million words. It conveys a feeling of approval, concern, and respect for the individual as well as his work.

Still another way to gain respect and to maintain discipline is to organize the classroom carefully, so that it is a pleasant and functional place in which to work. Artistic displays, good lighting, adequate ventilation, and orderliness help to make a room sufficiently comfortable for daily living. Unfortunately some art teachers seem to have the notion that squalor is essential to the production of art. They seem to feel that any responsibility for the care of tools, equipment, and property is an unbearable burden for the fragile and sensitive artist-teacher who must occupy himself with more profound aesthetic matters. But it seems a bit hypocritical to preach the importance of beauty in our lives while advocating sloppiness in the studio. Consequently, the persons who oppose orderliness should be required to show proof that slovenliness or dirtiness is more conducive to the creation of beauty than beauty itself. Until such proof is forthcoming, it seems more sensible to advocate neatness. But doing so does not mean that the classroom should have the antiseptic quality of a hospital. We mean that it should be orderly or thoughtfully arranged, so that students can clean up after themselves with relative ease. Tools and storage areas should be labeled, and working materials should be kept in open and accessible places. This makes it easier for youngsters to get materials without unnecessary commotion and helps the teacher to inventory his supplies at a glance.

In addition to arranging the classroom so that it will be pleasant and functional, the teacher is advised to plan the handling of supplies carefully. If he intends to introduce a papier-mâché project, he should figure out how to distribute wallpaper paste, how to keep furniture from getting pasty, how to store wet products so that they do not stick to anything, how to get the hands of the children clean, how to arrange the room for painting the products, how to distribute the paint, and how to manage other problems of that kind. By planning such things carefully the teacher will be able to eliminate many situations that could lead to disciplinary problems. Naturally, it takes a lot of work in the beginning, but if it is done well, it will not have to be done again, and it will also reduce the emotional strain on the instructor.

It is equally helpful if the teacher gives thought to planning the time of his art lessons, to the combination of students on cooperative projects, and to the variety of procedures and stim-

383

ulations that he presents. Children usually appear most alert and receptive to instruction in the morning. For that reason many teachers make a habit of teaching certain selected subjects at that time, and they reserve art instruction for a less desirable part of the day. They might make a practice of teaching art immediately after recess or after lunch, when deep breathing, active perspiration, or overeating make it somewhat difficult to concentrate and remain alert. Or they might teach art during the last half hour in the afternoon when youngsters are more apt to have their eyes on the clock and their minds on football. If art education is habitually confined to the less desirable hours, it is possible that it will fail to achieve interest and that discipline will be a problem. Hence it is recommended that teachers revise their teaching schedules from time to time, so that all subjects may enjoy the privilege of being taught at a choice hour.

Once in a while, the teacher may wish to have his class create a mural, a puppet show, or something else that requires group work and cooperation. If he does not plan the combinations of children in the work groups, he may run into trouble. Enemies usually produce a visual and theatrical flop, and groups without a leader are likely to sit around and wait for a miracle. This means that it is helpful to assemble reasonably congenial groups with at least one leader in each of them who can organize things and keep the project moving.

While we are on the subject of group work, it should be said that creating art with a committee is not easy, and there are some persons who believe it is impossible. But films are works of art, and they are almost always created by a "committee." The success of the film, however, is usually dependent upon a strong leader, such as the producer or director, who can estimate the abilities of the company, assign the members to the proper tasks, and get them to do their best work. Again, this merely emphasizes the need for leadership in group work and suggests that the teacher would do well to plan for leadership.

The teacher should also plan for a variety of art projects and a wide selection of stimuli, because variety adds excitement to learning and keeps youngsters from getting bored. A constant diet of crayon work, for example, is especially dull because crayons are commonly used by children from the age of three onward. Consequently, a balance of drawing, painting, print making, sculpture, crafts, art history, and aesthetics is necessary for maintaining interest and discipline as well as for general education in art.

Despite the fact that a teacher plans to avoid discipline problems and other troubles, something is still apt to go wrong. A child may spill a quart of paint or fill a silk screen with plastic glue instead of fish glue. The classroom teacher may disappear when the art teacher arrives, leaving him without any notion of what happened to a very necessary jar of paste, or some other unhappy thing might serve to fan the fire in thirty little hearts. But if such incidents do not occur regularly, the teacher must learn to accept them as part of the game of teaching, and he must not chastise his students and colleagues for them. This demands a measure of patience and good humor, but both qualities are recognized as essential in any occupation requiring close, continuous relationships with other human beings.

If the art teacher wishes to be admired so that his students will accept his valuation of the aesthetic as their own, he may succeed by doing the things that have already been suggested. But full success is bound to elude him if he fails to treat his pupils as respectable human beings whose appreciative judgments and creative products are worth hearing or seeing. "What is the use trying," they will say, "if the teacher does not listen to our ideas and look at our work with attentiveness and understanding? Why should we listen to him and accept his views if he fails to recognize that we are trying and that our struggle needs a little reinforcement?" In other words, a student is not apt to look kindly on the instructor if the latter is completely aloof, destructive in his criticism, and unmindful of the fact that a student is a student and not a teacher.

Up to this point we have tried to show that the teacher's job is to present himself as someone who values or is committed to the appreciation and creation of aesthetic objects. We also have tried to indicate that he must make himself respected and admired if he is to influence his pupils and cause them to have the same interest in the aesthetic that he does. But the teacher will have a hard time upgrading the cultural values of children if the values of the environment outside the classroom are different from the ones that the teacher is trying to develop. Unfortunately, that is the existing situation for most American teachers, and it means that many of them must try to affect the culture outside the school so that their teaching within the school will enjoy greater success. The recommended way of winning support from parents and other townspeople is to undertake a comprehensive public relations program of the kind described in Chapter 11, but the classroom teacher will do well to say a word or two in support of art during PTA meetings and parent-teacher conferences. At those times it helps to explain the value of art education and the goals that the schools are trying to attain. The parents must be given information about the nature of art and, especially, about the nature of the child's development in art. And if they want to know what they can do to help their children with the subject, the teacher must be prepared to offer suggestions. More recommendations on this matter will be made when we discuss the development of self-confidence in children, but at this point it can be suggested that parents help to develop the child's interest in art by showing some interest themselves. By this we mean that parents could take their children to museums and art exhibitions and view the displays as objectively as possible. They could also give more attention to the "look" of things by discussing with their children the appearance of flowers, insects, junkyards, city streets, and other aspects of life. They could attach more importance to the visual symbols that their youngsters create, and they could do so by displaying their work, by listening to explanations with patience, and by recognizing that the child is presenting himself for observation in the pictures that he paints. Parents could also provide the space and the materials for drawing and painting, and they could occasionally do a little creative work of their own. The only things needed for art activity are a few materials and a place to work that will not suffer seriously from the acci-

386

ART
EDUCATION

Fig. 8.18
*Parents help to build
interest and self-confidence in their
children by showing an interest in
the art that their children produce.
(Photo by Richard Hildwein.)*

dental spilling of paint or paste. Ideas about the materials that
a person might use may be obtained from Chapter 11, but a
good basic selection would include poster paint, newsprint or
used newspapers, bristle and hair brushes, crayons, paste, scissors,
colored paper, and all kinds of scrap materials. Working at an
easel is unnecessary because it is just as good or better to paint
and draw on a low table or on the floor. Further assistance for
parents in developing the child's interest in art may be obtained
from books devoted to the subject. The teacher is therefore
advised to have such books available so that parents can browse
through them. Probably two of the best-known books for parents

are *Your Child and His Art* by Viktor Lowenfeld[12] and *Art for the Family* by D'Amico, Wilson, and Maser.[13]

Finally, it is important to point out that the development of interest in the aesthetic dimension of experience is closely related to the development of confidence in the ability to make and to judge works of art. For that reason, we shall proceed to a discussion of the development of self-confidence in art.

DEVELOPING SELF-CONFIDENCE IN MAKING AND EVALUATING ART WORKS

If an individual is to make or appreciate art, he must feel confident of his ability to do so. Without that confidence he is apt to lose interest in the visual arts and turn his attention to forms of symbolization that offer a greater feeling of success or security. We know that a few children in all the grades of the public school exhibit a lack of interest in the visual arts, and we know that a large number of them begin to lose their interest during the late figurative stage of symbolic development. Without a doubt, much of their disenchantment with making and appreciating can be attributed to a lack of self-confidence. How can we avoid this deterioration in self-esteem? How can we make our students feel that they are capable of making and appreciating art?

From the start it seems clear that confidence in doing anything is aided by making it *possible* for a person to improve and to enjoy success, by *recognizing* his accomplishments, by *calling his achievements to his attention*, and by *complimenting* him. It is also clear that such treatment must start as soon as the child begins to make visual symbols, for the youngster who lacks confidence in ordinary, nonartistic symbolization is not apt to demonstrate greater confidence in the production of art. Thus the teacher of art must begin to develop the child's confidence in making the earliest forms of symbolization, even though the

[12] Viktor Lowenfeld, *Your Child and His Art*, The Macmillan Company, New York, 1954.
[13] Victor D'Amico, Frances Wilson, and Moreen Maser, *Art for the Family*, Museum of Modern Art, New York, 1954.

first scribbles are not apt to be works of art. Gradually, as the child matures and develops a knowledge of the nature of art, the teacher must make him feel capable of going beyond mere symbolization to the production of art.

Making success possible

To make the early scribbler or anyone else feel secure and satisfied with himself, the teacher is advised to provide tools and materials that permit the student to do what he proposes to do with his symbols. The scribbler, for example, is primarily interested in kinesthetic activity, in coordinating the hand and the eye, and in creating qualities of "thingness." For that reason it would be discouraging for him to work with watercolor, plaster, or papier-mâché, because they are too difficult to manage. He needs crayons, pencils, felt-tipped pens, tempera paint, absorbent paper, bristle brushes, and other tools and materials that permit him to make clearly discernible lines that do not run, drip, or merge with other lines. He needs to be able to see that he can repeat and control certain movements and that certain arrangements of lines produce a quality of "thingness." If his tools and materials do not permit the control that is necessary for such results, he may blame himself for lacking ability when the fault really lies elsewhere.

Even though appropriate tools and materials are provided, children may lose confidence in themselves if the teacher does not offer adequate instruction about the use of such things. It is not impossible, for example, to find kindergarten or first-grade youngsters who never have used a pair of scissors or a brush. This would clearly be the case with many culturally disadvantaged children, and the chance for their discouragement is very high if the teacher fails to show them how to hold a scissors or how to use a brush. For this reason, teachers must continually ask themselves if their students really have all the information it takes to carry out an assigned task. If they do not, the teacher obviously must provide it or assign a different task.

In addition to giving the required instruction about procedure, the teacher who wants to build confidence will find it necessary to let his students practice or work with a tool or material more than once, for it is the rare individual who creates a masterpiece the first time he has a brush in his hands. It takes practice to develop skill and to do the things one wants to do with visual symbols, but art teachers often forget that fact; they introduce new procedures and new tools and materials with increasing rapidity, and they frequently allow no more than twenty to fifty minutes for the children to get an idea and give it form. The outstanding exception to the continual introduction of new procedures is the teacher's repeated use of crayons. In that case he provides for too much practice, too little significant stimulation, and too little procedural instruction. As a result, children eventually become bored and frustrated with crayons because they have not been inspired and have not received sufficient help in exploiting the medium. Still, practice is one of the things that a student must have if he is to express what he wants to express. If he is unable to achieve the goal he has in mind, he simply loses confidence in himself as a maker of visual symbols.

Still another way of making improvement possible is to select topics for stimulation that are suitable for the child's stage of mental development. If they are not, the student will either fail to understand them, or he will not be interested in them. In either instance, the pupil is not likely to build the strongest form of self-confidence.

On the other hand, teachers may select topics for stimulation that are both interesting and familiar to their students, but some of the students may still be unable to draw as they want to. This leads to a loss of confidence in art; but in this instance the topic for stimulation may not be entirely responsible for the problem. Let us assume, for example, that the topic is horses. Each child in the class may have experienced a horse, and each may be able to talk about the experience in general terms. They may be able to say that a horse has four legs, a head, a long neck, a mouth, and a tail, but they may still be unable to draw a horse. If they do, it might look like a dog or a giraffe. They may say that they know exactly what they want to draw, and they may indicate that their problem is a lack of skill. That could be true, but their trouble is more apt to be a lack of concept development. The concept that they have is probably discursive in nature, which means that it can be stored in the mind in the form of words. To draw a convincing horse, however, they need a *visual concept* of a horse, the kind that is stored in memory as an image. Building such an image requires that a person actively engage in perceiving a horse and that he do so with attentiveness. The teacher may therefore help the child to draw a horse more naturalistically by requiring him to look at a horse attentively and in great detail. This means that direct experiences with a horse or with another object are the best means of building the highly detailed visual concepts that youngsters often need to satisfy their own desires in drawing. If direct experience is not feasible, the teacher may have to show the child a picture or a sculptural model of the object being drawn. The only other alternative is to suggest that the child draw something else. But the main point of this discussion is that a teacher may help to eliminate feelings of incompetence in art by doing things that will increase perceptual activity, and this is most easily accomplished while stimulating youngsters with direct experiences. It will build those concepts which permit youngsters to draw; and drawing what they want to draw will help them to feel confident.

Recognizing accomplishments and calling attention to them

Naturally, if a teacher is to make a student feel good about the work that has been done, he must be able to recognize the student's accomplishments. In other words, he must be sufficiently familiar with each child's visual symbols so that he can detect new feelings, new ideas, and new innovations in composition. He must be able to tell if an appealing use of line, color, or texture has been made, and he must be able to detect any new developments in the child's understanding of space. If the

Opposite page: Fig. 8.19
Exhibitions of child art
help to build self-confidence.
(Photo by Richard Hildwein.)

youngster creates a unique style or technique, it is important for the teacher to recognize that as well. But seeing such things requires a little more time and care than art is usually given in the public schools. Sometimes a remarkable change can occur in the way a leg or a nose is drawn, but if we have not been properly attentive to the child's work, we might easily overlook his achievement. It is not easy to prevent such an oversight, however, because the public school teacher often has too many other things to do or too many children to teach. Consequently, he is apt to notice only the most apparent successes. This is one of the unfortunate results of mass education, which can be overcome successfully only by reducing the number of pupils in a class or by eliminating some of the teacher's numerous duties. In any case, it is hoped that the teacher will do his best to study the work of his students for signs of improvement.

Having noticed their accomplishments, the teacher must make certain that the youngsters also recognize them. Sometimes students are so deeply involved in their work that they actually do not realize what they have managed to do. They may detect a slickness of technique or a greater degree of naturalism, but they may overlook a mood or a descriptive element that gives their work the mark of individuality. This suggests that a session of art appreciation following the completion of an art project would be most welcome. The session might be a private one or might involve the whole class, but the teacher's job would be to show and explain the good things he finds in the work of his students and to *compliment* them for their achievements. As he does so, it is absolutely essential that he speak with genuine sincerity because children are magnificent detectors of fraud. When they know a teacher's praise is insincere, they soon lose respect for him and for their own ability as artists. For that reason the teacher must know what he is talking about and offer compliments only when they are actually deserved. When they are appropriate, the compliments act as a reward or as a reinforcement of learning.

Praise for a student's accomplishment may also be given in a nonverbal fashion by slapping him on the back, winking,

nodding, or making some other gesture, including the victory sign. But one of the most common ways of showing admiration is to put the successful work on exhibit in the classroom (Figure 8.19). This is effective not only because it acts as a reward and aids self-confidence but also because it gives the children a chance to examine their own work leisurely and compare it with that of their classmates. It creates what Lowenfeld has called a form of "natural competition" and is educationally wholesome. Youngsters may discover any number of things in the creations of their fellow artists that can be used to improve their own future work. This is not to be construed as a suggestion that children should copy the work of their peers down to the last detail, but it is perfectly acceptable to get ideas from someone else. Grown artists do it all the time; in fact, there is not an artist in existence who does not obtain ideas, inspiration, technical information, or other assistance from fellow artists.

When exhibiting visual creations, the classroom teacher is likely to display the work of each child in his class, while the art teacher is more apt to show the most appealing work produced by a few children. Neither of the two practices is especially conducive to widespread improvement of artistic expression, although the classroom teacher is probably doing the more acceptable thing. He usually displays the work of all his students because it is the easiest thing to do, because he cannot tell the difference between art and nonart, because he cannot detect improvements, or because he does not want to discourage any of the children. All but the first reason are good ones, and they indicate that the teacher should continue to display all the work if he is unable to improve his own sensitivity to it. On the other hand, the danger that accompanies indiscriminate praise has already explained, and the display of all work is a form of compliment that is far from discriminate.

By exhibiting only the very best of visual creations, however, the art teacher is showing his biases. He is demonstrating his interest in art education as a means of encouraging and training a select group of people. At the same time he is showing that he is not interested in art education as a means of improving the aesthetic capabilities or the general education of all children. If he were, he would try his best to recognize and reward *all* improvements in visual symbolization; he would display any visual creation that indicates the deep involvement of the child. This is the practice that we most highly recommend, but in doing so it should be pointed out that an individual will probably not improve with each succeeding product and that measuring his degree of involvement is not easy.

The effects of criticism on self-confidence

It is part of the teacher's job to criticize the creative products and the reasoned judgments of his students. Only by showing them where and how to improve can the teacher help his pupils to grow in their productive and judgmental ability. But criticism can be a blow to self-confidence if it is not administered with care. Probably the most obvious of careful practices would be to offer criticism that is constructive, because such comments are both helpful and productive, and they leave the student with a feeling that success is possible. Destructive criticisms, however, leave no hope; they destroy self-confidence quickly and completely. Unfortunately, such criticisms occur far too often in the public schools. They are largely unintentional, of course, but they are no less destructive. Teachers simply do not realize what they are doing; they are not aware that theyare destroying self-esteem. Consequently, we shall take this opportunity to call attention to some of the more distasteful forms of critical behavior.

Comparing children's creations. It is not wrong to compare children's drawings. In fact, the following pages recommend that teachers compare the creative products of youngster's for the purpose of demonstrating how valuable it is to have a variety of styles in art. Comparisons are also helpful in pointing out the different kinds of achievement that students have made. But the instructor will *not* succeed in generating a broad feeling of self-confidence in his pupils if he compares the work of one child with that of another for purposes of showing how one is *superior* to the other. After all, a visual symbol is a presentation of the self; it is an exposure of personal concepts, emotions, and skills. For that reason an attack upon the symbol often is felt as an attack upon the person who made it. Thus the youngster who creates a visual image is not apt to "feel good" about himself if his expressive performances have been proclaimed inferior by someone he considers an expert. This is especially true if the proclamation is made in public. It is therefore recommended that teachers refrain from calling attention to failure in front of the class. If they simply point out the accomplishments that have been made, the unsuccessful youngsters will recognize their weaknesses without much trouble and will be spared the useless embarassment of public exposure.

In private conversations with a student, the teacher may occasionally find it necessary to point out weaknesses in the child's work. But his comments must leave the student with the feeling that not all is lost, that there are many more chances to succeed, and that the teacher has faith in him. Anything less than that surely will lead to discouragement. Yet any number of teachers and parents have been known to laugh at the creations of children or to make fun of them in public as well as in private. How they can expect youngsters to produce art after such behavior is hard to imagine.

Sometimes art teachers are guilty of projecting preferences and suggesting inferiority without a word being spoken. They do so by focusing their attention on certain students while ignoring the others. This is just as injurious to self-confidence as verbal comparisons of success and failure because it makes the ignored student feel that his work is without interest or merit. Consequently, it is important for the teacher to devote as much time and energy to one person as he does to another.

If the teacher is sensitive to the progress of his students and is careful about what he says, he can compare their work, publicize their accomplishments, and make suggestions for improvement without either emphasizing or ignoring failure. He can do this through a judicious combination of public and private utterances, but when he displays and discusses the work of the children before the whole group, he is inviting their comments to accompany his own. This can lead to unpleasant incidents, because children are not always kind, sympathetic, and understanding. They can be terribly cruel with their comments and comparisons, and they can destroy self-confidence as easily as any teacher. Classroom discussions are so important to the development of artists and connoisseurs, however, that talks must continue. But the instructor must see to it that the discussions assume a positive tone by urging the youngsters to find the beautiful instances of form, the strong presentation of mood or feeling, or the successful expression of an idea in visual terms. To keep such discussions positive in nature, teachers must begin in the early grades to teach their children that more progress can be made by mutual help, encouragement, and praise than by any amount of vituperation. And when nasty remarks do occur, he must squelch them immediately.

Art contests. Many administrators and a large number of art teachers are eager to initiate art competitions and to have their students participate in them. Unfortunately, their eagerness is not always motivated by the beneficial effects of the contest on children, but is frequently stimulated by the attention that is called to the school system, to the educational program, and to the instructional staff. This means that many youngsters are being exposed to a form of critical comparison that may have an undesirable effect upon their self-confidence in art. The effect is apt to be undesirable because a competition emphasizes the superiority of certain works and the inferiority of others, and the judges are usually regarded as experts by the participants.

It is true, of course, that a child whose painting is not rejected may feel that his work is good; and if he wins a prize or a ribbon, he may feel that he possesses superior ability. In other words, he may become self-confident. But few prizes are awarded in any competition, and if all submitted work is accepted and the child wins no prize, he may get the impression that he is incapable. He will certainly receive that impression if his work is rejected. The possibility that such a feeling might arise from a lack of success in contests is recognized by administrators and art teachers, but many of them seem to feel that the discouragements are minimal and that the benefits of the contest outweigh the disappointments in importance. What benefit is the child supposed to derive from competition?

It is said that a contest provides children with a challenge and a stimulus—which it does. But there are other ways of challenging and stimulating youngsters that do not place such a strong emphasis on success and failure. Furthermore, a contest gives no recognition to the child's expressive growth; it simply celebrates the work of the winner without considering the amount of progress he has made in relation to that of other children. Thus the child who has grown the most might be the one who is most discouraged when he fails to receive recognition.

It is said that contests expose the child to the cold competitive realities of life and that the elimination of contests would simply shield, protect, and coddle the child, making him unprepared for the cruelties of life that lie ahead. There is no doubt that competitions do expose the child to unhappy occurrences of the adult world. But the important question is whether the individual and his society will rise to greater heights by making certain children lose confidence in their expressive ability. In this writer's view, it does not seem probable, because the elevation of a culture is largely dependent upon improvement in the expressive abilities of *all* people, and improvement in anything is closely related to the feeling that a person is capable of improving.

Usually the person who speaks of contests as a way of exposing the child to reality is one who considers the goal of art education to be the preparation of future professional artists. A person with that belief is apt to feel that failure and criticism are good preparation for the artist because the life of art is full of discouragements and anyone who cannot maintain confidence in the face of failure is not destined to make a success of art. But the goal of art education in the public school is not the training of professionals. The aim is to produce nonprofessional artists and connoisseurs on a broad scale for the purpose of raising the level of the culture. We want to encourage expressiveness and recognize all forms of improvement without calling undue attention to the less successful statements. In that way we intend to preserve hope for self-improvement and to encourage continued expression. Without continued symbolization, improvement cannot occur.

By trying to avoid public proclamations of failure, we do not mean to suggest that the child should not experience failure or not recognize it. Naturally he must experience it and recognize it or he will not be able to detect the difference between the higher and the lower qualities of symbolization. But he must feel that he can fail without having his failure publicized; he must be shown the ways to improve; and he must feel that he is making progress. Such conditions promote self-confidence in spite of failure, but contests do not provide those conditions.

It is also said that competitions with big rewards give the financially disadvantaged child a chance to attend college. This is true, providing he is lucky enough to win a substantial prize. The chance of doing so is so rare, however, that the child can enter college more easily by practicing with the track team until he is able to pole-vault over 14 feet. If the financially disadvantaged child is to be helped, the help should come from the universities in the form of scholarships and grants-in-aid. This would permit the youngster who is interested in a professional artistic career to pursue it without discouraging the future nonprofessional artist from continuing his symbolic activity.

The use of dittoed drawings, coloring books, and numbered painting kits. One of the greatest discouragements to art educators is that classroom teachers and parents persist in giving their children large numbers of dittoed drawings, coloring books, and numbered painting kits. Sometimes they do it in the name of art, and sometimes they use such devices in the teaching of reading or arithmetic. Why do art educators object so strongly to such a practice?

To begin, the only thing that a person can do with a ready-made drawing is to color it. There is no opportunity to give

a · *b*

Color the dog brown.

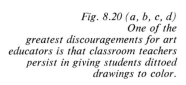

Color the ball green.
Color the bone yellow.

Color this picture any way you wish. Be neat.

Fig. 8.20 (a, b, c, d)
One of the greatest discouragements for art educators is that classroom teachers persist in giving students dittoed drawings to color.

form to concepts or emotions; there is no freedom to compose the elements within the picture; and in numbered painting the painter is not even permitted to choose his own colors. Consequently, the coloring of ready-made drawings is not an art activity, and if it is not an art process, it does not have the value of that activity. In fact, it is about as valuable as tracing a paragraph that has been written by someone else. It is nothing but "busywork." Yet parents and teachers insist that dittoed drawings and coloring books are valuable in developing artists, even though artists do not agree. They claim that the use of such devices helps to teach neatness and eye-hand control. But anyone who is slightly familiar with the creative mannerisms of the artist is immediately aware of the fact that neatness is not one of his virtues. Certainly it is rare for him to draw outlines of things and neatly apply color inside them; instead he works in a great variety of ways, many of which are sloppy rather than neat.

Eye-hand coordination can be gained just as easily by making and coloring one's own drawings, and surely there is no evidence of greater coordination in the coloring of pictures that have been made by someone else. In fact, the skill of coordinating the hand and the eye is more apt to develop if a person does his own work because there is more interest and enthusiasm

c

d

Color:
What color are horses?
Stay within the lines.

Our First President

involved in expressing personal ideas and feelings than there is in coloring someone else's.

In addition to the fact that the coloring of dittoed drawings, coloring books, and numbered paintings is not an art activity and not a means of developing characteristics peculiar to the artist, it does not lead to self-confidence in the making of visual symbols. It leads, instead, to a lack of confidence and to a dependence upon the teacher. Let us examine the reason for this. If a teacher presents his students with a dittoed drawing of a dog, he is telling them, in a nonverbal manner, that his method of drawing is the correct way to make dogs and that their own drawings are not so good. If their pictures were as good as the dittoed ones, the teacher would allow the youngsters to make their own. The children understand this implication very clearly, and many of them realize that they cannot draw a dog the way the teacher does. The result is that many sensitive youngsters begin to lose confidence in their own ability to make visual symbols. They may refuse to draw; they may ask for continuous help from the teacher; they may cry when materials are passed out; they may finish their drawings in a hurry to go on with something else; or they may behave in other ways that indicate a loss of faith in their own ability. These youngsters are usually very happy to continue using the dittoed drawings, and the teacher is even more willing to furnish them, because it relieves him of unhappy, complaining youngsters who are dissatisfied with their own creative work.

Moreover, there are some instructors who feel confident of their own ability in art and respond to the child's request for help by showing him how to draw a cat, a dog, or something else. Unfortunately this tends to make the child even more discouraged than he was after receiving the dittoed drawings. This is so because the teacher or expert has presented in a more *direct* fashion what seems to be the correct method of drawing. The teacher therefore gives the impression that the child should be able to do the same thing. But the child is unable to do so, and this is a dramatic indication to him that he is incapable in art.

Elsewhere in this book it is suggested that the teacher draw or create along with his students on certain occasions, but this is not to be confused with the act of drawing *for* them in such a way that they think they must imitate. Drawing *with* them is good because it gives youngsters the feeling that art is important to the teacher, but it can be done in an educationally profitable fashion only if the teacher lets the children know that their own symbols are just as wonderful as his own.

Psychologists would agree with the notion that youngsters need support from someone when they run into difficulty with the various forms of expression. But the wife of a psychologist once scoffed at the condemnation of dittoed drawings, and said that they offered the child the support and security he needed to maintain self-confidence in visual expression. It is hoped that the lady misunderstood her husband, because ready-made drawings of all kinds create nothing more than *false* confidence. If they did more than that, the children who use them eventually should be able to make their own symbols without finding fault with them, but they usually do not. Anyone who has worked as an art consultant or supervisor in the elementary schools is aware of the fact that children who have been exposed to large numbers of dittoed drawings are usually inhibited in their artistic activities. They are the ones who would rather do something else;

they are the ones who continually ask for help; and they are the ones who often require disciplinary action.

When we say, however, that ready-made drawings are harmful to self-confidence and artistic development, we do not mean to imply that they will affect all persons to the same extent. Many professional artists were exposed to ready-made drawings when they were children; yet they have managed to create art at a very high level for a long time. How they were able to maintain a belief in their own ability is not known; but it is possible that they received support and encouragement from someone whose opinion about symbolization meant more to them than their teacher's opinion. That they have been able to maintain their feeling of self-esteem does not, however, justify the use of noncreative or nonartistic devices in the aesthetic education of children, because our goal is improving the visual expression of *all* children. If any of them lose confidence and give up their creative activity in art, we cannot achieve this broad cultural gain that is so important.

When teachers recognize the harmful effects of dittoed drawings, they may try to stop using them, but such drawings are used extensively in the teaching of reading and arithmetic and for keeping students occupied while the instructor is busy with something else. In other words, the elimination of dittoed drawings is nearly impossible, especially if the art specialist offers the classroom teacher no assistance in getting rid of them. Unfortunately, this is too often the case. The art teachers merely complain about the situation without suggesting reasonable substitutes for the use of artistically inhibiting dittos. What substitutes can be made, or what can be done to remove the harmful effect of such drawings on child art?

In the teaching of reading, dittos are often displayed with the name of the pictured object at the bottom of the page, to facilitate a connection between words and their meanings. In that instance, it would be better, from the art educator's point of view, if the teacher would replace the drawings with photographs cut from magazines or, better still, with drawings made by the students. If for some reason dittos are absolutely essential in teaching reading, it is suggested that the teacher make them as complex and as detailed as possible, because youngsters will make less of an effort to copy them. It is also recommended that the students *not* be required to color the dittos, because coloring tends to suggest the idea of art when there is absolutely no art involved. The coloring has no educational value; it merely keeps the youngsters busy and out of trouble.

In the teaching of arithmetic, students often are given a drawing of something and asked to make a certain number of additional ones; or the pictures might be used to teach the concept of sets (sets of three or six units, etc.), the idea of more and less, and other fundamentals of mathematics. Again it would be helpful from the art educator's view if photographs could be used in place of drawings, or if drawings are essential, it would be better to use ones that are photographic in nature. Usually the pictured objects are recognizable as items that are experienced in everyday living. This is probably necessary if children are to remain interested, but it would be better for the child's artistic growth if triangles, circles, squares and other such forms could be used in place of naturalistic drawings. This is because the constant exposure to naturalistic sketches tends to condition the child to one form of symbolization, making it difficult for him to make or appreciate other forms of visual expression. Thus the use of ready-made drawings not only destroys self-confidence in many children but builds the wrong ideas about the nature of art. It gives the clear impression that art is a matter of portraying recognizable objects naturalistically or photographically. It suggests that art is the making of outlines filled with flat, colored tones. And when a person is conditioned to such ideas or to any other narrow conception of art, he is very resistant to instruction in aesthetics. This is another reason why art teachers find dittoed drawings and coloring books to be such an obstacle to art education.

Most critics of education would do well to spend a few days or a few months as teachers in the public school. Only then will they have a notion of how busy and how strenuous the teacher's life actually is. It is the amount of work and the amount of emotional strain that causes many teachers to use dittoed drawings. When they are working with reading groups, for example, they need to keep the rest of the class occupied, but they do not have the time, the energy, or the artistic background that would permit them to develop educationally worthwhile projects of an artistic nature that could be used to keep youngsters at work. The art teacher could therefore be of great service by helping the teacher to find substitutes for busywork. Among the best of substitutes are the art activities that are quiet and easy to undertake without close supervision by the teacher. Weaving, mural making, mosaics, individual dioramas, and certain kinds of constructions are especially good for quiet seatwork because the stimulation can be given and the procedure for doing the projects explained; the students can begin work, and then they can stop and go back to their other studies. When they need to be kept quiet and busy, the teacher can ask them to resume weaving or to carry on with their portion of a mural. Paper-cut murals are especially useful in this respect because each child can work on his assigned part of the mural at his own desk where paste, scissors, and pieces of colored paper can easily be kept. Naturally the materials that are needed for any quiet activity must be easy to obtain without commotion. For that reason it is recommended that storage areas be plentiful, open, accessible to children, and arranged in such a way that different items can be kept separate from others and clearly marked. This is so important that a good art supervisor could afford to spend time doing research on the efficient storage of art materials.

So far our comments about the harmfulness of ready-made drawings have been aimed at the practices of classroom teachers, but parents are equally guilty of furnishing such materials in the form of coloring books. As we criticize them, however, we are well aware of the fact that coloring books are everywhere and that parents cannot prevent their children from getting hold of such books even if they want to. But they can refrain from furnishing their children with such devices. And when the youngsters do obtain them, it is advisable not to make a fuss about them or take them away. On the other hand, it is not a good idea to compliment the children on the work they do in coloring books because it encourages them to do more. It would be far better to let them know that their own drawings are more enjoyable.

Copying. From what has already been said, it seems advisable for an art teacher to avoid art contests, dittoed drawings, coloring books, numbered painting kits, and uncomplimentary comparisons of children's drawings. It is also wise to discourage widespread copying. We know that a certain amount of acceptable copying goes on in artistic circles, and we know that it can be educational. It gives the copier a better understanding of the skillfulness that was required to produce an original configuration; it helps the imitator learn something about the procedure that was initially employed; and it may assist in developing an individual's concept of space. By imitating certain aspects of another man's work and combining them with his own ideas, an artist may also be able to create a new and unique model of the human condition, a new way of presenting concepts and feelings. But too much copying and too little of the student's own contribution can lead to low-grade art and to discouragement if the teacher is not careful. After all, art is the giving of pleasing aesthetic form to concepts and emotions, and a person is not giving form to those dimensions of his mind when he copies the work of someone else. And if the teacher continually encourages copying, it is apt to have the same effect as dittoed drawings. It may condition the copier to a few selected forms and techniques and to the notion that art is the task of creating only those particular forms. This, in turn, limits the things that the copier can say with visual symbols; it restricts his own personality development; and it decreases the freedom and self-realization of observers by depriving them of new models of thinking and feeling.

If the teacher demands too much copying, he may project the idea that the child's own symbols are inadequate or undesirable. This danger is even more acute if the instructor requires his pupil to imitate artistic works that are beyond the youngster's ability to reproduce. In other words, it can very easily lead to the destruction of self-confidence in art. Any copying must therefore be done sparingly, and the teacher must use great care and good judgment in assigning it. If the teacher is not qualified, by training or experience in art to make such judgments, he should not require his students to copy at any time. Practically speaking, this means that only art specialists are to use it in their classes, if it is to be used at all.

Tracing. Like copying and the coloring of ready-made drawings, the use of tracing as an educational device implies an unfavorable criticism of the student's visual symbols. It forces him into a comparison between the traced image and his own, with the suggestion that the reproduced symbol is superior. Otherwise there would be no point in tracing; at least there would be no need for it from the child's point of view, and this means that it should not be used by most teachers as an instructional device because it might lead to a loss of self-confidence in art.

On the other hand, it is difficult to ignore the findings of Piaget, who has discovered that perceptual *activity* is largely responsible for the child's conception of space. If that is so, the tracing and the copying of photographs and drawings should help to build the spatial concepts that are needed in drawing because tracing and copying demand a careful movement of the fingers and the eyes around, in, and between the objects being traced or copied. If the elementary school art teacher were to employ tracing for such purposes, he probably would have his pupils trace the naturalistic kinds of photographs and drawings that would aid in developing a visual concept of the spatial relationships which exist in visual reality. He would use tracing to help develop a *naturalistic* concept of space because this kind of concept permits the style of drawing that is most appealing to contemporary society. In other words, it permits a naturalistic form of art, the type that most children want to produce because of the taste that generally prevails in their environment. This does not mean that tracing would always have to be used to develop a *naturalistic* concept of space, but it is the kind that seems most appropriate for children in the elementary school. If they cannot produce naturalistic spatial relationships in a culture that values such relationships strongly, they are apt to lose their self-confidence and give up visual symbolization for another form of expression.

To develop a naturalistic concept of space is to build a concept of *projective* spatial relationships, and according to Piaget, that demands the prior development of *topological* and *Euclidean* notions of space. Topological and Euclidean spatial relationships are the only ones an individual needs to conceive if he is to create forms of art other than the naturalistic variety. Consequently, the teacher who succeeds in developing visual concepts of projective or naturalistic spatial relationships is a teacher who also has provided his students with the concepts of space that are needed for abstract and nonobjective art. By helping them to build a visual conception of projective relationships, or perspective, the instructor also increases their freedom of expression by making it possible for them to create naturalistic symbols. Without the ability to conceive such spatial relationships visually, an individual must limit himself to the content that can be expressed with abstract and nonobjective forms. Such limitations do not prevent the creation of art, but they do place a restriction on the self-realization of the artist as well as the observer; they restrict his freedom to say and to know.

From these remarks it is clear that the writer favors the development of the concept of projective spatial relationships in the public school. This means that he favors the teaching of naturalistic drawing and that he condones the limited and judicious use of tracing and copying with those youngsters who fail, after selected exercises in perception, to develop the naturalistic visual concept of space that they want to develop. But the judicious use of tracing, like the wise and careful use of copying, is apt to occur only if the teacher is trained for it. He must know what to have his pupil trace or copy; he must know when to have him do it; and he must be able to convince his student that the purpose behind the exercise is to help the student build the concept of space that the student wants to build in his own mind. The teacher must also be able to make it clear that good art does not have to be naturalistic. Doing these things well requires not only training and experience in art education but also a dedication to the subject of art. It is therefore suggested that the use of tracing and copying be left to the art specialist if it is used at all.

By this time the reader must be aware of a contradiction in the views that have been expressed about presenting youngsters with naturalistic models for imitation. On the one hand, it has been said that dittoed drawings, copying, and tracing lead to the destruction of self-confidence and to the formation of a narrow and inaccurate view about the nature of art; and we continue to believe that they usually do. On the other hand, the teaching of naturalistic drawing has been advocated, and it has been suggested that a *small* amount of tracing or copying *might* be educationally justifiable if it helps a child to develop the concept of space that is necessary for communicating the ideas and feelings he wants to express; however, because of the harm that might result, we do *not* recommend tracing and copying unless other methods of promoting concept development have failed. And we do not believe that naturalistic drawing should be taught to any child unless his questions and comments indicate that he wants and needs information about that kind of drawing. If we try to teach such a thing before there is a signal from the child that he wants it, we are apt to make him lose confidence in his ability. With this explanation, the apparent contradiction about the teaching of naturalistic art should disappear.

DEVELOPING AN OPEN-MINDED ATTITUDE TOWARD FORM OR STYLE

A person who is open-minded about form or style in art is one who recognizes and values the different shapes that art may take. Why is it important for art teachers to develop such an attitude in their students? The answer is that a person must be open-minded or tolerant of all art forms if he is to appreciate the contribution that each of them makes to the achievement of the good life. Lacking this attitude, an individual is not apt to expose himself to the concepts and emotions that are presented in a form that he does not like. This in turn leads to a lower degree of intelligence, less freedom in determining one's own fate, and less opportunity for self-realization. Obviously, such a lack of open-mindedness would not produce a connoisseur and would severely limit the artist. The artist would be restricted by narrow-mindedness about form because it would not permit him to change his style or to say things that his present style does not allow. In other words, Picasso could not have changed the form of his work and could not have managed to say so many different things if he had been narrow-minded about form. As we say this, however, we do not mean to imply that connoisseurs and artists must *like* every style of art in existence. That would probably be impossible. But we do hope that their preferences will be rather broad and continue to grow until they include the recognized masterworks of history. How do we develop this broad-mindedness in children?

The first task is to make youngsters realize that different styles actually exist. This can be done as we show them exemplars from art history and various works of modern times. At the same time, we can explain the values that people have received from the different forms of art, music, and literature. We can show, for example, that people would not have gotten the same ideas and feelings about light and atmosphere if the impressionists had painted in the style of Ingres or David. By the same token, we would not have the same understanding of the Spanish Civil War if Ernest Hemingway had written in the manner of Sir Walter Scott.

As the teacher looks at the work of many artists and discusses it with his students, he should not try to force his own likes or dislikes on the pupils by arguing with them or accusing them of a lack of taste. Such behavior will probably strengthen the child's resistance to the teacher's idea, or it might inhibit the child in expressing his own opinions. That would, indeed, be unfortunate. But if the teacher recognizes and accepts the student's view as legitimate, although different from his own, he may be able to win the student's agreement as he explains the reason for his own position. Some art educators, however, may object to the art teacher who voices his likes and dislikes about art because they feel that it might indoctrinate the students or unduly influence them. But what is the teacher supposed to do? He is supposed to act as an expert in art and raise the taste and creative abilities of his students. He cannot do that by remaining neutral, as Ennis has so ably pointed out.[14] He must explain his position as persuasively as he can, and yet he must recognize and call his student's attention to the significant aspects of art forms that he does not like.

When possible, it is an effective education for youngsters to discuss their likes and dislikes in art and to probe the attitudes and values that foster those opinions. In fact, it does no good to have students express their preferences unless they also are required to defend them. As they offer a defense, they often become aware of the weaknesses in their thinking and discover that habits and prejudices often color their views. They find that most forms of art have strengths as well as weaknesses, and they learn to respect the strengths for what they are worth. To make sure that they recognize strength, however, it is a good idea to have them identify both the strong and the weak points in art forms that they do not like. If they can see the value or strength in the things that they dislike, they are well on the way toward tolerance of form and style.

In addition to showing and discussing masterpieces of art that are different in form, the teacher can develop a greater tolerance for style by making each of his students feel that his own style is acceptable and worthwhile. He can compare finished products, not for purposes of praising the best and condemning the worst, but to point out the unique things that

[14] Robert Ennis, "Is It Impossible for Schools to Be Neutral," in B. Othanel Smith and Robert H. Ennis (eds.), *Language and Concepts in Education*, Rand McNally and Company, Chicago, 1961.

people have been able to say as a result of using different styles. This not only helps to develop an open-mindedness toward form, but it also assists in developing self-confidence in art. Consequently, finding something fine and worthwhile in the stylistic character of each child's work is one of the most important things that the teacher can do in teaching art.

DEVELOPING THE WILLINGNESS TO WORK HARD

One of the requirements for working hard in art is having something to say and feeling that it is important to get it said. As we have already mentioned, this indicates the need for stimulation by the teacher, because stimulation helps to create a motive for artistic self-expression. On the other hand, a person may be motivated and still lack the self-discipline that it takes to stick with a job and complete it. Self-discipline is a well-known but rarely mentioned quality that contributes to success in any endeavor. The willingness to discipline the self or to work hard is not easy to develop, but one thing that the teacher can do is to try and convince his students that the discipline of hard work is valuable, even essential, to their success in any enterprise.

The student must learn that art is rarely produced during fits of inspiration or insight. Inspiration may spark or stimulate creativity, but the job of realizing the inspiration in material form is plain, ordinary work. In other words, art is not something that a person produces only when he feels the urge. It is something that he must struggle to achieve; it is the result of effort that extends far beyond the moment of insight. And, strangely enough, the effort itself often provides the inspiration for more art. In fact, the spark that it takes to make art comes so rarely from waiting that students must recognize work as a major source of creative insight.

The artist receives a large measure of satisfaction from his creative activity, much of which comes from knowing the amount of time and labor that it takes to make art and from realizing that he has the strength of character to endure it. And for the artist the final product is a confirmation of that character which cannot be denied, and the feeling of self-fulfillment that follows its completion is more important to the artist than most of the social value it is apt to have.

Being told that satisfaction and success comes largely from work may cause some youngsters to enter the struggle that is art. But the teacher must realize that talking his students into the work is only part of his job. He must see to it that a sense of satisfaction actually does result from the student's labor. This feeling of fulfillment cannot develop unless there is a product— a product that is acceptable to the student. This means that the pupil must be able to find something worthwhile in the completed art object that justifies his hard work, and the teacher must help him to find that value. To do so, the teacher should look for concepts, emotions, and organizational characteristics that seem to be unique in each child's visual symbols. He should show that he recognizes and respects those singular qualities as well as the effort that it took to present them for others to see.

At the same time, the teacher must avoid destructive criticism because it not only destroys self-confidence but also dampens the respect for work. This respect is something that must be fostered, beginning in childhood, because it will aid the individual in mastering any of his future undertakings, including bicycle riding and reading, as well as art.

These comments do not mean that the teacher should cause children to slave over a hot drawing board; but they do mean that youngsters should be helped to see that concentration and persistence can be gratifying, and that other people will also recognize such effort and reward it for the results it brings.

DEVELOPING SKILL IN ART

Skill is the ability to use knowledge effectively. In art it is the ability to make effective use of what we know about life, formative procedures, composition, art history, and aesthetics. Thus skill in the productive aspect of art is the *technical proficiency* that permits a person to combine the various dimensions of his artistically relevant knowledge into a form that gives the observer an understanding of the concepts and feelings that the person experienced and grew to know.

Skill in the appreciative aspect of art is proficiency in experiencing art aesthetically. It is the indescribable technique of perceiving that permits an observer to grasp the human meanings or the concepts and emotions that exist in the "look" of an art object. It is the skill of the observer that ultimately permits the intentions of the artist to be realized.

Developing skill in both the productive and the appreciative aspects of art is largely a matter of giving students sufficient practice in making art and in looking at it. But, in addition to that, the growth of skill will be assisted if teachers do a good job of developing the knowledge and attitudes that have been discussed elsewhere in this chapter. Without the proper knowledge and attitude the individual would lack the motivation that is so essential for practicing creativity.

SUMMARY

In this chapter we have tried to show what the instructor can do to teach the structure of knowledge, attitude, and skill in art. In the past, art education has centered its attention on the development of only one or two of these structural elements, but rarely has it attempted to build all three. As a result, the production and appreciation of art have seldom been evident in the public schools. This means that the value of the art process and product has not been realized by most of our citizens. It also means that future instruction in the arts must cover *all* the characteristics that are fundamental to creativity in art: knowledge, attitude, and skill.

QUESTIONS FOR DISCUSSION

1. Try to give a detailed description of a street corner near your home. Does your description indicate that you have been visually sensitive? What is the cause of your sensitivity or lack of it?
2. What is the difference between fine art and popular art? Why do most people seem to prefer popular art? If you wanted children to develop a preference for fine art, what would you do?
3. Television is an audio-visual aid. How could it be used most effectively in teaching art to children? Could we do anything significant with portable tape recorders?
4. If students constantly go to their teacher for help in art, what does it tell you about the students? What does it tell you about the teacher?
5. List the materials that might be used in making sculpture in the elementary school. Try to make a plan for teaching sculptural procedures that will introduce new materials at each grade level.
6. Do the people in your hometown care about the appearance of their community? Are they bothered by blinking lights, neon signs, billboards, discarded trash, and cluttered business areas? If they are not bothered, what causes their lack of concern?
7. Some textbooks on art education tend to emphasize the therapeutic value of art. This textbook minimizes the therapeutic value of art and emphasizes its intellectual value. Why do we consider the latter position to be more appropriate for teachers in the public school?
8. Teachers frequently say that they know nothing about art, but in the same breath they are likely to insist that ditted drawings are significantly helpful in teaching art. What causes teachers to take this stand?

9. What would happen if a teacher never let a child know that his art work could be improved? What would this tell you about the teacher's educational goals?
10. Collect some children's drawings that were produced in response to a verbal stimulation. See if you can say something good about each of the drawings.

SUGGESTIONS FOR FURTHER READING

Barkan, Manuel: *Through Art to Creativity*, Allyn and Bacon, Inc., Boston, 1960.
This is a unique textbook in art education. It offers verbatim accounts of conversations between expert teachers and typical students in all the grades of the elementary school, and it touches upon many of the topics that have been discussed in this chapter. Chapter 10 of Barkan's book presents a short but accurate account of good teaching in art.

D'Amico, Victor: *Creative Teaching in Art*, International Textbook Company, Scranton, Pennsylvania, 1953.
A classic in art education. Especially pertinent at this point is the chapter on the child as a creator. There the author discusses sources of inspiration, training the visual memory, making the child conscious of art values, and other significant topics.

Erdt, Margaret: *Teaching Art in the Elementary School*, Holt, Rinehart and Winston, Inc., New York, 1962.
The author spent many years in the public schools as an art teacher. Consequently, this is a very practical book. Chapters 1 through 4 are especially good to read in conjunction with Chapter 8 of this textbook.

Jefferson, Blanche: *Teaching Art to Children*, Allyn and Bacon, Inc., Boston, 1963.
As a former public school art teacher and supervisor, Professor Jefferson offers a lot of practical advice to the reader. Chapters 1 through 7 contain information about methods of teaching, the values of creative expression, and other topics associated with instruction.

Linderman, Earl W., and Donald W. Heberholtz: *Developing Artistic and Perceptual Awareness*, William C. Brown Company, Publishers, Dubuque, Iowa, 1964.
The photographs and the lists of teaching aids in this book are excellent. Chapter 2 (on awareness) and Chapter 4 (on motivation) are very good.

Lowenfeld, Viktor, and W. Lambert Brittain: *Creative and Mental Growth*, The Macmillan Company, New York, 1964.
This is a revised edition of one of the great textbooks in art education. Chapters 1 through 3 cover the meaning of art for education, the importance of creative activity in elementary education, and the meaning of art in the classroom. All art educators should be familiar with this classic.

McFee, June K.: *Preparation for Art*, Wadsworth Publishing Company, Inc., San Francisco, 1961.
This book does a unique job of applying the findings of research to the teaching of art. The chapter on organizing the learning experience is appropriate if the reader is concerned with the practical aspects of teaching art.

Mendelowitz, Daniel M.: *Children Are Artists*, Stanford University Press, Stanford, California, 1953.
The introduction to this book covers such things as the influence of parents and teachers on child art, the nature of the "talented" child, and other interesting topics.

Chapter 9
A RECOMMENDED COURSE OF STUDY

In the ideal school system an art supervisor will plan a course of study with the assistance of art teachers, administrators, and classroom teachers. A plan that the supervisor might follow in developing such a program is presented in Chapter 11. At this point, however, it seems appropriate to outline a course of study that will give teachers an idea of what to teach their students when a planned program is not available. Perhaps the outline can also be used by supervisors to begin their work on curriculum development. We suggest that it be used only as a starting point, however, since it is not a comprehensive or highly detailed course of study because space does not permit the inclusion of more information and because the major portion of any art program should be determined by the persons who must live with it. The things that do appear in this outline, however, are sufficiently fundamental to be included in all courses of study, and they provide a clue as to what is artistically and educationally suitable at certain stages in the child's life.

Although the material in this guide is fundamentally important, the teacher should not interpret the grade placement of the content as a pattern that must be followed rigidly. To do so would be a terrible mistake because children grow and develop at different rates, which means that the recommended content will be mastered at different rates. This outline simply indicates the grade levels at which a given concept or a given activity is most likely to be successful.

SUGGESTIONS FOR NURSERY SCHOOL AND KINDERGARTEN

Teaching art at every educational level is a matter of developing artists and connoisseurs. The knowledge that is required to become an artist and a connoisseur is a knowledge of art history, aesthetics, procedures, composition, and life. If we wish to teach art in nursery school and kindergarten, we must provide youngsters with information from those five areas of knowledge and offer the kind of instruction that is appropriate for children who are three to five years old. What can we do that will be suitable for developing a knowledge of life?

Topics for stimulating development of a knowledge of life

When we say that a child must know about life if he is to make art, we mean that he must have concepts and emotions that he wishes to communicate. Making sure he has those concepts and emotions is a matter of stimulating him or causing him to pay attention to life. Among the various kinds of stimulation are direct experiences, audio-visual aids, verbal excitations, and interesting materials. But what experiences, aids, talks, and materials are most appropriate for nursery school and kindergarten children?

Most youngsters at the preprimary level are in either the scribbling stage or the emerging figurative stage of symbolic development. This means that most of the youngsters are interested in kinesthetic activity and in learning about the ordinary objects in their environment. The scribblers must not be asked to draw recognizable things because their inabiblity to do so would destroy their self-confidence. But direct experiences and other forms of stimulation will do them no harm. In fact, they might help the youngsters to develop concepts that permit the making of representational symbols. The direct experiences that would be most helpful to all the youngsters would be those with dogs, cats, rabbits, insects, flowers, people, vehicles, trees, chairs, and other common items. By looking at them carefully, touching them, and listening to them, they develop clearer concepts of those objects. The point is that preprimary youngsters will learn more satisfactorily from direct experiences with single objects than they will from experiences with combinations of objects. If there are too many things to see, young children often fail to perceive anything clearly. Thus it is appropriate to excite preprimary children by having them perceive a rabbit, but it is inappropriate to stimulate them by having them perceive a busy street corner.

The same may be said about audio-visual aids, stories, or poems as forms of stimulation for the nursery school and kindergarten. It would be most suitable to select films, recordings, and other forms of excitation that deal with a single object or incident in the child's environment. This means that a short film or story about a horse, an automobile, a kite, or a frog would be excellent, but a long, complex stimulation about all kinds of transportation would not be so good. A long, involved story or discussion is apt to present too many ideas and is not likely to develop any one of those ideas to the point where the child knows enough to create an artistic image. He is more likely to be confused and say that he does not know what to draw.

The following list of topics for stimulation has been prepared for those who expect to teach children in the nursery school and kindergarten. Perhaps it will give the teacher a few ideas about suitable direct experiences, visual-aids, teacher-pupil discussions, and readings.

I made a snowman	I felt the wind
My dog and me	My favorite toy
I watched a spider make its web	My house
The biggest building I know	My Christmas tree
I smell the flowers	My mother
My house in the snow	My father
I saw the moon and the trees	I am playing ball
A mother chicken and her babies	I can blow bubbles
I walked in the rain	I stood in the hot sun
I like to eat hot dogs	The bird I saw
My teacher	Our automobile
The goldfish and his home	I hurt my knee
The biggest grasshopper in the world	An old lady
Cats, cats, cats!	I hurt my finger

Materials are another source of stimulation for children. Indeed, there are many times when young people need nothing but materials for inspiration. Supplies not only help to generate ideas, but their presence usually makes a person want to play with them, handle them, or use them in some other way. It is therefore worthwhile to have a number of interesting and suitable materials on hand in all the grades. For children in the nursery school and kindergarten, the following items are especially good, but detailed information about other materials may be obtained from Chapter 11.

Tempera paint	Newsprint
Bristle brushes (¼ inch and ½ inch)	Newspapers
Finger paint and paper	Colored construction paper
Pencils	Kraft paper
Wax crayons	Drawing paper
Felt-tipped pens	Colored cellophane
Ball-point pens	Scissors
Paste	Vises, backsaws, hand drills
Clay	Hammers
Yarn and string	Scrap materials of all kinds

Suitable procedures

Before suggesting procedures to be taught at this grade level, it seems fitting to speak of the classroom and how to organize it for art activity. Without a doubt it is best to have furniture that is movable so that large amounts of table space or floor space can be obtained. Flat tables are better than ones with tilted tops or individual desks. Flat tops keep the tools from falling on the floor and provide more working space than desks. In addition, there should be plenty of space for storing art supplies either in the classroom or in a centrally located area in each school, or in both places. If no space is available in the classroom, there should be a convenient way of obtaining supplies from the central storeroom. Many school systems provide "art carts" that can be loaded with materials and wheeled to the classroom, but that is not a satisfactory solution for most schools with more than one floor. In those instances, storage within the classroom is a necessity unless central storerooms are provided on each floor.

Almost all schools lack sufficient storage space for unfinished art products. Planning committees and architects must have concluded that school art is done in miniature and stored in pillboxes, because there is practically no place to put thirty-five wet paintings or an equal number of prints, paper sculptures, or papier-mâché animals. And if each child in any class should happen to make two paintings or two prints, there would be no room to move without stepping on things or spoiling them. Consequently, drying racks and storage areas with adjustable shelving are necessary. Movable shelves provide a maximum of flexibility for the storage of supplies and unfinished work, and open drying areas of different kinds will allow the air to reach wet objects.

Another necessity is a sink that can be reached from more than one side. Without a sink, water must be carried in buckets, and a sink with only one approachable side is a bottleneck. In fact, a sink of that kind is almost a disaster area because it will accommodate only one dirty child; and thirty-five kindergarteners with finger paint up to their elbows can be terribly impatient. If the teacher has no choice but to work with a bucket brigade or a one-sided sink, he is advised to have a number of sponges and towels available. The sponges are helpful for washing hands or cleaning the room, and towels are useful for drying and for removing whatever the sponges have missed.

Still another suggestion is that each classroom be furnished with tables that have washable, stain-resistant tops. If that is not possible, it is recommended that plastic or oilcloth covers be made to fit each working surface. This will reduce the problems that arise when paint, paste, water, and clay are used on school furniture. It also will be helpful to have enough pressed-wood sheets so that each child in the class can have one to work on. They are especially useful if the class is working on clay objects, papier-mâché, or constructions that are not finished in one class session. They enable the children to carry their unfinished pieces to the storage area without breaking them or losing important parts. The sturdy sheets can also act as protective covers for the tables. In the nursery school and kindergarten the pressed-wood sheets are more convenient for the children if they do not exceed 12 by 18 inches. But in grades above that level the sheets are more useful if they are at least 18 by 30 inches in their dimensions.

Finally, it is wise for youngsters to wears smocks as protection for their clothing, and one of the best kinds is simply an old shirt, worn backwards. An old shirt costs nothing and can be taken home for washing.

Many other suggestions might be made regarding classroom management, but it seems easier to make them in relation to a specific art activity. For that reason, we shall turn our attention to suitable procedures for the preprimary level. They fall into five different productive categories: drawing, painting, sculpture, print making, and crafts.

Drawing. Drawing can be done with any instrument that makes a mark, but the tools most commonly used in the public school are pencils, crayons, chalk, brushes, charcoal, Conte crayons, sticks, ball-point pens, felt-tipped pens, and nibbed pens of many different kinds. Charcoal, Conte crayons, and nibbed pens are not appropriate for this level because they require treatment that little children cannot provide. Even chalk is considered by some teachers to be unsuitable, because children have a hard time keeping themselves clean when they use it. But the other drawing instruments mentioned above can and should be used in nursery school and kindergarten.

This writer makes a strong plea for the wider use of soft lead pencils, felt-tipped pens, and ball-point pens in all the grades, but especially at the preprimary level. The reason for this is that self-confidence and concept development are more apt to be served through the use of those instruments. The scribbling child obtains a lot of satisfaction and confidence from seeing the lines he makes. If the lines are clear and do not merge into one big area of color, the child can see his marks more clearly and learn to control them more quickly. Pencils, felt-tipped pens, and ball-point pens produce clear, permanent lines that do not run together. They also allow the child to make more details in his drawings of men, houses, trees, and other objects. Thus they allow him to engage in detailed perceptual activity or exploration, and Piaget has shown that perceptual activity is fundamentally important for concept development. He indicates that active perception will build concepts that are more highly differentiated, but it seems equally feasible that drawing itself will build concepts by requiring definitive activity from the eye and hand and by forcing a careful reexamination of the delineated object. If the child is not allowed to draw with pointed tools, however, he cannot engage in the detailed eye-hand activity that leads to a highly differentiated concept. Consequently, this writer believes that the emphasis upon large tools for little children is a mistake.

For a number of years educators have stressed the use of large crayons or brushes and the making of big drawings. But thick crayons and big brushes not only retard the development of conceptual images, but are not so easy for little people to manage as the experts maintain. At least, the writer's personal experiences with children indicate that youngsters have a much easier time managing skinny crayons. They may break, of course, but big crayons also break. Big crayons also have the disadvantage of being too large to color such things as the eyelashes on a baby dachshund.

The obsession of teachers for big drawings may have grown out of the ideas that prompted abstract expressionism, or it may have come from the notion that kindergarteners cannot make small drawings. But, whatever the cause, many teachers seem to give children the impression that it is almost a sin to make small pictures. They usually tell the child that he is "too tight," that he must "loosen up." Surely they must have forgotten that Giotto, Piero della Francesca, Pieter Brueghel, Paul Klee, and other distinguished artists made small pictures. It seems doubtful that anyone would accuse such masters of being "too tight." Consequently, it is recommended that teachers allow the student to use the various drawing instruments that have been suggested and that they permit the youngster to draw in any scale that seems natural to him.

When we say that an instructor must teach his students the various procedures for using drawing instruments, we mean that he must show them how to obtain different effects with a pencil, a pen, or any other tool. He might show them how to make wide lines, narrow lines, dots, and cross-hatching. He might show them how to darken an area by putting lines close together or demonstrate how to vary the width of a line from thick to thin. He might use the side of the tool as well as the point or show his students that it is possible to use more than one tool on a single work of art.

As he demonstrates the making of lines and textures, the teacher will want to give instructions about the proper care of the drawing instruments. He will want to caution the children against pressing too hard on felt-tipped pens, brushes, chalk, or crayons, as too much pressure may damage the tools. But too much fuss over unintended damage to the instruments may also destroy the beauty of the whole experience for children, because many of them do not have the muscle control that is needed to regulate pressure easily. Consequently, it is recommended that children be given periodic instructions about the care of tools, but complete adherence to those instructions should not be expected. If a few children are not physically capable of handling the instruments carefully, the situation is not apt to be serious, because the tools recommended here are very sturdy.

Painting. Preprimary children are vigorous and prolific painters, so they need strong bristle brushes and inexpensive, absorbent paper. The painting is usually done on easels, on flat tables, or on the floor, and each station has its advantages. At the easel, a child can reach all points of his painting easily, and the paints and brushes can be stored conveniently near the lower edge of his work. The disadvantages are that paint runs easily on a vertical surface and that most schools cannot afford the space or the money for each child to have his own easel in addition to a desk. Therefore, only a few youngsters can paint at one time, which means that the teacher must have another activity under way at the same time. Under such an arrangement, painting is not taught as often as it should be.

Working on tables usually means that more children will get to paint; but they occasionally have trouble reaching all points on their paintings, and the paints are not so conveniently placed in relation to their work. Sometimes it helps to mix the colors in containers that will fit inside a bread box, which will hold eight to ten containers. Several boxes can be placed on tables around the room, so that two or more children can share tables as well as paints.

Still another arrangement is to paint on the floor. Children can be grouped in twos or fours, with each group getting a box of paints, a can of brushes, a can of water, and some damp cellulose sponges. To do so, chairs and tables must be pushed aside; but if that is not possible or desirable from the teacher's view, the children may be stationed around the edges of the room, facing the wall, with their paints and other materials between them.

One of the most annoying jobs for teachers is the mixing

of powdered paint because it does not mix readily. The task may be made easier, however, if the powder is placed in a container with only enough liquid to make a *paste*. If the liquid is a little soapy, the paste can be made a bit faster. Then allow the paste to remain overnight in its covered container. The next day, by adding enough water to bring the paint to its proper consistency, it is ready to use. Keeping the paint from drying in its container is still another problem, but that may be solved easily by using plastic jars with covers that make them airtight.

Keeping bristle brushes in good condition is simply a matter of washing them thoroughly and storing them in a can with the bristles up. If the brushes are improperly stored, so that they stand on their bristles, the hairs of the brush will be permanently bent, and it will be hard to paint with them.

Having prepared his room and his materials, the instructor is ready to teach the procedures for painting. On the preprimary level, the teacher will be working with many youngsters who have not painted before, so he will have to start at the beginning. He will have to teach the children how to hold the brush, how to wipe excess paint off the brush, and how to keep themselves clean. He will also have to teach them how to paint with the tip of the brush, how to make thin lines, and how to make thick ones. After they have worked with the medium for a while, the teacher might show his students the difference between an opaque and a transparent area; he might also show them that the paint can be made transparent by adding water. Still another instructional possibility is to demonstrate how to paint one color over another after letting the first color dry. It is also worthwhile for the teacher or one of the students to show the others what happens when a wet color is placed next to another wet color or next to a dry one. Having covered that much, the teacher might demonstrate how to mix orange, green, and purple; and he might show how to make colors light or dark by adding white or black (see Plate 37).

Children will also enjoy combinations of drawing and painting procedures. They will be especially interested and pleased if the teacher shows them how to create a crayon resist by making

Pl. 37
Self-portraits by kindergarten
children, painted in tempera,
cut out, and mounted on colored paper.

a drawing with crayons and painting over it with tempera paint. The paint does not stick to the crayon marks, but only to the paper. The result seems like magic to children, and it is especially effective if the drawing is done with light-colored crayons on light paper and painted with dark paint (see Plate 54, page 472).

The teacher also might show preprimary children how to draw on top of a dry painting with crayons, chalk, or felt-tipped pens. Any such combination of media is perfectly acceptable as long as it looks pleasant to the sensitive observer.

Most of the painting that a child does in the nursery school or kindergarten will be done with tempera paint, because it is most suitable for his needs and abilities. But we cannot leave the subject of painting without making a comment about finger painting. Finger painting is not very useful to the instructor if he wants to teach art to preprimary children, because youngsters under five years of age do not use the medium to its best advantage. They play with it as they would if they were exploring any "gooey" substance. The slippery texture of the material is so fascinating that they smear it and resmear it without getting down to the business of making symbols. If they do make them, they usually do so with the tip of a single finger, which is not the way to use finger paint effectively.

On the other hand, it is important to have a variety of activities in nursery school and kindergarten. Finger painting does no harm and may have certain beneficial effects outside the realm of art. Consequently, it is recommended that finger painting be continued as an activity for preprimary children, but it should not be considered as an experience that contributes very significantly to the development of artists.

Print making. There are many ways of making prints, but one of the best procedures for very young children is the relief method, using scrap materials. In other words, color is placed on scrap material, and the scrap is pressed on paper to make a print. Because the *raised* portion of the scrap object is the part that makes the colored mark, the resulting composition is called a *relief* print.

Fig. 9.1
A finger painting by a girl
five years of age.

Fig. 9.2
This printed pattern was
made with paint and scrap
by a kindergarten child.

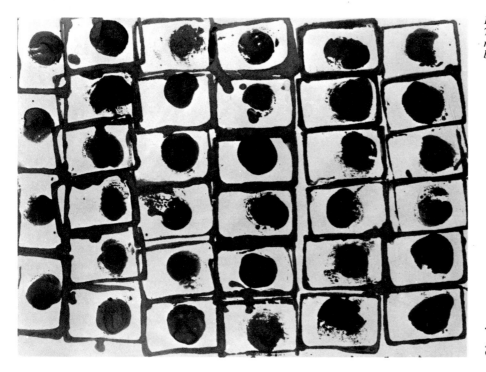

431

Print making with scrap is introduced most successfully after students have been taught the fundamentals of handling brushes and paint, since brushes are used to apply tempera paint to the scrap objects. Ordinarily, printing ink is used in print making, but children from three to five years old will have more success with tempera paint.

Preprimary children enjoy printing, which gives the art program some of the variety that is badly needed below the first grade. But the teacher will have to show his students how to paint the scrap and how to press it on paper. He will have to show them what happens when too much or too little paint is applied, and he will probably need to explain that the best impression is made with a scrap object that has a flat surface. Spools, scrap wood, tiny cardboard boxes, erasers, bottle caps, crumpled paper, the edges of cardboard, and many other objects make good printing instruments.

The teacher might also show his pupils that one print can be made on top of another. To do so, he might demonstrate how it is done or show them a print that was made earlier. Showing examples is usually a good idea when introducing a new procedure, but the teacher must be very careful to say things that will make his students feel confident that they can do as well as the person who made the example.

Sculpture. Sculpture, like print making, does not offer many procedures that can be taught successfully to youngsters in nursery school and kindergarten. But there are a few worthwhile things that can be taught, one of which is the procedure for working with clay. Children might be shown how to make designs by pressing objects into the clay; how to form clay into balls, coils, and slabs; and how to build with these elemental forms. They might also be taught that objects can be made by pushing and pulling on a single lump of clay or by starting with the parts and putting them together. Scribbling youngsters will probably do no more than pound and roll the clay, and they should not be urged to make things that are recognizable. In fact, no child should be pushed to make representational symbols of any kind. If he wants to make them, he will make them naturally without coercion (see Plates 38a, 38b).

The clay that is normally used in school either hardens as it drys or does not harden. The nonhardening type has oil in it, and the other type is mixed with water. Both varieties can be used over and over again; but the kind that hardens has an advantage, because it can be painted with tempera paint when it is dry. When it does dry, however, it is difficult to rejuvenate it for further use.

Both varieties of clay should be kept in covered containers if they are to function properly. They can be stored conveniently in a covered crock or in a small galvanized garbage can. In either case, distribution and cleaning up are hastened if the material is kept in its container in the form of balls that weigh about 1 or 2 pounds. If the clay is kept in that form, children can go to the container and get their clay without having to spend time digging for it. Then the clay can be carried to a working space that is covered with a small pressed-wood sheet, and work can begin with a minimum of fuss.

Nonhardening clay cannot be fired, whereas clay that hardens can be. Ordinarily, this is not an important consideration for the kindergarten teacher because firing seems unnecessary. On rare occasions, however, the teacher may wish to preserve the things that his students have made. In that case, firing will make the clay objects much stronger, but the pieces must be carefully constructed so that no air bubbles are trapped inside the clay. If they are, the clay will explode in the kiln. Having survived the kiln, they may be painted with tempera paint, but glazing is not recommended. The children are too young to control their glazes successfully, and the expense is too high to be justified at this level.

Another sculptural procedure that can involve the use of clay is the making of constructions. Constructions are simply combinations of materials arranged in a pleasing way. They might resemble objects in visual reality or they might not. But the teacher's job is to teach children the procedure for fastening things together and for making them stand up, hang from the

433

ceiling, or stick out from the wall. He might show his students how to make a clay base and how to put sticks in it. Then he might show them how to fasten things on the sticks and between the sticks to create a pleasing arrangement.

Still another procedure that might be called sculptural is the procedure for working with wood. Most teachers are surprised to learn that children can work with wood, but the fact is that youngsters have been working with it in nursery schools for years. They can be taught to use a backsaw, a hand drill, a hammer, and a vise when they are about four years old. They can saw pieces of wood and fasten them together with nails and with glue; they can drill holes and pound wooden dowels into them; and they can smooth the surfaces with sandpaper. When they are all done, they can paint their constructions with tempera paint. Although a heavy table or workbench is not absolutely necessary for woodworking, it is certainly helpful. It provides solid support for a vise, which is needed to hold the wood that is being sawed or drilled (see Plate 39).

Probably one of the most satisfactory but most neglected procedures for making sculpture with preprimary children is the procedure for working with cardboard boxes. In fact, few materials are more fascinating for children than corrugated cardboard boxes in a variety of shapes and sizes. Youngsters like to get in them and on them, and they can imagine the boxes to be anything from automobiles to tunnels. Consequently, the teacher is advised to take advantage of that interest by showing children how they can build three-dimensional forms with boxes.

Saying that the teacher might show children how to do something does not mean, however, that he should tell them what to make and how to make it in each instance. There are many times when he might ask the children what they think they could make with a given material, and he might ask them *how* they could make it. If their suggestions seem educationally profitable, the teacher might let them continue, giving help when it is needed. That system works very nicely with cardboard boxes. If the children suggest the making of buildings, animals, gigantic blocks, or vehicles, the teacher should let them try to make any or all of them. But, before they start, he might ask them how they would build such shapes with the boxes and how they would change the appearance of the boxes to make them look more like buildings, animals, or vehicles. In other words, he might get them to think about fastening boxes together, cutting holes in them, painting them, fastening things to them, and papering them. This would give the teacher a chance to demonstrate the use of gummed paper tape, scrap wallpaper, and wallpaper paste. If any cutting is necessary, the teacher will have to do it himself, because sharp cutting instruments are too dangerous for children of this age.

Crafts. When we speak of crafts we are speaking of a large number of activities some of which are hard to distinguish from drawing, painting, print making, and sculpture. Despite the large number of craft activities, not many of them are suitable for nursery school and kindergarten. Some of the procedures that are appropriate are: (1) simple finger weaving with cotton roving; (2) making collages with cut and torn paper and scrap materials; (3) mask making with paper bags, colored paper, and paint; and (4) puppet making with small paper bags, paper, paint, and scrap.

Of course, the teachers job is to show the children how to make the things that have been listed. But before he can do that, he needs to know the procedures himself. The information that follows is intended to meet that need, but the directions are not extensive. If the teacher feels that he needs more information about crafts, he may turn to one of the good books on the subject that are listed at the end of this chapter. Books that cover drawing, painting, print making, and sculpture are also included in the list.

As the teacher explains procedures to his students, it is important for him to give the names of the tools and materials that are being used, and it is necessary for him to demonstrate the most elementary things to preprimary children. He must show them how to cut with scissors, how to paste, how to clean their working areas, how to care for their brushes and other

435

Pl. 38 (a, b)
Clay plaques painted
with tempera and mounted on a
stained board. Kindergarten.

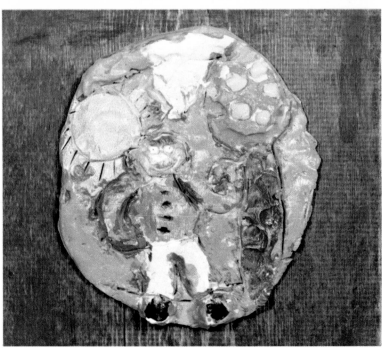

Pl. 39
Wooden animals painted with
tempera. First and second grades.

Pl. 40
An animal made with boxes,
paper tape, and tempera. Second grade.
(Photo by Barry Moore.)

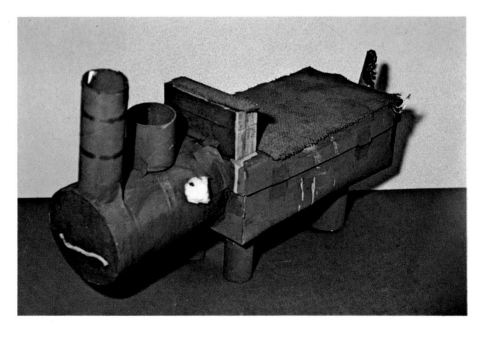

437
A RECOMMENDED COURSE
OF STUDY

tools, how to get the things they need, and how to put them away. With that introduction, let us proceed to a discussion of weaving.

Simple finger weaving can be done by five-year-olds if they are given a heavy weaving material and a properly constructed loom. The loom is started by nailing two wooden strips (about 1 by 2 by 12 inches) on top of two other wooden strips (about 1 by 2 by 14 inches) as shown in Figure 9.3. After wire brads have been nailed into the top two strips ($\frac{1}{2}$ inch apart), the warp thread or string is placed on the loom by tying it to one of the corner brads and by stringing it back and forth from one row of brads to the other until the last brad is reached. The warp thread is tied to the last brad just as it was tied to the first, and in both cases a piece of the thread, about 3 inches long, should extend from the knot. By tying each of the 3-inch pieces to the next parallel warp thread, the weaver prevents any unraveling when the weaving is finished. With kindergarten children it is also helpful to string the warp around the brads in such a way that the threads will be approximately 1 inch apart. If the threads are too close together, the youngsters will have a hard time weaving the yarn over and under the warp with their fingers (see Plate 52, page 468).

After the teacher has constructed the looms and helped with the stringing of the warp, he is ready to demonstrate the over-and-under weaving procedure. The best yarn for young children to use is a heavy cotton roving, and it is wise for the teacher to have the yarn cut into pieces that are about 3 inches longer than the width of the loom. If the yarn is not precut, the children have trouble controlling the tension of the yarn and are apt to produce a weaving that is narrow in the middle and wide on the ends. Finally, the teacher must show the children how to tamp weaving yarns (weft) close together and how to remove the product from the loom. The weaving is removed by slipping the warp threads over the tops of the wire brads, which have no heads. The looms may then be stored until another day.

A collage is an arrangement of various materials on a surface of two dimensions. It is an excellent activity for children of any age because it gives them a chance to have sensory experiences with a wide range of materials and gives them practice in cutting, pasting, and designing. The making of a collage is especially helpful to the child who says that he cannot draw because it does not require him to draw. It simply causes him to cut materials and paste them on pieces of stiff paper or cardboard in such a way that the arrangement looks nice. Scrap materials of all kinds may be used, but the teacher must remember that kindergarteners will have difficulty cutting heavy materials and fastening to the background objects that cannot be pasted with ease (Figure 9.4).

A cut-paper picture or a torn-paper picture is a type of collage, and it is perfectly satisfactory to make such a picture in the nursery school or kindergarten. It is also interesting to have children make individual cut-paper objects instead of pictures— in other words, to have them make flowers, people, animals, insects, birds, wagons, and other objects of their own choosing by pasting pieces of paper together. Children who scribble will not, however, make recognizable objects. They will paste

Fig. 9.3
This child is using a homemade loom suitable for the preprimary and primary grades.

Fig. 9.4
A paper collage of the human figure by a girl five years of age.

pieces of paper to other pieces of paper. The teacher merely demonstrates how it can be done and urges the children to make their own pictures and objects. In addition, he will find that collage activities are easier for all concerned if the many scrap materials and papers are sorted and stored in separate boxes. Such a system allows the children to find the materials they want more easily.

Mask making is still another craft activity that is suitable for early childhood. The best materials to use are large paper bags, colored paper, paint, paste, scissors, and yarn. The teacher must show the children how to put the bag over the head, how to feel for the eyes, and how to mark the location of the eyes with a piece of chalk. The bag is removed, the eyeholes are cut, and the teacher indicates that paper can be pasted to the bag to make eyes, ears, nose, mouth, hair, teeth and other facial features. Or if he chooses, the teacher might show his students that the bag can be painted to make a mask. In either case, the project is simple enough to be carried out by youngsters of nursery school age.

Paper bags also lend themselves to the making of simple puppets, but they must be small bags instead of large ones. The child simply uses paper or paint to make the bag look like a head or a full figure, and then he puts on a little puppet show for the rest of the class. The teacher will probably find that cooperative puppet shows are not very successful below the second grade because the children are too highly egocentric to work well together. Consequently, nursery school and kindergarten teachers are advised to have their students put on individual performances with their puppets (see Plate 48).

Suitable information on composition

Very little needs to be done with composition at the preprimary level. The children are experiencing art materials for the first time and are learning how to manage their tools. They are thrilled with the idea that they can make visual symbols which communicate simple concepts and feelings. Any attempt to teach them composition in a formal manner would take the fun and excitement out of these early experiences with symbolization. Furthermore, the children are still too immature to understand most of the information that can be given about composition. This being so, what, if anything, can the teacher do to improve pictorial arrangement?

One thing he can do is to cause the children to look at natural objects very closely. He might take them outside to look at trees, bushes, weeds, seashells, birds, and other such things. He might let them look at other things through a magnifying glass or a microscope, as a close inspection of nature might give them a feeling for elemental forms and relationships, a feeling that could be helpful in organizing visual symbols. The effect is not apt to be great on such young children, but it may be helpful. About the only other thing that the teacher can do about composition is to make suggestions about balance and the use of space. By this we mean that a teacher might ask a child what he is going to do about the vacant spaces on his paper, or the teacher might tell him that his paper seems a little too heavy on one side. In this way the instructor can make an informal attempt to get him to balance his work and to make use of all his space. Otherwise there is not much that a preprimary teacher can or should do about composition.

Appropriate information on art history

When it comes to art history, about all the teacher needs to do at this level is to show the children a variety of pictures and to talk about them. The age of the picture or the style of painting is not important, but it is a good idea to show a wide assortment of art objects, so that children will come to understand that all art looks different. If the art was made from a special material such as egg yolk, marble, wood, oil paint, or some other substance, the teacher might give that information to the children along with any interesting items about the artist and the time in which he lived. Beyond that there is very little the teacher needs to do about art history.

Topics to cover in aesthetics

Teaching aesthetics to youngsters who are three to five years old is not difficult. It is simply a matter of adjusting the material to their level of understanding, and it can be taught most effectively while looking at the work of the children or at reproductions of masterpieces. It involves a discussion of the following questions:

1. *What is art? What is an artist?*
2. *Why does an artist make paintings, drawings, statues, prints, and other objects?*
3. *Does an artist help us by making such things? How does he help us?*
4. *As you look at this work of art, what do you see?*
5. *Does this work of art look happy, sad, cool, warm, hard, soft, calm, exited, clean, dirty? What makes it look that way?*
6. *Do you like the picture? Why?*
7. *Are you an artist?*

It is important to let the children speak in these discussions, but it is also important for the teacher to present ideas that the youngsters have overlooked. He might use the ideas about art and artists that are presented in this book, if he simplifies them a bit. In addition, he might invite a grown artist to visit the class, talk to the children, and create for them. The presence of such a person is usually an exciting experience that stimulates a lot of activity in art.

SUGGESTIONS FOR THE PRIMARY GRADES

When we speak of the primary grades, we refer to grades one, two, and three. Most children at those levels are in the mid-figurative stage of symbolic development, but the rest of them are apt to be in either one of two other stages. A few youngsters from the first grade are likely to be in the emerging figurative stage, and a small number of the people in grade three may be in the late figurative stage. The possibility of such a wide range

442

of development in the primary grades was taken into account in the following recommendations.

Topics for stimulating development of a knowledge of life

The direct experiences that are used in stimulating nursery school and kindergarten youngsters may continue to be used in the primary grades, where the children are still quite egocentric and are still striving to learn the nature of single objects. In other words, it is perfectly appropriate to continue stimulations that center on only one item. By mixing such experiences with those which are more complex the teacher will meet the needs of all the children and help them to grow conceptually.

The relatively complex direct experiences that are most suitable for primary children are experiences involving several objects and the relationships among them. This means that the teacher might take his students to a busy intersection of streets so that they can see, hear, and touch the things they find there. In addition, the teacher might call attention to *relationships* of size, color, texture, speed, and sound, or he might challenge the children to describe all the details they can find in a telephone pole, a store window, or a building. He also might call attention to the mood of the intersection and ask the children to describe it and to identify the things that create it. Describing a mood and identifying its cause will not be easy for primary youngsters, but there is no harm in getting them to try. If the teacher is successful in all these efforts to increase perceptual activity, the children should develop concepts and emotions that are clear enough for symbolization.

In selecting visual aids for stimulation, the teacher is advised to continue with one or two films that concentrate on a single object or a single idea. But it is also recommended that he begin to use aids that present experiences of a more complex nature. This means that they might cover life on a farm, a day at the police station, or animals in the zoo. The reason for this, once again, is that primary children are concerned with the relationships between things as well as with the objects themselves.

Pl. 41
Portrait of a friend.
Emphasis on facial features
and color mixing.
First grade.

Pl. 42
Birds and animals, drawn with
felt-tipped pen. Second grade.

Pl. 43
Washing the car, drawn with
felt-tipped pen and crayon.
Emphasis on composition.
Second grade.

Pl. 44
A Viking ship, painted with
tempera. Second grade.

445

A RECOMMENDED COURSE
OF STUDY

Similar comments might be made about the topics of verbal stimulations. In other words, it is advisable to make some of them cover a broader range of concepts and emotions than the stimulations for nursery school and kindergarten. Several suggestions for suitable stimulations are listed below:

I am tying my shoes	*A trip to the zoo*
I am buttoning my shirt or blouse	*A fire drill*
I am combing my hair	*We are jumping rope*
I am brushing my teeth	*A trip to the circus*
A visit to the furnace room	*The houses on my street*
A visit to the fire station	*A picnic*
Playing in the school yard	*Visiting the newspaper office*
Riding my bicycle	*The Halloween parade*
Doing push-ups	*We are ice-skating*
At the swimming pool	*Crossing a busy street*
Going over a bridge	*Shopping with mother*
Eating at a restaurant	*Helping to wash the car*
Sledding in the country	*Playing on my street*
I saw a fight	*The time I was afraid*
My street at night	*Playing in a vacant lot*
Trash	*Weeds*
Self-portrait	*Washing windows*

When it comes to materials as a source of stimulation, it is recommended that primary children be given the same tools, supplies, and equipment that are given to youngsters in the nursery school and kindergarten. In addition to those items, it is suggested that the following art materials be available:

Large-eyed needles (third)	*Staplers*
Plastic glues	*Tracing paper*
Printing inks	*Bogus paper*
Rubber brayers	*Oak tag*
Wallpaper paste (third)	*Chipboard*
Colored chalk	*Glazed colored paper*

There are other materials that might serve to stimulate children in the primary grades; but it is important not to introduce all available supplies in the first two or three grades, so that there will be something new to interest the children when they reach the upper grades.

Suitable procedures

The classrooms for the primary grades present even more problems than the rooms for nursery school and kindergarten. The reason is that the rooms are usually filled with desks rather than tables, which means that the working surfaces are reduced in size. To make more working space, the teacher might obtain a few 4- by 8-foot sheets of Celotex or Homosote and place them on top of the desks. The sheets can be stored against the wall by standing them on edge, and they can serve as bulletin boards by placing them on chalk trays. If such sheets are not available, the teacher might move desks together in groups of four so that they form islands. Such an arrangement does not create more working space, but it does make it easier to supply the children with art materials. Boxes of paints, scrap materials, or paper might be placed on each island, so that they can be obtained without walking around the room and without trying to store everything on each desk. If this does not appeal to the teacher, he can always arrange to have the children work on the floor, as we already have suggested for kindergarten.

Drawing. Everything that has been said about drawing in nursery school and kindergarten may also be said about drawing in the primary grades. In fact, the first-grade teacher may have many children in his classes who have not been to nursery school or kindergarten, and many of them may never have used a felt-tipped pen or a paintbrush. The teacher must find out what their experiences have been; and, if necessary, he must start at the beginning to explain how the various drawing instruments are used (Figure 9.5).

All the drawing tools that were recommended for preprimary children are highly satisfactory for primary youngsters, but it is also quite possible to draw with chalk. The dustiness of chalk, which is often offensive to teachers, can be reduced considerably

Fig. 9.5
Drawing with crayons
in the first grade.

Fig. 9.6
Drawing figures in action
is a good art activity for children
in the primary grades. This drawing
was made with a felt-tipped pen.

Fig. 9.7
One of several action
drawings made very quickly with a
pencil and a felt-tipped pen
by a child in second grade.

by drawing on wet or moist paper. Bogus paper is especially good for this purpose, and so is colored construction paper. Chalk looks especially nice on a colored surface, and the children will notice the effect and enjoy it.

It is also possible to use chalk and keep things reasonably clean by taping the paper to the chalkboard so that the dust falls into the chalk tray. But keeping things immaculately clean is not one of the goals of education. We expect to keep things reasonably neat, but we are more concerned about giving youngsters experiences with the tools and materials of self-expression. Chalk is one of those materials, and it does make moist little hands quite colorful, especially if the teacher wishes to show the children how to use chalk on dry paper. He might show them that they can rub it with their fingers or with a paper stump (tightly rolled paper) to create certain effects; or he might show them how to blend two colors. When they are done, the teacher probably will want to demonstrate how to spray the drawings with a fixitive that keeps the chalk from rubbing off the paper. Spraying fixitive is very difficult for primary children, unless the schools system is able to afford the kind that comes in pressurized cans. Consequently, chalk drawings are not apt to be fixed unless the teacher does the fixing.

So far it has been suggested that children be stimulated in some way prior to drawing; the impression that young children should draw solely from memory was not intended. In fact, we strongly advocate the practice of drawing from the environment once in a while, because that is one way to develop the conceptual images that are so important for art. In other words, it is a good idea to have children look at a house, a tree, an automobile, or a fellow student as they draw them. The previously mentioned pressed-wood sheets are handy for such work because the children can take them outside and use them as supports for their drawing paper. The paper, as well as the drawing tools and erasers, may be taped to the board with masking tape before leaving the classroom. If such an activity is planned periodically, the children will enjoy it, and the teachers are apt to be amazed by the maturity of the finished drawings.

9.5

9.6

9.7

Painting. Again, the things that have been said about painting at the preprimary level may also be said about painting in the primary grades. It is a good idea to repeat many of the things that were taught to the children below the first grade. Having accomplished that, the teacher might give them more information about controlling the paint and the brush. He might show them how to pick up a puddle of wet or runny paint with a facial tissue or an absorbent paper towel. He might demonstrate how to scumble by dragging a brush (with a bit of paint left in it) over an area that has already been painted. Or he might demonstrate the effects that can be obtained with brushes of different sizes.

At this point it should be emphasized that it is very worthwhile to have children look at some of the things they are painting as they paint them. The process of drawing or painting the immediate environment has virtually disappeared from American public schools; but there was a time late in the nineteenth and early in the twentieth century when it was a common practice. At that time the photographic reproduction of landscapes and still-life arrangements was the ideal in art. Children could not

Fig. 9.8
This drawing was made
with a felt-tipped pen by a
boy in second grade.

meet that standard, however, and they could not understand the rules and regulations for painting a naturalistic pussy willow, a cat, or a house. Consequently, they usually hated art lessons, and the lessons were ineffective.

After a while, art educators realized that photographic reproduction was not a reasonable goal for art education, so they turned to drawing and painting from memory. They failed to realize, however, that working from the immediate environment aids the child in recalling things and in building his imagery. Thus we strongly recommend a certain amount of painting from nature or from the things found in the classroom itself, but without stressing photographic reproduction.

In the third grade the teacher is advised to give a little more emphasis to the mixing of colors. By taping a 6- by 12-inch strip of tinfoil to the pressed-wood sheet or to any other working surface, the child will have an area for mixing his colors. When he is finished, he can crumple the tinfoil and throw it away. As the teacher demonstrates the mixing of different colors, he should also begin to show his students the effect color can have on the expressiveness of their work. He might show, for example,

Fig. 9.9
In this drawing by a boy in second grade we see the result of the teacher's advice about using all the space on the paper.

451

that blues, purples, and greens can produce a cool, fresh, or regal feeling. He might speak of the softness of pastel hues, the warmth of yellows and oranges, and the eeriness of yellow-green. By doing such things, he helps his students to put more meaning into their work. Ordinarily we do not expect children to use color very expressively before the age of eleven or twelve, but it does no harm to mention the effects of color to eight-year-olds.

Print making. Printing with tempera paint and scrap materials, which has been advocated for nursery school and kindergarten, is also suitable for the first and second grades. If the children have engaged in that activity, however, there is no reason to repeat it, because there are several other printing procedures that are appropriate for the primary grades.

Probably the reason that printing has been so largely ignored in the elementary school is that classroom teachers feel incapable of managing so many tools and messy materials; however, the job is not that difficult. The secret of doing it with little or no trouble is to organize the room very carefully. If possible, it helps to plan and equip about ten inking stations. Each station might have a metal cookie sheet for rolling out the ink, a tube of oil-based printing ink, and a rubber brayer. At their desks the children might have some small sheets of thin oak tag, scissors, an inexpensive spoon, some plastic glue, pieces of newsprint, and a 4- by 8-inch sheet of heavy oak tag or light chipboard. For his own use the teacher should have some old rags and a small can of turpentine or mineral spirits.

Having arranged the room, the teacher might demonstrate how to cut shapes from the thin oak tag and glue them to the heavy tagboard or chipboard. Then he can take the chipboard and go to an inking station where he can show the children how to ink a brayer by rolling it in ink on a cookie sheet. After demonstrating how to roll the ink on to the chipboard with the brayer, the teacher can return to one of the desks, place some newsprint over the inked chipboard, and rub the back of the paper with a hand. When the paper is peeled off, the print is

Pl. 45
A tempera painting illustrating
a portion of *Pecos Bill*. Emphasis on
color mixing. Second grade.

Pl. 46
A tempera painting illustrating
a portion of *Pecos Bill*. Emphasis on
color mixing. Second grade.

453

A RECOMMENDED COURSE
OF STUDY

finished, and the teacher has a sample to show his students. This system allows the student to spend a good share of his time at his own desk and eliminates the need for large numbers of brayers and other tools.

At each inking station it is a good idea to cover the working surface with oilcloth, a large sheet of chipboard, newspapers, or kraft paper. And when the printing is completed, the teacher and a few capable children can clean the ink from the cookie sheets and brayers with old rags that have been moistened with turpentine or mineral spirits. The trouble with using oil-based ink and cleaning it from the tools is that it can be difficult to remove from clothing. It is the only ink, however, that is reasonably easy to use and gives good results. For that reason oil-based ink is highly recommended as long as the children wear protective smocks.

The printing operation described above can be managed by youngsters in first grade. In the second or third grade the same basic procedure may be used again, but materials other than oak tag might be glued to the chipboard, including string, assorted scraps of cloth, ribbon, rickrack, yarn, leaves, and weeds. A variation on this project is also suitable for primary children. For example, they might glue materials to the chipboard, place newsprint over the materials, ink the brayer, and roll the brayer over the paper. Or they might make a print by running an inked brayer over a plain piece of paper in a variety of ways to make a design. Other possibilities for printing with a brayer may be found in books on elementary printing techniques, some of which are listed on pages 529–531.

Monoprinting is another procedure that deserves to be mentioned here because it is a relatively simple process. It requires that ink be rolled out on a cookie sheet. After that, the child places his newsprint on top of the ink and draws on the paper with a pencil or a stick. Then he removes the paper and places it somewhere to dry. This is one of the easiest of printing projects, and it is relatively clean. The teacher must remember, however, that all the work is done at the inking stations, which means that the children must take turns working on the project.

9.12   9.13

9.14

Fig. 9.10
Gluing paper to a piece
of chipboard before inking and
printing in the first grade.

Fig. 9.11
Examining a print that has
just emerged from the printing press.
First grade.

Fig. 9.12
This print was made in
first grade by following the
procedure illustrated
in Fig. 9.10.

Fig. 9.13
The plate that produced
this print was made by gluing yarn
to chipboard. Second grade.

Fig. 9.14
A monoprint made by
drawing on the back of paper that
has been placed on a surface covered
with colored petroleum jelly.

Sculpture. The sculptural projects that were recommended for the nursery school and kindergarten may be continued in the primary grades, but the teacher may wish to carry them a little further. When working with clay, for example, the instructor might show the children how to add pieces of clay to the objects they are building by using clay slip. He also might stress the importance of keeping air bubbles out of the clay if the clay is to be fired in a kiln. Firing is a good thing to do in the primary grades and above. A fired object does not break as easily as an unfired one, so the child can take his work home more easily without breaking it. Fired objects can also be painted very beautifully with tempera paints. Glazing is not recommended at this level because the child will have trouble controlling it; it is expensive and seems to serve no useful purpose (see Plates 38a, 38b).

The teacher might also show his students how to make pinch pots, slab constructions, and figures with textured surfaces, and the finished work might be painted. If the teacher does not know how to make such things with clay, he can consult the books listed at the end of the chapter (Plates 47, 50).

Next to clay one of the best sculptural materials for the primary grades is paper. The teacher might ask his students how they could make a piece of paper stand up. Hopefully, they will think of a way; but if they do not, the teacher might show them how to make simple cylinders, cones, and open-ended boxes. With this as a starting point, the teacher might encourage the children to add other materials to those forms to make them more like a person, an animal, a house, a tree, or some other object. The teacher might restrict them to using paper, or he might permit them to use yarn, cloth, or other materials. Restricting them once in a while is a good idea because it forces them to get the most from a given material. To help them use a material such as paper effectively, the teacher might demonstrate a few of the things that can be done to paper. He might show how to curl it, fold it, fasten it, and punch holes in it, or he might show how different kinds of paper can be used to give a different color, texture, or pattern (Figure 9.15; Plate 48, page 460).

Pl. 47
Ceramic pot made from
slabs and decorated with iron oxide
and clear glaze. Second grade.

If paper sculpture is to be an art activity, however, the student must be required to make more than a vague generalization of a face, an animal, an insect, or some other object; he must be required to embody some conceptual and emotional content in his work. To encourage that embodiment, the teacher is advised to ask that the student make a *particular* object with *character* or *personality*. In other words, he should make such things as doctors, firemen, dachshunds, lions, or pine trees; and they should look happy, sad, sick, frightening, or wealthy. To make a special kind of object with a particular personality, the child must try to think of the identifying characteristics in that special object, and he must discover the things that make the object look happy or sad. If he does not try to give his dog any doggish characteristics, he is likely to produce a stiff, nondescript object that could just as well be a cow or a horse because it does not look like anything but a four-legged piece of paper.

The same comments apply to the making of art from papiermâché. The teacher must offer the kind of stimulation and the kind of procedural information that will cause a child to put

Fig. 9.15
The beginning of a
paper head in grade two.
(Photo by Barry Moore.)

458
**ART
EDUCATION**

concepts and feelings into his work. If he can do so, the child will deliver the kind of highly expressive product shown in Figure 9.16 instead of the insensitive kind of object in Figure 9.17.

Art educators in public schools are frequently criticized or ridiculed by artists or by art students because they use such materials as papier-mâché. But such critics lack an understanding of children and of public school finances. Elementary school youngsters are not capable of producing sculpture in marble, rosewood, or welded steel; yet they need to work with something other than clay if the art program is to remain interesting to them. The sculptural materials that they use must also be inexpensive because the art program is already a costly portion of the educational enterprise. Papier-mâché is not only manageable by children and different from clay but is also inexpensive. Consequently, it is used extensively in the public school.

It is probably best to begin using papier-mâché in the third grade because younger children usually have a hard time manipulating it and keeping it off their elbows, faces, and clothing. Even at the third-grade level, the teacher must provide a fair amount of assistance if the children are to enjoy success. This suggests that the papier-mâché projects for the third grade should be relatively simple; one of the easiest of those projects is the making of a head-shaped plaque to be hung on the wall. The first step is to prepare the materials and the classroom. The children should be asked to bring quantities of newspaper to school, and the janitor may be asked to furnish a package of paper towels. When free time is available, the pupils may be given the job of tearing the newspaper into small pieces no larger than 1 inch square. Tearing the paper is important because cut paper leaves ridges that show in the final product; and small pieces are desirable because they give a smoother finish than large pieces.

The next step is to prepare a quantity of wallpaper paste. The paste may be obtained in any paint store, and a 5-pound bag should be more than enough for one class of thirty students. The dry powder is mixed with water to the consistency of heavy cream. If the classroom is arranged so that the children can work

in groups of four, the wallpaper paste can be distributed conveniently in plastic bowls. Next to the bowls, there could be a cardboard box filled with torn newspaper, and each working surface could be covered with chipboard, cardboard, or pressed-wood sheets. A roll of masking tape for each group of children also would be helpful.

With everything ready, the teacher should demonstrate how the paste is mixed. Then he should show his students how to crumple newspapers into the shape of a fat pancake about 2 inches thick. This crumpled lump is then wrapped with another sheet of newspaper so that the loose ends of the paper can be fastened in back with a piece of masking tape. The lump is placed on the working surface, pieces of paper are dipped in paste, and the top side of the lump is covered with those pieces. Other wet pieces of paper may be crumpled into the shape of a nose, ear, lip, or eye and stuck to the original pancake shape. Additional pieces of papier-mâché are used to fasten those parts to the basic head-shape, and a final layer of torn paper toweling gives the plaque a smooth finish. At this point, the teacher should warn the children against using too much paste, especially in the final layer of paper. If the paste is used too freely, it will produce a crackled surface that may not be desirable. Four layers of papier-mâché are probably sufficient. When finished,

Fig. 9.16
This papier-mâché dog contains a few doggish characteristics. It was made by a girl in third grade.

Fig. 9.17
Almost no doggish traits appear in this papier-mâché dog. It is merely a stiff, four-legged piece of paper.

461
A RECOMMENDED COURSE
OF STUDY

the teacher can show the children how and where to store their sculpture to dry, and he can show them how to fasten a piece of string to the back of the plaque with papier-mâché. The string permits the head to be hung on the wall.

The children are then ready to begin their own work; and when they finish with the last layer of paper, they must let their sculpture dry for about three days. At the end of that time, the teacher should show them how to paint their papier-mâché heads and how to add materials to them to make them more expressive. The object in making the head, painting it, and adding materials to it is to present the idea of a particular person with a specific character. If it is done successfully, the room will be a very interesting and attractive place.

Another kind of sculpture can be created with boxes, as has already been mentioned in connection with the nursery school and kindergarten; but children in the primary grades can work with small as well as large boxes. Shoe boxes, matchboxes, cigar boxes, oatmeal boxes, candy boxes, and other small cardboard containers can be glued together or to larger boxes to make automobiles, wagons, airplanes, houses, trucks, or non-representational constructions. If the boxes are not covered with wax, they can be painted or paper can be glued to them. Such objects can be made to look new, old, fancy, plain, or rich. In other words, they can be made to say something visually. The teacher should strive for that end, although it will not be easy for young children to make more than a general statement (Figure 9.18).

It is also possible to add papier-mâché to the boxes after they have been glued together. They become very strong and can be painted and decorated quite easily. Still other sculptural procedures are possible with children, and instructions for them may be found in the books listed at the end of the chapter.

Crafts. The number of craft projects that might be undertaken at the primary level is large, as any book on the subject will indicate. Consequently, only a few of the more common projects will be listed and described here. Nursery school and kinder-

Fig. 9.18
*Painting an animal
that has been made with small boxes
and papier-mâché. Grade four.
(Photo by Richard Hildwein.)*

Fig. 9.19
*Making a puppet with
a Plasticine head on the end
of a stick. Grade two.
(Photo by Barry Moore.)*

463

**A RECOMMENDED COURSE
OF STUDY**

garten craft activities may be offered if the children did not attend preprimary classes. In addition, the teacher will find the following projects very suitable:

Papier-mâché puppets   *Cut-paper pictures or murals*
(third grade)
Stuffed paper animals   *Elementary ceramics*
(third grade)
Crayon and pencil rubbings   *Elementary weaving*
Paper costumes   *Appliqué*

A simple papier-mâché puppet may be started by rolling a piece of newspaper into a tight, strong tube that is taped to hold its shape. A sheet of newspaper is crumpled into the shape of a ball and fastened over one end of the paper tube with masking tape. Papier-mâché is then added to the crumpled head-shape and to the tube so that the two are securely fastened together. After the papier-mâché dries, the head may be painted, and materials such as yarn and buttons may be added to give the head character. A hole is cut in the bottom of a small paper bag, and the tube is inserted in the hole. Thus the bag becomes clothing for the puppet, and the child can manipulate the puppet by holding the tube that is inside the bag.

Stuffed paper figures are enjoyable to make in the third grade or above. A sheet of 24- by 36-inch kraft paper is folded in half and a simple animal or other object is drawn on the paper. The teacher must emphasize the importance of keeping the contour of the object very simple and the legs or other appendages quite wide. If those directions are not followed, the children will have difficulty stuffing and sewing their figures.

Having drawn the figure, the folded paper is held securely with paper clips, and the figure is cut out. Then, the outer sides of the two pieces of paper are painted. When the paint is dry, the sewing begins. With a large-eyed needle and yarn, the two pieces of paper are partially sewed together, stuffed with crumpled newspaper, and sewed some more. A running stitch, a blanket stitch, or several other stitches may be used to sew the papers together, but it is important to do the sewing at least one-half inch from the edge of the paper. After the sewing and stuffing is finished, the children may add cloth, yarn, buttons, paper, and other materials to give their stuffed figures more richness and personality.

Making crayon and pencil rubbings is an activity that might build a greater sensitivity to patterns and textures in the environment. To make them, the teacher must show his students how to search for an interesting texture, how to place a piece of thin paper over it, and how to rub the paper gently with the side of a crayon or a pencil. When they understand the procedure, the teacher might give each of them several sheets of paper to take home and ask them to make rubbings of as many interesting textures as possible. The rubbings they bring to the classroom could be displayed, and the children could try to guess where they were obtained. The project is easy, but it is very fascinating for youngsters in the primary grades. It is not actually an art project, of course, but it is a useful exercise if it makes children sensitive to textural pattern.

A collage, a torn-paper picture, or a cut-paper picture is a suitable project for the primary grades. It is simply a matter of pasting pieces of paper or other materials to another piece of paper to make a work of art. The teacher's job is to show the students how to cut, tear, and paste the materials, and it is also his job to show them what effects can be created with a variety of papers and other substances to make the pictures interesting to perceive. Consequently, it is helpful to have wallpaper scraps, glazed paper, colored construction paper, cloth, and other such items available (see Plate 53).

A project that is similar to collage is appliqué, which involves the sewing or pasting of cloth on another piece of cloth. If the pieces are sewed instead of pasted, appliqué should begin at the third- or fourth-grade level. Children in the second grade are still unable to thread needles, so the teacher should do it for them. But in the third grade the teacher should be able to teach them how to thread big-eyed needles, how to sew things securely, how to use the thread or yarn as a linear element in

465

their work, and how to achieve variety by using a number of different kinds of cloth.

Murals are nothing more than large drawings, paintings, collages, appliqués, or mosaics that are made on a wall or attached to a wall. In the primary grades, a cut-paper mural is appropriate and so is a large appliqué. The teacher's first job is to decide upon a theme and to make a list of the things that might appear in the picture. The children should help with the list and should be allowed to volunteer for making the things that appear on the list. When everyone has been assigned a portion of the mural to make, each child can work at his own desk to complete his task. As people begin to finish with their pasted or sewed pieces, they may tape them temporarily to the kraft paper or to the cloth that forms the background for the mural. When all the pieces are in place, the teacher may discuss the arrangement with the class to see if any changes are necessary. The pieces then may be pasted or sewed in place permanently (see Plate 51).

Sometimes it is necessary to prepare a background for all the pieces that go on a mural. If so, a few children can be asked to volunteer for that job. In other words, they might agree to make mountains, fields, sky, water, or other large background elements in the mural.

Suitable information on composition

The suggestions that already have been made about the teaching of composition in the preprimary classes also apply to the primary grades. But there are a few more things that can be done with youngsters in the first, second, and third grades. As the teacher exposes his students to work of art, he might point out the formal elements that exist in those works. This means that he might call attention to different kinds of lines, textures, patterns, colors, and shapes; and he might have his students make thick and thin lines, light and dark colors, big and little shapes, smooth and rough textures. The object, of course, is to get the youngsters to understand the meanings of the terms that are used in talking about composition. Once they have learned the meanings of the terms, it is a good idea to ask them to put some patterns, some light and dark colors, or some thick and thin lines in their art products; however, the teacher should make such a request once in a while, not all the time, because too much of it would take the enjoyment out of the art activity for primary children.

Still another recommendation for teaching composition is that the children be given opportunities to arrange a bulletin board, a science display, or some other exhibit. As they do so, the teacher might call attention to instances of imbalance, of unused space, or of cluttered areas.

As the children draw, paint, arrange displays, or create in some other visual way, the teacher should continue to help them control their tools and materials, because a lack of control can lead to products that look messy. This means that instruction in procedure is closely related to success in composition.

These suggestions lead, admittedly, to an elementary kind of instruction in composition, but art educators seem to agree that formal lessons on composition are almost certain to kill enthusiasm for art in young children. At least, formal lessons did have that effect during the last half of the nineteenth century and the first half of the twentieth.

Appropriate information on art history

Children in the first and second grades will have difficulty understanding concepts of time. For that reason, it is not advisable to attempt the teaching of historical developments or sequences in art below the third or fourth grade. It is advisable, however, to build the understanding that there is history in art, that some works of art were produced long before others, and that men always have created visual symbols of one kind or another. It is also a good idea to show all different kinds of art to children and to let them see works from all the major periods in art history. By doing so, the teacher continues to build the idea that there is no single art form that is correct for all human beings

Pl. 51
Detail of a cut-paper and
tempera mural. First grade.

Pl. 52
A weaving produced after
instruction in the making of
patterns. Second grade.

Pl. 53
A collage. Second grade.

and to emphasize the fact that there are as many different art forms as there are people. This is an important point for children to learn, and the sooner they learn it the better. If we postpone such instruction until youngsters have developed the erroneous idea that there is only one acceptable art form, we will have a hard time establishing the correct view.

In the primary grades, it is not too early to mention that art has served different purposes through the years. The students might be taught that art has been made to tell stories, to decorate buildings, to beautify cities, to sell merchandise, or simply to please people. Most children are especially surprised to learn of the many things for which art is used today. Such information leads quite naturally to the discussion of artists and what they do. Students will be interested in learning something about the daily lives of a few outstanding painters and sculptors, and, if possible, they will enjoy visiting a local artist in his studio. After all, they study the fireman, the grocer, the teacher, the farmer, and other community workers, so it seems quite natural to study the artist and the part that he plays in the community. While covering such material, the teacher might compare the life of the contemporary artist with the life of an old master.

Topics to cover in aesthetics

In teaching aesthetics, it is perfectly proper for the primary teacher to cover the same questions that were proposed for study in nursery school and kindergarten, but he can expect the primary children to discuss those questions in more depth and for longer periods of time. In addition, the teacher might raise the following questions with his students:

1. *As you look at these two paintings, do they look the same? What makes them look different?*
2. *Is it good to have pictures or statues that look different? Why?*
3. *Can you tell us about something in our town that does not look nice? How does it make you feel when you see something that does not look nice? What could you and I do to make our town look better?*

4. *Is this object a drawing, a painting, a piece of sculpture, a print, a piece of architecture, or a craft object? How can you tell?*
5. *Here is a rock. Is it pleasing to look at? Is it a work of art? Why?*
6. *Here is a weed. What do you see in this weed? Does it look strong or weak, friendly or unfriendly? Does it look young or old? What makes it look that way?*

As these questions are covered, the teacher will naturally offer instruction in aesthetics in accordance with the suggestions offered in the previous chapter. He will also contribute to the student's understanding of aesthetics by doing the things that have been recommended for the teaching of content, procedure, composition, and art history.

SUGGESTIONS FOR THE INTERMEDIATE GRADES

Grades four, five, and six are called the intermediate grades. Several children in those classes will be in the mid-figurative stage of symbolic development, and some of them may reach the stage of artistic decision. But most of them will be in the late figurative stage, especially in grades five and six.

Topics for stimulating development of a knowledge of life

There are very few restrictions to be placed upon direct experiences as a form of stimulation in the intermediate grades. It is not advisable, however, to have students blow their noses, comb their hair, or engage in similar activities to build their imagery or refresh their memories of noses, hair, and arms, because the students will consider such actions childish. They will respond much more favorably to visits to the local newspaper, the courthouse, the department store, the sewage treatment plant, the automotive repair shop, the animal hospital, the factory, and other such places. As they make their visits, it is important to have them search for any mood or atmosphere that seems to be present and to identify the cause of that mood. The visual contributions to the nature of the experience are especially

471

Pl. 54
A clown, in crayon resist.
Third grade.

Pl. 55
Bicycling, a watercolor
painting. Third grade.

important to observe. In other words, it is essential for the children to become aware of the differences in atmosphere between a courtroom and an automotive repair shop and for them to see how the "look" of the two places contributes to those differences. At that time, it is appropriate for the teacher to point out how important visual appearances actually are. He might extend the discussion to include comments about personal appearance as well as the appearance of the environment. As he does so, he will not only stimulate ideas for the content of child art, but he will engage in aesthetic education.

In the intermediate grades the teacher can also give special attention to the patterns that can be seen in the neighborhood. There are patterns made by the clouds, by the bricks in a masonry wall, by the trees against the sky, by the windows in an office building, and by the automobiles in a parking lot. Patterns of that kind might be used in works of art to increase their complexity and their visual appeal.

Having visitors who wear distinctive uniforms in their occupations come to the school to talk with the children is another direct experience that is very worthwhile. But in place of such visitors, films can be used quite effectively. Children in the late figurative stage of symbolic development are beginning to identify themselves very closely with their own sex and are developing a keen interest in the occupations performed by the members of that sex. If the occupation requires a uniform, the interest is especially strong. Consequently, films that depict the life of a nurse, an airline pilot, a railway conductor, a ballerina, or a police officer will be especially stimulating, and they will help to build the knowledge of content and subject matter (life) that is so necessary for the creation of art. Films about life in the circus, in the newspaper business, in art, or in some other colorful profession will be equally well received by students, and so will a film that covers swimming, boxing, or tennis. As direct experiences, ausio-visual aids, or other forms of stimulation are selected, however, it is not wise to choose ones that simply "gild the lily." In other words, a stimulation is better if it is reasonably true to life instead of completely glamorous.

When it comes to verbal stimulations, the teacher will find that clowning or overly dramatic presentations are not especially successful with children in the intermediate grades. The teacher can be amusing and joke with the children, but when he is trying to impress them with the nature of an experience such as an auto accident, he must speak to them seriously and in a mature fashion. In fact, most fifth- and sixth-grade youngsters will prefer to discuss life's experiences in a fairly mature fashion, although they will not be capable of handling abstract ideas with much success.

Poems, stories, newspaper accounts, or parts of stories are useful as verbal stimulations at this level, but they must be moving and persuasive accounts that deal with topics that are interesting to the students. A few topics of stimulation that have demonstrated their usefulness are listed below:

Doctors and nurses at the hospital	*Hard work*
My favorite sport	*Shopping at a supermarket*
The greatest show on earth	*Riding on a crowded bus*
Tug-of-war	*Working in a drugstore*
Things that jump and crawl	*A long line of stores*
This is kindness	*A flower garden*
The ugliest thing I can imagine	*The chef*
Helping the wounded	*A crowded elevator*
Lost in a great forest	*This is fun*
Life as an astronaut	*The boxing match*
The garbage collector	*Swimming*
The view from an anthill	*Holding my breath*
The most peaceful place in town	*The department store*
The telephone repairmen after a	*Trucks, cars, and motorcycles*
storm	*Helping the victims of a flood*

Materials are just as stimulating for children in upper elementary grades as they are for younger ones. In the intermediate grades, students may use all the tools and materials that have already been recommended for the earlier grades, and in addition they may be given the items that are listed at the top of the next page.

Charcoal pencils	*Linoleum or 3M Printmaker's Plate*
Oil crayons	*Linoleum-cutting tools*
Pressed crayons	*Plaster*
Watercolor paint	*Colored tissue paper*
Hair brushes (sizes 3, 7, 12)	*India ink*
Rulers	*Lettering pens*
Oragami paper	*Wire*
Waxed paper	*Charcoal erasers*

Suitable procedures

The room arrangement in the intermediate grades may be handled in the same way that was suggested for the primary grades (Figure 9.20), and many of the same procedures might be taught. But the activities mentioned in the following pages are especially appropriate for grades four through six. The teaching of those procedures might be enhanced through the occasional use of films or television. Better films are being introduced every day, and school systems may either buy or rent them. Many states, in fact, make it possible for schools to obtain educational films at a reasonable cost from the film libraries of their state universities and state libraries. To use such visual aids, of course, the teacher must plan far in advance so that he will be able to obtain the film he wants at the time he wants it.

The advantage of film or television is that it gives each child a chance to see a demonstration of a procedure by a qualified person without having someone get in the way. If there are any questions about the process that is being demonstrated, the teacher must be able to answer them after the show has ended. Obviously, such an aid cannot possibly act as a substitute for the teacher, because it cannot offer the highly personalized instruction that is so essential to the production of art after the students have begun working. Some persons, for example, may express a dissatisfaction with their work. The teacher must find out what they dislike and help them to achieve their goals, or they are apt to become discouraged with art and lose interest in it.

Fig. 9.20
This room is arranged
conveniently for painting and
other art activities.
Grade six.

Drawing. Children in the intermediate grades are more likely to become dissatisfied with their drawing and painting than with anything else. Frequently, their unhappiness stems from an inability to produce the naturalistic forms that the culture seems to demand. It is hoped that the kind of art education that has been advocated in this book will help to reduce the feeling that naturalism is the only acceptable art form. But the desire for naturalism will never be completely eliminated, and it probably should not be, since it is an inherent desire. Children struggle for it not only because of cultural demands, but also because it is a way of learning about themselves and their environment; it is a form of self-adjustment. For that reason the teacher should be prepared to help his students produce naturalistic symbols if that is what they want to do. It may mean that he will have to teach perspective and proportion because those are the things that will be most helpful in making symbols that approach visual reality. Unfortunately, classroom teachers lack the information that is needed to teach perspective and proportion, because teacher training programs ordinarily do not include it. It is important, therefore, to upgrade teacher training programs if art instruction by the classroom teacher is to improve.

Meanwhile, the only thing that the classroom teacher can do is to consult books on drawing and painting or leave the instruction in perspective and proportion to the regular art teacher. Instruction of that kind should not be given formally to a whole class, however, because it may cause contented children to become dissatisfied with their own work. It is far better to offer such help only to those who indicate they need and want it.

By the time children reach the fourth or fifth grade they are usually tired of the drawing tools they have been using. Thus it is wise to introduce a few new ones so that the old, familiar tools need not be used so often. Oil crayons, pressed crayons, charcoal, hair brushes, and lettering pens are drawing instruments that older children can manipulate with interest and satisfaction. The teacher's job is to show the youngsters a few of the things that can be done with such instruments. He might show them how to blend colors with crayons by rubbing the colored surface with a finger or how to create interesting textures by building up layers of color with the oil crayons. Because the colors in the new crayons are quite intense and different from the colors of ordinary wax crayons, the teacher might show his students how to create visually rich effects by using more than one kind of crayon in their pictures.

Charcoal pencils are nice to use because they produce a very black color that can be shaded rather easily by rubbing it with a paper stump (a tightly rolled piece of paper). The teacher can demonstrate how to shade, how to sharpen the point of the pencil with sandpaper, and how to keep from smudging the drawing. Smudging may be avoided by resting the hand on a piece of clean paper that has been placed over the colored area. When the drawing is complete, it can be protected by spraying it with fixative in the same manner that was described in the discussion on the protection of chalk.

When working with chalk and charcoal, the teacher will find it helpful to distribute charcoal erasers and to demonstrate their use. The new eraser is pulled apart and kneaded like dough, and it is then pressed against the colored area to remove the pigment. To keep it clean and useable, it must be kneaded again after each erasure. The eraser itself is so different from other erasers that the children will be fascinated by it and want to use it.

Charcoal paper is too expensive to use in the elementary school, but bogus paper, oatmeal paper, and ordinary manila drawing paper are quite satisfactory for use with chalk and charcoal. The teacher will find, however, that it is much more difficult to erase on these papers. Consequently, it is a good idea for the teacher to show his students the degree of erasing that can be achieved on the paper they are using.

Youngsters will also enjoy using India ink and nibbed lettering pens of various kinds. Each child will need some good white drawing paper, a bottle of ink, a pen, and possibly a damp

Fig. 9.21
A portrait in charcoal
and white chalk by a boy
in fifth grade.

Fig. 9.22
A self-portrait made
with a felt-tipped pen by a boy
in sixth grade.

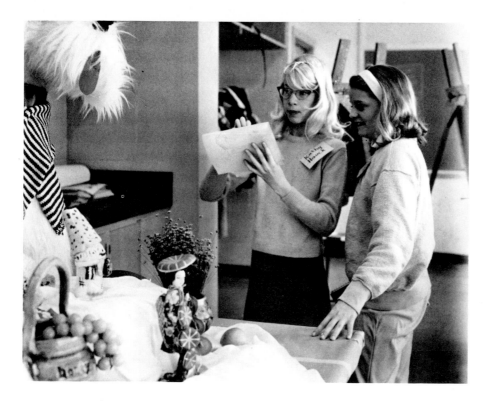

Fig. 9.23
*Examining and sketching
a still-life arrangement in sixth grade.*

sponge. With the materials passed out, the teacher might demonstrate the way to make lines of differing widths by varying the pressure on the pen, and he might show the effects that can be achieved by stippling, crosshatching, and drawing on wet paper. And to keep the tools in good condition, he might indicate how to clean the pens with a damp sponge, a cloth, or a paper towel.

Drawing with a brush may also be done in the intermediate grades. Two brushes made of hair, sizes 3 and 7, as well as some good drawing paper, would be useful. Either India ink or tempera paint might be employed, but tempera is much more economical. The teacher's job is to show his students how to use the tip of the brush or the side, depending upon the effect that is desired. He might show them how to lighten the color with water, how to draw on wet and dry paper, how to fasten the paper to the pressed-wood board with masking tape, and how to paint with a semidry brush. Distinguishing between this procedure and paint-

Pl. 56
Chalk drawings of
the human figure.
Fifth grade.

Pl. 57
My Teacher. A drawing made
with felt-tipped and nylon-tipped pens.
Fourth grade.

ing is not easy, but drawing with a brush usually involves a concentration on line rather than area.

As teachers introduce these various procedures, they must remember to give their students time to practice with their new tools and materials, and they must arrange to give them more than one experience with the medium. Without a doubt, some of the activities will cause them to draw from memory while others will require them to draw from the environment. It is important, however, to continue the effort aimed at increasing perceptual activity. The teacher must therefore try various ways of getting the children to explore an object carefully with their eyes as they draw it. One method of doing so is to engage them in an exercise called contour drawing. The exercise requires them to keep their eyes on the object they are drawing and not on their paper. As they carefully move their eyes around the contour of the object, they also move their hand and the drawing instrument. The first drawings will look very strange and incompetent to the children, and they will laugh. But if they do it several times, the naturalistic quality of their drawings will improve, and so will their mental images of the object being drawn. Such an exercise is not exactly an art activity, but it is the kind of drill that can be useful in concept development and eye-hand coordination if it is not overdone. The creative teacher may think of other ways to involve the student in careful preceptual activity.

Finally, it is a good idea to show children examples of different drawing techniques as they are exemplified in the work of well-known artists. It is good, for example, to show drawings by Picasso, Ingres, Shahn, Leonardo da Vinci, Dürer, Matisse, Toulouse-Lautrec, and certain oriental artists. Each of them uses a different kind of line, and seeing those differences will give the children a notion of what can be accomplished in drawing.

Painting. Tempera paint is without a doubt the most suitable kind of paint to use in the elementary school, but watercolor may also be used successfully if the instructor can teach the proper procedure for handling it. Watercolor is normally given to schoolchildren in tiny pans enclosed in a metal box. By

Pl. 58
Girl in a flowered hat, drawn
with oil crayons. Fourth grade.

Pl. 59
The figures in this collage were
painted with black tempera and colored
with oil crayons. Then they were cut out
and mounted on a background.
Fourth grade.

Pl. 60
As in Pl. 59, this collage was
made with an emphasis on the action of
the figure and pattern. Fourth grade.

483

adding water to the color in the pans, the painter obtains a medium that is both transparent and free-flowing. The adult artist usually tries to take advantage of those characteristics to produce a painting that has sparkling transparencies and a feeling of spontaneity. The child artist, on the other hand, is apt to use watercolor opaquely, and he is not likely to respond favorably to its free-flowing qualities. If he cannot be taught to use watercolor in a manner that is more conducive to its nature, however, he might just as well continue to use the more inexpensive tempera paint, which is the practice that is recommended below the fourth grade. After the age of eight, the child still may have trouble manipulating the medium in a completely satisfactory way, but he usually is capable of profiting from instruction. Consequently, the teacher in the intermediate grades might find it worthwhile to demonstrate some of the fundamental procedures of painting with watercolor. He might show how to make a watercolor wash (an even tone over a broad surface) or how to deal with accidental configurations that occasionally develop as a result of the free-flowing quality of the medium. He might also show how to create tints, shades, and gradations of tone. He might indicate the effects that can be produced by using cleansing tissue, erasers, pins, sandpaper, and pens on both wet and dry painted surfaces, and he might tell his students about the advantages and disadvantages of tipping the painting surface and of taping the watercolor paper to a pressed-wood sheet.

Real watercolor paper is too expensive to use in the elementary school, but a white drawing paper of high quality will work satisfactorily. Hair brushes, of course, must be used for watercolor painting, and it is also recommended that they be used for tempera painting in the intermediate grades. The reason for the change from bristle brushes is that the children in grades four to six are capable of making details and usually want to produce them in their paintings. The only brushes that will permit such work are hair brushes, because they are the only ones that come to a point. If they do not come to a point, they are not good brushes. Good ones are not inexpensive, so the teacher

must show his students how to care for them. The students should not scrub with them; they should wash them and draw them to a point after using; and they should store them with the hairs up. If the teacher keeps sizes 3, 7, and 12 in stock, he will have the brushes necessary for producing a wide variety of effects.

Children in grades four through six usually want to maintain absolute control over the medium they use. Consequently, they tend to become discouraged with watercolor because it is difficult to control. Therefore, the teacher's job is to help the children understand that accidental effects are to be expected because it is the nature of watercolor to be free-flowing and somewhat unpredictable. To help students become accustomed to the accidental and to help them make the best of unintended configurations, the instructor might have his students make accidental forms on purpose and build a meaningful image out of the unintended shapes. In other words, he might have the children wet some paper and touch it in various places with brushes full of color. The color will disperse in various directions, and when it

Fig. 9.24
Using the crayon resist
technique of drawing-painting
in the fourth grade.
(Photo by Barry Moore.)

Fig. 9.25
Painting with tempera
in the sixth grade.

Pl. 61
My Secret Hiding Place.
An x-ray painting in watercolor.
Fifth grade.

Pl. 62
Casein painting.
Fifth grade.

Pl. 63
Casein painting.
Sixth grade.

dries, the students might try to figure out what the resultant forms suggest. After that, the teacher might have them make the suggested content more apparent by requiring them to draw or paint on top of the accidental forms with ink or tempera paint. Such an exercise, if repeated more than once, may help students to accept a certain amount of guidance from their tools and materials.

Print making. Gluing materials to heavy cardboard, inking them, and pressing them on paper is a printing procedure that has been described and recommended for the primary grades. The same procedure and the same room arrangement may be used satisfactorily in the intermediate grades, but is a good idea to introduce new materials and equipment. Inner tubes from automobile tires, for example, may be cut into different shapes and glued to wood or heavy cardboard. Like other materials, the tubing may be inked; paper may be placed on top of the inked tubing; and the back of the paper may be rubbed with a hand. Instead of using the hand, however, the teacher is advised to demonstrate the use of a printing press and to let the children use it for the first time.

There are two kinds of presses that might be used. The first is equipped with two sturdy metal plates that can be separated in different ways, depending upon the construction of the press. The inked printing block, topped with a piece of paper, is placed between the metal plates, and a magazine or a piece of felt is placed on top the paper. The two metal plates are then forced together to make a very tight sandwich. When the pressure is released and the plates are opened, the inked block is taken out and the printed paper is removed from the block. To make another print, the block must be inked again and placed in the press once more. Such a procedure allows the student to see what happens when heavy pressure is applied to a printing surface with a printing press.

To let the children know that there is more than one kind of press, the teacher might fasten an ordinary, old-fashioned, hand-operated clothes wringer to a table. He might obtain a sheet of pressed wood that is just narrow enough to fit through the wringer. The inked block is topped with printing paper; a magazine or a piece of felt is placed on top the paper; the pressure on each end of the wringer is equalized; and, finally, the whole sandwich is placed on the pressed-wood sheet and run through the wringer. Such a printing press is not the best, but it is relatively inexpensive and offers an introduction to the better kind of printing equipment used in the secondary school.

Another printing procedure that is suitable for children in the intermediate grades is linoleum-block printing. Probably, the easiest kind of linoleum to use at this level is the kind that can be purchased from school supply houses, but battleship linoleum, obtained from local stores, is excellent. In addition to a piece of linoleum about 3 by 4 inches, each child will need a set of linoleum-cutting tools and a piece of tracing paper. With the materials in readiness, the teacher is ready to demonstrate the printing procedure. The first step is to show the students that they must draw their visual symbols within a space that is the same size as the linoleum block. Tracing paper is placed over the drawing; the drawing is traced with a soft, dark lead pencil; the tracing paper is turned over; and the drawing is traced through to the back of the tracing paper. The next step is to place the tracing paper, front down, on the linoleum block and to trace over the lines on the back of the paper once again. This will cause the original drawing of the symbol to appear backward on the linoleum block. The teacher must be sure to emphasize that the drawing should appear backward on the block, for if it did not, the final print would be backward.[1]

After the drawing has been transferred to the linoleum, the teacher must show his students how to cut away the portions of the block that should not print. He should be especially careful to mention the importance of cutting away from the hands and should suggest that the cutting be done by moving the fingers rather than the whole arm. Such instructions will

[1] Block printing has been simplified in recent years by the introduction of 3M Printmaker's Plate, a substitute for linoleum.

tend to reduce accidents and give the student more control over his work.

With the cutting done, the teacher is ready to ink the linoleum block with a brayer and to print. The printing may be done either by rubbing the back of the printing paper with a hand or by placing the block and paper in a printing press. When the printing is finished, the oil-based ink should be cleaned from the block with turpentine or mineral spirits, and the prints should be hung or placed in a well-ventilated place to dry.

If the teacher gives his students several opportunities to print with linoleum blocks, he will find that he can teach them to do more intricate work. They are capable of printing with more than one color by making a block for each color, and they are able to create different visual effects by experimenting with different kinds of paper. The time to do such things should be provided because it gives the creator a sense of accomplishment and a feeling for exploration (see Plate 69, page 503).

If the teacher wishes to try another printing procedure with his students, he might teach them a simplified method of making a screen print. It involves stretching a piece of tarlatan, organdy, or orlon net across an opening such as the one found in an embroidery hoop. The design to be printed is cut out of a piece of waxed paper or a piece of stencil paper, and some powdered soap is mixed with tempera paint until the paint reaches the consistency of pudding. The stencil is a placed on the printing paper; the embroidery hoop with its stretched organdy is placed on the stencil; and a tablespoonful of paint is placed inside the hoop. A piece of stiff cardboard is used to drag the paint across the tarlatan and across the opening in the stencil that is underneath. This action causes the paint to go through the stencil and onto the printing paper; as a result, the stencil adheres to the bottom of the tarlatan. With the stencil and screen joined, it is a simple matter to make more prints. And when the printing is finished, the stencil may be peeled from the tarlatan and the screen may be washed by holding it under a faucet.

To cut a design out of wax paper or stencil paper, the student must use a sharp instrument such as a stencil knife.

Fig. 9.26
This girl is drawing on an inked surface in the process of making a monoprint. Grade four. (Photo by Richard Hildwein.)

489
A RECOMMENDED COURSE OF STUDY

Many teachers will permit their students to use sharp instruments after giving a careful lecture on safety, but the matter of using such tools should be discussed with the school administration before the tools are given to children. If it seems inadvisable to use such instruments, screen printing can still be done by eliminating the stencil. This means that the teacher will have to show the children how to draw their designs on the tarlatan by pressing heavily with waxed crayons. The paint will go through the uncolored portions of the tarlatan to make the print. The paint may then be washed from the screen, as before, with water, but the crayon will have to be removed by rubbing the screen with alcohol.

Sculpture. Clay is always an excellent sculptural material to use at any stage in the child's development. In the intermediate grades the teacher is advised to continue with the teaching of the procedures that he initiated in the primary grades. He might continue to help his students perfect their techniques for building sculptural forms with slabs and coils, and he might show them how to give the surface of their work a texture. The surface can be pricked, paddled, brushed, and scraped with a broken hacksaw blade, or it can be textured by pressing objects into it. Firing the finished product is still advisable, if the work is to be made strong enough to preserve. Glazing, however, is still expensive. But if the materials for glazing are available, it is a good idea to have sixth-grade children learn the process. After all, they must have experiences with such an important procedure if they are to have an adequate base for making decisions about ceramics in the future. The directions for glazing usually come with the glazing materials.

Another sculptural medium that is appropriate for the elementary school is a mixture of 2 parts of Zonolite, 1 part of molding plaster, and enough water to give it a thick, slushy consistency. Zonolite is an insulating material that can be obtained, along with the plaster, from a building supply store. It should be mixed with the plaster and water in a plastic bucket so that any of the mixture that remains can be removed from the

Fig. 9.27
Making an abstract
construction with clay slabs.
Grade five.

Fig. 9.28
Bisque-fired clay heads
that were made over a damp,
crumpled-paper core or armature.
The paper burns out in the kiln.
Grades six and seven.

Fig. 9.29
Bisque-fired clay animals
ready for glazing or painting.
Grade four.

Fig. 9.30
Bisque-fired clay heads
ready for glazing or painting.
They were made over a
crumpled-paper core. Grade six.

bucket without damage to the container. After it is mixed, it can be poured into half-gallon, cardboard milk containers, where it can stay until it hardens. As soon as the mixture becomes hard enough to hold its shape, the milk carton may be torn away and the sculpturing may begin. Carving with a dull knife is especially easy while the medium is still warm, but becomes a little more difficult as the material cools and hardens. The Zonolite lightens the mixture and makes it possible for children to carve, but it also has a tendency to produce crumbling as the carving proceeds. Because of the crumbling, details are quite difficult to carve and should be avoided in most cases.

Naturally there is a possibility that some of the carved waste will fall on the floor. The teacher must see that the floor is covered with kraft paper or a large sheet of plastic, or he must take special precautions to see that the waste does not reach the floor in a large quantity, because plaster on the floor can dirty a room and a school corridor more quickly than almost anything.

Although plaster can be messy, children must be allowed to use it if they are to learn the various sculptural procedures that lead to three-dimensional art. One of the most appropriate things to teach them in the fourth, fifth, and sixth grades is a procedure for making plaster bas-reliefs. To engage in the process, each child needs a cardboard box approximately 8 by 11 by 2 inches deep and a quantity of oil-based clay. The teacher's job is to demonstrate how the clay is pressed into the bottom of the box to a depth of about 1 inch. After smoothing the clay, the teacher must show his students how to dig it out, how to draw in it, and how to press objects into it to make depressions of different heights. When the picture or design is finished, it is painted with liquid soap, and liquid plaster is poured over the clay until it almost reaches the top of the box. Paper clips are partly inserted in the wet plaster so that the finished bas-relief can be hung on the wall. When the plaster hardens, the clay can be separated from the plaster, and the plaster can be painted with shellac or with plastic glue. Shellac or glue will keep the plaster from absorbing moisture, so that the bas-relief can be painted with tempera paint. The tempera will adhere to the plaster more satisfactorily, however, if it is mixed with a little plastic glue.

The teacher will need to demonstrate the painting procedure, and he will probably have to mix the plaster, unless he can find one or two children who are capable of doing such a ticklish job. Mixing plaster is a task that requires attention because the proportion of plaster to water must be reasonably accurate, and the mixture must be poured into the boxes as soon as it reaches the proper consistency. It has reached that stage when a finger mark can be made on the surface; and if it is not poured quickly, it might harden in the mixing container. Consequently, it is a good idea to mix it in a plastic bucket, so that it can be removed if it hardens too fast. The proper proportion of water to plaster is 1 quart of water to 2 pounds and 12 ounces of plaster.

Unlike plaster, paper is a sculptural medium that is useful in all the grades. Any comments that have been made about its use at the primary level apply equally to the fourth, fifth, and sixth grades. But students at the intermediate level are capable of building bigger and more complex structures than they could as younger children. For that reason it is suggested that pupils be urged to do more than simply add pieces of paper to a single cylinder-, cone-, or box-shape. They might *combine* such elementary forms in the construction of full-standing human figures, animals, buildings, and other objects. The teacher might suggest that possibility and demonstrate various ways of fastening the parts together. As he does so, he should encourage the youngsters in their efforts to invent new forms and fastening devices. As the children succeed in their sculptural efforts with construction paper, the teacher might introduce chipboard, illustration board, and corrugated cardboard as sculptural materials. With such sturdy supplies it should be possible to create sculpture of a fairly large size. Bigness is not necessary for art, of course, but it does permit the student to experience the problems and possibilities of large size. It gives him a chance to paint his sculpture and presents him with more difficult problems of fitting and fastening the parts. Instead of using glue and tape, for example, he might be forced to use wire, metal eyelets, cloth joints, or string. Although

Pl. 64
A seated figure, in terra-cotta.
Fourth grade.

Pl. 65
A plaster sand-casting
mounted on stained wood.
Fourth grade.

the possibilities with such materials are enormous, the teacher will find that not all sixth-grade children will be able to use the materials with ease. For some youngsters the problems of cutting and fastening may be more than they can manage. Consequently, the teacher must make a careful decision about whether it is advisable for him to introduce large-scale paper sculpture to his students.

Another procedure that might be taught in the intermediate as well as the primary grades is the procedure for working with papier-mâché. The method to be taught is still basically the same, of course, but instead of having the children in the upper elementary grades begin with a simple crumpled-paper core, the teacher might show them how to begin with a wire armature. This will require each child to bring two coat hangers made of the thinnest wire they can find (coat hangers made of heavy wire are difficult to cut). In addition to the wire, the children will need to bring a piece of wood about 6 by 8 inches. Some of the huskier students can score the wire with wire cutters and break it. That will provide pieces which, when straightened, are about 3 feet long. With the wire, wood, and newspaper in readiness, the teacher might show the children how to bend the wire with pliers, how to nail or staple the bottom ends to the wooden base, and how to bend the upper ends to act as supports for arms, heads, tails, necks, or other portions of a figure. Newspaper may then be fastened to the wire with string or tape, to give substance to the various parts and to act as a base for papier-mâché. When the students have proceeded that far with their individual figures, the teacher might see that papier-mâché is prepared and demonstrate how to apply it to the covered armature. From that point on, the student's job is to paint his sculpture and add things to it, so that it has character and presents a unique reaction to experience.

Using a wire armature is valuable because it permits students to experience an important sculptural procedure, but it can be difficult for children if the teacher is not careful. Cutting, bending, and fastening the wire can be an especially frustrating job if the wire is hard to cut or bend. And the whole task can be a

Fig. 9.31
*Papier-mâché animals
by youngsters in fourth grade.
(Photo by Barry Moore.)*

failure if the wire is so weak that it will not support the weight of the papier-mâché. Consequently, the teacher must check the wire carefully, and he must be sure that he has a sufficient number of wire-cutting pliers, hammers, nails, and staples.

Crafts. Because the children in the intermediate grades are physically and mentally more mature than the youngsters in the primary grades, it is possible to engage in a wide variety of craft activities during the last three years of the elementary school. The number of worthwhile activities is, in fact, so large that only a few projects are listed here:

Dioramas	*Mosaics*
Puppets	*Stitchery*
Murals	*Pottery*

The making of dioramas is suggested for the intermediate grades. Children in those grades are capable of making the detail that a diorama requires simply because they have more control over their small muscles. This means that they can build things small enough to create a model of a scene inside a small box. By building the scene at one end of the box and cutting a peephole in the other end, they can make a simple peep show of aesthetic merit. They can create an atmosphere or mood by cutting holes in the top and sides of the box to admit light, and the total effect of the scene can be altered by changing the location of the holes or by covering the openings with colored cellophane or tissue paper. Still other results can be obtained by removing the top of the box and covering the opening with transparent or transluscent colored paper. The teacher's job, of course, is to show the children how different effects can be created and how important it is to make imaginative use of materials. A peep show that he had already created would be very useful for such purposes because it would allow him to demonstrate lighting effects, the use of weeds for trees, and other such things.

Murals can be made in both the primary and intermediate grades, but the older children can make them with less supervision from the teacher. Murals may take the form of a collage, an appliqué, a mosaic, a low-relief sculpture, or a painting. In each case it is a good idea to make the mural on a 4- by 8-foot sheet of plywood, pressed wood, Celotex, or Homosote. By doing so, the murals can be displayed more easily and attractively in choice locations throughout the school, and they can be taken down and replaced. Celotex and Homosote make good foundations for tempera painted murals, but they usually need a coat of flat white paint before the tempera is applied. Such murals are relatively inexpensive to make because the paint can be washed off and a new mural can replace it.

Appliqué may be used effectively with any of the materials that have been mentioned, but mosaics and low-relief sculptural constructions may need the support of plywood or pressed wood. Small mosaics make excellent hot dish pads, and they are made in the same way as a mural. The pads require that each child be given a pressed-wood sheet 9 by 12 inches. The sheets can be sawed at a lumberyard, and a quantity of vinyl floor tile and grout can be secured from a store that sells floor

497

coverings. After cutting the tiles into small (about ½ by ¼ inch) pieces on a paper cutter, the teacher is advised to separate the pieces and to put them in boxes according to color. The students may then be taught to make the sketches for their designs directly on the pressed-wood sheets by using felt-tipped pens. The next step is to show the students how to glue the vinyl tesserae to the board so that there is about one-sixteenth or one-eighth of an inch between the pieces. If any of the vinyl needs to be cut into different shapes, heavy scissors or a pair of tin snips will do the job. Having fastened the pieces to the board with waterproof plastic glue, the teacher is ready to mix the grout according to the directions that come with it. The mixture is rubbed into the openings between the tesserae, and the whole mosaic is cleaned as much as possible with a damp sponge. After the mosaics have dried, they may be cleaned again with a dry cloth.

By the time youngsters reach the fourth grade, they are able to thread large-eyed needles with yarn. Consequently, it is a good time to introduce stitchery. This means that the teacher will have to provide each child with a piece of burlap (about 16 by 22 inches), a large-eyed needle, and a selection of colored yarns cut in pieces 3 feet long. In addition, the task will be made easier for the children if frames can be used to stretch the burlap. Good 14- by 20-inch frames can be made from 12- and 20-inch lengths of wood that are 2 inches wide and 1 inch thick. Making the frames is a little extra work, of course, but they can be used again and again without rebuilding. The burlap is stretched across the frame and fastened with thumbtacks or staples, and the design for the stitchery is drawn on the material with a piece of white chalk. Naturally, the teacher explains or demonstrates those steps and shows his pupils how to make different kinds of stitches. When the students have finished their work, the burlap must be removed from the frame so that the edges can be hemmed or finished in some other way.

The making of puppets is a fine artistic activity. There are a great many different kinds of puppets that can be made in the intermediate grades. One of the most popular is the sock puppet,

Pl. 66
Glazed ceramic figures.
Fifth grade.

Pl. 67
Seated human figures,
in terra-cotta.
Fifth grade.

because it makes possible a wide range of facial expressions. To make one, each child needs a sock, a 3- by 6-inch piece of red felt, scissors, a needle, some thread, and some scrap materials, such as buttons, yarn, and cloth. His first job is to make a mouth. There are at least two ways that he can do it. He can sew a piece of red cloth (not the felt) over the toe of the sock and push the toe back in so that only the edge of the red cloth shows. The toe will be in the palm of the hand that is inside the sock, and by opening and closing the hand, the mouth can be made to do many things. Another way to make a mouth, however, is to lay the sock on its side and to cut a slit 3 inches long (starting at the toe and cutting up the middle) in it. The next step is to draw a 3- by 6-inch oval on the 3- by 6-inch piece of felt and cut it out. The sock is then turned inside out, and the felt is sewed to the opening in the sock. When that is finished, the sock is turned right side out, and the mouth is complete. Having used either method of making a mouth, the child proceeds to sew other materials to the sock, to make eyes, nose, hair, and other such features. Students will find their puppets to be delightful characters, and they will get a great deal of enjoyment from using them in a puppet show that they have written themselves.

Suitable information on composition

By the time the child reaches the intermediate grades, he may begin to find fault with the appearance of his visual symbols. One thing that a teacher can do to help him develop a more positive attitude toward his work is to help him with composition. The child should have learned the meanings of the terms that are used in talking about composition by the time he reaches fourth grade, and he should be able to manipulate the formal elements of art. This means that the teacher can talk to him about lines, shapes, colors, textures, and patterns, and that he should be able to see the effect of his talk in the adjustment of those formal elements within the child's art work. If the teacher is able to do such things, it is an appropriate time for him to increase emphasis on balance, unity, and variety.

In the earlier grades the teacher was advised to mention the need for balance and to suggest things that would lead to unity and variety. But such things were not to be emphasized, and the instruction was to remain very informal. To change instructional tactics at this point, however, and to stress composition a little more heavily does not mean that the teaching of composition should be done through a series of formally presented lessons that require the child to engage in a lot of exercises devoted exclusively to design. The teacher may occasionally speak to the whole class about common compositional problems, but the majority of his instruction on the subject of design should occur in private, informal conversations with each student. The reason for such a tactic is that design achieves meaning and significance only if it is related to the expressive purpose of the student's own personal work. The teacher must help the student to recognize imbalance, disunity, and a lack of visual excitement in his work, and the instructor must convince him that he will be more effective in reaching and impressing the observer with the content of his work if he can overcome those compositional weaknesses. Furthermore, the teacher must make suggestions that will help the student to do the job.

To help a child achieve balance or uniformity of opposition in his work, the teacher might point to the disturbance caused by a dominating size, color, shape, direction, or texture, and he might indicate how and where to counter it with an opposing element. As he does so, he may be able to show the child that a circle does not need to be opposed or balanced by a circle, a red color by a red color, or a big shape by a big shape. He might demonstrate that a circle can he opposed by a square, a red color by a green one, or a large shape by a lot of little ones. In other words, he might show the child how to create balance without resorting to symmetry. And it is understood that his suggestion must not lead to a distortion of the concepts and feelings that the child is trying to convey.

If there is disunity in a child's work, the suggestions that the teacher makes will depend upon what is causing the difficulty. The teacher might suggest that the child repeat certain colors,

501

A RECOMMENDED COURSE
OF STUDY

Pl. 68
Chalk drawing of a classmate.
Sixth grade.

Pl. 69
A paper collage. Fourth grade.
(Photo by Barry Moore.)

Pl. 70
A block print made with 3M
Printmakers. Plate.
Fourth grade.

Pl. 71
A papier-mâché mask made
over a large balloon. Fourth grade.

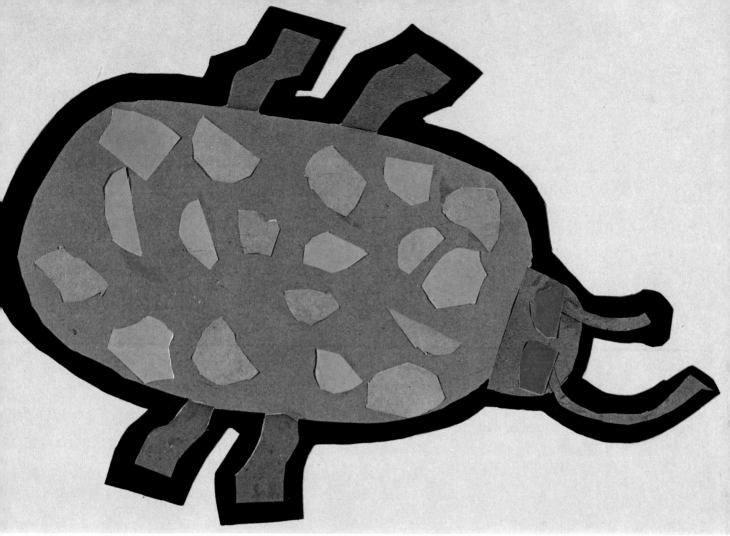

Pl. 69

Pl. 70   Pl. 71

values, intensities, sizes, lines, shapes, textures, or directions in various parts of his work. The resultant similarities among the parts will cause the observer to perceive the units as a group or a whole, which is a step toward unity. Further improvement in that direction may be forthcoming if the teacher advises his students to use space that has been neglected or to reduce the size of that space by placing the elements of the work closer together. As the units move closer to each other, the observer will tend to perceive them as a group and not as separate parts; hence the action is a contribution to unity.

The teacher can also help to achieve stability, order, or coherence by recommending that certain formal elements be rearranged to keep the eye moving from place to place within the art object, but not outside it. By creating a path of implied continuity that begins and ends at the same point, the artist not only keeps the eye from wandering away, but he permits the observer to experience closure in the perception of the art object. Closure is a matter of seeing wholes instead of parts; thus it is an instance of unity.

It is quite possible, however, to achieve a high degree of unity while producing an object that is visually boring. If that happens in the classroom, the teacher must try to help the student introduce variety in his work. To do that, the teacher might suggest that the student add or change certain formal elements to create more shapes, sizes, colors, values, intensities, lines, textures, or directions. As variety increases, however, there is apt to be a reduction in unity. This means that the teacher and the student must be careful to maintain enough unity to balance the variety. When too much of the latter is created, the result is chaos.

Two other ways of increasing visual variety are to place a *few* of the formal elements a little farther apart and to give different degrees of emphasis to different parts of the art object. Emphasis or attractiveness is created by making a certain portion of an object different from the surrounding areas. Bright colors, unusual shapes, lots of detail, sharp contrasts, and many other things can give emphasis to an area if the surrounding space does not exhibit the same characteristics.

Finally, the teacher can help the child to achieve variety in his work simply by urging him to avoid symmetrical arrangements. If he can succeed in getting children to improve their compositions with such elemental advice, he will be doing about as much as he can expect to do with youngsters in the elementary school.

Appropriate information on art history

By the time youngsters reach the intermediate grades, they should have been exposed to art from most of the major periods in art history and should know that some art forms were made long before others. And they should have heard about the lives of several famous artists. With that background the child is ready to learn that there is a sequential order to the different periods in art history, and he is ready to learn more details about artists and about the work of art historians.

As the teacher covers the sequence of periods in art history, it is not advisable for him to include all developments and all details. In fact, it is far better for him to limit his instruction to a simplified sequence such as the following: primitive art; Egyptian; Greek and Roman; Medieval; Renaissance; eighteenth- and nineteenth-century European; modern European; and American. If the students happen to show more interest in certain periods than in others, it is a good idea to let them spend more time on them. Perhaps they could delve more deeply into the lives of artists who interest them; or they might study the patrons of the arts or the social, political, and religious climate of the time.

Although students should be allowed to spend their time on the aspects of history that interest them, the teacher should make an effort to see that the significant features of major periods are covered, and he should make sure that the lives and contributions of at least two to four representative artists from each period are discussed. To make this material interesting, the teacher is advised to use reproductions, films, and slides to full advantage. Films on the lives of artists would be especially worthwhile.

Taking classes to art museums is also valuable because it gives children a chance to see original works, to examine them carefully, and to see more work from a given period than the teacher has shown in class. Because most museums group art objects according to the periods in which they were produced, the museum makes it possible to compare periods more easily and to recognize that changes from one to another were gradual instead of abrupt. The museum also affords youngsters an opportunity to take tours conducted by experts in art history, and it permits them to hear authoritative lectures and to ask questions that the teacher has been unable to answer.

As we have mentioned before, it is important to expose children to experts because it is from the authorities that young people will get the most accurate impressions of the artistic profession. Thus it is recommended that teachers invite art historians to their classes when the occasion permits. The historians might talk about art and artists in history, of course, but they also could and should talk about the job of being an historian. What does such a person do? Why does he do it? What is interesting and exciting about the work? What do you have to do to become an art historian? Why do we have so much art in museums instead of elsewhere? Why do the major museums happen to be in their present locations? What is the difference between an historian and a critic? Obviously, there are many more questions of a similar nature that an art historian could answer as no one else could. To ignore that fact and to ignore the historian would be a shame.

Topics to cover in aesthetics

Again, it is expected that teachers in the intermediate grades will cover the same questions that were covered by instructors in the earlier grades, but it is also expected that the level of the discussion will be higher. As the teacher faces these questions with his students, both parties will discover that answers can be very complex and that more than one answer is possible. This should lead to interesting debates among the students and leave them with the feeling that there is a highly important intellectual frontier to be explored and conquered.

If the questions that have been asked at the preprimary and primary level are not sufficient to maintain interest, the following queries might be helpful:

1. *Why do businessmen hire artists rather than nonartists to design automobiles, billboards, and cereal boxes?*
2. *Are beautiful things good for us? Are they* always *good for us?*
3. *Here is Gainsborough's* Blue Boy. *Do you believe that this painting affected boys and girls in Gainsborough's day in the same way that it affects you? Why?*
4. *Here are two paintings (with exactly the same subject matter but a completely different formal structure). Would you say that they are the same or different? What is similar or different about them?*
5. *Is it worthwhile for people to make art objects that deal with the same subject matter? Why?*
6. *Is it worthwhile for one artist to employ the same style as another artist? Why?*
7. *In how many different ways can art be valuable to us?*
8. *You have looked at a number of reproductions of paintings. Which one do you like best? Which one do you like least? What is it that causes you to like or dislike paintings? To what extent does our environment affect what we like and dislike?*
9. *If we are to fully appreciate a work of art, should we let our environment affect us as we perceive the work?*
10. *If two average citizens happen to disagree about the worth of an art object, is it possible to determine if one is more nearly correct than the other? How?*

SUGGESTIONS FOR THE JUNIOR HIGH SCHOOL

If art is taught in the junior high school, it usually is taught by professional art teachers who have been trained in the procedures of art. Consequently, it seems unnecessary to include the same amount of detailed information that was provided for the preprimary, primary, and intermediate grades. Instead, we shall restrict our comments to the listing of recommended activities and the justification for those activities.

Topics for development of a knowledge of life

By the time youngsters reach junior high school, they have learned basic, concrete information about themselves, about the objects in their environment, and about the relationships among those objects. They become interested in ideas that are more complex and more profound. They begin to think abstractly, to examine values, and to commit themselves to causes of one kind or another. In other words, they begin to concern themselves with many of the same things that occupy the minds of adult men and women. It is true, of course, that adolescents will often act as children one moment and as adults the next. But if the teacher wishes to interest them and spur them onward to artistic activity, it is probably wise to treat them more like adults than like children. This means that the teacher's stimulation must be of the sort that might interest grown men and women.

Direct experiences or confrontations with the environment are still appropriate as stimuli for developing a knowledge of life. But the teacher must be careful not to conduct tours or sketching sessions in such a way that he creates an image of little children being guided by their teacher to see things that are really very ordinary. The direct experience must seem like a serious and mature venture if it is to be successful.

Visual aids and verbal discussions also continue to be useful in stimulating the growth of knowledge; and, as usual, it is very important to select topics that actually concern the students. The following subjects are especially pertinent:

The slums	*The pleasure of work*
Forms of brutality	*The problems of the minority*
The realities of war	*Industry*
Justice	*An imaginary world*
The goodness of the earth	*Gentleness in people*
Places where peace can be found	*Hate*
Sources of happiness	*Intolerance*
Fear and how it shows	*Impressions of our town*
Machines in our lives	*Noontime*
The characteristics of morning	*Pleasurable patterns*

An instance of despair	*The young and the old*
Plain and fancy things	*The theater and its stars*
The ideal man	*Speed in our lives*
Being poor	*Being hungry*
Being rich	*Patriotism*
Being nobody	*People with character*
Being somebody	*Fair play*
You and me	*Friendship*
People I admire	*Hypocrisy*

Having selected a suitable topic, the teacher might discuss it with his class as a whole, and by so doing, he might get them started on an idea for their creative work; or he might mention *several* topics to the group and allow each individual to work with the one that seems most appealing. In either case it is very important to give the student time to think about the topic and to make a few preliminary sketches. It is also important for the teacher to engage in private conversations with individuals, so that he can familiarize himself with each student's orientation to the topic. Private discussions are vital because they give the instructor a basis for making meaningful suggestions and let the student know that the teacher is advocating the assertion of individuality through art. Adolescents want to be recognized as individuals and as reasonably independent persons. Consequently, the teacher wins the pupil's support by showing that individuality is actually expected and encouraged in art. Getting each student to make the most of his individuality, however, is especially difficult in a large class because little time can be spent with each pupil. Classes should not exceed twenty or twenty-five students.

Tools, materials, and equipment still continue to stimulate young people to creativity. For that reason it is advisable to add the following items to the lists provided for the earlier grades:

Vine charcoal	*Drypoint needles*
A variety of pencils	*Plastic sheets for printing*
The best pastels	*(drypoint)*
Conte crayons	*Printing presses*
Sculpturing tools	*Wood blocks*
Charcoal paper	*Wood-carving tools*

509

Quality drawing paper   *Polaroid cameras*
Jigsaws   *Moving picture cameras*
Acrylic paints   *Box cameras*

Suitable procedures

Art is usually taught in a special art room in the junior high school. This means that the furniture and equipment are specially selected to facilitate the teaching of art. There are several books and articles available to the inexperienced teacher that will help him choose and arrange the furniture and equipment in a new art room. These references are listed at the end of the chapter. At this point, however, it is sufficient to say that the room should resemble a workshop rather than a study hall, and it should be arranged to permit freedom of movement, maximum safety, and easy access to tools, materials, and storage.

Drawing. For many years, Edward Rannells has emphasized the importance of drawing in the junior high school; he also has stressed the need for teaching representational drawing. Speaking of the student in the junior high school, he says:[2]

> The rapidly expanding world of early adolescence is not merely mental, it is spatial. This is the larger "reality" he experiences now, and it poses a problem for art in the junior high school. Before he can cope with this spatial world in a way that enables him to possess it and know it, as I believe he can through representation, the young adolescent needs entirely new skills. The simple skills that came so easily in childhood no longer suffice. He sees more and knows more than he can draw. He needs direction of a positive kind to develop skills for spatial representation.
>
> It would be an evasion of responsibility to expect him to discover these particular skills for himself. This just does not happen; at least it never happens soon enough. What has to be pointed out, demonstrated, and taught are skills for realizing projections and recessions in depth, and for spacing intervals between them, ultimately finding rhythmic continuities through space as well as on the surface—all of which is more than just "perspective." It is art.

[2] Reprinted from Edward W. Rannells, "Thoughts on the High School Art Program," *The School Review*, vol. 72, no. 3, 1964, pp. 354–355. (By permission of the University of Chicago Press. Copyright © 1964 by the University of Chicago).

In this text we have stressed the importance of drawing in all the grades and have advocated the teaching of representational drawing to individuals when their comments indicate that they want and need such instruction. It is hoped that such a program will bring about the gradual development of representational skills needed by youngsters in the junior high school. At the very least it should provide a good foundation for the kind of drawing experience that Rannells so wisely advocates for the seventh, eighth, and ninth grades. In other words, it should prepare the student for instruction in perspective or in the handling of three-dimensional space.

Learning perspective is important to the adolescent because it gives him more freedom in his expression. It allows him to say things that he could not say if he knew nothing about the handling of three-dimensional space. Learning about perspective, however, is not always easy. In fact, some persons find it very difficult. How can the teacher make this learning as easy as possible?

Probably he should very carefully explain that perspective is *not* being taught because anyone believes that naturalistic art is superior. It is being taught because it will permit people to draw naturalistically if they want to and will help all persons to create a three-dimensional quality in their work. Following such an explanation, the teacher might offer a little information about perspective and then ask the students to apply that information as they draw their environment. Drawing things that can be seen is better than drawing from memory because it allows the instructor to point to the instances of color, angle, size, and overlapping that produce the appearance of three-dimensional space in the environment.

While drawing the things around them, young people should also receive instruction in proportion. They should be taught the proportions in natural objects, such as the human figure, and they should be taught to compare the lengths, widths, heights, and angles of lines, shapes, and volumes. The purpose, once again, is to provide the student with information that will free him to draw naturalistically when he wishes to do so.

In addition to teaching naturalistic drawing, the teacher should show his students that they can depart from naturalism to create certain desirable effects. He should show them how to create distortions, effects of light and shade, and effects of pattern and texture. In other words, he should help his students to produce the nuances of form that are necessary for the presentation of particular concepts and emotions. Perhaps the basic difference between instruction in the intermediate grades and instruction in the junior high school is that the latter is more *complex* and slightly more formal; information about perspective, proportion, and other technical matters is directed at *all* students instead of a few. The theory behind such practice is that junior high school students are ready and able to understand technical instruction; they are able to see its value for certain kinds of expression; and they are able to receive it without feeling threatened by it (see Plates 74, 75).

To emphasize drawing, however, as the most fundamental dimension of productive art, the teacher must find ways of adding variety to the task. He can do that by having the students draw from memory as well as from the environment; he can offer exercises in contour drawing, quick sketching, and shading; and he can introduce new drawing materials, such as vine charcoal, high-grade chalk, and Conte crayons.

Painting. As in drawing, many of the painting procedures begun in the elementary school may be continued in the junior high school. But, it is expected that the teacher will assist his students in developing more subtlety, complexity, and control in the handling of paint. It is also recommended that the instructor continue to have his students paint from memory and imagination as well as from the environment. And he should try to help them use the formal elements of art more expressively than they did in the past. In that respect it is appropriate for him to explain how color can be used to create depth or a feeling of three dimensions; and it is fitting to encourage the production of richer, more subtle, or more complex textures and patterns.

As far as *new* painting procedures are concerned, the introduction of both encaustic painting and acrylic painting are recommended. Each procedure will increase the student's potential range of expression, and the new and different effects that can be obtained will be exciting. By melting old crayons the teacher can make a perfectly satisfactory medium for early experiences in encaustic painting, but acrylic painting must begin with the same paints that are used by professional artists. Acrylic paints have a great advantage over oil paints in the secondary school because they dry quickly.

Probably the most widely used paint in the secondary school is ready-mixed poster paint. It is commonly referred to as tempera, which is a mistake. Real tempera is made with egg yolk, linseed oil, and other ingredients; the recipe for making it is described in books on painting techniques.[3] Making tempera is an activity that junior high school students enjoy, and it helps them to appreciate the achievements of the old masters who used tempera regularly before the invention of oil paint. It is especially good as a project for youngsters who are ahead of the rest of the class.

Another activity that is especially appropriate for the junior high school is the making of murals. Or if the administrator is one who worries about his walls, it is equally worthwhile to make large easel paintings for prominent places in the school. Libraries, cafeterias, seminar rooms, entrance halls, and offices are excellent places for murals or big paintings; and the use of such display space tends to encourage the students and make the art department more visible.

Murals might be painted directly on a wall or on 4- by 8-foot Masonite or Celotex panels. The second idea, however, is probably the better of the two. Panels can be inserted in specially constructed frames that are fastened to the wall, so that the paintings can be removed whenever new ones are created. Such a system increases the number of paintings that a school can accommodate and eliminates the need to paint in hallways, offices and other places where painting can create a disturbance.

[3] For example, see Ralph Mayer, *The Artist's Handbook of Materials and Techniques*, The Viking Press Inc., New York, 1940.

Pl. 72
Girl after a tiring day,
made with chalk and oil crayon.
Junior high school.

Pl. 73
Chalk drawing.
Junior high school.

Pl. 74
A tired and unhappy girl,
in chalk and crayon, by a girl in
junior high school. From the
stage of artistic decision.

Pl. 75
A tired and unhappy girl,
in chalk and crayon, by a boy in
junior high school. From the
stage of artistic decision.

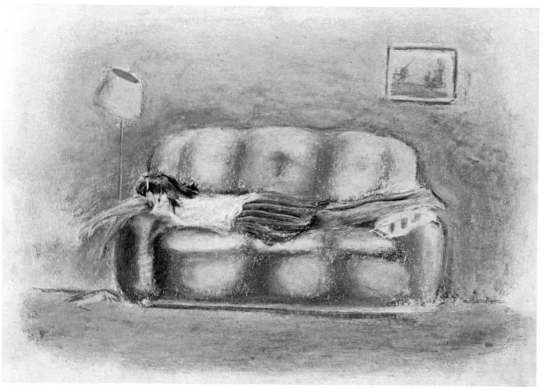

*Fig. 9.32
This tempera
painting about war was produced
by a girl in seventh grade.*

*Fig. 9.33
A mural painted in
tempera on heavy paper
by students in junior high school.
(Photo by Barry Moore.)*

Print making. The printing processes recommended for the intermediate grades may be repeated successfully in the junior high school, especially if the teacher shows his students how to make variations and improvements. Linoleum-block printing, for example, is perfectly suitable for repetition because the students can be taught to print with more than one color, to improve textural effects, and to utilize the special qualities of different printing papers.

As far as new procedures are concerned, we recommend the introduction of wood-block printing and drypoint. The wood-block process is a natural follow-up to linoleum printing, and drypoint is an entirely new and different method of reproduction. It is wise, however, to use sheets of plastic in place of metal plates for the drypoint. Plastic is far less expensive (see Plate 76).

Sculpture. By the time youngsters reach junior high school, they are old enough, strong enough, and responsible enough to carve wood. They might carve in relief or in the round, but in neither case is it necessary to work with gigantic blocks of wood. Pieces that are 4 by 4 by 12 inches or 2 by 4 by 12 inches are large enough for work in the round, and pieces that are 2 by 8 by 12 inches are large enough for relief. The teacher must make a special effort to give instructions on safety because carving tools are sharp. And if he feels that he needs advice on the matter, he should consult the school administrator and the industrial arts teacher who handles dangerous tools in every class.

Earlier we suggested the use of plaster in the intermediate grades, but we also recommend that it be used in junior high school. Students may continue with the making of relief sculpture, and by doing so, they will develop more and more skill. But it is also fitting to begin making plaster sculpture in the round with an armature. The teacher might show his students how to build a chicken wire armature, how to add burlap strips dipped in plaster, how to add metal rods for reinforcement, and how to use plastering tools to add more plaster. The procedures for removing, texturing, and finishing plaster may also be taught in junior high school.

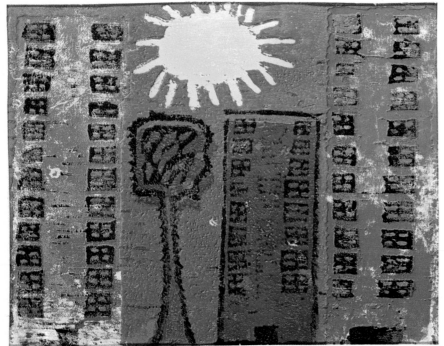

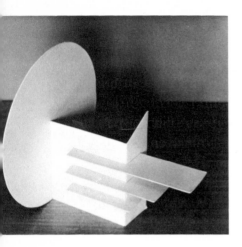

Fig. 9.34
*Abstract sculpture
made with illustration board
in the ninth grade.*

Making plaster casts is interesting and exciting for young people, and it gives them a little insight into the more complicated casting of metal. They can be taught how to make waste molds and piece molds and how to fill them with cement as well as plaster. In most instances the sculpture to be reproduced with molds is sculpture that the student has made out of clay. Hence clay or ceramic sculpture is also recommended as an ideal activity for junior high school youngsters.

Ceramic sculpture should be fired in the secondary school, and the students should be taught different ways of finishing the work. They might be shown, for example, how clay looks when it is unglazed, glazed, or painted with acrylic paints; or they might be shown how it looks mounted on wood, adorned with metal, or combined with other materials (see Plate 77).

Crafts. There are, of course, a great many crafts that might be included in the junior high school program. But research indicates that art education is more successful when it offers instruction in depth rather than instruction in breadth.[4] Consequently, it is better if the instructor confines himself to the teaching of two or three outstanding craft procedures. Pottery and photography are crafts of extraordinary merit, and we believe them to be of great interest to young people.

Making pots is absolutely fascinating to students in the secondary school. They enjoy making them from slabs and making them on the wheel; but wheel-thrown pottery is probably their favorite. If wheel-throwing is to be introduced in the junior high school, however, it probably should not be started below the ninth grade. It requires time and patience to learn the necessary skills, but once they have been acquired, students have difficulty staying away from the art room.

Photography is equally attractive. In fact, several art educators maintain that photography is *the* art form of the twentieth century. They believe that it is the one art form that young

[4] Edward Mattil et. al., "The Effect of a Depth Versus a Breadth Method of Art Instruction at the Ninth Grade Level," *Studies in Art Education*, vol. 4, no. 1, 1962.

people naturally appreciate because it is familiar to almost everyone. We agree with that appraisal and believe that art educators should take advantage of such widespread appreciation. Hence photography might be taught as a serious art form, and it might be used to build sensitivity to other art forms.

Polaroid cameras are especially useful because they eliminate the need for developing and printing, and give the students a chance to see immediate results. For a simple and almost fool-proof camera, however, it is hard to beat the old box camera. It is easy for children to use, and the film is relatively inexpensive. With such cameras, students might be asked to take pictures of peacefulness, happiness, sadness, ugliness, busyness, and other such qualities. They might be asked to do a documentary series of still pictures on their town or neighborhood. They might take photographs of a busy, noisy street corner and tape-record the sounds that occur there. Then they could display the pictures and play the tapes in some appropriate place.

Motion pictures, of course, create all kinds of possibilities for expression, and they are ideal for junior high school. Students could act in their own films; they could make films about their school, their town, or their neighborhood; or they could write a story, illustrate it with many paintings, and photograph the paintings. Such a film, combined with a tape recording of the story, could be very exciting. And there are many other possibilities for making motion pictures that the students will discover for themselves.

If the teacher needs any assistance in the teaching of photography, it is recommended that he write to the Society for Photographic Education, Department of Photography, George Eastman House, Rochester, New York. This society is trying to do everything possible to improve the teaching of photography all over the world.

The craft procedures that a teacher covers in the junior high school will undoubtedly depend upon the teacher's own background of experience. It is completely unrealistic to expect any given art teacher to be an expert in all crafts. If he knows two of them reasonably well, that is about all that we can expect.

A RECOMMENDED COURSE
OF STUDY

We happen to believe that pottery and photography are especially good for the junior high school, but we know of several instances in which weaving, rug hooking, jewelry making, and copper enameling have been taught with great success.

Suitable information on composition

It is not necessary to tell the prospective junior high school art teacher what to teach in the area of composition, because his training should provide him with a thorough understanding of design or structural organization. But it is important to repeat two very important points: (1) composition should not be over-emphasized; and (2) it should not be taught in isolation. This means that visual organization should not be made more important than the presentation of concepts and emotions, and it should not be taught without relating it to the communication of such information. The teacher should therefore be interested primarily in the ideas and feelings that his students are trying to convey. And his instruction in composition should help the students to understand that design is the grammar of art and that the success of art is largely dependent upon that grammar.

Appropriate information on art history

While discussing a course of study for the intermediate grades, it was suggested that youngsters be taught the characteristics and the sequences of the major periods in art history, and it was proposed that they be taught information about two to four interesting artists from each period. Now we recommend that the same treatment be continued in the junior high school. This means that there should be a review and a refinement of the content covered in grades four, five, and six; and, in addition, several other artists and their works should be studied.

If emphasis is to be placed on a particular portion of art history, we believe it should be placed on art in America. After all, young people in the junior high school are at an age when they begin to identify themselves with groups, countries, causes,

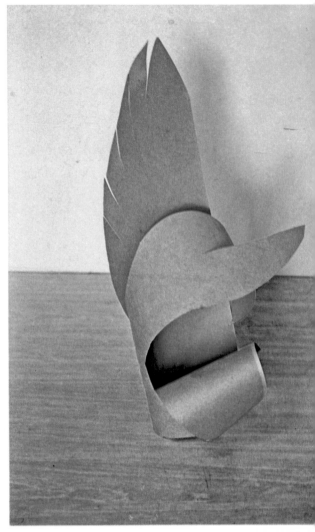

Pl. 78
Head of a woman,
of polymer acrylic on ceramic.
Seventh grade.

Pl. 79
Abstract paper sculpture.
Junior high school.

and ideas. They begin to consider ways in which they can assert themselves and have an effect upon their environment. Hence it seems fitting to show them the work of American artists and to explain the effects that the artists were trying to achieve. They might study the work of George Caleb Bingham, George Bellows, John Sloan, Thomas Eakins, Ben Shahn, James Whistler, Charles Sheeler, John Marin, Hans Hofmann, and other prominent painters. The work of equally famous sculptors, printmakers, and craftsmen would also be appropriate. Naturally, it should be understood that the aim is to show young people how the spirit of America is revealed in the expressive presentations of artists.

It would also be worthwhile to discuss some of the following questions:

1. *Why did George Caleb Bingham and his contemporaries not paint in the manner of a Hans Hofmann or a Gyorgy Kepes? Was it simply a matter of cultural pressure?*
2. *What was the Ashcan School? Why was it called by that name?*
3. *When we speak of regional painters in referring to American artists what do we mean? Give an example of a regional painter.*
4. *What is a primitive artist? Have any Americans become famous as primitive artists? Who?*
5. *What was the WPA Art Project? What did it accomplish? How is it different from the federally supported art projects of the 1960s?*
6. *Is there such a thing as American architecture? What is unique about it? Who are the giants of American architecture?*
7. *Have wealthy businessmen played a part in the development of the arts in this country? Explain.*
8. *Has religion played a part in the development of the arts in this country? Explain.*
9. *Who are the famous female artists of America? Why have there been so few?*
10. *What does a person do if he wants to become an artist, an art historian, or a critic?*
11. *What is the difference between the art programs in universities and the art programs in professional art schools? Where are the prominent art schools located?*
12. *Where were the prominent art schools located during the early years of art instruction in America?*
13. *How did we happen to get the National Gallery of Art in Washington? the Metropolitan Museum in New York? the Chicago Art Institute?*

14. *Who was Joseph Duveen? What influence, if any, did he have on art in America?*
15. *Why would anyone want to preserve old buildings or old murals?*

The questions listed above are only a small sample of the many interesting topics that a teacher might discuss under the heading of art history. It is an area of instruction that has been badly neglected for years, but this neglect should not continue. The future art teacher in the junior high school can help us to inaugurate a new era of interest in art history.

Topics to cover in aesthetics

In our discussion of the topics to cover in aesthetics at the primary and intermediate levels, it was indicated that the same subjects could be covered again and again, as long as the students discuss them with increasing maturity at each grade level. And we believe that those same topics may be covered in the junior high school together with questions of the following types:

1. *As you look at this work of art, what seems to be the artist's chief objective? What is the nature of the information he is presenting? Does he present it in a pleasurable way, or do you find it to be disturbing? What makes it pleasing or displeasing? Would you say that the content of the work is simple or complex? Does the complexity of the content have any effect upon the quality of a work of art? If so, how?*
2. *If the artist happens to focus his attention on composition rather than subject matter, would it affect the complexity of the content in his work? Why?*
3. *Which is more interesting in this particular work of art—the composition or the content?*
4. *Can you describe the organizational system that the artist used? Does he repeat formal elements? If so, where? Does he have a center of interest? If so, how does he achieve it? Is variety evident in the work? If so, how is it achieved?*
5. *Examine paintings by Grant Wood. Are the compositional techniques highly apparent, or are they difficult to pick out? What does the artist do with the formal elements of art to create unity?*
6. *As you look at this work of art, can you discern a mood within it? How does the artist create that mood?*
7. *What does the artist do with lines, colors, textures? Does he seem to handle them consciously?*

Pl. 80
Abstract wood sculpture.
Ht., 5 ft. Sixth grade.

Pl. 81
Abstract wood sculpture.
Ht., 4 ft. Seventh grade.

8. *Is there any distortion from visual reality? What is the purpose of that distortion? Could it be accidental? Could it develop from a lack of skill?*

9. *Where is the foreground? the background? Is the work symmetrical or asymmetrical?*

10. *Are the outlines of things clear and sharp, or are they fuzzy and ambiguous? Do you suppose that there is any reason for it? What could the reason be?*

11. *Do you like the looks of your community? What do you dislike about it? Do you believe that the appearance of the city has an effect upon you and me? What do you think the people of this town should do about it?*

12. *Why do we try to preserve certain sections of the country in their natural state (for example, seashores, prairies, mountain areas, etc.)? If a person does not object to the destruction of natural beauty, does this mean that he favors such destruction?*

13. *What makes a person want to become an artist? Is it because he is a little odd? Is it because he is idealistic, shiftless, or incapable of doing anything else?*

14. *What motivates an artist? Is he moved by sounds, sights, tactile sensations, or inner conditions of the viscera?*

15. *Would you say that this work of art is loud or quiet in its presentation? Is loudness preferable to quietness? Why? What makes a visual statement powerful and bold? What makes it gentle? Would it make sense to speak of a gentle line, a bold color, or a powerful shape?*

16. *Do you find any contrast in this work of art? What causes it? What is its function?*

SUMMARY

In this chapter we have tried to suggest appropriate informational material in the areas of stimulation, procedures, composition, art history, and aesthetics. The aim was simply to offer a *guide* for curriculum development from nursery school through junior high school; and the task of completing the guide is left to those who eventually must live with it. In other words, the job of building a comprehensive course of study is left to the art teachers and classroom teachers in local school districts all over America. If this brief outline helps them in their task, it has served its purpose.

QUESTIONS FOR DISCUSSION

1. Examine six courses of study from as many states. How many of them recommend art activities for specific grades? What are the reasons for making or failing to make such recommendations?

2. Take a procedure such as painting and develop a list of words and definitions (a vocabulary) that would be suitable for use in the teaching of painting at each of the various grade levels in the public school. Do the same for sculpture, print making, and the other dimensions of art.

3. Try to develop a set of teaching materials that would be helpful in teaching composition in the elementary school (charts, slides, transparencies for overhead projection, models, etc.).

4. Examine the field of children's literature, and see if you can locate books on the lives of famous artists. In what grades would they be appropriate for children to read?

5. What could you tell children about color that would help them to produce depth in their paintings?

6. The mismanagement of materials and equipment is one of the greatest barriers to success in art education. How would you manage materials if you wanted to make plaster reliefs in the intermediate grades? Remember that you must make the plan simple enough so that you will feel that you can actually carry it out. Try making similar plans for other activities.

7. In your own words, explain why the teaching of drawing is so strongly emphasized in this book as one of the most essential elements in art education.

8. Using information in Chapter 11 as an aid, make a list of art materials that might be stored in each classroom of the elementary school. Which materials should be stored in a central storeroom in each school?

9. In what way would an overhead projector be of assistance to you in teaching art to children? What about a tape recorder, an opaque projector?

10. Explain in your own words why it is important for children to engage in a given procedure more than once.

11. Pick some art activities that are not mentioned in this chapter, and see if you can decide upon the grade level at which they should be offered. You might do so by comparing them with the activities that are mentioned in this chapter.

12. Suitable tools and materials have been recommended throughout this chapter. See if you can add to the list.

SUGGESTIONS FOR FURTHER READING

Anderson, Donald M.: *Elements of Design*, Holt, Rinehart and Winston, Inc., New York, 1961.
A book dealing with composition.

Andrews, Michael: *Creative Printmaking*, Prentice-Hall, Inc., Englewood Cliffs, New Jersey, 1964.
This book contains a wealth of information about practical print-making procedures that might be taught in the public schools. An excellent book.

Baranski, Matthew: *Graphic Design*, International Textbook Company, Scranton, Pennsylvania, 1960.
Another fine book on print making, or graphic design. The comments about composition are especially helpful to the classroom teacher.

Beitler, Ethel Jane: *Create With Yarn*, International Textbook Company, Scranton, Pennsylvania, 1964.
Stitchery, rug hooking, and weaving are the procedures that are emphasized in this book.

Collier, Graham: *Form, Space, and Vision: Discovering Design through Drawing*, Prentice-Hall, Inc., Englewood Cliffs, New Jersey, 1963.
A helpful book on composition.

D'Amelio, Joseph: *Perspective Drawing Handbook*, Tudor Publishing Company, New York, 1964.
A fine book on perspective for the classroom teacher.

D'Amico, Victor: *Creative Teaching in Art*, International Textbook Company, Scranton, Pennsylvania, 1942.
The chapter that deals with the child as a painter is especially pertinent.

Dibble, George: *Watercolor: Materials and Techniques*, Holt, Rinehart and Winston, Inc., New York, 1966.
An excellent book for beginners in watercolor.

Duncan, Julia Hamlin, and Victor D'Amico: *How to Make Pottery and Ceramic Sculpture*, Museum of Modern Art, New York, 1947.
A practical book on pottery for the public school teacher.

Faulkner, R., Edwin Ziegfeld, and Gerald Hill: *Art Today*, Henry Holt and Company, Inc., New York, 1956.
This book emphasizes the many ways in which art affects men. It will be helpful to the teacher in discussing the nature of art and the value of art.

Gombrich, E. H.: *The Story of Art*, Phaidon Publishers, Inc., New York, 1966.
One of the finest art history books available.

Hoover, F. Louis: *Art Activities for the Very Young*, Davis Publications, Inc., Worcester, Massachusetts, 1961.
A marvelous book of art activities suitable for children between the ages of three and six.

Hopper, Grizella: *Puppet Making through the Grades*, Davis Publications, Inc., Worcester, Massachusetts, 1966.
This book explains a variety of ways for making puppets.

Kenny, John B.: *Ceramic Design*, Chilton Company–Book Division, Philadelphia, 1963.
A widely used elementary text on ceramics.

La Mancusa, Katherine: *Source Book for Art Teachers*, International Textbook Company, Scranton, Pennsylvania, 1965.
As the title suggests, this book supplies the reader with a wealth of information about art terms, procedures, materials, and tools.

Lyons, Nathon (ed.): *Photographers on Photography*, Prentice-Hall, Inc., Englewood Cliffs, New Jersey, 1966.
An anthology of personal statements about photography by twenty-three famous photographers. It gives the reader some insight into photography as a fine art.

Lyons, Nathon (ed.): *Seeing Photographically*, Prentice-Hall, Inc., Englewood Cliffs, New Jersey, 1966.
Prepared with the help of teachers of photography throughout the United States. It is illustrated with 200 photographs and presents the reader with problems aimed at building his visual awareness.

Mattil, Edward L.: *Meaning in Crafts*, Prentice-Hall, Inc., Englewood Cliffs, New Jersey, 1965.
Probably one of the most popular, comprehensive, and practical craft books for the elementary school teacher. Everything in this book has been done successfully with children.

Mayer, Ralph: *The Artist's Handbook of Materials and Techniques*, The Viking Press, Inc., New York, 1940.
Written for the professional artist, but it explains a technique for making tempera paint that might be used in the junior high school.

McIlvain, Dorothy S.: *Art for the Primary Grades*, G. P. Putnam's Sons, New York, 1961.
Another highly practical book on methods, materials, and projects for the kindergarten through third grade.

Moseley, Spencer, Pauline Johnson, and Hazel Koenig: *Crafts Design*, Wadsworth Publishing Company, Inc., Belmont, California, 1962.
Contains excellent procedural information on printing, dyeing, paper construction, weaving, stitchery, serigraphy, pottery, enameling, mosaics, and other suitable art activities.

Nicolaides, Kimon: *The Natural Way to Draw*, Houghton Mifflin Company, Boston, 1941.
A famous book on drawing.

Pattemore, Arnel W.: *Printmaking Activities for the Classroom*, Davis Publications, Inc., Worcester, Massachusetts, 1966.
The print making activities explained in this book are excellent for the elementary school.

Rainey, Sarita R.: *Weaving without a Loom*, Davis Publications, Inc., Worcester, Massachusetts, 1966.
Procedures for weaving and rug hooking are clearly explained in this fine book.

Randall, Arne W.: *Murals for the Schools*, Davis Publications, Inc., Worcester, Massachusetts, 1956.
Aimed at mural making in the elementary school.

Rottger, Ernst: *Creative Paper Design*, Reinhold Publishing Corporation, New York, 1961.
An excellent book on the use of paper as an artistic medium. Suitable for the junior high school.

Rottger, Ernst: *Creative Wood Design*, Reinhold Publishing Corporation, New York, 1960.
One of the few books dealing with wood as an artistic medium. Suitable for the junior high school.

Schinneller, James A.: *Art: Search and Self-Discovery*, International Textbook Company, Scranton, Pennsylvania, 1961.
One of the best books of its kind. It is useful to the teacher in the areas of art history, art appreciation, and aesthetics.

Schultz, Josephine Burley (ed.): *Planning Facilities for Art Instruction*, National Art Education Association, Washington, D. C., 1960.
A booklet dealing with the organization of art classrooms.

Smith, Ralph A.: *Aesthetics and Criticism in Art Education*, Rand McNally and Company, Chicago, 1966.
An anthology of high caliber that may be useful in teaching aesthetics. Difficult for persons unfamiliar with art or with philosophical material.

Wachowiak, Frank, and Theodore Ramsay: *Emphasis: Art*, International Textbook Company, Scranton, Pennsylvania, 1965.
This book contains excellent information on methods, materials, and curriculum in the elementary school.

Watson, Ernest W.: *How to Use Creative Perspective*, Reinhold Publishing Corporation, New York, 1955.
A book on perspective for the art teacher.

Zim, Herbert S., and R. Will Burnett: *Photography: The Amateur's Guide to Better Pictures*, Golden Press, New York, 1956.
A clear, concise, and practical book dealing with technical photography. Very helpful in the junior high school.

Chapter 10
EVALUATION AND REPORTING TO PARENTS

The primary aim of art education is the development of non-professional artists and connoisseurs; or, to put it differently, the major objective is to develop persons who can make visual forms for aesthetic experience and appraise such forms with taste. If educators fail to develop such persons, a considerable amount of time, effort, and money will have been wasted and society will have lost an important opportunity to better itself. Obviously, losses of that kind must be avoided, and it is the teacher's job to see that they are. To be sure that he is fulfilling that obligation, the teacher must devise a continuous system of evaluation that will permit him to appraise himself, his program, and his students. And he must report his findings to parents if mothers and fathers are to make responsible decisions about the artistic progress of their children. But how should he measure achievement? How should he report to parents? In answering those questions, let us begin with the problem of assessing student progress.*

* A large portion of this chapter appeared for the first time in *Art in the Elementary School*, published by the National Art Education Association, Washington, D.C., 1967. It is used with permission of the National Art Education Association.

EVALUATION OF STUDENT ACHIEVEMENT

Obviously, responsible evaluation cannot occur in the absence of clearly formulated goals. For that reason it may be helpful to review, briefly, the difficulties associated with formulating goals in art education.

A brief review of objectives and associated problems

It is not enough to say that we intend to produce nonprofessional artists and critics, because a statement of that kind does not tell the teacher how such persons act or how their products look or sound. Formulating goals of a more useful, detailed, or descriptive nature is not, however, an easy task. The difficulty arises, in part, because objectives must be developed in accordance with the nature of art, the nature of the artist, and the nature of child. This means that the educator must have a reasonable philosophy of art and a point of view about the unique characteristics of an artist before he can fashion goals that are rational and justifiable. He must also have knowledge of the needs and abilities of children if he is to adapt the needs of the subject to them. Naturally, the children change and mature with each succeeding year. Hence it is necessary to reconstruct the objectives for different levels of the educational program, but not necessarily for each grade. Children grow and develop slowly enough that it is perfectly satisfactory to indicate how the educated child should act at the beginning of the first, fourth, seventh, and tenth grades. Using such standards as a guide, individual teachers may then proceed to write their own goals for each grade level.

When we say that objectives must be written with the needs and abilities of children firmly in mind, we refer to the characteristics of the majority. In other words, we believe that goals should not be fashioned to suit the abilities of atypical youngsters. If aims were adapted to the characteristcs of the gifted, for example, parents and teachers would probably expect a degree of achievement that most children are not able to attain. And if the abilities of slow learners were used to establish the goals, most children would in all probability not be sufficiently challenged. Thus the characteristcs of the majority should be the ones that influence objectives.

As aims are constructed, further difficulty is apt to arise simply because objectives can be stated at different levels of specificity. We might say, for example, that the educated child, upon entering the seventh grade, should act like an artist by making graphic prints; or we might declare that he should behave like an artist by making linoleum-block designs. The former goal is obviously less specific than the latter, and the goal writer has the knotty problem of deciding which way the aim should be stated. As he makes that decision, he must continually remind himself that general or vague objectives are nearly useless because they fail to indicate exactly what is to be accomplished; yet highly specific or overly detailed goals rob the individual teacher of his freedom to make pedagogical decisions.

Another thing that makes the formulation of goals difficult is the fact that some of them must be cognitive while others must be affective and psychomotor. In other words, youngsters must know and understand certain things about art; they must have relevant attitudes and values; and they must possess certain skills. Their knowledge must cover life (especially the asethetic dimension of life), artistic procedures, composition, art history, and aesthetics. Their attitudes must include an interest in the making and appreciating of art, confidence in their own ability to make and appraise art, tolerance of the various forms that art might take, and a willingness to work hard. And their skill must center around the efficient manipulation of art tools and materials.

To know about life is to be sufficiently aware of the self and the environment so that one can give visible or audible shape to his reactions and share them with others. Knowing about artistic procedures is possessing sufficient information about how an art object is made so that one can either make art or explain the process to others. Knowing about composition is a matter of understanding how to organize lines, shapes, colors, textures, and volumes to create a pleasurable structure with a particular meaning. To know something about art history is to possess enough information about specific works of art, about artists, and about sequential periods of artistic development to make reasonably accurate verbal presentations of the material. And to know about aesthetics is to understand the nature of art, the value of art, and the nature of aesthetic experience well enough to explain such things to others and to make tasteful judgments.

A person displays an attitude of interest in art if he makes it or looks at it frequently and seriously. He is confident in art if he makes it or offers competent judgments about it without inhibition or without feelings of inferiority. If he is able to demonstrate, through his choices and comments, that he recognizes and values the different shapes that art may take, we may say that he is tolerant of form or style; and a willingness to work hard is revealed in concentration, persistence, and constructive artistic activity.

A person is skillful or technically proficient as an artist if he uses the tools and materials of art efficiently. To use them in that way is to communicate what was intended with forcefulness and with structural beauty, but without calling attention to technique. Skillfulness in the appreciative aspect of art, however, is proficiency in experiencing art aesthetically. It is the ability to grasp the full meaning that resides in the "look" of an art object, and it is revealed through the making of tasteful choices as well as through verbal and written responses to works of art.

Goal writers face the problem of spelling out in more detail the manner in which knowledge, attitudes, and skills manifest themselves; they must also see that each dimension of artistic ability receives the proper amount of emphasis. If knowledge is overemphasized at the expense of attitude, we may develop youngsters who know a little bit about art and yet may dislike it intensely. Or if skill is stressed as a goal, students may become technically proficient without knowing anything about art history or aesthetics.

If the reader desires assistance in formulating goals, he is advised to turn to Chapter 7, where appropriate objectives are spelled out with the proper degree of specificity. Separate and sufficiently different aims are listed for the first, fourth, seventh, and tenth grades. At the end of each objective, the information in parentheses indicates what kind of knowledge, attitude, or skill is exemplified by the described behavior.

Using the objectives in Chapter 7 as a guide, and keeping the various problems of goal building in mind, administrators, art specialists, and classroom teachers can advisedly *cooperate* in developing detailed objectives for each grade in the school system. The art specialist is probably the most logical leader of the group because of his training and experience in art. He can offer expert advice on the nature of art and artists, and he can provide information about the nature of child development in art. The other members of the team can serve an important purpose by making sure that objectives are written with enough specificity to be useful to educators and meaningful to parents. They can also make sure that the aims for the second grade are different from the aims for the third grade. And they can check to see that the objectives are realistic for the majority of children. With these ideas in mind, let us turn to the problem of evaluation.

Evaluation in relation to objectives

Emphasis has been placed upon the formulation of specific goals simply because they act as a standard for the evaluation of a child's progress. If the child behaves or creates expressive form in accordance with the objectives for his educational level, we may conclude that he is performing satisfactorily in a manner that is expected of most students. If he exceeds the standard or fails to achieve it, we may conclude that he is either ahead of the majority or behind it. But it is important to realize that a person might meet the standard in skill, exceed it in knowledge, and fail to reach it in attitude. Likewise, a person might attain the established goals in certain aspects of knowledge, attitude, and skill, but not in others. The existence of carefully prepared and published objectives makes the detection of such uneven achievement more probable. In the absence of complete and specific goals it is too easy to evaluate artistic growth on the basis of either knowledge, attitude, or skill alone, and that, unfortunately, is what happens in a number of school systems.

As the teacher evaluates each student in relation to stated objectives, he is able to decide what his course of action should be in furthering the pupils development. Most educators would agree with the purpose behind such evaluation, but some of them would caution the teacher against letting the student hear of his own weaknesses. But how does a teacher with that view get his students to improve as artists and critics? What does he say to his pupils if they ask him how they can improve? Or if the students remain ignorant of their own failures, how are they to recognize success? How are they to know if they should pursue a career in art? The answers to such questions are difficult to construct if the teacher does not admit that the results of evaluation must eventually reach the students. Fortunately most teachers do recognize the need to inform youngsters of weaknesses. Some of them, in fact, make it a practice to share the task of evaluation with their students, and the experience seems to be valuable for both parties. Among other things, it helps the teacher to find out more about the personality of each student, and it helps the student to develop a deeper knowledge of the standards for successful performance and how to achieve them.

Naturally the teacher must act wisely when he informs his pupils of their weaknesses, for if he is careless, he can easily cause them to lose their self-confidence in art. In general, it is wise to explain such matters in private, and to leave the child with the feeling that he knows how to improve and that he is able to improve. It is also essential for the teacher to emphasize the good aspects of the student's work and to make him feel that the teacher is interested in him and confident that he can succeed. If the instructor crushes him with derogatory criticism and leaves him without hope, there is not much chance that he ever will improve. And if such behavior occurs in front of a class, the damage to the student will be very difficult to rectify.

REPORTING TO PARENTS

Probably the best way to give evaluative information to parents is to present it verbally during a face-to-face meeting. By speaking directly to the parent, the teacher is able to clarify information that is misunderstood and to preserve the confidential nature of the material he wishes to communicate. But, for various reasons, some parents cannot or will not meet with teachers to discuss their children. As a consequence, educators are forced to use report cards if they expect to get evaluative information to parents without meeting them in person. The trouble with report cards is that they make it difficult to communicate easily, accurately, and fully. If the teacher, for example, were to write the same things that he would say to a parent, it would take too long to fill out the report cards. Even then he might be misunderstood, and there would be little opportunity for him to correct the misunderstanding. If symbols are used to indicate achievement, the chances of inaccurate communication are increased. A grade of B in art fails to indicate how a student is doing in the various aspects of the subject. Hence a parent would not know if his child needed to improve in knowledge, attitude, or skill, and he would not know how to advise the child. Furthermore, a B does not say if the child is average in relation to classmates, to children in the local school system, or to children in the state or nation; and it does not indicate whether the evaluation of the child is based upon a recognized standard of any kind. In other words, a mere symbol is nearly meaningless.

If the teacher wishes to inform parents more satisfactorily, it might be advisable for him to create a special report card similar to the one presented on page 540. A report card of that kind allows the teacher to indicate if a child is equaling, exceeding, or falling below a definite standard. The standard, in this case, happens to be the objectives outlined in Chapter 7. Those objectives, in all their detail, do not appear on the report card, but they should be made available to parents upon request. There should be an accompanying note indicating that the goals are based upon the nature of art, the nature of artists, and upon

STUDENT PROGRESS REPORT

Name .... Subject ....

Teacher .... Evaluation Period Ending ....

    The objectives of art education in this community are based on recognized developmental norms and the recommendations of experts in art education. The estimates of achievement reported here are based upon that standard. Copies of the standard may be obtained from the school that your child is attending.

	Below Standard	Standard	Exceeds Standard

KNOWLEDGE OF:

Content and subject matter (life) . . . .

Procedures . . . .

Composition . . . .

Art History . . . .

Aesthetics . . . .

ATTITUDES:

Self-confidence in art . . . .

Interest in art . . . .

Willingness to work hard . . . .

Tolerance of style in art . . . .

SKILL:

The ability to handle materials efficiently . . . .

Comments:

recognized developmental norms. In other words, it should be clear to parents that the evaluational standard is not entirely local in origin and that children who reach the objectives will compare favorably with the majority of children elsewhere in the country.

Perhaps, in time and with cooperative study by art educators, objectives will be developed that will serve as a *national* standard for evaluation in art. The desirability of ascertaining and reporting progress in relation to a national measure seems clear. After all, a local or community standard of evaluation does not tell parents how their child is doing with respect to children elsewhere in the country. It may tell the mothers and fathers of Slippery Rock that Johnny is doing better work than Myrtle; but how meaningful and how important is that information? It is practically useless. Knowing that Johnny is doing better than other children of his age according to a national measure of achievement is far more helpful to the parent who wants to advise his child and plan for the future. Furthermore, there is no good reason for the standards in Slippery Rock to be different from the objectives in New York, San Francisco, or any other place. Consequently, we recommend the acceptance of national goals in art education.

As we recommend a national standard for judging achievement, however, we know that many teachers will object. Some will say that the important consideration is the amount of personal progress that a child has shown and not his progress in relation to a norm. But a common measuring device does not eliminate the teacher's opportunity to estimate and report the amount of growth that has taken place in any given child. In fact, we believe that such information *should* be given to parents and have provided space for it (under comments) on the report card. If this is the only information that parents receive, however, it is not especially useful, because all it lets them know is whether or not their child has changed since he started school. Needless to say, the change may be from bad to poor or from good to excellent. Surely most parents would prefer to know how far their youngsters have progressed in relation to a meaningful standard, because the mere knowledge that they have made some headway is mighty small comfort. For that reason, the report form in Figure 10.1 has been designed to permit comparisons with a standard as well as comments about personal improvement.

If the report form presented here is reasonable and useful, there should be no reason for changing it from one grade to another. The lack of change would be a good thing for teachers and for parents. It would require less explanation from teachers and give parents about twelve years to figure out what the terms really mean.

Although the recommended report form is superior to many others, it still has a few weaknesses. The most apparent of them is that the report will require more of the teacher's time than he ordinarily gives to evaluation in art. On the other hand, it is difficult to see how a clear and comprehensive report can be given if the amount of time required for reporting is decreased.

EVALUATING THE INSTRUCTION AND THE CURRICULUM

By evaluating the behavior and the products of a single student, the teacher will learn how to treat that student, and he will prepare himself for reporting to parents. But it is the careful study of *all* his students as a *group* that gives the instructor the best indication of his own effectiveness. If the group as a whole shows progress under the teacher's guidance, he may conclude that his teaching has been influential, and the amount of the group's achievement will indicate the extent of his effectiveness.

As he judges his own effectiveness, he must be careful not to give himself credit for *developmental* characteristics that would normally occur without guidance from anyone. For example, he must not assume, without careful consideration, that his teaching has caused students to move from the use of a base line to the use of planes and overlapping in their drawings. Such a conclusion would be warranted only if the students as a group were much more advanced developmentally than a person would normally expect.

Unfortunately, too many teachers judge themselves and their programs according to the achievement of a few advanced students (and it is clear that those teachers wish to be judged by the work of such pupils if they fail to display the creations of other students in public). Such teachers frequently fail to ask themselves if the growth of the advanced students is merely developmental. Therefore, administrators could do a great service to art education by reminding the teacher that the progress of the *group* is the most meaningful indication of success.

Another point for teachers and administrators to consider is whether a change in the curriculum might bring about a greater degree of achievement. It is important, for example, to think about the relative educational value of different projects and to decide if the sequence of activities could be arranged in a way that would make the attainment of objectives easier and more efficient. As educators make changes in their program, however, it is advisable not to make them continually. Program changes must be given an adequate time to have an effect, and the effect must be measured with a certain amount of care. If the teacher constantly changes his program, he has no way of knowing if the alteration is actually an improvement.

SUMMARY

This chapter has tried to show that sensible evaluation is dependent upon the existence of clear and specific objectives, and it has been recommended that the objectives in Chapter 7 be used as a standard for measuring achievement. If educators wish to have goals of a more detailed nature for grades two, three, five, six, eight, and nine, it is recommended that they develop those goals cooperatively in their own communities.

After careful study by experts in art education, it is suggested that objectives be developed that will eventually become a national standard for evaluation in art education. Along with such a standard, we recommend the use of a new report card for reporting to parents because we believe that most of the report forms now in use are absolutely meaningless.

Finally, we suggest that teachers judge their own effectiveness by studying the progress of groups rather than the achievement of a few students who might be advanced developmentally. Careful evaluation is the key to success in art education. Consequently, it deserves more attention than it has received in the past.

QUESTIONS FOR DISCUSSION

1. What would happen if the standard for evaluation was different from the objectives of art education?
2. Assume for a moment that sensibility is a goal of art education. Would such an objective be useful in evaluation? Why?
3. What would happen if every city in the United States had a different set of objectives for art education?
4. If a teacher wishes to let parents know about the effort that their children put forth in art, where would he give that information on the report card recommended in this chapter?
5. How difficult do you think it is to ascertain the progress of individual children between September and June (assuming that they enter the class at different levels of achievement)? Why do you say so?
6. What would happen if separate reporting forms were used for each subject in the curriculum?
7. How many art teachers you have known tend to measure their own effectiveness by studying the progress of the *groups* that come under their guidance?
8. What are the arguments against a national standard for evaluation in art education? What are the arguments against national standards in other subjects?

9. Goals that are more highly detailed than the ones in Chapter 7 may be needed. Why should the more highly detailed or more specific objectives be developed in local school systems?
10. Make a survey of textbooks in art education. How many of them list specific objectives for art education?

SUGGESTIONS FOR FURTHER READING

Conrad, George: *The Process of Art Education in the Elementary School*, Prentice-Hall, Inc., Englewood Cliffs, New Jersey, 1964.
One of the most recent attempts to solve the problem of evaluation in art. Appendix 1 is especially pertinent.

De Francesco, Italo L.: *Art Education: Its Means and Ends*, Harper and Brothers, New York, 1958.
Chapter 7 deals with evaluation in a different way from this textbook. The difference is probably caused by a different set of objectives.

Erdt, Margaret: *Teaching Art in the Elementary School*, Holt, Rinehart and Winston, Inc., New York, 1954.
Chapter 11 contains some very helpful suggestions for evaluation in the elementary school.

Keiler, Manfred L.: *The Art in Teaching Art*, University of Nebraska Press, Lincoln, Nebraska, 1961.
A fine book that takes up the question of self-evaluation on page 95.

Linderman, Earl W., and Donald W. Herberholz: *Developing Artistic and Perceptual Awareness*, William C. Brown Company, Publishers, Dubuque, Iowa, 1964.
This book provides a list of specific evaluational criteria for use in the elementary school, but it leaves several essential items unmeasured.

McFee, June: *Preparation for Art*, Wadsworth Publishing Company, San Francisco, 1961.
A short but concise account of evaluation. It does not include the evaluation of achievement as a connoisseur.

Reed, Carl: *Early Adolescent Art Education*, Chas. A. Bennett Co., Inc., Peoria, Illinois, 1957.
Chapter 11 covers evaluation in the junior high school.

Chapter 11
THE SUPERVISION OF ART IN THE PUBLIC SCHOOLS

Public school administrators are charged with the responsibility of managing the total educational enterprise. This means, among other things, that they are ultimately responsible for the instruction that occurs under their direction. But the management of a school system or of a single school has become so complex that a superintendent or principal is unable to give adequate direction or supervision to all aspects of the educational program. It is especially difficult for one or two individuals to offer the proper guidance in all subject-matter areas when the knowledge in each of those areas is expanding more rapidly every day. As a result, administrators have found it necessary to delegate part of their responsibility to instructional specialists, called supervisors, who automatically become representatives of the administration. Their ultimate goal is better education for all children through improved teaching.

The supervisor of art oversees all or part of the instructional program in the visual arts for the purposes of giving direction, assisting progress, and evaluating accomplishments. The title given 547 to such a person might vary from one school system to another depending upon the size of the community and upon the nature and extent of his responsibility. He might be called a director, a supervisor, a consultant, a helping teacher, a coordinator, an adviser, or any of several other names. He might direct the teaching of art in one or two schools, in all elementary schools, in all secondary schools, or in all the schools of a given community. In any case, the job requires that other persons be given help and direction. This means that instructional aid might be given to classroom teachers, to art teachers, to other supervisory personnel, or to all these groups. Such a service might be completely administrative or might involve the direct teaching of children. Customarily the administrative duties occupy a larger part of the supervisor's time if a full range of supervisory services is desired. But what are those services? What does a supervisor do to improve instruction if he acts in his full capacity as a supervisor?

Such a person assists in the fundamental task of formulating a philosophy of art education, and he uses that philosophy in developing an art curriculum. To facilitate the practical application of the philosophy within the framework of the curriculum, he manages an in-service education program for those who work under his direction. He tries to maintain a pleasant and effective relationship with administrators and teachers, and he tries to keep the people of the community informed of developments in the art program. In addition, the supervisor makes an effort to obtain and use advantageously the best equipment and supplies that funds allow. This means that a considerable portion of his time is devoted to budgetary matters, to inventories, and to the efficient storage and distribution of materials. He also keeps himself informed of professional developments in art education, and he tries to find and repair weaknesses in the total art program through on-the-job research. Finally, the art supervisor works continuously at the problem of evaluating himself, the teachers, the program, and the children.

From this account it is evident that a full range of supervisory service entails considerable work. The extent of this work and the kind of person needed to do it will become even more obvious as we explore the duties of the supervisor of art in more detail.

CURRICULUM PLANNING

Effective supervision begins with careful planning, but plans that effectively promote education in and through art are not apt to be made if the planners are poorly prepared. For that reason, a period of self-preparation is vitally important for the art supervisor, who, in all likelihood, will be called upon for leadership in planning the art curriculum.

In preparing himself for such a role, the supervisor might very well clarify his thoughts on the subjects covered in this book. To begin, it is essential that he develop his own point of view about the nature of art. Then, he must decide if artists have any special characteristics that lead to the production of art. If they do, the supervisor must determine how those characteristics are developed and, especially, how they can be developed through teaching. He must also consider the nature of the child's visual symbolic development, and the various physiological, psychological, and sociological explanations for that development. After that, the supervisor must decide what to expect in the way of art from children at different stages of development; he must determine the most appropriate time for teaching things that lead to the production of art and artists; and he must develop suggestions about methods of teaching.

Forming a curriculum committee

Having prepared himself in the proper manner, the art supervisor is ready to assemble the curriculum committee with the assistance of administrative superiors. One might wonder why such a committee is necessary when the supervisor has already organized a curriculum in his own mind. The answer is that education is a complex enterprise involving numerous problems that are not all apparent to one individual. Thus a specialist needs the expert advice of his colleagues so that he can avoid errors which might hurt his program or interfere with other offerings in the total curriculum. Such advisers are not only valuable in formulating a good, workable program, but they are essential in winning wholehearted acceptance of it. The composition of the curriculum committee is therefore vitally important to the success of the art program. The supervisor must exert all possible influence to see that the group is composed of capable advisers who have a highly professional attitude toward education and toward curriculum development in particular. They should be bright, forthright persons who are capable of working in a cooperative and nondictatorial manner. They should be open to new ideas, and they should be influential leaders who have gained the respect of their colleagues. Such persons are admittedly rare and hard to obtain, but efforts to secure them should always be made.

To operate effectively, there should be at least five persons on the curriculum committee. A smaller number usually means that some important element in the school system is not being adequately represented. When that happens, there is always the possibility that a highly significant view of the art curriculum has been neglected and that it will ultimately rise in opposition to the program. Thus it is important to make sure that all groups having a relationship to the art program be represented on the curriculum committee.

On the other hand, the supervisor should not allow the group to become too large. Seven members, including the art supervisor, are about as many as efficient cooperation will permit. Undoubtedly a committee of that size still will need to consult many other persons and work closely with them. But the main body of the curriculum group must remain small if the supervisor is to utilize the talents of each individual member, a point of considerable importance. After all, a committee member wants to feel that he is making a meaningful contribution. Such feelings are not apt to develop in a large committee in which individual participation is restricted. Consequently, a curriculum group of five to seven members is highly desirable. But who should the supervisor place on the committee; why should he include them; and how should he select them?

Perhaps the first person that the supervisor should consider is a representative, other than himself, from the administrative ranks of the school system. A *principal* would be an ideal selection, for he would bring to the group a knowledge of the educational objectives of the school district as well as a wide background of experience in curriculum organization. A principal would be familiar with the needs of other subject-matter areas, with the strengths and weaknesses of his teachers, with the extracurricular program, and with problems of scheduling. Furthermore, the principal can "make or break" an art program. If he feels that art education is valuable and that the program is a good one, he can do a lot to solicit cooperation from classroom teachers and from other administrative personnel. By the same token, he can reduce the effectiveness of art education if he thinks it is relatively unimportant. Consequently, a principal should participate in the formulation of the art curriculum because he is not apt to reject something that he has helped to create.

If the supervisor is one whose responsibilities for curriculum extend from the kindergarten through the high school, it is desirable that he have both an elementary and a secondary school principal on his curriculum committee. It is not necessary, however, that they both be on the committee at the same time. The administrator from the elementary school would be most effective when program considerations applying to his realm of responsibility are being considered, and the same would be true for the representative from the secondary school. Both of them can return to the committee in the final stages of planning so that they can get an overall picture of the total curriculum.

Another administrative official who can and should contribute to the planning of the art program is the *curriculum coordinator*. In large school districts, the curriculum coordinator might be an assistant superintendent of schools with responsibilities for the educational offerings in all twelve grades. Smaller districts might place this burden on the building principals, or they might employ a coordinator for the elementary schools. Other organizing arrangements might also exist, and in some cases the presence of a curriculum coordinator might lead administrators to eliminate art supervisors. This is rarely done, however, without losing the special knowledge and talent that an artist contributes to art education.

Assuming that the need for both a curriculum coordinator and an art supervisor is recognized and that both are employed, the supervisor definitely should make use of the coordinator's knowledge and experience. In fact, it would be difficult to ignore it because the coordinator is usually responsible for giving unity and coherence to the combined offerings of the school district. Like the art supervisor, he attempts to improve the program, keep it up-to-date, and give it direction. But, unlike the supervisor, he is concerned with all areas of instruction. He could help the art curriculum committee to solve problems and make decisions that satisfactorily integrate art with instruction in other subject-matter areas. He could make suggestions for the use of teaching aids and other resources available to the school system. In short, he could judge the overall feasibility of the curriculum proposal and offer valuable suggestions simply because of his broad experience with such matters.

Although curriculum coordinators are thoroughly familiar with children and with the principles of curriculum organization, it would be very unusual to find one who knows enough about art and artists to decide what and how to teach. To make these decisions, the committee needs the services of an *artist-teacher*. Naturally, the supervisor himself fills this requirement. But support for his cause will increase and pleasant relationships with the rest of the art staff are apt to improve if art teachers from the elementary and secondary schools are invited to participate directly in curriculum planning at the "summit." In addition, the presence of art teachers who work with children every day is helpful in the construction of a workable program. Without such persons it is possible to develop an overly theoretical or impractical aid to instruction.

The elementary and secondary school art teachers, like the principals, need not be present on the committee at the same time, but it is imperative that both attend meetings during the final stages of planning, to assure that a meaningful sequential program exists from the kindergarten through the high school. In fact, a great contribution to art education would be made if the art curricula of the elementary and secondary schools were more close integrated. A more widespread use of curriculum committees would help to bring about that improvement.

If for some reason the committee should seem too large to include the art teachers, they certainly should be consulted on a regular basis. In fact, the art supervisor should go over his ideas with the art teachers on the staff before he begins meeting with the committee. This should be done even if art teachers are to be present as members of that group, because it allows the art department to settle disagreements and to repair weaknesses in their thinking before their proposal is offered to the committee. After all, a well-informed group of art educators with a common point of view is much more persuasive than a group of individuals who disagree.

Still other persons who should be represented on the curriculum committee are the *elementary and secondary school classroom teachers*. Again they need not appear at the same time, but their services are certainly important. Like the art teacher, the classroom teacher is one who ultimately puts the curriculum into practice especially in the elementary school. If the teacher does not understand it, or if he does not approve of it, he is not likely to make it a success. Consequently, no one can afford to ignore the views of the classroom teacher. But there are large numbers of such people, and the views of some are more helpful than the views of others. How does the supervisor select the ones that will be most useful?

There are two methods that the supervisor can use. He can ask principals, other supervisory personnel, and the curriculum coordinator to help him identify the most capable teachers. The judgment of such persons is valuable because they have had the opportunity to work with all the teachers and to watch them

553

teach. But it is also important to obtain committee members who have the respect and confidence of their fellow teachers. For that reason it is often wise to have the instructors select their own representative to the curriculum committee. This method is more apt to eliminate teacher resistance to committee proposals and is strongly recommended as the better of the two ways of selecting representatives. The committee can always consult other teachers, anyway, if it wishes to do so.

With the addition of classroom teachers, the main body of the curriculum committee is formed, and it includes those persons whose services are most essential during all phases of curriculum development. Yet there are other individuals who can help immeasurably to create an outstanding program and to win its acceptance. One such person is the state director of art education, who knows more about art offerings within the state than any other individual. One visit would probably be sufficient for him to evaluate the committee's proposals and to offer the views of his office with respect to curriculum.

Equally valuable help may be obtained from janitors, secretaries, cafeteria superintendents, and other nonacademic personnel. In fact, art educators are dependent upon the help of such persons in many things that they do. They need the janitor's cooperation in keeping classrooms clean, in shipping materials from school to school, in constructing puppet stages or display units, and in visiting the boiler room. The janitor can offer formidable resistance to such activities, as well as to the use of clay, plaster, papier-mâché, colored chalk, lacquer thinner, and other art materials. Thus consultation between academic and nonacademic personnel is essential if the two groups are to perform their duties cooperatively and without unnecessary interference. If janitors and others are recognized by the art curriculum committee as important to the success of the educational program, they may become enthusiastic supporters as well as cooperative co-workers.

Another important person for the committee to consult is the guidance counselor from the junior or senior high school. Without a doubt he will have ideas about the function of art classes in the secondary school, but in some instances his views may be contrary to the best interests of art and of education. He might view art as a form of therapy or as a device for keeping troublesome students occupied. Such views play havoc with a serious art program and need to be brought into the open. If they are exposed and defeated by the curriculum committee, they are less likely to cause trouble in the future.

Other persons that can be helpful in curriculum development are the supervisors in other subject-matter areas, including librarians. These people can help the committee keep abreast of the latest curriculum developments in other subjects, and they can offer advice based upon their own experiences in program development. They are especially helpful when the committee discovers a conflict between the proposed art program and the teaching of social studies, reading, industrial arts, or some other dimension of the curriculum. Conflicts usually arise from a lack of understanding. If they can be eliminated in the early stages of program development, they will not have an opportunity to grow into major problems.

Librarians can be especially helpful by maintaining reference books on art for both teachers and students. They can also bring new books to the attention of the art staff and suggest ways of getting more use out of the library. By inviting the librarians to participate in curriculum decisions the art department gains a strong and helpful ally.

Still another individual to be consulted by the committee is the educational director of the local museum. Most school systems do not take full advantage of museum resources when they have them at their disposal. One of the major reasons for this is a lack of communication and a lack of cooperative planning between the two educational institutions. If museum personnel are permitted to join in curriculum discussions, the school and the museum can avoid unnecessary duplication of instruction, and each institution can develop its program in the direction that seems most appropriate for its facilities and the capabilities of its staff. Cooperation between the school and the museum can not only save money but it can provide a broader array of facilities for the teaching of art history and aesthetics, and it can increase the instructional staff.

Still other sources of help to the curriculum committee are children and their parents. Youngsters are most apt to be helpful when they reach high school age and look back upon their experiences in art. Their observations and suggestions are frequently so clear and sensible that an adult wonders why he did not think of them.

Parents probably feel more useful and actually contribute more to the educational program when they act as consultants to curriculum committees than they do as members of the PTA. They are important to the committee because they bring the educator into closer contact with the ideas, attitudes, and needs of the community.

Additional help can and should be obtained from the curriculum materials put out by other communities and other states. Some of these materials are excellent, but they should be examined with care. The same advice may be applied to the information on curriculum that is contained in textbooks on art education. The supervisor should give it all considerable thought.

Finally, the superintendent of schools should be given an opportunity to study the curriculum proposal and to offer suggestions or criticisms. No program would be complete without his endorsement.

Working with the curriculum committee

Having formed a curriculum committee and assembled a group of consultants for the committee to interview, the supervisor is ready to begin the task of program development. Without a doubt there are a number of ways to approach this task, but one way to begin is to uncover the strengths and weaknesses of existing art programs by listening to the comments and criticisms of committee members. To encourage the full exposure of their views, the supervisor might come to the first meeting with a list of pertinent questions. Perhaps the following questions would be appropriate.

1. *What do teachers and administrators believe to be the goals of art education? What should they be?*

2. *Do classroom teachers understand what is to be taught in art lessons? Are their ideas about content similar, or are they different? Should their ideas about content be different?*

3. *Do we have any problems in adapting content to specific grade levels? Do teachers have any difficulty in selecting art activities that are appropriate for children at the various grade levels?*

4. *Should appropriate projects be suggested for the grades, or should the teachers be allowed complete freedom of selection?*

5. *Do teachers feel a need for new and different art activities? What are the reasons for this desire? Should it be satisfied? How?*

6. *What are some of the present trends in curriculum development outside the field of art? If these developments seem fruitful, do you think that similar directions might be worthwhile for us to follow in the formulation of an art curriculum?*

7. *Do we offer enough courses in art at the secondary level? What, if anything, should we add or eliminate? Why?*

8. *Do college entrance requirements have any meaning for us in the development of an art curriculum?*

9. *If our classes constitute the end of formal education for any of our students, should we take this into consideration in our curriculum?*

10. *How do teachers feel about the relative importance of drawing, painting, crafts, and art appreciation? Are we weak in any of these areas?*

11. *Should we make a greater effort to integrate art with other subject matter? Do teachers need any help with such integration? What problems might be encountered?*

12. *What problems, if any, do art teachers create for the person who must teach other subjects? What can be done about these problems?*

13. *What criticisms do administrators have of the art program? Have the art specialists been sufficiently helpful in providing administrators with justifications for the program?*

14. *How do parents feel about the art curriculum?*

15. *Are guidance counselors familiar with the goals of the art program? How can the art specialists help the guidance counselors?*

16. *Should the art program be adjusted in any way to meet the needs of gifted children, slow children, average children, the culturally deprived, the culturally affluent, the handicapped?*

17. *How do teachers and administrators feel about art as therapy?*

18. *Are after-school enrichment programs desirable?*

19. *Are we making sufficient use of local resources such as museums and industries?*

557
THE SUPERVISION OF ART
IN THE PUBLIC SCHOOLS

20. *What problems, if any, do we have with the selection and distribution of materials? Could we enrich our program by adding any equipment or materials?*
21. *Should we emphasize either the fine or the applied arts?*
22. *Is our exhibition program adequate? How could the program be improved?*
23. *Do we have an adequate selection of visual aids? Could we make better use of slides, reproductions, films, charts, examples of finished projects, or books?*
24. *Do we need to study the scheduling of art classes or the scheduling of visits by the art teacher? Does scheduling interfere with art instruction in any way? What about bus schedules and lunch schedules?*
25. *Is there any needless duplication of instruction from grade to grade or among our classes in art, industrial arts, and homemaking?*
26. *To what extent should the art curriculum become involved with plays, holiday decorations, and contests?*
27. *To what extent should the curriculum be based upon the needs of the subject; upon the needs, interests, and abilities of the child; upon the need for social reconstruction?*
28. *Do we have any problems in our relationships with other staff members that need attention if our curriculum is to be accepted?*
29. *How can information about the art curriculum be given to teachers in a form that encourages its use?*
30. *Are our elementary and secondary school art programs meaningfully related to each other?*

Without a doubt there are other questions that the supervisor might ask to get at the ideas and attitudes of the staff about art education. The supervisor should pursue this questioning until he feels that he has obtained as much information as he can from the committee. The information is then duplicated and distributed to the group for further examination, additions, or deletions.

Using the corrected material, the supervisor and the art teachers should reexamine the curriculum proposal they had formulated prior to meeting with the committee. If the committee's suggestions seem feasible, the proposal should be adjusted to incorporate them. If they are not feasible, the supervisor should prepare a statement that indicates why the suggestions are not being followed.

Having prepared himself as fully as possible, the supervisor is ready to present his proposal to the curriculum committee. He and his art teachers bear the burden of presenting the first draft of the curriculum because they are probably the only committee members who know enough about art and art education to organize content into a meaningful program. If the whole committee were to participate in framing the first draft, valuable time would be lost and interest would decline.

As he presents his program, the supervisor must exert his full measure of ability as a leader. He must explain with care the reasoning that went into the curriculum proposal, and he must argue vigorously against any suggestions that would alter the goals of art education or weaken the chance of attaining those goals. The integrity of the subject matter must be defended, and the supervisor and the art teachers are the experts who must do it. If they cannot gain acceptance of a program that leads to the production of artists and connoisseurs of art, any further reference to *art* education would be meaningless.

Upon hearing the proposal, the committee may ask for clarification or offer suggestions and criticisms. They may disagree about the suitability of recommended materials and projects for the various grades. They may question the practicality of certain things in view of the time required or the teachers' abilities. These and other comments are highly desirable, and the supervisor must see that they are thoroughly discussed. When it is agreed that changes are necessary in the proposal, those changes should be made and the committee could assist in the rewording.

A careful examination of the curriculum cannot be made, however, unless adequate time is allowed to study it. For that reason it is a good idea to let the committee go over the proposal for several days at their leisure. After that, further corrections can be made, and the committee can proceed to interview other persons and solicit reactions to the proposed program.

When the committee and its consultants have thoroughly reviewed and corrected the new proposal, it is ready for presentation to the superintendent, to the board of education, and to the rest of the school staff. When the new art program finally reaches the school faculty, it has already become the official curriculum. Consequently, the supervisor must present the art program to the staff, and he must explain it, justify it, and do all he can to make it successful. This easily becomes the supervisor's most time-consuming job, and it requires a variety of in-service educational activities and the best of personnel relationships. We shall discuss these methods of presenting and implementing the program in the pages that follow. But the *writing* of an art curriculum has been emphasized so heavily in discussing the work of the curriculum committee that it seems fitting, at this time, to discuss the most effective method of presenting the program to the teachers in written form.

The curriculum guide

Emphasis has been placed upon the *writing* of a curriculum proposal with its rationale because teachers and administrators are in need of a permanent statement for frequent reference. Verbal accounts of the program and its goals are too easily forgotten. Consequently, school systems that operate without the benefit of a written curriculum are apt to have more aimless and inappropriate instruction.

Apparent as this may seem, the National Education Association reported in 1963 that sequential courses of study in art were being used in only 38.5 per cent of the elementary schools in the United States. Similarly, the NEA said that only 57 per cent of the secondary schools offering art were using a written curriculum.[1] The absence of such instructional aids is partially explained by the fact that teachers rarely use them. But why do they fail to use them?

One reason is that permanent statements of the art curriculum are often written without the classroom teacher in mind. They are frequently the esoteric products of a dedicated but overly theoretical curriculum committee. For that reason it is highly recommended that the supervisor keep the need for a *practical* curriculum statement in mind at all times. This means that the official program proposal should be rewritten and

[1] The National Education Association, *Music and Art in the Public Schools*, Research Monograph 1963-M3, Washington, D.C., 1963.

abridged, if necessary, in the form of a clear, concise, and pointed guide for the classroom teacher. After all, a busy teacher is not apt to study long involved educational documents when his most pressing need is to obtain pertinent information in a hurry. With this in mind the following suggestions for the content of a curriculum guide are recommended:

1. *Table of contents* — This is essential if the teacher is to find the necessary information quickly.

2. *Directions for use* — Guides can be used in ways that might be undesirable. The supervisor should therefore provide brief directions concerning its use. He might point out, for example, that the document is merely a guide and that rigid adherence to recommended projects does not give the art program the flexibility it needs. Different but related experiences initiated by the teachers might be encouraged so as to avoid the lock-step kind of program that can result from following a curriculum guide without imagination.

3. *Statement of basic philosophy* — A statement of the basic philosophy of art education is important so that teachers will come to understand why they teach art and why they are expected to do certain things and avoid others. Such a statement would include a definition of art and a comment about why art is important as a part of general education. It would include the view that our major goal is the development of children as artists and connoisseurs of art in accordance with their levels of growth and development. The statement must be brief and to the point or teachers will not read it.

4. *Characteristics of children* — It is important to describe the characteristics of children and of their visual symbols during each of the developmental stages. This gives the teacher some idea of what to expect from his students and why. It helps him to understand why certain materials and projects are appropriate while others are not.

5. *Stimulation and content* — A statement about the role of stimulation and the various kinds of stimulation is necessary, but we want the teachers to know that there is content to be covered in an art class. Mere stimulation is not enough.

6. *Grade-level aids* — A teacher is more likely to use a curriculum guide if he can turn quickly to a section devoted to his grade or to a suitable group of grades (primary, intermediate, junior high, etc.). Each section should contain a list of the goals to be attained. They might be similar to those outlined in Chapter 7, but they could be listed in greater detail. In addition, each section might well contain the following information:

(a) A list of appropriate topics or experiences for stimulation.

(b) A list of the most desirable art equipment and materials.

(c) A list of suggested art projects or activities together with instructions for carrying them out. The supervisor must be careful, at this point, to avoid the kind of step-by-step instructions that restrict the child's freedom of choice or result in products that all look alike. The importance of individuality should be emphasized.

(d) Photographs that help to clarify the text are helpful, but funds may not permit their use. Drawings do not add expense, however, and they are always helpful to the teacher.

7. *Evaluation* — The teacher's evaluation of himself and of his students is always one of his most difficult problems. The supervisor must make every effort to suggest evaluative techniques that can be used by teachers who are nonartists. The purpose of evaluation also should be stressed.

8. *Reporting to parents* — An explanation of reporting procedures in art would be helpful. Emphasize the importance of making a conscientious report of progress to parents. Teachers must be made to feel that careless reporting in art is a disservice to parents who are interested in discovering the unique abilities and weaknesses of their children.

9. *Parent-teacher conferences* — It would be helpful to a teacher to know what he can suggest to parents who would like to help their children. Information about instruction outside the school might be useful, or a list of art education books for parents might be appropriate.

10. *Exhibits* — A section devoted to the exhibition of child art might contain suggestions for mounting pictures, arranging bulletin-board displays, and making educational displays for parents. The use of libraries, hallways, and cafeterias as exhibit areas might be suggested. Keep the exhibition techniques easy.

11. *Integration of subject matter* — A section on the integration of art with other subject-matter areas should emphasize that art is not be the handmaiden of the social studies or a visual aid to health education. Samples of worthwhile integration should be given so that teachers can understand what good integration really means.

12. *Supplementary teaching materials* — A list of books, films, pamphlets, slides, filmstrips, recordings, and reproductions that are available in the school system would be most welcome. It is especially important to indicate how they are obtained.

13. *Seasonal activities* — Teachers are always in need of suggestions for holiday activities. The supervisor can use the guide as a way of introducing more worthwhile experiences, and he can warn against an art program that is oriented to the holidays.

14. *Supplies and equipment* — A list of available supplies and equipment should be provided together with information about where they are stored and how to obtain them.

Curriculum guides are usually provided in mimeographed form because it is a relatively inexpensive way of getting information to the teachers. Some supervisors find it advantageous to present this material on large charts, but mimeographed pages that are offered in a loose-leaf notebook are much more efficient.

563

New pages can be added or removed easily, and a greater amount of information can be provided.

In some school systems separate guides are furnished for the elementary and secondary schools, but there is an advantage to combining all the information in one volume. It costs a little more, but has the virtue of providing teachers at both educational levels with an overview of the whole curriculum. Teachers need this understanding of the total art program, but they have isolated themselves at either the elementary or secondary level for many years. Their consequent lack of understanding of the whole art curriculum is one of the major weaknesses in contemporary art education. If art educators are to offer meaningful learning experiences to children, they need to know more about the instruction that precedes and follows their own.

Having produced an official art curriculum, the supervisor and his committee should give it a fair trial. This means that it should be used for at least two years or perhaps three. If changes are made year after year, it is very difficult to evaluate the total offering. After two or three years the committee might meet again to appraise their work. By that time the teachers and administrators will have developed points of view about the program that will be helpful in making further improvements.

Upon the completion of the original curriculum plan, the supervisor must be ready to implement it in as many ways as possible, and it is a good idea for him to let the committee know how he intends to do it. The guide for teachers is, of course, one of the devices he may use, but there are several others. What else can a supervisor do to make his program succeed?

PERSONNEL RELATIONSHIPS AND IN-SERVICE EDUCATION

The duties of the art supervisor may be completely administrative or may involve the teaching of children. In either case the acceptance and eventual success of the art curriculum are largely dependent upon the supervisor's ability to maintain pleasant relationships with the rest of the staff. At the same time he must offer the guidance and supporting services that lead to improved instruction. Accomplishing both objectives is especially difficult because of the many personalities involved. How can the supervisor do the job?

Working with the administration

Maintaining pleasant relationships with administrators is extremely important.[2] The time may come when a supervisor needs to ask a principal or a superintendent of schools to assert authority or to approve a budget. But he cannot expect their full support unless he convinces them that he is doing a good job; this is largely a matter of keeping them up-to-date on the aims and accomplishments of the art department as well as its major obstacles.

One of the best ways to keep them informed is to submit an *annual report* to all administrators. It takes time, but the work can be reduced if the supervisor keeps a daily record of the accomplishments in his department. A chart for recording routine information might be developed to simplify the record keeping. At any rate, answers to the following questions would be most desirable in the annual report:

1. *What are the long-range objectives of the art program?*
2. *What were the immediate objectives of the department for the last year?*
3. *What was accomplished in the elementary schools during the last year?*
   (a) How many demonstration classes were taught by the art supervisor?
   (b) How many classes were taught by art teachers?
   (c) Approximately how many art lessons were taught by classroom teachers?
   (d) Were any of the classroom art activities worthy of special note? What were they?
   (e) Were any special school-wide or community-wide projects undertaken? What were they?
   (f) How many exhibits of student work were offered?

[2] The writer is deeply indebted to Professor Edward Mattil of Pennsylvania State University for many of the ideas about working with administrators presented here.

(g) How many field trips were conducted?

(h) How many workshops were offered for the benefit of classroom teachers? How many teachers attended? What was accomplished?

(i) How many school-wide, grade-level, and personal meetings did the art supervisor have with classroom teachers?

(j) Were extracurricular or enrichment programs in art offered by the art department? Did other groups offer such instruction? What were the results?

(k) How does the work of elementary school youngsters as a whole compare with the standards adopted by the school system? Is there evidence of especially good work? In what way is the work of our youngsters weak?

4. *What was accomplished at the secondary school level during the last year?*

(a) How many courses were offered by the department, and what was the enrollment in each course?

(b) How many service projects were completed in the junior high school and senior high school? How many posters, banquet decorations, dance decorations, building decorations, signs, programs, menus, and sets for plays were produced?

(c) How many requests for service were refused? Why?

(d) How many "problem" students were placed in art classes during the year? What were the results?

(e) How many high school art students went to art school?

(f) What kind of recognition has been received by art students (scholarships, prizes, exhibitions)?

(g) How many exhibits of student work were offered?

(h) How many field trips were conducted?

(i) What was done to provide students with more and better information about schools of art and jobs available to artists?

(j) How much service was offered to other subject-matter areas? How many art history lectures were given for the history department, etc.?

(k) How does the student work in the secondary school compare with the standards adopted by the school system? Is there any evidence of special strength? In what way is the work of our students weak?

5. *What were the other accomplishments of the art department during the year?*

(a) What was the art supervisor's schedule for time in the office (preparation, research, reports, ordering supplies, inventories, school visits, teachers' meetings, demonstration classes, and other activities)?

(b) What were the schedules of the other art teachers in the department?

(c) How many schools did the art supervisor visit outside his own school system? What were the purposes and the results of those visits?

(d) Were any articles or publications produced by members of the department?

(e) Did any art teachers exhibit their own work?

(f) Were art clubs sponsored by people in the department?

(g) Did members of the department teach courses in adult education?

(h) Were any research projects inaugurated? What were the results?

(i) Did the department undertake studies of evaluation, courses and curricula, etc.? What were the conclusions?

(j) What was achieved in the way of public relations? Did the art department contribute to parent-teacher meetings in any way?

(k) What improvements were made in integrating the elementary and secondary school art programs?

(l) Were any speakers or consultants employed this year?

(m) Did any members of the department act as critic teachers in teacher-education programs of the local colleges?

(n) Did any members of the department lecture at other schools?

(o) Did any of the art teachers engage in advanced study or travel?

(p) Were any improvements made in in-service education (orientation, curriculum guides, newsletters, resource materials, demonstration teaching, workshops)?

(q) Were any improvements made in the management of equipment and supplies? Was the department able to save the school district any money?

(r) In what way did the staff participate in the work of professional organizations?

6. *What improvements can be made in the future?*

   (a) What would the department like to accomplish in the near future?

   (b) What would help the department to achieve its immediate goals and to develop a better art program (not supplies or equipment)?

   (c) What supplies and equipment are needed for a broader, more extensive program?

   (d) What could the administration do to improve the work of the department?

   (e) Suggest the administration feel free to make suggestions for improvement.

7. *Acknowledge assistance from all other departments. Mention classroom teachers, art teachers, janitors, cafeteria workers, and other persons who are doing an excellent job and have helped to make the art program more successful. If you cannot say something positive, say nothing.*

If information of this kind is given to the administrator in an annual report, he will remain alert to the aims and needs of the art department, and he will know that the art staff is "on its toes." Together with a statement of the art curriculum and its rationale, the annual report gives the administrator a basis for supporting the art program verbally and financially. Furthermore, a written report is not as easy to forget as a verbal one. Thus the reluctant administrator cannot delay action as easily if he does not wish to appear inefficient.

On the other hand, an annual report of accomplishments is

nothing but idle chatter unless the administrator can see definite achievement in the growth and development of children. For that reason the art supervisor should take every opportunity to point out the concrete signs of progress as they occur in the classroom. He should invite administrators to exhibits and take them into the classrooms to see the children at work. He should introduce them to outstanding art students and point to evidence of growth.

Finally, the supervisor's relationship with the administration will improve if he is able to work cooperatively and successfully with the rest of the staff and fulfill his other responsibilities satisfactorily. How can be improve his relationship with his co-workers?

Working with other supervisors and with art teachers

Supervisors in all subject-matter areas are eager to promote their own subjects, and they frequently do so with unrestrained vigor. Such enthusiasm is highly desirable, but it may have unhappy consequences if the supervisors do not work together.

Specialists who keep to themselves often find that their activities conflict with those of other departments. The supervisor of home economics, for example, may discover that her after-school cooking club conflicts with orchestra rehearsal or with girls intramural sports. To avoid such troubles with scheduling, the art supervisor must arrange meetings with administrators and with colleagues in other subject-matter areas. Conflicts of interest are bound to arise; however, with a certain amount of compromise, a fair and impartial calendar of activities can be arranged. Scheduling courses and after-school activities is such a monumental task, however, that some schools are using computers to do the job. The subject-matter specialists merely indicate their needs, and the computers figure out how to satisfy those needs within the limits of a school day.

By planning with his colleagues the art supervisor will also gain an understanding of the total educational program and have an opportunity to explain the place that art occupies in that program. He will find that his aims and problems are similar to those of his colleagues, and he will learn to respect other subject-matter areas. In an atmosphere of recognition and respect, supervisors can help each other with problems of handling supplies, evaluation, reporting to parents, demonstration teaching, and pesonnel relationships. They are most likely to succeed in such discussions if they begin with the idea that *there is no hierarchy of subjects.*

Building and maintaining pleasant relationships with art teachers is also a continuous job. It begins during the interview for employment. At that point, it is advisable for the supervisor to question the applicant thoroughly to ascertain his philosophy of art education. Future conflicts can often be avoided by hiring art teachers who subscribe to a philosophy similar to that of the supervisor. For this reason supervisors should make every effort to be included in the interviewing procedure. If not, they should let their desires be known to interviewing officials.

Having employed a new art teacher, the supervisor must help him in his orientation to the new job and to the school system. If the position is in the elementary schools, the new art teacher might be included in the orientation program for new classroom teachers. At any rate, he should be given enough information about his duties so that he can begin work with a minimum of apprehension.

Periodically thereafter, the supervisor ought to arrange informal staff meetings to provide further information and guidance for the new teacher. Staff meetings should also be used to give all art teachers a part in the making of significant decisions that affect the art program. By using the democratic process each teacher has the opportunity he needs and deserves to influence the course of art education. If he does not get it, the teacher loses interest in his work and education suffers. But education can also suffer if decision making by the democratic process lacks dymanic leadership. Consequently, the supervisor must come to his staff meetings prepared to accomplish something. He must make the problems clear, list some of the things that have a bearing on the problems, and suggest alternate solutions.

He must come with pertinent questions and any figures or facts that might be helpful. In short, he must be prepared to keep the meeting moving, for his example will determine the level of thinking and involvement that occurs. If he allows the meeting to succumb to idle chatter, it will be a waste of time, and his future meetings will be doomed to failure.

On the other hand, the supervisor must be careful to avoid a dominating attitude or a tendency to exert power. The reason for this is simple enough: the supervisor has no power. He must lead by the force of good ideas, good example, hard work, and persuasion. If he attempts to lead by exerting power he does not have, he is sure to fail.

Once the supervisor and the art teachers have decided on a course of action, the supervisor should charge the teachers with certain responsibilities and leave them alone to carry out their work. Observing them at their jobs is not a good idea, unless they request it, because it makes them uncomfortable and gives the impression of recognized superiority. Trust, respect, and the anticipation of good work are much more effective in winning the good will of the art teacher and causing him to meet or exceed expectations.

Finally, the supervisor must praise his colleagues when praise is warranted, and he must make a special effort to mention their good work to administrators and townspeople.

Working with classroom teachers

Establishing a pleasant but effective professional relationship with classroom teachers is one of the supervisor's most difficult yet essential jobs. His work is made easier, however, if he begins to cement relationships as soon as the teacher is hired. A new staff member usually appreciates assistance because he is unfamiliar with the art program; he does not know what he should teach; he does not know what the children have already covered; and he probably has doubts about his own artistic judgment. Usually, he does not know what materials are available or how to obtain them. Consequently, he needs the supervisor's help and must not be allowed to drift until the semester is well under way. Clearly, an orientation program is in order for all new art and classroom teachers. In the best school systems this would be a cooperative venture undertaken by all supervisors. What should be covered?

Orientation programs for new teachers. In the first place, the program is most useful if it is initiated at the earliest possible time, preferably before classes begin. The supervisor should seek out the new teachers, introduce himself, and arrange for a private or group meeting. Waiting for the teachers to request a conference is not advisable. Furthermore, the meeting ought to be friendly and informal, and it should offer the new teacher plenty of time to ask questions and to indicate his expectations or preferences regarding supervisory assistance. If the teacher has definite opinions about the role of the art supervisor, they should be remembered and respected when school begins. After all, the supervisor gains nothing by offering unwanted supervisory services or by denying services that are fully expected.

Despite the new teacher's opinion or lack of opinion about the supervisor's job, the specialist must let it be known at the orientation meeting that he is not a boss but a co-worker. He should make it clear that he is interested in providing the best possible art education for children and that the school system has given its endorsement to the art program and to the philosophy that supports it. Perhaps it would also be wise to give the new teacher a copy of the system's philosophy of art education together with a curriculum guide. Both documents could then be discussed and their practical significance for the teacher could be emphasized.

At these meetings it is appropriate for the supervisor to describe the nature of his job and the services he can offer to classroom teachers. It is equally appropriate to mention the things he cannot do, and why. He may wish to point out, for example, that he cannot teach all the art and that he cannot assist with an art project at a moment's notice. But he should let the teachers know how to reach him if they need help.

Another useful addition to the orientation meeting would be an exhibit of child art from all the grades. Colorful displays are always helpful in building early enthusiasm, in describing the caliber of work that can be achieved, and in suggesting uses for various materials. The teachers, of course, will want to know what is available in the way of supplies and equipment. They will want to know where such things are stored and how they can be obtained. If possible, the supervisor might take the group on a tour of a typical elementary school and point out the central storeroom, the classroom facilities, and any handy arragements that the system might have for storing scissors, brushes, colored paper, and other materials.

By providing information of this kind to new teachers, the supervisor begins his relationship with them in a helpful and professional manner. He is already "paving the way" for improvement of instruction. But a single meeting does not bring the orientation program to an end. The program continues as part of all the services that the supervisor can offer.

Classroom visitations and demonstration teaching. The supervisor's personal visit to the classroom for consultation or demonstration teaching is probably his most effective method of improving instruction, but it is also the most difficult. He has to work with numerous personalities, and it is not easy to adjust to all of them with equal success. Yet the supervisor is expected to strive for that adjustment simply because a pleasant professional relationship is more apt to foster improved instruction. His success is partially determined by his ability to accept the teachers as they are and to build from there. If he recognizes certain strengths, he attempts to develop or expand them. If he detects a weakness in teaching, he tries to reduce or eliminate it. In either case he must accept the teacher and offer helpful support in a positive or constructive manner.

It may take a long time to eliminate weaknesses in instruction, expecially if habits and attitudes are deeply engrained. Consequently, patience is a virtue that should be cultivated. Much too often, supervisor's expect teachers to change their personalities at the drop of a hat, the assumption being that change can and should occur when the need for it is logically pointed out. The trouble is that habits, attitudes, and mannerisms usually change gradually if they change at all. Logic is certainly helpful in initiating such conversions, but it rarely causes immediate alterations in behavior.

Supervisors sometimes try to exert pressure on the teacher when they become impatient with the slow effects of logic and persuasion. But power or force is not effective in dealing with teachers for at least two reasons. The first is that the supervisor has little or no power to apply. Consequently, any attempt to exert pressure places the supervisor in the same position as the general who rattles his cannon without ammunition. The slightest resistance leads to a resounding defeat.

Let us assume for a moment, however, that the supervisor does have power and that he uses it. It is still ineffective, even if it causes a rapid change in teaching behavior. It is ineffective because it results in compliance on the surface without full acceptance or commitment, and actions that are forced and unnatural are seldom convincing or permanent. Furthermore, a show of force from anyone creates a barrier between the teacher and supervisor that is practically impossible to remove.

As a result the supervisor is urged to be patient and to avoid a show of power. He stands a far greater chance of improving instructional behavior if he uses logical persuasion, provides pertinent information, and sets a good example. For this reason it is highly recommended that the supervisor devote his classroom visitations to consultation and demonstration teaching rather than to observation of the teacher. Anything he needs to know about the instructor's work can usually be obtained from conversation and from the work that students produce. If the supervisor watches the teacher work, the teacher is certain to be uncomfortable, unnatural, and filled with feelings of inferiority or contempt. Besides, the real inspiration that a supervisor must create does not come from teacher-watching. It comes from great teaching. But how does the supervisor arrange for such demonstrations?

Probably his first job is to plan a schedule of regular visitations to each teacher in the elementary schools. During the first two or three weeks of the year it might be advisable to arrange weekly visits to new teachers as part of the orientation program. The remainder of the scheduled calls for the year would then be divided equally among all the instructors. The frequency of those visits will depend upon the number of persons offering supervisory service as well as the number of teachers. Once a month should be often enough, but supervision loses its effectiveness if calls by an art specialist are made less than once every two weeks. A supervisor tends to lose his effect on the art program by spacing his visits a month apart unless an art teacher is scheduled to appear as a reinforcement several times a week, once a week, or once every two weeks. It is hoped that the supervisor will have the assistance of enough art teachers so that he will not be forced into frequent visitations that prevent him from offering other supervisory services.

If possible, the supervisor should plan his time for regular visitations in such a way that he has free time available each week for assisting the teachers who ask for extra help. If requests for assistance are not forthcoming, the supervisor always can use the time on other worthwile tasks. But free time is essential for good supervision. Without it there is no opportunity for flexibility.

Having planned and distributed his schedule to teachers, the supervisor begins his round of visitations. It is most advisable, however, for him to discuss the demonstration lesson with the classroom teacher before he comes to teach. Advance consultation gives both the supervisor and the teacher an opportunity to select a lesson that is in keeping with the other things that the children are studying. It also gives the supervisor a chance to explain the purpose of his lesson. After all, he must make it clear that art instruction is more than keeping children busy with art materials.

As the supervisor explains the goal he hopes to achieve with the children, he should point out any aspects of the lesson that he thinks might be interesting or helpful to the regular teacher.

For example, he might indicate that the demonstration will make use of (1) new materials or techniques; (2) a different method of distributing, collecting, and managing materials; (3) a different motivational technique; (4) group work; (5) new ideas on the display of finished products; or (6) integrative techniques.

Naturally the demonstration will not serve its purpose as an aid to the improvement of instruction if the teacher does not remain in the room. The supervisor must therefore encourage the teacher to remain, even if it necessitates giving him some responsible job in the art activity. A helping hand can always be used in the management of equipment and materials.

The supplies that will be necessary for the proposed art lesson can be discussed with the classroom teacher prior to the lesson. If the materials are available in the classroom or in the school to be visited, the supervisor may ask the teacher to have them ready when he arrives. Sometimes a mimeographed list of common supplies can be given to the teacher with the necessary items checked off. This helps him to remember the demonstration and to have everything ready. Such a form is even more helpful when advance consultations cannot be held, and it is simply sent by messenger or through the mail. A sample form appears on page 576.

As the supervisor makes his visits, it is definitely advisable to arrive for appointments on time. The elementary school teacher is a busy individual with a tight schedule who is forced to improvise or to rearrange his carefully prepared plans when a demonstration is late. Consequently, the supervisor who wants and needs the teacher's cooperation must be considerate. He must be prepared as well as prompt. He must have the whole lesson carefully organized; if unrequested materials are necessary, he must furnish them. Equipment and materials should be smoothly and efficiently distributed; the stimulation and directions should follow, and the children should begin their work while the supervisor offers individual instruction. If he has time and the situation permits, the supervisor would do well to compliment the teacher warmly on any deserving art work that is on display. But his major occupation should be the teaching of children.

When they have finished their work, he should take the time to discuss it with them and with the teacher. This is really crucial to improved instruction. After all, any teacher must be able to judge instruction through the effects that it produces.

If the supervisor's teaching is not fully successful, the fact must be admitted and the two teachers must try to figure out what went wrong. Such an arrangement is superior to teacher-watching as a supervisory technique because it allows the supervisor to be as critical as he wishes. His comments will not hurt or insult the teacher because they are directed toward his own teaching.

Finally, the supervisor should make sure that equipment, materials, and finished products are collected in an orderly manner and returned to the proper places. The most sacred of rules in demonstration teaching (if there are any) is that classrooms must be cleaned before you leave them. If the teacher is left in an arty mess, his enthusiastic endorsement of the art program is bound to fade away.

Workshops. Next to demonstration teaching, the art workshop is probably the supervisor's most effective instrument for improving instruction, but it presents several serious problems, one of which is getting full attendance by classroom teachers. The fact that teachers are hardworking, underpaid individuals who receive little or no recognition for their effort is well known. Consequently, they resent being asked to attend workshops on their own free time without pay or without educational credit. They also rebel against meetings that do not offer practical solutions to everyday problems, and they detest any professional activity that is so poorly timed and located that it seems to be a case of planned inconvenience. After all, any educational function for teachers that is arranged without regard for their welfare is a clear and ringing announcement that the teacher is no more than a lightly valued friend.

Keeping these attitudes firmly in mind, the supervisor is urged to begin the planning of any workshop by seeking the opinions of the teachers themselves. He might ask what kind of workshop activities would be most useful if such meetings could be made satisfactory in all other respects. If the teachers offer no ideas, the supervisor might present a few of his own and listen to the reactions. Naturally, the amount of time provided for the workshop will affect the number and nature of the topics that can be covered, but any of the following activities would be worthwhile.

1. Participation in drawing, painting, or craftwork is especially helpful to teachers if it is related to the teaching of youngsters in the elementary school. It would help the teachers to learn more about composition, materials, and general procedures, and it could help them with classroom management.

2. A field trip to a local museum would help the teachers to learn how they can use the museum as a community resource in the development of art appreciation or connoisseurship. Museum officials could be asked to conduct tours and to discuss art, as well as to offer suggestions for the visits of schoolchildren to the museum.

577

3. A field trip to an artist's studio, an architect's office, a department store, an advertising agency, or to some other place where art is being produced for daily consumption would help the teacher to see the place of art in contemporary society. It would also provide insight into the life of the artist. Visits to high school and college art departments would give the teachers an idea of the training that lies ahead, which could serve to emphasize the importance of their own teaching.

4. A visiting artist could bring to the workshop some of the advantages obtained from a trip to his studio. This saves time, and it is especially good if trips cannot be made. But it obviously lacks the benefits received from meeting the artist in his working environment.

5. Films, slides, filmstrips, recordings, reproductions, and other audio-visual aids could be fully explored. These devices could be used to inform the teacher on almost any subject connected with art education, or the supervisor could demonstrate how to use them in teaching art to children.

6. A group of about twenty-five children could be taught by the supervisor while the teachers observe. After the lesson is over and the children have left, the supervisor could lead a discussion based on observations. The subjects for discussion under such circumstances are almost unlimited. With the equipment now available, sessions with children could be filmed and recorded on tape so that a later discussion might be enlivened with audio-visual aids. In fact, art lessons occurring in the classroom could be filmed, taped, and brought to the workshop for analysis and discussion.

7. A visiting art educator might be invited to present the latest views or developments in art education and to relate them to the work of the classroom teacher. He might be asked to supplement his speech with an informal discussion period.

8. Evaluation would make a useful topic for a workshop. The supervisor might make use of the art work of several children to demonstrate evaluation.

9. Children might be invited to discuss the art program at a roundtable. High school children are especially enlightening if they are asked to assess the meaning of art in their lives or to evaluate the kind of instruction they have received.

10. Art history or art appreciation would offer a wealth of content for teachers to use in their classrooms. The supervisor might devote a workshop to the lives and works of several key figures in the history of art, and the teachers might be asked to read a book or two for background prior to the workshop. To add interest and variety, the subject need not be limited to artists. Consider, for example, the exciting life and great influence of Duveen as an art dealer.

11. The philosophies of art and of art education could easily occupy the minds of workshop participants for several hours.

12. Sometimes a new face with new or different ideas is stimulating. For that reason a neighboring art supervisor, a museum instructor, or a college professor might be invited to lead the workshop or to participate in it. This is a possible solution for the overworked, overextended supervisor who simply does not have the time to do both the planning and the teaching in the workshop. Still another solution for such a busy person is the commercial art workshop conducted by trained representatives and financed by the manufacturers of art materials. Such workshops are very popular, so they must be planned a year or more in advance. The supervisor must be careful, however, not to let the commercial workshop become a regular habit. The person who knows the strengths and weaknesses of the local school system is the one who is most apt to provide for the special needs of the teachers.

13. Workshops can be arranged for instructors who work at a specific grade level; or the meetings can be geared to a single school or to several schools. There are advantages and disadvantages to each arrangement. A restricted workshop allows teachers to work at problems peculiar to their grade level or to their school, but it does not allow them to see what is going on elsewhere and to exchange ideas with persons from other schools. A community-wide workshop, on the other hand, does expose the participants to a wide variety of ideas and activities, but some of the instruction may not be appropriate for the teacher of a given grade level. The supervisor needs to take this into consideration and make plans to offer instruction that is as appropriate as possible for each teacher. He might arrange a community-wide meeting, for example, but instead of teaching all the participants in a single group, he might divide them according to their common interests and place a workshop instructor with each group.

14. Refreshments and social activities can hardly be called a part of the educational content of a workshop, but they do play an important role in establishing the friendly relaxed atmosphere that makes a workshop popular as well as informative. Coffee or tea and a light snack may be all that is needed to make a professional meeting most enjoyable, but the supervisor may be able to arrange meals and a musical program as well. Usually the need for such things will increase as the length of the workshop increases.

15. Any combination of the activities listed above would be perfectly acceptable, and such a combination might give the meeting a variety that is highly desirable.

Perhaps there are other educational projects that the supervisor could suggest to teachers as worthwhile activities for a workshop. But having made his suggestions, he must accept the verdict of the teachers regarding the merit of the proposals. They are apt to say that philosophical talkathons are not desirable and that how-to-do-it sessions are much more welcome. Whatever the consensus of opinion may be, the supervisor should orient the workshop around it. He may feel that other things would do more to improve instruction, but he must honor the teachers' wishes if he hopes to win their attendance and their attention. He can always work his ideas into the program, anyway, while featuring the educational flavor that the teachers prefer.

After assembling opinions on content, the supervisor must give some thought to the location of the workshop. A highly desirable location would be a large art room in one of the schools, as the art room provides handy access to tools, materials, equipment, and storage. Since such rooms are often too small to accommodate large numbers of teachers, the workshop might be held in a cafeteria, a gymnasium, a church basement, or in any other room large enough to hold the anticipated crowd. If large rooms are not available, the attendance will obviously have to be limited, or the group will have to be divided and placed in several rooms.

In any case, the room or rooms must be centrally located with ample parking and transportation available so that teachers do not find it inconvenient to attend. The room must also contain a sink and a sufficient number of tables and chairs, and there should be adequate lighting, ventilation, rest rooms, telephones, dining facilities, and coffee-making equipment. School cafeterias often can be put into operation to handle meals, if there are not restaurants nearby, but this increases the cost of the workshop. When cost is a primary problem, coffee should still be furnished, but teachers can be asked to bring their lunches.

In addition to such requirements, the meeting room should contain a small blackboard and a large amount of bulletin-board or exhibition space. The display space is especially important because it permits the use of educational exhibits and allows for the exhibition of finished work.

With certain tentative locations in mind, the supervisor is ready to plan the length of each individual session as well as the number of sessions. Howard Conant and his students have recommended a number of satisfactory arrangements in their useful *Art Workshop Leaders Planning Guide*.[3] Their strongest recommendation is that sessions should be one and a half to three and a half hours in length. Shorter meetings do not allow enough time to do an adequate job, and longer sessions are too long to maintain interest and enthusiasm. In fact, any meeting that lasts over two and a half hours should be interrupted by a coffee break or a period of relaxation.

Conant and his students also recommend most strongly that workshops be offered in double sessions (A.M and P.M.) for two to five days. Considering the problems connected with planning workshops, any program that lasts over three days would very be difficult to arrange.

This brings us to a related issue: the question of whether a teacher should be expected to attend workshops on his own free time and without pay. Naturally, and rightfully, the answer from the teacher is no, and it is the only answer that deserves serious attention. Administrators or laymen may feel that it is the teacher's duty to improve himself on his own time and at his own expense, but the merit or lack of merit in such an argument is a meaningless academic question when you consider that people rarely improve themselves under conditions they strongly dislike. Recognizing this, many school systems are wisely offering some form of compensation to teachers for attendance at workshops if the meetings occur outside school hours. Some systems provide additional pay, and others award educational credits that result in a salary increase for the teacher when sufficient credits have been obtained.

Usually the best teachers attend the workshops, and the less capable teachers stay home. When attendance affects salary, however, many of the persons who are most in need of training will appear. This is highly desirable as long as it pays off in the classroom. In fact, the ultimate measure of success for any form of in-service education is the teacher's performance in the class-

[3] Howard Conant (ed.), *Art Workshop Leaders Planning Guide*, Davis Publications, Inc., Worcester, Massachusetts, 1958, p. 19.

room. His exposure to in-service instruction is merely an encouraging sign.

Some school systems avoid the problem of extra pay for workshop attendance by providing released time for such events. In other words, classes are dismissed for a day, a part of a day, or for parts of several days so that teachers can attend professional meetings. Other school systems schedule workshops during the early orientation period prior to the time that classes begin in the fall. These two arrangements are especially desirable because they do not require the teacher to sacrifice his own time or to give up the opportunity to do what he wishes with that time. Under such favorable conditions he is treated as a professional educator and not as a professional martyr.

Naturally administrators will be concerned about the cost of a workshop, but they are apt to look at it much more favorably if they see that the supervisor has planned in advance and that he has exercised judgment in the tentative selection of supplies the arrangements for meals, and other costly elements. Wages are, of course, the largest expense in any educational endeavor. Consequently, a good reason for scheduling meetings during the working portion of the day or year is that the payment of additional wages for workshop attendance will not be necessary.

With tentative arrangements in mind, the supervisor is advised to meet with the art teachers and with a few selected classroom teachers to have his plans evaluated. With their approval and their help, he can proceed to work out a list of the necessary supplies with the cost of each item indicated. By adding the various expenses the total cost of the workshop can be estimated. Then the supervisor is ready to present his proposal to the appropriate administrator and to discuss it with other supervisory personnel. If the proposal is presented far in advance, the administration will be able to study it carefully and to adjust the budget to include it, whereas a last-minute request does not provide that opportunity.

Sometimes administrators oppose workshops because of the difficulty of planning them satisfactorily. But they have a hard time refusing a workshop that already has been planned in such a way that it takes into account the wishes and concerns of the whole staff. When official approval is received, the supervisor will need to arrange further meetings with art teachers and with key classroom teachers. Together they can decide upon the number of workshop leaders that will be required; they can plan a variety of activities that will make the workshop interesting and exciting; they can plan ways and means of organizing the rooms, supplies, and equipment; they can provide for cleaning up afterward; they can arrange for publicity; and they can take care of any of the other numerous details that remain.

When the time of the meeting draws near, the supervisor should make a special effort to invite administrators and school board members to participate actively in the program. Their presence gives the meeting a special air of importance and offers the supervisor a chance to sell the school board on the educational merits of art.

Another important task is to develop a system for evaluating the workshop. The ultimate measure of its value is, as we have said, the quality of the teacher's performance in the classroom and the growth of the children as artists and connoisseurs of art. But it is also helpful to know which aspects of the workshop are most pleasurable for teachers and which are least pleasurable. Naturally the supervisor will want to eliminate the unpleasant portions of the program in future workshops if it does not adversely affect the improvement of instruction in the classroom.

One way to obtain reactions to a workshop is to mimeograph an evaluation form that can be filled in anonymously at the end of the last session. A form similar to the one that appears on page 585 might be used.

While the workshop is still in preparation, the supervisor must make sure that it will be followed by plenty of support as the teachers try to put their learnings into practice. Schools must be stocked with the necessary equipment and supplies, and the teachers must be informed of their location. The supervisor is also advised to arrange his post-workshop schedule so that he will be free to assist teachers in applying their new ideas.

Finally, the art supervisor should see that the names of

MY EVALUATION OF THE WORKSHOP

I would rate the various portions of the art workshop as follows:

	Very helpful	Moderately helpful	Least helpful	Should be eliminated

1. **Participation in art activities** . . . .

2. **Field trip** . . . .

3. **Speakers** . . . .

4. **Films and filmstrips** . . . .

5. **Tape recordings** . . . .

6. **Demonstrations** . . . .

7. **Discussion periods** . . . .

8. **Suggestions for:** . . . .

   (a) classroom management . . . .

   (b) evaluation . . . .

   (c) stimulation . . . .

   (d) art projects . . . .

   (e) appreciation . . . .

9. **Children** . . . .

10. **Exhibition** . . . .

11. **Refreshments** . . . .

12. **Meals** . . . .

13. **Entertainment** . . . .

14. **Transportation** . . . .

15. **Parking** . . . .

16. **Location of workshop** . . . .

17. **Length of sessions** . . . .

18. **Number of sessions** . . . .

19. **Dates of sessions** . . . .

Suggestions for improvement:

workshop participants are made known to administrators so that persons with highly professional attitudes may be recognized. And future workshops should not be planned at such frequent intervals that they become unpopular with the conscientious teachers. The frequency with which they occur should depend upon the time that is available, the other demands on the teachers' time, the recognized need for improved instruction, and the nature of previous workshops.

Newsletters. The purpose of the newsletter is to provide the teacher with up-to-date information on art education. When such information is not available, the classroom teacher often turns elsewhere for ideas or for assistance, and some of his sources do not provide the kind of help that is beneficial to art education. For that reason it is recommended that the supervisor use a regularly published newsletter to supplement the curriculum guide and to suggest new ideas or techniques for drawing, painting, crafts, art history, aesthetics, exhibitions, evaluation, or any other subject that might be helpful.

The supervisor may wish to have portions of the newsletter placed in the curriculum guide. Consequently, information about art activities should be written in the same style as the guide; its proposed location in the guide should be properly indicated; and any necessary holes for loose-leaf notebooks should be prepunched. These details may sound unnecessary, but such things usually determine the difference between using and not using printed materials.

Staff meetings. Some supervisors use staff meetings to provide information and instruction relevant to the art program. But as a method of in-service education, the faculty meeting is the least popular with classroom teachers. The situation is usually too formal and too closely associated with the unpleasant aspects of everyday work. Yet the supervisor might use such a meeting to present some new, major innovation like a curriculum guide, a newsletter, of the announcement of a workshop. It is wise, however, to keep the presentation very short, and to supplement it with further information elsewhere.

Exhibits. More will be said about exhibits later on, but we make a special point of mentioning them here because they are not used as extensively as they might be in the in-service education of teachers. It takes time to arrange them, of course, but once an exhibit has been assembled it can be used over and over.

Any good display is instructive and inspiring, but the best exhibit for improving instruction is one that is intended for that purpose. Such a display might describe the characteristics of symbolic development or the procedure for carrying out a new art project. Sometimes it is worthwhile to show work completed before and after a good job of teaching, because it helps teachers to see clearly the effects of superior instruction. In any case, it is especially important to indicate the level at which the work was produced and to label everything clearly.

Exhibits for teachers are quite appropriate during an orientation period just prior to the opening of school. They are effective at teacher's professional meetings, and they are very useful as visual aids to workshop education. More extensive use of them should be made.

Visiting authorities. Guest speakers or consultants always add variety and a sense of reality to in-service education in art. They give teachers, as well as children, more of a feeling for the artist as a human being who makes important contributions to society.

Speakers might be invited to appear for PTA meetings, staff meetings, workshops, assemblies, high school career meetings, or individual classes at both the elementary and secondary level. Whenever speakers can be obtained, it is most advisable to have them talk directly with students; this does not minimize the educative effect that they have on teachers.

Persons who might be utilized as speakers or consultants are advertising designers, industrial designers, interior decorators, dress designers, architects, landscape architects, city planners, art historians, museum directors, illustrators, medical artists, sign

587

painters, display artists, fine artists (painters, sculptors, etc.), and art teachers.

Reading materials and audio-visual aids. The supervisor has not provided a full range of in-service education if he fails to supply each school with a selected professional library of reading materials on art education. The teachers' lounge or a restricted section of the library might be an appropriate place.

In addition to providing reading materials, the supervisor should see that the school system owns (or rents at appropriate times) slides, films, and filmstrips that are meant for the education of teachers and parents. A visual aid that covers any aspect of art will be useful as an in-service aid to the education of teachers, but a few films that deal specifically with teaching will be especially helpful.

MANAGING EQUIPMENT AND SUPPLIES

The educational program in any school system is revealed in financial form by the budget, and administrators are continually attempting to evaluate the various aspects of their programs as a basis for allocating available funds. Consequently, the supervisor must work diligently to develop, implement, and promote a first-rate program in art education. If he is successful, he still may find that he incurs administrative opposition with his requests for equipment and supplies. This is most probable if his requests are large and unexplained. Thus it is important for him to give careful attention to the proposed expenditures of his department, so that he can justify the need for them and show that they are economically sound. To do this he must be familiar with prices, with inventories, with the rate of consumption, with the local distribution of supplies, and with the care of materials. He must know how much material is required for a minimal but sufficient program in art, and he must make every effort to save money by carefully studying the quality of his materials and his purchasing procedure.

In 1957, an educational cost analysis of thirty Illinois school districts indicated that instructional expenses for salaries and materials exceeded all other costs (general control, operation and maintenance).[4] But the study also showed that, although the cost of salaries and materials had nearly quadrupled since 1935, salaries were being allotted a smaller proportion of the budget than in 1935, and materials were receiving a larger proportion. Despite the possibility that the trend may have changed since 1955, there is no denying that an increase in expenditures for materials is apt to affect the funds available for teachers' salaries. Again, this means that the supervisor, for his own good, must exhibit thrift in purchasing and using art supplies.

As we all know, many administrators place an emphasis upon the use of scrap materials in the art program. Without a doubt their views are based upon economic considerations, but they insist that a good art teacher can develop a good art program with junk. Teachers customarily admit that a few worthwhile art experiences can involve scrap materials, but certain essential experiences in art can only be enjoyed with purchased equipment and materials. After all, there is no substitute for paint, colored paper, brushes, and similar supplies. Consequently, we shall turn our attention to budgets, supplies, and equipment.

The budget

Occasionally we hear administrators speak of the art budget in terms of a lump sum. They may say that there is $3,000 or $5,000 to spend on art supplies, but such figures do not indicate the adequacy of the funds. It is much more meaningful to speak of the amount spent per pupil, because a budget of $5,000 is obviously more generous for 1,000 students than it is for 10,000 students. Furthermore, the number of youngsters being served should be figured on the basis of enrollment rather than average daily attendance. If the average daily attendance is 10,000, a

---

[4] William P. McLure, *Educational Cost Analysis*, Bureau of Educational Research, University of Illinois, Urbana, 1957, pp. 20–22.

budget of $5,000 will provide less than 50 cents per pupil because it will have to serve more than 10,000 persons.

Studies of art expenditures have been made, but they are rare. In 1952, Elizabeth J. Foster made a study of basic costs per pupil for an effective art program in the first to sixth grades. We do not know what was considered an "effective art program," but the data were gathered from ten selected cities in Indiana. The average expenditure per child for art materials in the ten cities was $3.20. The city with the lowest art budget spent $1.34 per child, while the city with the highest art budget spent $5.32 per child.[5]

In 1956, the state director of art education in Illinois, William Bealmer, conducted a survey to determine art budgets.[6] He found that the *mean*, or average, disbursement for art materials was $1.21 per pupil, but the range of expenditure was from 30 cents to $6.00 per student. Like the Indiana survey, this one was conducted at the elementary school level. Any account of art costs at the secondary level should be given separately because not all secondary school youngsters participate in the art program. Furthermore, the costs per pupil being served at that level are apt to be higher because the materials and equipment are quite different and more expensive. High school students, for example, might be furnished with potter's wheels, gas kilns, jewelry equipment, welding tools, silk screens, and other costly items.

In 1962, the Research Division of the National Education Association conducted a survey of music and art programs in the elementary and secondary schools of the United States. The results, published in 1963, do not provide us with an account of art expenditures in the elementary schools, but they do show how much was being spent in secondary schools for consumable art supplies. The *median* disbursement per pupil enrolled in art was $3.72, a modest sum indeed when you consider that a box

[5] Elizabeth J. Foster, *A Study of Basic Costs Per Pupil for an Effective Art Program in Grades One to Six*, The Related Arts Service, New York, 1952, p. 11.
[6] William Bealmer, *Art Education Resource Guide No. 4*, Office of Public Instruction, Springfield, Illinois, 1959, p. 8.

of watercolors in 1962 cost 90 cents, a tube of inexpensive cadmium red oil paint cost $1.40, and a box of twelve good pastels cost $1.40.[7]

Some school systems could not provide the NEA Research Division with information about art expenditures because such items were not given a separate listing in the budget. This is evidence that more school districts are gaining extra flexibility in their budgets by doing away with fixed allotments of funds to separate departments. They know that expenditures in any department will vary from year to year depending upon enrollment and upon the need to replace or add equipment. If the art department happens to need an electric kiln in a year when another department needs less than usual, the kiln may be purchased if the school system has a flexible budget. But if the art department has a fixed budget, it may take a year or more before the kiln can be obtained, even if sufficient funds are available and unused in the allotment to another department in the school system.

Despite the interesting information that has been obtained on art expenditures, we still do not know how much money per pupil is required for an adequate but unpretentious program in art. Surveys have not indicated the quality of the art programs whose costs have been studied, or if quality has been mentioned, the criteria for judging it have not been provided. Furthermore, it is difficult to determine actual expenditures because some communities do not furnish all art supplies to their students. Some of them require the children to furnish their own materials, and others charge an art laboratory fee. But if an accurate figure could be obtained on art expenditures, it would be helpful to an art supervisor as an index of his own efficiency. Naturally the figure would vary from year to year with fluctuating costs, but once it was obtained, it could be adjusted in accordance with current prices.

[7] Prices were obtained from a Dick Blick catalogue for 1961–62. The prices were lower when materials were ordered in quantity, but the figures provide some indication of how far $ 3.72 would go in purchasing materials in 1962.

Ordering supplies and equipment

Supplies are materials that last for less than three years, but equipment lasts for more than three years. When the time for ordering such items arrives each year, the supervisor is responsible for seeing that an accurate inventory is taken of materials and equipment. Then, using the order for the previous year as a guide, he tries to determine how much must be purchased to meet the needs for the next school year. He consults classroom teachers to see if there are any special materials that they would like to have, and he reviews the requests of secondary school art teachers. When the art department agrees on the items to be purchased, an order form is carefully prepared and submitted to the proper administrator, who is usually the business assistant to the superintendent of schools. The name, quantity, and price of each item should be furnished, as well as the name of the company that sells it. Appropriate catalogues should be given to the business manager, and the pages on which certain items appear should be indicated.

If the business manager is not provided with the necessary information, he might order the wrong things. But it is not impossible for him to ignore the best instructions and order an inferior product to save money or time. When that occurs, the supervisor must register a firm complaint. If the supervisor has done his job well, the business manager will not be able to buy comparable merchandise at a lower cost, and the supervisor must make this clear. But how does a supervisor, especially a new one, prepare an order that he can defend?

If the art program is new, the supervisor probably will not have the art request from the previous year upon which to base his estimate of material needs. In that case he is advised to consult almost any school supply catalogue. Most of them contain charts that show the materials that are required for youngsters in the elementary and secondary school, and they make suggestions about the number to order for a class of a certain size. With a little simple arithmetic, the supervisor can then calculate the total amount he will need and the cost.

Although the school supply catalogues are helpful, the supervisor must examine their recommendations carefully. Sometimes they suggest materials that are not essential for a good art program, such as sets for textile stenciling; or they might recommend a paper cutter for each classroom or a box of watercolors for each child. Desirable as those items may be, their cost might be too much to bear in one year. As a result the supervisor might decide that a paper cutter and enough watercolors for two classes be kept in a central storage area in each elementary school. Such an arrangement permits the sharing of certain expensive items for a few years until a more extensive inventory can be built up. In fact, the sharing of any item is to be encouraged if it does not interfere with the business of teaching.

If possible, the supervisor should test the materials that he intends to buy before he submits his request, because the material with the lowest price is not necessarily the most economical to buy. It may lack the color, the strength, the erasability, or the lasting quality of the higher-priced material. On the other hand, the more expensive items do not necessarily constitute wise purchases either. A lot depends upon the youngsters for whom the materials are intended. It would be a waste of money, for example, to buy high-quality white drawing paper for the kindergarten or first grade, where youngsters normally need a large quantity of absorbent paper. Newsprint and lightweight manila would be more satisfactory and less expensive.

A complete list of appropriate art materials for the elementary and secondary school would be too long to discuss here, but it does seem fitting to give some attention to the items for which we spend the most money. The Indiana study by Elizabeth Foster indicated that more money was spent (in the elementary school) for paper, paint, and crayons than for any other supplies.[8] Since the largest expenditure was for paper, the kinds of paper that are normally used are listed on pages 594–596.

[8] Foster, *op. cit.*, p. 10.

1. *Newsprint* — This is the most inexpensive paper available, unless the supervisor chooses to use old newspapers covered with print. Unused newsprint is especially good for painting in the kindergarten and in the first and second grades, where the children use large quantities of paper. Its absorbent quality helps to reduce the puddling and running of tempera when painting, and the paper can also be used for drawing and printing. In the secondary school it is used extensively for sketching. It comes in a variety of sizes, but the most useful are 12 by 18 inches and 18 by 24 inches.

2. *Manila drawing paper* — This is the next most inexpensive and most widely used paper. It comes in several weights, and the lighter weights are the flimsiest. Light, flimsy paper is perfectly acceptable in the first and second grades, but the heavier weights are required for older children because the permanency of the final product is more important to older youngsters. Manila paper continues to be used quite extensively in the junior and senior high school. The most popular and most useful sizes are 12 by 18 inches and 18 by 24 inches, because they fit standard desks and tables most satisfactorily.

3. *White drawing paper* — This paper is used if white color is desired and if the work to be done warrants a better grade of paper. The lightweight variety is again acceptable in the lower grades, but a paper that will not take erasing is to be avoided. The 12- by 18-inch and 18- by 24-inch sizes are the handiest. This paper is used extensively for drawing and painting, but it is quite versatile, and it can be used with a variety of media.

4. *Colored construction paper* — This is expensive, and it should be used and stored with care. The weight to buy is about equal to that of heavy manila. It comes in a variety of colors, but the eight basic colors are usually enough. The supervisor might buy a few packages of the more unusual colors for special occasions. It can be used with tempera, chalk, charcoal, and printing inks, and it is employed in paper sculpture and bulletin board displays.

Teachers like to use this paper more than any other. The 12- by 18-inch size has more possibilities for application than any other size, but the 18- by 24-inch size is useful for painting.

5. *Poster paper* — This lightweight colored paper is especially suitable for cutting and pasting. Many teachers feel that it is superior to construction paper for that purpose. The most useful size is 12 by 18 inches.

6. *Bogus paper* — This is a heavy (80-pound) gray paper with a textured surface that lends itself to painting and to drawing with chalk and charcoal.

7. *Kraft paper* — This is indispensable at any level in the public school. It comes in rolls that are 36 inches wide, and it is best at a 40-pound or 60-pound weight. The heavier weight can take a lot of punishment before it tears. It can be used for many things, including murals, scenery, desk covers, and floor covers. It comes in sheets (24 by 36 inches) as well as rolls. The sheets are very convenient if each child is to have paper of the same size.

8. *Finger-paint paper* — This is of some use in the nursery school, kindergarten, and first grade if it is heavy in weight. Sheets that are 16 by 22 inches are most convenient. Glazed shelf paper can be used as a substitute however, and some manufacturers sell finger paint that does not require special paper.

9. *Tracing paper* — This paper is easier to use (for preparing linoleum blocks, etc.) if it is purchased in packages rather than rolls. Onionskin is a perfectly acceptable substitute.

10. *Oak tag* — This is the stiff, cream-colored paper from which manila folders are made, and it comes in several weights. The 150-pound weight is quite adaptable. It can be used for stencils, signs, folders, and three-dimensional constructions. Its main virtue is its stiffness. The sizes most frequently used are 12 by 18 inches, 18 by 24 inches, and 24 by 36 inches.

11. *Illustration board (white pebbled finish)* — This board is used primarily for matting work that is to be exhibited. It is expensive and must be used wisely. Melton mount also is used for this purpose. Usually it is best to order the large sizes and cut them to order.

12. *Newsboard or chipboard* — This is a heavy gray cardboard that has many uses. It is employed in folders, constructions, models, and displays. It also can serve as a desk cover and as a moveable surface for papier-mâché and clay work. A 28-by 34-inch size is common.

13. *Special papers* — The supervisor will also find it helpful to have a variety of special papers on hand. Glazed, metallic, crepe, colored cellophane, oragami, and colored tissue papers are always useful. Wallpaper sample books are also handy, and at the secondary level there will be a special need for charcoal paper, detail paper, oatmeal paper, watercolor paper, printing papers, and a variety of other special items.

According to Elizabeth Foster the material for which the second largest sum is spent is paint.[9] Most of our money goes for tempera and watercolor paints, but a certain amount is spent for finger paint and oils. What should be considered in buying these paints?

1. *Powdered tempera or poster paint* — This is the most widely used paint in the elementary school, but it is not as suitable for the secondary school. It comes in a number of different qualities, and the supervisor usually profits from testing it. The *undesirable* varieties will not cover as much surface as the better kinds, and the poor types are apt to cover unevenly, show streaks of different colors, rub off, or dry in light and dark patches. Powdered tempera is sometimes a bit difficult to mix, but it helps to start the

[9] *Ibid.*

mixing with a small amount of water and add more water when the mixture becomes smooth and wet. Although it is a little troublesome to mix, it is more inexpensive than ready-mixed paint. This makes it suitable for the elementary school where a large quantity of tempera is used each year. It comes in many different colors, but it is most important to have red, yellow, blue, green, orange, purple, brown, black, and white. Black and white are consumed more rapidly than the other colors, and brown and purple are used the least.

2. *Liquid tempera paint* — Jars of this paint are available in sizes that contain from three-quarters of an ounce to one gallon. Because it is better and more expensive than powdered tempera, it is used most frequently at the secondary level, where the students need paint of higher quality. Usually it pays to buy the paint in large jars, but they should not be given to students who are apt to forget about replacing the caps. Once it dries up, it is hard to recondition. Consequently, many teachers buy the large jars to save money and then pour the paint into syrup dispensers, plastic catsup containers, or other small jars for the students to use. When comparing liquid tempera paints, the supervisor should make the same tests that he does for powdered tempera. He should check the relative strength of the color, and he should be sure that there is no cracking, flaking-off, or glossiness when dry.

3. *Watercolor paint* — It pays to buy a good quality of watercolor from an established company. In the elementary school it is used quite often from the third to the sixth grade. It is more suitable for the secondary school, however, because younger students tend to use it like opaque tempera paint (which is more inexpensive). At any rate, the watercolor that is most useful in the public schools is the kind that comes in metal or plastic boxes. The metal boxes are more apt to rust. Although it comes in boxes of sixteen colors, an eight color container is sufficient. The paint should be smooth and free from grit. It should produce a wash without specks or streaks and dissolve readily enough

that a full brush of color can be picked up. It is equally important that the color buttons be shaped so that the paint can be completely removed. If the color in the buttons cannot all be used, the supervisor is losing money.

4. *Finger paint* — The use of finger paint is justified in kindergarten and the primary grades because it adds variety to the art program. But it is not the best medium for children to use in producing art because its tactile quality is distracting. It comes in moist or powder form, and in most cases it must be used on finger-paint paper or glossy paper. Some of the new varieties, however, can be used on any paper—an obvious advantage. Some teachers save money by making their own finger paint. The easiest method is to add powdered tempera paint to a quart jar of heavy, cold starch. A quart is enough for a class of thirty children if a heaping tablespoon of starch is placed on each paper. The best results are usually obtained with dark colors.

5. *Oil paints* — These paints are used occasionally at the high school level, but they are expensive and must be used with care. The most inexpensive brands are usually good enough. They can be used on shellacked illustration board if canvas, canvas boards, or other materials are too expensive for the budget.

Elizabeth Foster indicates that the material for which the third largest amount of money is spent is crayons.[10] There are several different types that are useful in the public schools.

1. *Wax crayons* — Crayons are used extensively throughout the elementary school because they are easily managed by young children and provide inexpensive color. Crayons should *not* be weak in color, waxy, gritty, or bendable. They should cover the paper evenly without streaks and without piling up. Boxes that contain eight colors are perfectly adequate, but money can often be saved by purchasing the crayons in bulk without the

10 *Ibid.*

cardboard boxes. Other containers can be used for storage in the child's desk (cloth bags with drawstrings or hard-cover cigarette containers).

Many teachers feel that large kindergarten crayons are best in the primary grades, but this writer feels that they are too large and clumsy. The child who wishes to color a small area cannot do it with such a big instrument.

2. *Oil crayons* — These crayons contain a certain amount of oil that allows a shading and blending that cannot be obtained with wax crayons. The color is also more intense, but the crayon does not last quite as long as the wax variety and is not as clean to handle. As a result, oil crayons are used more successfully in the upper elementary grades and in the secondary school.

3. *Pressed crayons* — These crayons are not so widely used as others, but they are excellent for children in the upper elementary grades and in secondary school. They are made with a clay base and with heavy pigmentation. They are hard; they last longer than wax or oil crayons; they do not smudge easily, although they blend nicely; and they can be erased.

The Foster report shows that two-thirds of the average art budget goes for paper, paint, and crayons, while the remaining third is spent on clay, chalk, paste, brushes, and miscellaneous materials.[11] What can be said about the items that consume the remaining third of the budget?

1. *Chalk* — The chalk discussed here is the kind used for drawing, but not the type used on chalkboards. It should be strong in color and free from grittiness. It should blend nicely when rubbed with a paper stump and should be strong enough to resist breaking in ordinary use. Chalk is not especially popular with teachers because it rubs off on clothing, colors moist little hands, and powders onto the desk and floor. Yet it is an excellent

[11] *Ibid.*

art medium, especially for use above the fifth grade, because it facilitates shading more readily than tempera paint. If a good quality of chalk is used, as well as good paper, it will not powder excessively.

2. *Oil modeling clay* — Teachers generally prefer a clay that contains oil for kindergarten and the first and second grades because it is clean and does not require as much preparation and care as ordinary clay. It stays in working condition indefinitely and can be used over and over again. In cold weather it sometimes hardens, but it can be softened again with a little heat. Too much heat, however, tends to remove the oil. It is more expensive than ordinary clay flour, so it is good to protect it by keeping it in a container with a lid. It also helps to order only one color, so that a gruesome mixture of hues cannot be made. Naturally, the finished product cannot be fired.

3. *Clay flour* — This clay can be purchased in powdered form or mixed with water. If you buy it moist, you will be paying shipping charges on water, but the moist variety does save the effort of mixing. Children can mix it themselves, however, by filling a plastic bag about half full of clay, adding water, squeezing out the air, placing a rubber band around the top, and kneading the mixture right in the bag. Mixing larger quantities alone and without the proper equipment is more difficult, but it can be done in a garbage can or crock. If a sidewalk is available, the dry clay can be poured out, sprinkled with water and raked until it reaches the right consistency; then it can be picked up and kept in plastic bags. This clay will dry hard. It can be fired in a kiln and be glazed or painted. Glazing would seem to be an unnecessary expense, however, because painting the clay is just as effective aesthetically and gives the children more control over the appearance of the end product.

4. *Brushes* — In the kindergarten and primary grades, bristle or easel brushes are the most satisfactory; they are most useful in one-quarter or one-half inch widths. After all, one cannot

paint a little, lovable ladybug with a 1-inch brush. But a few wide ones are helpful for big painting jobs.

Camel's hair brushes are most necessary from the third grade upward, because older youngsters make more details in their paintings. Consequently, they need a brush that comes to a point. If it does not do so, it is not a good hair brush. Both easel and hair brushes are better if they are made with seamless ferrules that hold the bristles and hairs tightly. And it is equally important to buy a brush with a handle that cannot be twisted into pretzel shapes by inventive youngsters who forget how difficult it is to put a pretzel into a watercolor box. As far as size is concerned, hair brushes in sizes 5, 7, and 10 are perfectly adequate for the public schools. Inexpensive shellac, stencil and oil-painting brushes (secondary level) are also useful.

5. *Scissors* — Five-inch scissors of good quality are indispensable. They come with round or sharp points, and the latter are much less frustrating. The supervisor should make sure that left-handed scissors are available for those who need them.

6. *Paste and glue* — Ordinary school paste is another necessity, but it should not be dry or flaky. If strong bonds or quick-drying adhesives are necessary, the teacher should be supplied with rubber cement, vegetable or fish glues, airplane cement, and plastic glue. In the intermediate grades, wallpaper paste is needed for papier-mâché.

7. *Wood and wood tools* — Wood for the elementary school can usually be obtained in scrap form from lumberyards. Supplemented by spools, broom handles, dowels, cigar boxes, and other wooden materials, the scrap is perfectly satisfactory. The woodworking tools should include vises, backsaws, jigsaws, hand drills, coping saws, hammers, nails, screws, screwdrivers, wood clamps, and sandpaper.

8. *Yarn and string* — In both the elementary and secondary school it is necessary to have rug yarn, knitting yarn, and carpet

warp for weaving, stitchery, and rug hooking. In the primary grades, youngsters will have more success if they weave with cotton roving. All yarns come in a variety of colors and are fairly expensive, so they should be used sparingly.

9. *Cloth* — Stitchery, appliqué, collage, and other activities require cloth. Perhaps the most useful materials for such purposes are burlap, muslin, and monk's cloth, together with scraps of all kinds. Burlap comes in a variety of grades and colors, and it should be examined carefully for strength and texture before it is purchased. Two-thread monk's cloth is highly recommended for rug hooking.

10. *Other tools and materials* — The teacher also will find it necessary to have rulers, knives, thread, needles, pins, linoleum, printing ink, brayers, linoleum-cutting tools, masking tape, brown kraft-paper tape, lettering pens, India ink, shellac, denatured alcohol, staplers, paper clips, turpentine, pliers, tin snips, pipe cleaners, looms, paper cutters, tongue depressors, aluminum foil, paper cups, newspaper, paper bags, plastic bags, sponges, cotton, tin cans, wire, string, sand, plaster, inner tubes, ribbon, shoe boxes, and cardboard boxes.

The alert supervisor will agree that many more materials can and should be used in the elementary school. He will also agree that a high school program requires far more in the way of supplies and equipment, but many of the necessary items are expensive. But figures are not available to indicate where we spend most of our money at the high school level. Our comments about elementary school supplies, however, should be sufficient to encourage careful selection at any level.

PROFESSIONAL OBLIGATIONS

If the art supervisor wishes to maintain an outstanding art program, he must keep himself up-to-date on ideas, research, and other developments in the profession. This means that he should visit other school systems, visit museums, read professional publications, and attend professional meetings. But some art educators neglect these duties and remain cheerfully undisturbed and self-confident in their ivory classrooms. A few may read books and magazines on art, and they may go on an occasional pilgrimage to museums and galleries. When they do, they certainly are making a partial attempt to better themselves. Yet many of the same persons fail to read anything about art education, and they fail to attend professional conferences. Why do they neglect such matters?

One reason for such neglect is that some teachers wish to be pictured as artists and connoisseurs rather than as educators. And they feel that a cultured image, like a cultured pearl, is not apt to grow in the wrong environment. The odd part of it is that most artists cannot avoid being art educators, even if they want to, because it is the only way that most of them can earn a living. It would therefore seem wise to swallow one's image and meet with other art educators in an effort to improve the common lot.

But the desire to maintain an artistic image is not the only thing that keeps people from exposing themselves to the professional organs of art education. Some art teachers who are deeply committed to education avoid the literature and conferences in their field because they feel that the content of both leaves something to be desired. What they fail to understand is that improvement can hardly be made if those who recognize the need for better conventions stay home and ceremoniously cancel their subscriptions to professional journals.

Reading the literature and attending conferences are professional obligations because they are means of self-improvement and because in the long run they are two of the best ways to better the whole profession on a national scale. We realize that an uninformed but intuitive and capable art supervisor can do a lot to raise the quality of art education in his local community. But we also know that he is likely to accomplish a whole lot more by keeping himself informed and by accepting the support of a strong professional organization. Five thousand voices are usually more persuasive than one.

It should also be noted that mere reading and mere attendance at business and cultural events are not enough to satisfy the need for excellence in art education at either the local or national level. If the profession is to improve, its members must participate *actively* in its affairs. They must write articles as well as read them, and they must respond to ideas publicly as well as privately. They must give speeches, participate in discussions, conduct research, produce works of art, and contribute to our knowledge and understanding in any other way that they can. Smiling, nodding, and shaking the head, however, are not forms of active participation, and neither is clapping, waving the fist, or expressing disgust to a companion. Reminiscences and curiously irrelevant remarks in scheduled presentations are not especially conducive to excellence either, although they might be classified as a kind of verbal activity.

Perhaps the lowest level of truly active and useful participation in the business of art education begins with asking significant questions about some aspect of the profession. Yet many of us feel that we are meeting our professional obligations if we devote most of our conference time to raising questions. It is difficult to criticize such a display of curiosity because it is important to point to the things we still have to learn about art education. The trouble is that we need more persons to give answers. We know so little about the teaching of art that questions about it are relatively easy to formulate. It is the answers that stump us. Consequently, all art educators have a professional obligation to think of *answers* to the questions that stare them in the face. They have the further obligation to make their thoughts known through contributions to the literature and through presentations at conferences. It does no good to go home and argue a cause with your wife, unless she happens to be influential in education; but it does help to present your views in a recognized professional forum.

Having presented his views and argued their merits in the proper meetings and publications, the art supervisor should abide by the considered opinion of the profession (if it can be obtained). If he does not accept and uphold the position of the profession as a whole, he serves to divide the group and weaken it. All the members of the American Medical Association may not agree with the expressed decisions of their organization, but they abide by those decisions. The resultant unity gives the group the strength it needs, but it does not prevent individual members from continuing to battle for the acceptance of their views within the organization.

Art education, however, seldom presents a unified front. Individual teachers feel no obligation to abide by the decisions of national organizations. As a consequence, the group loses its effectiveness. As an illustration, consider the reaction to a statement by the National Committee on Art Education condemning art contests for youngsters in the public schools.[12] Hundreds of teachers refused to accept the position of the committee and continued to endorse contests. The result was a blow to group effectiveness.

Cases of this kind cause national art organizations to refrain from taking a stand on anything, because failure emphasizes their ineffectiveness. But the ineffectiveness of the group merely reflects the lack of professional loyalty and the absence of professional obligation on the part of individual members. This is one of the great weaknesses in art education. The conscientious art supervisor should not contribute to the propagation of it.

PUBLIC RELATIONS

If the quality of art education is to grow and develop, people must feel that it is sufficiently worthwhile to receive their support. To decide that it is valuable they must have information about its accomplishments. This means that the art supervisor must maintain a public relations program for the purpose of keeping

---

[12] National Committee on Art Education, "Contests and Competitions," mimeographed digest of a discussion held at the Museum of Modern Art, New York, May, 1959.

his community informed.[13] Some supervisors, however, are reluctant to undertake public relations because they dislike persons who "blow their own horns." But there is a difference between giving information and bragging. The latter usually concerns the personal accomplishments of the teacher, whereas information about the art program presented in a factual manner is actually a kind of public service that permits the community to make better decisions about education.

Information can be provided through newspaper articles, radio announcements, television announcements, exhibits, posters, demonstrations, leaflets, newsletters, magazine articles, and speeches. It should reach all the people, including teachers, administrators, and children. In fact, school children are usually our best salesmen. If they are satisfied, happy, and enthusiastic about art activities, you can be sure that their parents will know it.

Some school systems assign a staff member to the job of preparing news releases for the mass media. This is a good idea because it tends to improve the relationship with newspapers, radio, and television by increasing efficiency. A person who regularly acts as liaison between the school and the mass media is much more capable of preparing the news in a way that is both convenient and useful. If such a person is not employed by the school system, the supervisor must find out how to prepare his news releases in an acceptable fashion. He must also find out how much advance notice is required if his information is to be announced by the media on a certain date. After all, the news must be adjusted to the schedules of writers, commentators, and photographers and to the space and time available. Sometimes the public information media are reluctant to give coverage to events that have already taken place. Consequently, an early annoucement to the media of a coming event will give them an opportunity to decide if the event should be covered before or after it has passed.

[13] For many of the ideas on improving public relations presented here, the writer is indebted to Fred G. Attebury of Wayne State University.

There are many things that would be appropriate for public announcement in the mass media. Exhibitions, art club activities, field trips, awards, public demonstrations of art activities, displays, speeches to parent-teacher and civic organizations, the visit of an artist, innovations in the art program, and outstanding work by students are a few examples of interesting news that should be released to the public. If an exhibit should prove to be especially nice, it would be worth the effort to ask that a qualified person review the show, and the supervisor could offer to accompany the reviewer for purposes of providing information and helping with photographs. As any public relations man knows, photographs give the news an added punch, so their use should be encouraged whenever possible.

Exhibits are, of course, a means of informing the public about the art program, even if they are not covered by the mass media. Exhibits can be set up in the public shools, in bank lobbies, in department store windows, in civic centers, in local museums, at county fairs, or in any building that is visited by large numbers of people. An alert supervisor might get in touch with his local chamber of commerce to see if a vacant building could be used for the purpose, or he might ask local contractors if he could place outstanding student work in model homes.

Any exhibit that is meant for the public should be carefully planned. Display units should be constructed so that they show the work to advantage, and they should be sturdy units that can be used again and again in a variety of locations. If they are not adaptable, they are not especially good.

Most supervisors are qualified to put up an attractive exhibit, so they do not need a lecture on pleasing arrangement. But they do need to remember that a crowded presentation is not desirable, even if there is an urge to show the work of as many youngsters as possible. Naturally we want to show the work of many students, but a crowded arrangement simply does not convey the impression that good taste will be developed in art classrooms, and it does not allow the high quality of individual works to be perceived. Therefore, it is better to have several exhibits than to have one crowded one.

In addition to proper spacing, an exhibit should be arranged with an educational point of view in mind, and the point should be made clear with short, explanatory statements mounted in appropriate places. The supervisor might wish to show the artistic development that occurs over a period of time, or he might want to show the procedure used in making a silk-screen print, a papier-mâché mask, or a stenciled fabric. He might wish to point out the variety of stylistic features in student work or to emphasize the wide variety of art media used by the students. If printed explanations do not make important points sufficiently clear, arrows can be used to point to significant things and students or art teachers can provide guided tours.

Exhibits that simply present representative work by elementary, junior high, or high school youngsters are especially informative when they are circulated from school to school within the community. As students and teachers become aware of art activities at more advanced grade levels, they are more apt to include art courses in their plans for the future. And high school students are educated in the ways of young children when they are permitted to see exhibitions of work from the elementary school. This is important because many high school students are planning for teaching careers, and they are sure to take a serious interest in the work of young children.

Youngsters and their parents are also interested in the accomplishments of teachers. They like to feel that instructors are capable people, and for that reason, an exhibit of creative work by art teachers is usually well received. Parents and interested citizens have even been known to buy paintings and sculpture from such exhibits for themselves and for the school system.

Public demonstrations of art activities are probably as helpful as exhibits in presenting information to the community. Throwing pots on the potter's wheel, sculptural techniques, graphics, drawing, painting and many other activities can be demonstrated at PTA meetings or in any of the locations that were previously listed as being appropriate for exhibits. Demonstrations always provide an attraction because people like to observe art in the making. It is something they rarely see, and they are fascinated by it. In fact, hundreds of people have been drawn to the making of pottery as a result of watching demonstrations.

Organizing exhibits and demonstrations for the PTA and for service groups like the Kiwanis Club or the Rotary Club has been suggested, for the reason that such organizations are made up of persons with community spirit and civic pride. They are interested in schools and in helping the youth of the community to receive the best education possible. In many instances these organizations award scholarships to deserving students who need financial aid, and they offer important encouragement to administrators in adding art facilities to new buildings or in expanding the art curriculum. Consequently, students, teachers, or supervisors should be well prepared when they appear before such groups to speak, exhibit, or demonstrate. People who are serious enough to join service organizations are people who respect a person who knows his business and shows his knowledge through a businesslike presentation. Finally, it helps to invite the members of such groups to the school so that they can get a look at the art program in action.

Information about the art department can be given to more parents by issuing an occasional mimeographed leaflet that can be taken home by students. This is especially important if a field trip is being arranged or if outside work will be required for a certain art project. The leaflet might explain the itinerary of a proposed trip and the spending money that will be required, or it might explain the hours during which children will be decorating store windows and building scenery. In short, a leaflet often can save parents from the unfortunate experience of receiving garbled or erroneous information from a youngster whose skill at verbal communication is not always topnotch.

News about the art department can be sent to teachers, administrators, and children through the regular art department newsletter, through assemblies, or over the public address system found in many new schools. But it is especially important to see that the administration knows what is going on. The annual report is vital of course, but the administrator should also be informed of current happenings. The art supervisor should make sure that principals, superintendents, and curriculum coordinators see exhibits and demonstrations, and he should point out the purposes behind the shows as well as any nuances that might be overlooked.

The supervisor is also urged to offer student works of art as decorative appointments in corridors and administrative offices. Drawings, paintings, pottery, and prints provide a little of the elegance that institutional architecture so rarely enjoys.

As a final suggestion, it is certainly desirable to promote the good will and respect of other subject-matter specialists in the school system, and this can be done while improving public relations. It would be a fine idea, for example, to invite the home economics and industrial arts departments to cooperate with the art department in arranging an exhibit or to design the covers for dramatic and musical programs, or it would also be a good idea to invite the English department to write the script for a puppet show. The cooperation could take place within a single school or between the high school and the elementary school. Once again we mean to suggest that great things can be accomplished if all subject-matter areas and all levels of the school system work together.

EVALUATION

It is the art supervisor's ultimate responsibility to see that the growth of our youngsters in art is properly evaluated. We have discussed this problem elsewhere (Chapter 10), but the point to be made here is that evaluative criteria and techniques are subject to change. Esoteric knowledge of one epoch is sometimes common knowledge in the next. As we learn more about ourselves and about our world, we realize that the objectives of education have to be altered and that similar alterations must be made in the curriculum. Consequently, the art supervisor must remain alert to changes in objectives so that he can help to initiate changes in the curriculum and in evaluative criteria.

Developing an adequate method of evaluating growth in art is a difficult and complex job, and the formulation of criteria for judgment is only one of the baffling tasks that confront the educator. He may find that tests and records are necessary to measure growth based on a certain criterion, or he may decide that careful observation is all that is necessary. Decisions of that kind depend upon his objectives. But the adequacy of his decisions, his tests, and his records can be measured through empirical research. This means that an alert supervisor is likely to be involved in on-the-job research of some kind almost continuously.

The need for constant research is emphasized because the growth of youngsters is not the only thing that must be evaluated. Many systems of reporting to parents need careful examination. We need to study our art programs and our teaching methods to make sure we are doing as much as possible for slow learners, for the gifted, the dropouts, the handicapped, and the culturally disadvantaged.

Naturally the growth of our youngsters in art is the ultimate measure of success in education. But we also have to evaluate our programs, our supervisory practices, and our teaching if we are to aid instructors who are not achieving the desired level of artistic competence in their students. Thus the supervisor is confronted with a wide assortment of evaluative problems that demand careful investigation or research. If he does not handle these problems with the care that research requires, he is almost certain to waste his time and place the art program in jeopardy. For that reason it seems fitting that we turn our attention to research in art education.

SUMMARY

This chapter has attempted to describe the duties of an art supervisor and has offered some suggestions for fulfilling those duties. The reader will find that there are differences of opinion regarding the suggestions that have been made—and that is all to the good, as the ensuing debate will perhaps lead to improvements in art education.

The major theme of this chapter, however, is one that should receive the wholehearted support of all art educators. In short, the point is that an art supervisor should act as a leader and not as a faceless individual who behaves largely in response to the ideas and policies generated by others. The art supervisor and his corps of art teachers must take the initiative in developing an art program simply because they are the persons whose training and experience qualify them for the job. If they fail to exert that leadership, art education will come to an end.

QUESTIONS FOR DISCUSSION

1. We have suggested that art educators abide by the decisions of their professional organizations. Can you think of an opposing argument?
2. What is the consultant system? What are the advantages and disadvantages of the consultant system?
3. Assume that you have been asked to begin an art program for the elementary schools (grades one to six) in a small rural community. The enrollment is 1,000 students equally divided among three schools, and the art budget is $ 2,000. There are two classrooms for each grade in each school. What would you include on your list of supplies and equipment? How much would you buy? Why?
4. If a classroom teacher on tenure refused to follow the philosophy of the school system in teaching art, how would you, as the art supervisor, handle that teacher?
5. Interview an art supervisor from a large city; then interview another from a small village. How do their jobs differ? What are the problems that seem most outstanding in each situation?
6. What are the requirements for certification as an art supervisor in your state?
7. What are some of the problems that might arise if an administrator does not give support to the art supervisor?
8. In some communities the recruitment of art teachers is a major problem. What could a supervisor do to aid recruitment?

9. Examine several curriculum guides or courses of study in art. Try to identify their strengths and weaknesses. Consider their value from the classroom teachers point of view as well as from the art teachers point of view.
10. What could a supervisor do to assist in the training of future classroom teachers and art teachers?
11. Supervisors often become involved in the planning of new school buildings. Find all the information that you can on the planning of an art room in the secondary school.
12. Approximately how many art teachers would be needed at the elementary school level if a good art program is desired in a community that has sixteen elementary schools, each containing about three-hundred students? Explain the reasoning that caused you to arrive at your conclusion.
13. What are the names and the characteristics of the professional publications that an art supervisor should read?
14. After reading this chapter, could you make a list of the characteristics that are necessary in a good leader? What are they?

SUGGESTIONS FOR FURTHER READING

Beelke, Ralph G.: "Supervision in Art and the Improvement of Instruction," *Art Education*, Sixty-fourth Yearbook of the National Society for the Study of Education, Part II, University of Chicago Press, Chicago, 1965, pp. 175–200. *This is a comprehensive article on art supervision in contemporary American schools. It tends, however, to be more descriptive than prescriptive.*

Baumgarner, Alice A. D.: "Getting an Art Program in Motion," *This is Art Education,* Kutztown Publishing Co., Kutztown, Pennsylvania, 1951, pp. 105–113. *This article contains some practical suggestions for the implementation of an art program.*

Conant, Howard (ed.): *Art Workshop Leaders Planning Guide*, Davis Publications, Inc., Worcester, Massachusetts, 1958. *A fine booklet on planning workshops.*

Conant, Howard, and Arne Randall: *Art in Education*, Chas. A. Bennett, Co., Inc., Peoria, Illinois, 1959. *This is one of the most practical books available for the beginning teacher.*

De Francesco, Italo: *Art Education: Its Means and Ends*, Harper and Brothers, New York, 1958, pp. 505–557. *One of the few recent textbooks in art education to cover the role of the art supervisor.*

Chapter 12

RESEARCH IN ART EDUCATION

Research has been defined in a variety of ways, but for our purposes we shall call it the pursuit of knowledge through systematic inquiry. Naturally its importance to art education is based on the fact that it can provide additional information about art and the teaching of art.

Since the end of World War II there has been considerable research in art education as compared with previous years. Thomas Munro, Viktor Lowenfeld, Kenneth Beittel, June McFee, Manuel Barkan, Jerome Hausmann, Robert Burkhart, Elliot Eisner, and several others have been among its most enthusiastic supporters; yet a number of art educators remain highly critical.

One of the interesting aspects of the debate about research is that both the favorable and unfavorable comments have centered chiefly around the subject of experimental investigation. Thus an inaccurate impression may have been given regarding the nature of research in art education. Certainly the search for knowledge is not restricted to the experimental system of inquiry. If it is not, what are the other types of scholarly investigation? *615*

TYPES OF RESEARCH

Any typological classification of research is likely to be confusing because there are several ways of classifying it. It is not uncommon, for example, to speak of basic and applied research. Basic research is the kind that may have no immediate practical application, but is pursued simply because it is interesting or challenging. Applied research, on the other hand, is undertaken because of a recognized need.

It is also possible to classify research according to: (1) the field in which it is conducted (physics, psychology, education); (2) the place in which it is conducted (field, laboratory); or (3) the most prominent method of collecting data (historical, experimental). Although this is not an exhaustive list of the various ways to classify research, it does show that the system employed in this chapter is merely one of many.

Using data-gathering techniques as a means of classification, we may say that traditionally there have been about five types of research: historical, philosophical, creative, experimental, and descriptive. *Historical research* is an effort to get accurate information about some aspect of the past, and its purpose might be to help us understand the present and provide for the future. The historical method of gathering data is largely a library method, employing first-hand and second-hand resources or records and occasional archaeological finds. There is no better example of the fruits of such research than the book by Frederick Logan called *The Growth of Art in American Schools.*[1]

Philosophical research is an attempt to achieve truth through the study of metaphysics, epistemology, logic, ethics, and aesthetics. The data for such work consists in principles, laws, rules, theories, hypotheses, inferences, conclusions, judgments, and opinions. It makes use of scientific facts, when possible, but extends beyond them. Again, the philosophical method of securing data is largely a library method plus analysis and experience.

[1]Frederick Logan, *The Growth of Art in American Schools*, Harper and Brothers, New York, 1955.

Such research was employed by John Dewey when he produced his now-famous *Art as Experience*.[2]

Of course, all research is creative, but in art education the term *creative research* refers to the search for truth through the production of forms for aesthetic experience. The making of a painting is an example of this type of inquiry. As a way of obtaining data, it might be called the method of experience in living. Its result is obviously a work of art.

Experimental research, which has received so much attention, is simply an attempt to gain information through controlled trials and operations. Such a method involves doing things under regulated conditions in order to ascertain causes, effects, relationships, and characteristics with the greatest possible precision. The work of Sina Mott is an example of experimental research.[3] By carefully controlling classroom conditions, including stimulation, she was able to show that the movement of body parts brings about a more comprehensive drawing of those parts by children.

As a method of gathering data, *descriptive research* is different because it is actually many methods gathered together for the purpose of obtaining information about the existing nature or status of something. Data may be collected through surveys, case studies, developmental or longitudinal studies, activity analysis, and library work. Tests, interviews, and other devices are frequently employed, depending upon the situation being explored. The work of Helga Eng serves as an example of such research.[4] She studied and collected the creative drawings of her niece for many years in an effort to describe visual symbolic development in children.

While it has been indicated that there are several types of research, it should be understood that accurate and precise description of them is difficult because of the elements they

[2] John Dewey, *Art as Experience*, Minton, Balch and Co., New York, 1934.
[3] Sina Mott. "Muscular Activity an Aid in Concept Formation," *Child Development*, vol. 16, pp. 98–108, March–June, 1945.
[4] Helga Eng, *The Psychology of Child and Youth Drawing*, Routledge and Kegan Paul, Ltd., London, 1957.

frequently have in common. Tests and surveys might be used, for example, in experimental as well as descriptive research, and historians might very well make use of interviews. The purpose in mentioning various types of research is simply to indicate that the heavily criticized experimental system of inquiry is only one of several methods.

CRITICISM OF RESEARCH IN ART EDUCATION

Anyone who has attended professional meetings and read professional periodicals in art education is aware of the condemnation that has been placed upon research. But, despite the criticism, it is significant that the amount of systematic inquiry in art education has increased year by year. Even the U.S. Department of Health, Education, and Welfare is making large sums of money available to persons who are capable of developing acceptable research proposals in the visual arts, and hundreds of projects are under way. There is evidently a widespread recognition of the need for research and a growing body of interested investigators.

Like the research in other professions, some of the completed studies have been well done and some have not. Among the good and the bad are several types of inquiry. Consequently, any comments or criticisms that refer to the sum of the investigations should be offered with great care, for they must apply with fairness and accuracy to all studies and all types of investigation. This has not been done. Praise as well as criticism has been placed, like a blanket, on the total research effort in art education, although most of it should have been leveled at specific experimental or descriptive studies. As a result it has not been accurate or fair. When such generalizations cannot be made with accuracy, then the critic has a duty to be more specific. It is especially unjust to attack the quality of research without being specific about where, when, how, and by whom errors are being made, for such attacks punish those who are doing superior work.

When we act as critics, we should think about another thing: the nature of criticism. Criticism is the "art of judging with knowledge and propriety." Propriety is the quality of being proper, fitting, or suitable. One who judges with propriety maintains decorum. He does not engage in judgments that extend beyond his subject, to questions of the investigator's sincerity, intelligence, achievement, or general character.

Keeping these thoughts in mind, let us examine some of the criticisms that have been leveled at research in art education since World War II. There seem to be about ten of these objections, which are in many respects similar to criticisms that have been made of art education itself.

The *first objection* is that art is too elusive, too subjective, or too personal to yield to systematic investigation. But if art is so individualistic and so intangible, how do we manage to teach it? How do we decide what to say and do to our students? How do we determine if our students are producing art? Surely the fact that we do these things cannot be denied, for art has been taught for hundreds of years, and anything that has been taught for so long a time would seem to be sufficiently objective for systematic study. Furthermore, if things like art are too subjective for investigation, how does a person explain the progress made in psychology? Surely psychology deals with things that are as subjective as art.

One must also remember that research in art education need not and does not deal exclusively with the art process and product. It might, quite legitimately, deal with materials, budgets, curriculum, visual aids, classroom management, art room planning, and other practical problems.

In summary, the idea that art is too personal to serve as a subject of research is not a sound one. If it were accepted, there would be no art history, no aesthetics, and no art. Under such circumstances there would be no need for art education and no call for investigation into the practical matters of teaching.

The *second objection* to research in art education clearly refers to experimental and descriptive methods of inquiry. The criticism is that tools of research (especially statistics) are not compatible with art. In other words, one cannot express emotions, intuitions, and similar elements in mathematical, logical, or scientific terms. That, of course, is true; the concepts and emotions expressed through art cannot be fully expressed in another medium. But no evidence has been provided to indicate that researchers have attempted to restate the meaning of a given work of art, and no evidence has been given to show that the meaning in art has been reduced to statistics. Thus the second objection to research in art education seems as unsound as the first.

The *third objection* is that persons who do research move into the domains of other disciplines where they are not competent. It has been said, for example, that researchers invade such areas as psychology, sociology, and mathematics when they lack ability in those subjects. That is quite probable; the secrets of art are closely associated with matters of a psychological and sociological nature, and mathematics is one of the fundamental tools of research. Consequently, art educators are apt to stray into the domains of those subjects. Being as ill-equipped in such disciplines as outsiders are in art, the average art educator is apt to make mistakes. When such errors occur, the critic has every right to criticize the researcher. But the critic must be able to spell out specific cases of irresponsibility or he has no legitimate ground for complaint. That has not been done.

Nevertheless, students of art education can profit from such accusations of incompetence by making certain that they obtain help from qualified specialists in other disciplines when it becomes necessary to draw upon the knowledge in those areas. The importance of doing so has long been recognized. In fact, it is the primary reason for placing educators, statisticians, psychologists, historians, philosophers, and other specialists on doctoral committees.

Criticism of research is unfounded, however, if it is merely an objection to studies that involve other disciplines. If we did not allow the mixing of disciplines, we would not have astrophysics, biochemistry, art history, industrial design, sociology, cybernetics, psychiatry, or education. We must make use of this knowledge in other academic fields, but we must do so with care.

The *fourth objection* to research is that it might result in a formula for the production of art or the teaching of art. Without a doubt the chance for such an occurrence exists and the consequences might be harmful. But the possibility of developing a formula for teaching exists whether we do research or not. After all, a formula is simply a system for doing something. We have always had systems for drawing, painting, brushing our teeth, or performing other tasks, because the absence of systematic behavior invites chaos or chance behavior. For that reason, formulas or systems for doing things are likely to continue. The important thing for us to do is to make sure that we develop good systems of behavior which are conducive to the full and unique development of the individual in his quest for the good life. The function of research is to help us develop better and better systems, and because research is a carefully reasoned activity, its ability to do so is far better than chance.

A *fifth objection* to research is that the subject of much investigation is insignificant. Again, critics have not directed their comments toward any particular study or studies, but there are undoubtedly subjects that would appear relatively valueless. The trouble is that it is too easy for a person to draw his own personal line between what is significant and what is not; the line frequently indicates personal bias or lack of foresight rather than any separation of the important from the unimportant. In fact, the label of insignificance has been attached to many discoveries in the past, only to be proved wrong later. It is a label that is often attached to basic or pure research because of the fact that a practical application of the results is not immediately apparent. Actually, the value of such research may not be fully appreciated until time has passed and further investigation has taken place.

Perhaps it is natural that we should place the greatest value on research findings that prove to be correct after sufficient replication, but studies that prove to be wrong may also have a certain amount of value. They may provide new ideas or techniques that can be used in later attempts at systematic inquiry, and they may stimulate our thinking. For that reason we need to be cautious about complete condemnation of any scholarly investigation.

The *sixth objection* to research in art education is that researchers are naïve or unsophisticated in art. This objection is probably directed toward experimental and descriptive forms of inquiry, but the instances in which investigators have been naïve is not indicated. As a result the comment could be understood to apply to all research, including painting, drawing, and other forms of creative inquiry. Without a doubt there are painters who are naïve and unsophisticated in art, but that does not mean we should do away with painting. It does not mean that other research should be discontinued either, even if it can be proved that a few researchers are unknowledgeable in art. Thus the criticism of such investigators does not constitute an argument against research; it merely argues for more sophisticated investigators.

The *seventh objection* to research is more specific and more constructive.[5] It refers primarily to experimental studies that require the teaching of art and the evaluation of a finished product. The criticism is that experiments are often conducted without the benefit of stated assumptions about the nature of art and the nature of teaching. As a result the investigator is apt to go through the motions of an activity that he calls teaching without having given careful thought to the question of whether he actually *is* teaching, and if so, whether he is teaching *art*. Furthermore, an accurate evaluation of the final product as a work of art depends upon what the researcher believes art to be. If he has not given careful consideration to the nature of art, his evaluative criteria may measure something other than the artistic quality of the product.

An example of these errors may be found in the writer's own research. He wanted to determine the effect, if any, of

[5] See Kenneth M. Lansing, "A Reaction to Research in Art Education," *Studies in Art Education*, vol. 3, no. 2, pp. 3–5, Spring, 1962.

class size and room size on the drawings of fifth-grade children.[6] Consequently, he arranged to have teachers provide selected stimulations to students and collect the resultant drawings. The drawings were evaluated, and the scores were treated statistically, yielding conclusive data. But the nature of art and of teaching was not given careful consideration through the formulation of definitive statements. Consequently, the so-called teaching involved in the study was little more than stimulation. No concerted effort was made to see that the stimulation was followed by instruction that promoted the creation of art.

In like manner the evaluation of final products was based upon developmental criteria that were not necessarily measures of artistic quality. Under such conditions it would be a mistake to conclude that class size and room size have no effect on child art. No one knows what the result would have been if art had actually been taught and if the evaluation had been based on criteria that measure quality in art.

The *eighth objection* to research in art education deals with the length of time that investigators have provided for the creation of art.[7] In experimental studies such as those conducted by Lansing,[8] Jones,[9] Kendrick,[10] McVitty,[11] Eisner,[12] and many others, children have been required to produce finished visual symbols, called art, within a very short time. Probably the children were not given more than fifty minutes to an hour to complete their work. Apparently researchers have believed it possible by

[6] Kenneth M. Lansing, "The Effect of Class Size and Room Size Upon the Creative Drawings of Fifth Grade Children," *Research in Art Education*. NAEA, Ninth Yearbook, Kutztown Publishing Co., Kutztown, Pennsylvania, 1959.

[7] See Kenneth M. Lansing, "Editorial," *Studies in Art Education*, vol. 4, no. 1, pp. 1–3, Fall, 1962.

[8] Lansing, *op. cit.*

[9] Clyde Jones, "Relationships Between Creative Writing and Creative Drawing of Sixth Grade Children," *Studies in Art Education*, vol. 3, no. 2, pp. 34–43, Spring, 1962.

[10] Dale Kendrick, "The Influence of Teacher Motivation and Non-motivation on the Overall Aesthetic Quality of the 'Whole' and the 'Parts' of Cutpaper Art Products," in *ibid.*, pp. 52–63.

[11] Lawrence F. McVitty, "An Experimental Study on Art Motivation at the Fifth Grade Level," *Research in Art Education*, NAEA, Ninth Yearbook, Kutztown Publishing Co., Kutztown, Pennsylvania, 1956, pp. 74–83.

[12] Elliot W. Eisner, "A Typology of Creativity in the Visual Arts," *Studies in Art Education*, vol. 4, no. 1, pp. 11–22, Fall, 1962.

that method to measure accurately such things as creativity, the effects of stimulation, the effects of school environment, and other factors. This raises at least three important questions: (1) Is there any reason to expect an immediate reaction to a stimulus? (2) Is fifty minutes to an hour long enough for each individual to give form to his unique reaction to a stimulus? (3) Is there any reason to assume that an individual will do equally well in all media?

If an experience can have a delayed reaction, if some artists work more slowly than others, and if artists are not necessarily proficient in all media, we can have serious doubts about the research in question. Therefore it would be wise in the future to extend the time allowed for creative behavior and to collect a number of final products for evaluation. Work might be gathered over a whole semester or a year, so that a variety of media could be employed. Such an arrangement would allow instructional techniques, environmental conditions, and student personalities a reasonable length of time to affect visual symbols and works of art.

The *ninth objection* to research in art education is that sufficient attention has not been given to the problem of judging visual symbols. The same criticism could be made of the evaluation that occurs in art classrooms day after day. In both instances, evaluation is one of the keys to success, but it is frequently undertaken without consideration for the nature of art, the adequacy of judgmental criteria, and the ability of the judges.

The first and most important need in research is for a statement about the nature of art. It would allow the investigator to develop criteria capable of separating art from nonart. Once he has accomplished that, he must refine the criteria so that they distinguish between great art and art that is not so great. Then he must train his judges to make evaluations as he would make them himself. The fact that judges might agree with each other is not enough. Their judgments, based on a given criterion, must be in accordance with the intention of the investigator or the results are likely to be misinterpreted. In fact, we might say that the only ability that a judge needs is the ability to evaluate in accordance with the wishes of the person conducting the research.

Beittel[13] and Linderman,[14] among others, have recognized the critical importance of judgment in teaching and research, and their efforts at improving evaluative techniques are steps in the right direction. Beittel points out that judgment in the arts is always relative to something,[15] by which he means that evaluation is relative to such things as time, place, and the personality of the judge. Beittel believes that judgments may suffer from such relativity. But the evaluations made by the investigator in establishing his criteria and by the judges in applying the criteria will not cause serious problems, if the researcher reports the basis for his decisions and shows that the judges are acting in accordance with his wishes. Under such conditions the investigator and his judges are not apt to get away with inconsistent or unreasonable decisions. No, the real danger in research does not come from the making of relative judgments. It comes, instead, from making evaluations without explaining the judgmental criteria and the basis for selecting those criteria.

The *tenth objection* to research in art education is that the language from the beginning of a study to the conclusion is often too imprecise. This is an important and justifiable criticism as the editors of our professional journals can testify. But art educators often resent the editor's request to clarify language, and they dislike editorial corrections in their writing. This is extremely unfortunate because the improper or imprecise use of language in the conduct and reporting of research is an indication that the research itself is equally improper or imprecise. Thus it is important for art educators to remember the old adage "clear writing is a sign of clear thinking."

Without doubt there are other criticisms to be made of research in art education, but the ten that have been mentioned

[13] Kenneth Beittel, "Molesting or Meeting the Muse: A Look at Research on 'Creativity' in the Visual Arts," *Studies in Art Education*, vol. 1, no. 1, pp. 26–37, 1959.
[14] Earl Linderman, "The Relation of Art Picture Judgment to Judge Personality," *Studies in Art Education*, vol. 3, no. 2, pp. 46–51, Spring, 1962.
[15] Beittel, *op. cit.*, p. 27.

here provide an important basis for improvement. Some of them are inaccurate and unfair because they fail to specify the instances in which errors were allegedly made, and some of them offer little or nothing in the way of constructive criticism. Others make more of an attack upon the character of an investigator than they do upon the specific mistakes in his work. In spite of this, they have been presented here, along with more useful comments, to show that criticism itself can stand improvement. The art educator who is interested in research can profit from the better criticism by making sure that the same objections cannot be raised about his investigations. But mistakes are apt to appear from time to time despite the effort to eliminate them. This is to be expected, for all persons who explore, invent, and originate make errors. They may lead us to the wrong answers—which is unfortunate,—but this does not mean that formal research should be abandoned. It means instead that we should exercise greater care and inquire in many different ways. After all, research is not to be feared any more than reading is to be feared. It is a form of systematic inquiry that will gradually provide us with more knowledge about art and art education and increase the efficiency with which we teach.

THE APPLICATION OF RESEARCH FINDINGS

Although research is a method of creating new and potentially useful knowledge in art education, the teacher in the public school is apt to be slow in making use of the results in his teaching. Why is application of these findings likely to be slow?

The first, and perhaps the most obvious, reason is that the teacher is simply too busy to make use of research findings in their present form. Teaching is a full-time job, and any nonteaching time that the art instructor may have is sufficiently occupied with routine chores, extracurricular activities, committees, guidance, and preparation for the next day. Outside the school the majority of teachers have the same responsibilities to fulfill as other people do. They have homes and families to maintain, and they frequently find it necessary to take additional jobs to supplement their low incomes. Consequently, it is highly unrealistic to expect teachers to engage in an extensive search for research.

Research findings are too difficult for busy teachers to obtain because they are reported in publications that are not normally found in public school or village libraries. Information is scattered through a variety of publications such as the *Journal of Aesthetics and Art Criticism, Studies in Art Education*, the old yearbooks of the National Art Education Association, the old *Eastern Arts Bulletin*, the old *Western Arts Bulletin*, unpublished doctoral dissertations, and numerous books and pamphlets both inside and outside the field of art education.

Even if those sources of knowledge were made available in public school libraries, the teacher would have trouble applying the information that he found. The reason for this is that the fruits of systematic inquiry are often unrelated to the teacher's immediate problems. When they do have an immediate application, however, the relationships between those findings and the teacher's problems are rarely spelled out with sufficient clarity. Thus the information is not apt to be used because the teacher does not have time to ponder over its application.

When research findings and their practical applications are indicated, it is still necessary for the teacher to evaluate the studies to determine if the results are worth applying. But if most teachers are not trained to find research, they are certainly not trained to evaluate it and wisely avoid trying to do so.

From these comments we can understand why teachers are not likely to use the results of research in their teaching. With this understanding we can proceed toward a solution of the problem—a solution that is necessary if we expect progress in art education to keep pace with advancements in other curricular areas. Fortunately, at least seven possibilities are immediately apparent as partial answers to the problem.

Foremost, and most obvious, is the suggestion that we train future teachers to find, evaluate, and interpret research. This could probably be done, but it has several disadvantages.

It would require more courses in an already crowded teacher-training program or would mean eliminating some of the present offerings. In addition it would not affect those who are presently employed in the public schools. This means that it would take years to fill the ranks with persons capable of finding and interpreting research, and when the ranks were filled, the teachers would still be too busy to make use of their special training.

A second suggestion seems more feasible. Investigators could present research information in such a way that the practical applications, if any, are absolutely clear. One can hardly argue against such an improvement, but it does present certain problems. In the first place, researchers are not all familiar with the trials and tribulations of the classroom. Consequently, they are not always aware of the educational utility of their work. In the second place, research and the knowledge resulting from it could be worthless and still be clearly explained and applied to the classroom situation. For that reason the teacher must still have the ability to evaluate the work.

Because most art instructors lack the time and the training that are necessary for the evaluation and interpretation of research findings, a *third* suggestion for helping the teacher is even more feasible. A person with classroom experience who has been trained in art education and research could review pertinent research, evaluate it, and summarize the applicable findings in terms that are clear and understandable to laymen. This would be a substantial task. It would require time, care, and the services of a very capable person; but it could provide the busy teacher with a clear, meaningful account of the latest practical information about such things as curriculum development, stimulation, developmental stages, art room planning, rewards and competitions, class size, creativity, and other important subjects. Assuming that such reports could be written, how could we get them in the hands of the public school teacher?

Perhaps one of the professional publications in art education could be utilized for such purposes, since the regional art bulletins have been discontinued, and *Studies in Art Education* is highly technical and should remain so. The latter provides an excellent place for research specialists to report their work and debate the issues, but it does not serve the needs of the public school teacher. This leaves the yearbook of the National Art Education Association and *Art Education*, the journal of the N.A.E.A. Since 1954, several issues of the yearbook have been devoted to the reporting of research on alternate years. Now that *Studies in Art Education* has taken over that function, the yearbook could be used for the purpose we have been discussing; or, as an alternative, the journal of the N.A.E.A. could devote one issue a year to the same purpose. The only disadvantage of this system is that both professional publications go only to those who belong to the professional associations in art education.

To overcome this single disadvantage, a personal supplement to the printed word could also be offered. For example, the information published in professional journals could be brought to teachers through the field-services divisions of the state universities. This has been done for many years in the field of agriculture and has been extremely successful in keeping farmers up-to-date on the latest research. The personal contact between the university specialist and the expert farmer helps to keep them both well informed, and the same thing could happen in art education. An annual or biannual visit by the university specialist could serve to keep art teachers abreast of developments in their field and stimulate them to use such information. In return the specialist would keep in touch with the realities of the classroom. As an alternative to the participation of universities, the same service might be offered through the state offices of public instruction; but the benefits that are likely to come from closer contact between universities and public schools are certain to cause greater advancements in art education.

The sixth suggestion for getting teachers to use research information—which may be the most effective means of all—is to get teachers involved in systematic inquiry into their own problems. An individual's own professional troubles are always of more interest to him than someone else's problems, and he probably would be more eager to accept and put into effect the results of his own investigation into those difficulties. But what about the art teacher who is untrained in research techniques? Could he actually do research?

Most teachers are capable of doing research of an informal type, and it is possible for them to participate in the more formal variety. In fact, teachers engage in informal research all the time. Even those who criticize research will find that they participate in a form of studious inquiry themselves. They might collect descriptive information about their students in an effort to understand them better, and the teacher, on the basis of that information, might change his way of working with his students. Then he might examine the results to see if his new method is superior to the previous one. This would be an example of informal research. The only difference between such activities on the part of the teacher and work that we normally call research is that the latter is more studied, more formal, and more controlled or more precise.

With the help of someone like a visiting specialist from a state university, the public school teacher should be able to carry out formal investigations. The teacher could identify the problems, and the research specialist could develop and explain the appropriate method of collecting data, the method of treating data, and the way to evaluate the results. Together, they could decide what the results mean for teaching, and by discussing the research as it goes along, both partners could grow in their knowledge of children, of teaching, of research, and of education in general.

Naturally, since research takes time, the teacher would not be able to participate for extended periods. For this reason, assistance in the form of a trained specialist is recommended. The bulk of the work would fall on the expert unless the teacher elected a problem that did not lend itself to such an arrangement. For example, a teacher might decide to make a systematic study of the philosophy of art education because of its fundamental importance in his teaching. In that case the burden of the research would fall upon the teacher, and he would simply have to decide how much time he could devote to it. The specialist could still be helpful as a resource person, a listener, a sympathetic critic, or a questioner. Sometimes the presence of such an individual can stimulate research activity that otherwise would not have occurred.

The seventh and final possibility for getting teachers to use research findings is to provide them with that information at professional meetings. Persons who have completed research might report on their work, or informed specialists might summarize the information from various studies and explain its practical application. Again, this form of personal exchange between the specialist and the teacher has an advantage that the printed word does not: more enthusiasm is generated; there is an opportunity for questions; and the person who makes the presentation has more of an opportunity to use all his teaching skills.

Verbal presentations of research by artists, architects, educators, psychologists, and research technicians are already quite common at professional meetings, which are being attended with growing regularity by hundreds of teachers from coast to coast. There are indications, however, that such presentations are not a complete success. Listeners applaud politely, hurry to shake the lecturer's hand, and enthusiastically assure each other that the talk was interesting and provocative. Yet many persons—perhaps the majority—come away from such meetings with erroneous ideas about the quality of the research, the conclusions to be drawn from it, and its practical application. Others persons leave without being able to restate a single idea that they had obtained after an hour of attentive listening. What are the explanations for such a failure, and what can be done about it? To answer this question we must turn our attention to the pursuit of meaning in research presentations.

GETTING THE MOST FROM RESEARCH PRESENTATIONS

Making verbal or written reports on research is never easy, but the difficulty is sometimes increased by the nature of the audience for whom the report is intended. If the audience is composed of colleagues who understand the techniques and jargon of research, the task is relatively easy. But if the audience is made up of persons who are unfamiliar with such things, communication becomes more difficult.

When a research specialist speaks to teachers, for example, he is addressing persons whose talents usually do not lie in the realm of formal research. Consequently, he must make a determined effort to be understood. If he has done a good job, his audience should be able to restate, in a few sentences, the major points in the speaker's presentation. They should feel that necessary frames of reference were clearly established and that unfamiliar terms were adequately defined. They should recognize that one or more ideas had been clearly developed and that the speech was not simply a random collection of observations, jokes, and anecdotes. They should feel that the speaker's methods of collecting data were sound, that his conclusions were justified, and that he did not speak with "tongue in cheek." Finally, it is a poor researcher who seems overly eager to impress his audience with statistics. It would be far better if the audience were impressed by the care, logic, and understanding that is demonstrated in the *total* research activity.

The person who does not understand or feel satisfied by a research report *should not accept* its conclusions without further investigation. Accepting research on faith would be the educational equivalent of voting for legislation that one cannot comprehend. Consequently, the teacher should question the researcher vigorously. Among other things he should ask for the basic assumptions upon which the research was based. He should ask for the definitions of unfamiliar terms and should find out why the researcher thinks the answer to his problem is important. Having asked his questions, he should be critical of the answers. If the researcher uses any of the following tactics in response to queries, the teacher may be justifiably skeptical of the researcher's work.

1. The speaker avoids the question but makes a strong statement about something else.

2. The speaker answers the question with a question. Although this can be an effective response, it is often used to avoid expressing an opinion.
3. The speaker rephrases the question and returns it to the questioner. By doing so, he places the burden of the argument upon the questioner—who, incidently, is not being paid for his comments.
4. The speaker obscures the question with a long, wandering oration that involves numerous irrelevancies and fails to come to grips with the issue. It is an important tactic to watch, because there is a growing tendency for art educators to value such tactics as a form of divergent thinking. The trouble is that the difference between constructive divergent thinking and scatterbrained thinking has not been made sufficiently clear. A creative, constructive divergent thinker is one who can crystalize his thoughts and come up with several possible answers to questions or problems. The scatterbrained thinker, on the other hand, is someone who cannot organize his thoughts well enough to give a coherent answer. Obviously the person who allows his mind to wander aimlessly in response to questions, is not apt to do research with greater precision.

If teachers listen critically, ask clarifying questions, and demand responsible answers, the quality and value of verbal research presentations is likely to improve. Teachers who willingly spend large sums of money for the services of experts have every right to that improvement.

NEEDED RESEARCH

As we approach the end of this textbook, it seems appropriate to suggest topics in art education that are badly in need of research. Systematic inquiry, up to now, has been relatively scarce in art education; this means that a great many things need to be investigated. We do not intend to list them all, even if we could, but it may be helpful to persons entering the profession if a few of the things that are desperately in need of research are mentioned.

Probably the area that most urgently needs to be studied is *curriculum development*. We need to work with experts in drawing, painting, printmaking, sculpture, crafts, art history, and aesthetics to develop sequential programs in each of those areas from kindergarten through the high school. As the programs develop, we must try them in the public schools, and change them when changes seem necessary. Without such programs, education can be terribly wasteful and inefficient, and it may not reach the goals that we have set for it.

Secondly, we would be a lot better off in training teachers and in developing curricula if we knew more about *how children develop in responding to works of art and in making three-dimensional visual symbols*. Most of the descriptive research in art education has focused on how youngsters develop in the making of drawings and paintings. But what should we expect from children in the second or sixth grade if we cause them to work with clay? What are they apt to see in a painting? What do they say about sculpture?

Thirdly, we could profit from much more investigation into the *methodology* of teaching art. It seems clear, for example, that we know very little about the use of audio-visual aids in art education. Could we reach our goals more efficiently if we used films, filmstrips, reproductions, slides, tape recordings, videotapes, and teaching machines? What is the best way to use such devices in the art class?

What are some specific techniques for developing highly differentiated percepts and concepts? How can composition be taught without destroying the student's interest and enthusiasm for art? How can we cause the student to apply his art learning to life situations?

A fourth area that needs research is *evaluation and reporting to parents*. Perhaps this area should be studied in connection with the development of the curriculum and the formation of objectives, but it is obvious that research is badly needed. Evaluation is frequently unrelated to what is taught. Sometimes it focuses on effort instead of on achievement, and, many times, it is based on standards that have nothing to do with art. With that kind of evaluation, art education can hardly improve.

A fifth subject that needs investigation is the *administrative arrangement for teaching art*. We need to know whether art education is best if it is offered under the team-teaching arrangement, the consultant system, the self-contained classroom, the traveling art teacher, or under the guidance of an art teacher in an art classroom. We need to know more about the in-service education of teachers and how to improve it. In fact, we need to study all aspects of supervision in art to make sure that time and money is being well spent.

A sixth area that requires study is *classroom management*. Many of the difficulties that teachers have with art are difficulties that arise from poor classroom management. The teachers need to know how to organize their rooms for art activities. They need to know how to handle supplies efficiently, how to store tools and materials, how to clean up, how to display finished work, and how to use the total resources of the school most effectively. If they knew how to do such things, a lot more art would be taught, and the instruction would improve.

Finally, it would be very helpful to know more about the effects of the environment upon the child's development in art. When does the environment have its most pronounced effect? What effect does it have? Would knowledge of such things cause us to change what we teach and when we teach?

From these few comments it should be clear that art education is a "new frontier." There are so many things we do not know and so many worthwhile things to be done that new teachers are really pioneers. Their future is promising and exciting, and we wish them the best of luck.

QUESTIONS FOR DISCUSSION

1. Writers and researchers in art education occasionally use new words to refer to old concepts. Consequently, they give the impression that they are speaking of something new and different. Why is that a bad practice?
2. Why does so much research deal with small, delimited topics?
3. Why is it helpful to replicate certain kinds of research?
4. Do you believe that a good teacher should be able to explain his research to college graduates? Why do teachers frequently fail to understand research presentations?
5. Several books have been written concerning the different types of research in education and the social sciences. How do they classify the different types of research?
6. What effect has research had upon education? Consider the information you have obtained from your instructors about teaching. How much of that information was based on research? How much of it came from experience?

SUGGESTIONS FOR FURTHER READING

Eisner, Elliot W., and David W. Ecker: *Readings in Art Education*, Blaisdell Publishing Company, Waltham, Massachusetts, 1966.
This excellent anthology contains many research reports that are relevant to art education. The introductory chapter is especially worthwhile.

Feldman, Edmund: "Research as the Verification of Aesthetics," *Studies in Art Education*, vol. 1, no. 1, pp. 19–25, 1959.
An article that explains how aesthetics can play an important role in research in art education.

Harris, Dale B.: *Children's Drawings as Measures of Intellectual Maturity*, Harcourt, Brace and World, Inc., New York, 1963.
This book summarizes most of the research that has been done on children's drawings. It is written by a developmental psychologist who is one of the country's outstanding authorities on child art.

Kaufman, Irving: "Some Reflections on Research in Art Education," *Studies in Art Education*, vol. 1, no. 1, pp. 9–18, 1959.
An example of some of the writing that has been critical of research in art education.

Kiell, Norman: *Psychiatry and Psychology in the Visual Arts and Aesthetics*, University of Wisconsin Press, Madison, 1965.
This is a bibliography of books and articles that deal with the relation of psychology and psychiatry to fine arts and aesthetics. It is a wonderful resource for anyone interested in doing research in art education.

Meier, Norman: "Recent Research in the Psychology of Art," *Art in American Life and Education*, Forty-first Yearbook of the National Society for the Study of Education, University of Chicago Press, Chicago, 1941, pp. 379–400.
This article gives the reader an indication of the artistically relevant research that was going on in psychology during the years just prior to 1941. The author of the article was one of the foremost authorities on the subject.

Munro, Thomas: *Art Education: Its Philosophy and Psychology*, Liberal Arts Press, Inc., New York, 1956, pp. 191–208.
A fine early comment (written in 1933) on tests and research in art education by one of the professions most outstanding figures.

Munro, Thomas: *Scientific Method in Aesthetics*, W. W. Norton and Company, Inc., New York, 1928.
One of the early pleas for systematic inquiry in the arts.

A Seminar in Art Education for Research and Curriculum Development, United States Office of Education, Cooperative Research Project, Edward L. Mattil (project director), no. 5–002, Pennsylvania State University, University Park, 1966.
A verbatim account of a seminar devoted to the stimulation of research and curriculum development. Full of interesting and provocative ideas.

Valentine, C. W.: *The Experimental Psychology of Beauty*, Methuen and Co., Ltd., London, 1962.
This book gives an account of experiments with responses to objects that are called "beautiful". It is likely to be very useful to anyone interested in studying aesthetic experience.

INDEX

PRINTED IN ITALY BY OFFICINE GRAFICHE ARNOLDO MONDADORI - VERONA

Designers: Fiorenzo Giorgi, Maurizio Turazzi
Editorial Supervisor: Robert Brainerd